NORTH AMERICAN
MOOSE

RANDOLPH L. PETERSON

UNIVERSITY OF TORONTO PRESS

IN CO-OPERATION WITH THE ROYAL ONTARIO MUSEUM

FOREWORD

It is with a feeling of deep satisfaction that I am privileged to introduce this the first comprehensive book of its type on North American moose. The majestic moose is as much a Canadian heritage as the dark spruce forests of the north. Our native Indians and the early explorers lived on his flesh and used his skin for articles of clothing. Our sportsmen have prized him above all other beasts of the chase, and our campers and tourists have rejoiced to see his tracks in the earth, or, less often, to come in view of the great deer himself.

A few years ago it was suggested by some that the moose was faced with certain extinction, yet no one was sufficiently familiar with this great animal to evaluate the many factors which seemed to threaten its existence. Fortunately, the timely studies of Doctor Peterson have produced the facts necessary for a sound management programme for its continued conservation. The future prospects for moose now look much brighter.

Thoroughly trained in the field of wildlife conservation, matured by travel and field work, a specialist in the study of mammals, the author is particularly well qualified to carry out the challenging task of producing this vastly important contribution. How well he has carried out this exacting task will be apparent to the readers.

I wish to congratulate the Royal Ontario Museum and Doctor Peterson on a great accomplishment. It has often been our privilege to work with them, and this book will be a source of special satisfaction to men of the Department of Lands and Forests scattered throughout the homeland of the moose.

W. J. K. Harkness
Fish and Wildlife Division
Department of Lands and Forests
Province of Ontario

v

ACKNOWLEDGMENTS

ACKNOWLEDGMENT, with sincere thanks and appreciation, must be extended to the great number of persons who have helped to bring together the results of this study. In fact, so many people have extended their whole-hearted co-operation in the course of this work that I find it a most difficult task to attempt to express my indebtedness to each individual without surely overlooking some. To all those whose names are not specifically mentioned I wish to humbly signify my utmost gratitude for their interest, support, and assistance.

The Carling Conservation Club deserves great credit in making possible this study through its financial support in the form of a research grant to the Royal Ontario Museum of Zoology. The proper appreciation of the necessity of long-continued research, on the part of the Carling representatives, has greatly facilitated the progress of this project. Their far-sighted policy of undertaking a campaign directed toward the cause of wildlife research and the conservation of natural resources deserves special mention.

The Department of Lands and Forests of the province of Ontario has extended much co-operation and many services which have made possible the completion of this study. The Honourable H. R. Scott, former Minister; Mr. F. A. McDougall, Deputy Minister; Dr. W. J. K. Harkness, Chief of the Fish and Wildlife Division, and Dr. C. H. D. Clarke, Supervisor of Wildlife, together with many of their field representatives through the northern part of the province, have all assisted in making possible a much more extensive and thorough study of moose in the field than would otherwise have been possible. During the period from 1949 to 1951, the author had the pleasure of serving the Department in a consultant capacity in carrying out a province-wide moose investigation programme. Mr. A. T. Cringan of the Fish and Wildlife Division and Mr. R. C. Passmore of the Research Division were instrumental in bringing together many specimens for our studies of tooth development and wear as indications of age.

In the field, Mr. Thomas McCormick, Jr., acted as guide for two seasons, Mr. Dalton Muir acted as general assistant and photographer for two seasons, providing many of the photographs contained herein, and Mr. V. H. H. Williamson assisted in studies of the food habits of moose during one season and carried out detailed examinations of moose stomachs and droppings in the Wildlife Food Habits Research Laboratory at the Royal

Ontario Museum of Zoology, under a research grant from the Research Council of Ontario.

Dr. A. Murray Fallis and Dr. J. F. A. Sprent of the Ontario Research Foundation identified internal parasites and assisted in moose autopsy work. Dr. J. H. Soper of the Department of Botany, University of Toronto, checked the identifications of many botanical specimens. Dr. M. L. Prebble, former Officer-in-Charge of the Forest Insect Laboratory at Sault Ste Marie, Ontario, supplied information on the ecology, distribution, and spread of the spruce budworm in Ontario, and his staff of Forest Insect Rangers provided valuable data on the numerical status of moose in the areas where spruce budworm investigations were carried out.

Mr. Laurits W. Krefting, Regional Biologist, Fish and Wildlife Service, United States Department of the Interior, who has done much research concerning the Isle Royale moose population, accompanied me on a brief inspection of that area and also provided many helpful suggestions, especially with reference to moose winter browse analysis.

Dr. Walter P. Taylor, former Senior Biologist, Fish and Wildlife Service, United States Department of the Interior, reviewed most of the manuscript and provided many helpful suggestions.

I would like to express my sincere appreciation for the splendid co-operation and assistance given me by the entire staff of the Royal Ontario Museum of Zoology (and Palaeontology) under the directorship of Professor J. R. Dymond and later Dr. F. A. Urquhart.

My wife, Elizabeth Taylor Peterson, was a constant assistant in compiling data and preparing the original manuscript. Without her unceasing encouragement and support this work would not have been possible.

R. L. P.

CONTENTS

CHAPTER ONE

INTRODUCTION

. . . there is, also, the elk, which strongly resembles our steers, except that it is distinguished by the length of ears and of the neck. There is also the achlis, which is produced in the island of Scandinavia; [achlis and elk are considered to be the same animal by translators, i.e. European elk or moose] it has never been seen in this city, although we have had descriptions of it from many persons; it is not unlike the elk, but has no joints in the hind leg. Hence, it never lies down, but reclines against a tree while it sleeps; it can only be taken by previously cutting into the tree, and thus laying a trap for it, as otherwise, it would escape through its swiftness. Its upper lip is so extremely large, for which reason it is obliged to go backwards when grazing; otherwise, by moving onwards, the lip would get doubled up. (Written in the first century A.D. by Pliny the Elder; Bostock and Riley, 1855, p. 263)

The *Moose* or *Elke* is a creature, or rather if you will a Monster of superfluity . . . their horns . . . very big (and brancht out into palms) the tips whereof are sometimes found to be two fathom asunder . . . and in height from the toe of the forefoot, to the pitch of the shoulder twelve foot, both which hath been taken by some of my *sceptique* Readers to be monstrous lyes. (Josselyn, 1674, p. 88)

The most admirable Creature is the Mose which Josseline thus describes, in his New-England Rarities. T'is about 12 Feet high, with four Horns, and broad palms, some of 12 feet from the Tip of one Horn to that of the other. . . . His tail longer than a Buck's, . . . He shoots his Horns every four years. (Oldmixon, 1741, p. 187)

When chased by the Indians, its horns are laid back upon its shoulders, and in this posture its strength and velocity are so great as to break down and destroy small trees and branches of a considerable size. (Hollingsworth, 1787, pp. 85–86)

It has been pretended that the orignal, or elk, is subject to the epilepsy, and when he is seized with any fit, he cures himself by rubbing his ear with his left hind foot till the blood comes; a circumstance which has made his hoof be taken for a specific against the falling sickness. This is applied over the heart of the patient, which is also done for palpitation of the heart; they place it in the left hand, and rub the ear with it. . . . This horny substance is also believed to be good in the pleurisy, in cholic pains, in fluxes, vertigoes, and purples, when pulverized and taken in water. . . .

The Indians look upon the elk as an animal of good omen, and believe that those who dream of them often, may expect a long life; . . . There is also a very diverting tradition among the Indians of a great elk, of such a monstrous size, that the rest are like pismires in comparison of him; his legs, say they, are so long, that eight feet of snow are not the least incumbrance to him; his hide is proof against all manner of weapons, and he has a sort of arm proceeding from his shoulders, which he uses as we do ours. He is always attended by a vast number of elks which form his court, and which render him all the services he requires. (Written by Charlevoix about 1721. Kellogg, 1923, vol. 1, pp. 183–184)

MANY AUTHORS have given various other accounts of the superstitions and supernatural beliefs of Indians concerning moose. Many of their ideas have been accepted as factual by various white men who, having even less understanding of moose and their habitats, have been guilty of expanding and perpetuating, or creating their own, fantastic accounts of unnatural history.

From the beginning of the white man's explorations and settlement of North America, the majestic moose has been a familiar figure in the northern wooded part of the continent. Such a conspicuous animal could hardly fail to impress the pioneers and consequently it has been mentioned in the records of many of the early writers. Notable among these are the writings of the Jesuit missionaries of the seventeenth century. Figuring prominently as a source of food, clothing, and many other necessities, as well as being an object of sport and recreation, the moose has been the subject of innumerable accounts in the subsequent pages of literature. A great influence has been wielded by the works of Audubon and Bachman (1851), Powell (1855), King (1866), Grant (1902), Hornaday (1904), Merrill (1920), and Seton (1927). Even the later of the above authors were influenced by the earlier accounts, especially by those of Audubon and Bachman, and of Powell, for their works contain many statements which show little deviation from the early writings. Passing from an era of casual and uncritical natural history, the first extensive scientific study of moose in North America was carried out by Murie (1934) on Isle Royale, Michigan. Following this period, there was a growing scientific interest in moose which culminated with the appearance of several serious studies following the close of the Second World War. The author had the extreme good fortune to be provided with an opportunity to devote the major portion of his time and effort to a study of moose from 1946 onward. Although most of the field studies were confined to the province of Ontario, it was soon apparent that if a thorough understanding of moose and the factors which affect them was ever to be reached, it would be necessary to seek out data from every available source. A vigorous search of the literature and unpublished files, and the accumulation of original data, subsequently resulted in a multitudinous mass of information. The desirability of subjecting these data to critical examination and bringing them together in some organized and usable fashion presented such a challenge that the following report has resulted. In many respects, it is merely a preliminary report on our present state of knowledge of this animal, for studies are under way which will enlarge our understanding of certain factors, fill in existing hiatuses of knowledge, and modify some of the concepts expressed here. It is felt that we are merely approaching a scientific understanding of moose. If this report can in any way assist and stimulate others, the many hours of pleasant toil in its preparation will be considered to have been a most rewarding privilege.

CHAPTER TWO

TAXONOMY AND DISTRIBUTION

A TAXONOMIC REVIEW of the living representatives of the genus *Alces* has been provided in an earlier paper (Peterson, 1952). A brief synopsis of this work follows.

Genus **Alces** Gray
Moose, Old World Elk

1821. *Alces* Gray, London Med. Repos., vol. 15, p. 307.
1827. *Alce* H. Smith, Griffith's Animal Kingdom, vol. 4, p. 72; vol. 5, p. 303.
1841. *Alcelaphus* Gloger, Handbuch Naturgeschichte, p. 143 *nec* Blainville, 1816.
1857. *Alces* Blasius, Säugethiere Deutschlands, p. 34.
1902. *Paralces* Allen, Bull. Am. Mus. Nat. Hist., vol. 16, p. 160. (Substitute for *Alces* proposed on the assumption that this is a homonym of *Alce* Blumenbach, 1799.)
1945. *Alce* Simpson, Bull. Am. Mus. Nat. Hist., vol. 85, p. 155. (Proposes acceptance of *Alce* Frisch, 1775.)
1948. *Alces* Hershkovitz, Journ. Mamm., vol. 29, no. 3, p. 273. (Shows *Alce* Frisch, 1775, to be non-Linnaean and unavailable; *Alces* Gray, 1821, should stand.)

Type Species. Cervus alces Linnaeus.

Geographical distribution. Circumpolar in the boreal coniferous forests of both the Old and the New World (Figure 1).

Characters. The moose (and Old World elk) is readily distinguished by its large size (the largest living Cervid; about the size of a saddle horse), heavy body, long legs, high shoulder region, short tail, broad overhanging muzzle, large ears, short neck, and unique dewlap or "bell." The nose is covered with short hair except for a bare spot between the nostrils which is usually more or less triangular in shape. Adult males develop extremely large antlers which are characteristically broad palmate blades with projecting tines.

The upper part of the body is quite dark in new spring pelage, appearing almost black in some individuals, and in others varying towards dark brown, reddish brown, and greyish brown. The underparts of the belly and lower legs are distinctly lighter, usually either greyish or brownish in colour, sometimes almost whitish. There is a gradual fading in body colour during summer, fall, and winter to produce a more greyish effect by early spring.

In addition to the general characters given above, *Alces* may be distinguished by skull greatly lengthened in premaxillary region; nasal region shortened with sizable nasal aperture; distance from front of nasal to front of premaxilla about equal to that from back of nasal to back of occiput;

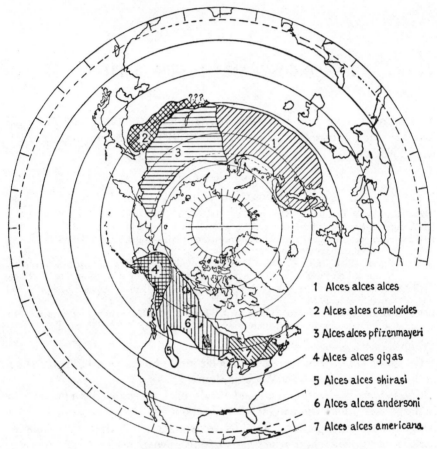

FIGURE 1. World-wide distribution of moose

1 Alces alces alces
2 Alces alces cameloides
3 Alces alces pfizenmayeri
4 Alces alces gigas
5 Alces alces shirasi
6 Alces alces andersoni
7 Alces alces americana

vomer lower posteriorly, not dividing aperture of posterior nares; lacrimal vacuity widely open, the pit well developed, maxillary canines usually absent in both sexes; lower canines incisiform, incisors but little differentiated; molars and premolars rather broad and low crowned. Median metacarpals united as a cannon bone; lateral metacarpals strongly attenuated, rudimentary, with only distal ends developed as styloid vestiges (teleometacarpalian). Metatarsal gland absent; front hoofs larger than posterior ones, both long, narrow, and pointed.

Alces alces alces (Linnaeus)

European Elk

1758. *Cervus alces* Linnaeus, Syst. Nat., 10th ed., vol. 1, p. 66.
1910. *Alces machlis typicus* Ward, Records of Big Game, 6th ed., p. 66.
1913. *Alces machlis uralensis* Matschie, Veröff. Institute Jugdkunde, vol. 2, p. 155.
1913. *Alces machlis meridionalis* Matschie, *ibid.*, p. 156.

1914. *Alces machlis tymensis* Zukowsky, Archiv. f. Naturgeschichte, 80 Jahrg., Abt. A, H. 9, p. 42.
1914. *Alces machlis angusticephalus* Zukowsky, *ibid.*, p. 44.
1915. *Alces alces alces* Lydekker, Cat. Ungulate Mamm. Brit. Mus. (Nat. Hist.), vol. 4, p. 232.

Type specimen. Unknown.

Type locality. Sweden.

Geographical distribution. Northern Europe and western Siberia, eastward probably as far as the Yenisey River and Altai Mountains (Flerov, 1931).

Characters. A relatively small animal with a broad nasal process of the premaxillary bone extending well up the rim of the nasal aperture (Figure 2). The skull averages relatively short (adult males 550–580 millimeters) with the antorbital region being noticeably shorter than in other races. The pelage averages more greyish brown in colour than North American races and usually lacks the blackish tints found in other races.

Alces alces cameloides (Milne-Edwards)
Manchurian Elk

1867. *Cervus cameloides* Milne-Edwards, Ann. Sci. Nat., Zool. ser. 5, vol. 7, p. 377.
1868–74. *Cervus alces* Milne-Edwards, Recherches pour servir à l'Hist. Nat. des Mammifères, p. 181.
?1902. *Alces bedfordiae* Lydekker, Proc. Zool. Soc. London, vol. 1, p. 109 (indefinite locality, possibly applies to this form).
?1908. *Alces machlis bedfordiae* Lydekker, A trip to Pilawin, p. 85.
?1915. *Alces alces bedfordiae* Lydekker, Cat. Ungulate Mamm., Brit. Mus. (Nat. Hist.), vol. 4, p. 234.
1931. *Alces alces* subsp. ? Flerov, Comptes rendus de l'Acad. des Sci. de l'URSS, p. 74.
1940. *Alces alces cameloides* Allen, Mamm. China and Mongolia, Am. Mus. Nat. Hist., vol. 11, pt. 2, p. 1205.

Type specimen. Unknown (?). Supposedly one or more antlers in the Paris Museum.

Type Locality. Manchuria (?).

Geographical distribution. Limits of range unknown. Supposedly from the Amur River region of extreme southeastern Siberia, northern Manchuria, and northeastern Mongolia.

Characters. The status of this form remains uncertain. Presumably it is a relatively small animal.

Alces alces pfizenmayeri Zukowsky
Siberian Elk

1910. *Alces pfizenmayeri* Zukowsky, Wild und Hund, 16 Jahrg., Bd. 11, p. 807.
?1902. *Alces bedfordiae* Lydekker, Proc. Zool. Soc. London, vol. 1, p. 109.
?1908. *Alces machlis bedfordiae* Lydekker, A trip to Pilawin, p. 85.
1911. *Alces machlis jakutskensis* Millais, Field, vol. 118, p. 113.
?1915. *Alces alces bedfordiae* Lydekker, Cat. Ungulate Mamm., Brit. Mus. (Nat. Hist.), vol. 4, p. 234.
1931. *Alces alces pfizenmayeri* Flerov, Comptes rendus de l'Acad. des Sci. de l'URSS, p. 73.

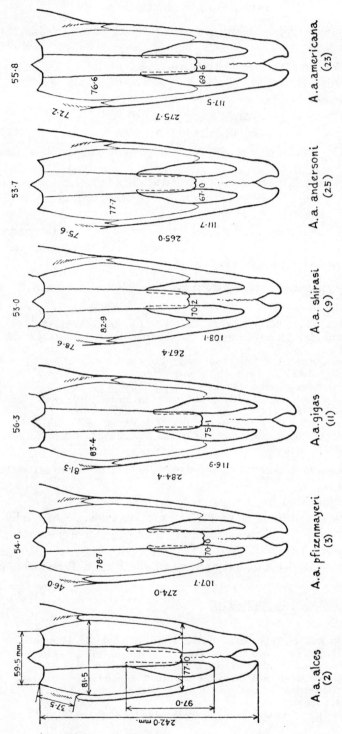

FIGURE 2. The average size and shape of the nasal apertures of the races of *Alces alces* (adult bulls). Figures in parenthesis refer to the number of specimens averaged

Type Specimen. Unknown (?).

Type locality. Aldan River, Yakutia, Russia.

Geographical distribution. Northern Siberia, eastward from the Yenisey River (Flerov, 1931), probably south to Sayan, Yablonovyy and Dzhugdzhur mountain ranges.

Characters. A relatively large and dark form, similar to the Alaskan race, *A. a. gigas,* but with the nasal processes of the premaxillary bone extending further up the rim of the nasal aperture.

Alces alces gigas Miller

Alaskan Moose

1899. *Alces gigas* Miller, Proc. Biol. Soc. Wash., vol. 13, p. 57.
1901. *Alces machlis gigas* Lydekker, Great and Small Game of Europe, etc., p. 49.
1902. *Paralces gigas* Allen, Bull. Am. Mus. Nat. Hist., vol. 16, p. 160.
1904. *Alces americanus gigas* Osgood, N. Am. Fauna, no. 24, p. 29.
?1907. *Alces columbae* Lydekker, Field, vol. 9, p. 182 (thought at first to be from somewhere in British Columbia).
1915. *Alces alces gigas* Lydekker, Cat. Ungulate Mamm., Brit. Mus. (Nat. Hist.), vol. 4, p. 237.
1924. *Alces gigas* Miller, U.S. Natl. Mus., bull. 128, p. 491.
1929. *Alces americana gigas* Anderson, Natl. Mus. Can., bull. 56, p. 105.
1950. *Alces americana gigas* Peterson, Roy. Ont. Mus. Zool., Occ. Pap. no. 9, p. 3.
1952. *Alces alces gigas* Peterson, Roy. Ont. Mus. Zool. and Paleo., Contrib. no. 34, p. 21.

Type specimen. U.S. National Museum, no. 86166.

Type locality. North side of Tustumena Lake, Kenai Peninsula, Alaska.

Geographical distribution. Forested areas of Alaska, western Yukon, and northwestern British Columbia.

Characters. Largest of living forms with massive skulls with a high occiput and relatively wide palate.

Alces alces shirasi Nelson

Yellowstone Moose

1914. *Alces americanus shirasi* Nelson, Proc. Biol. Soc. Wash., vol. 27, p. 72.
1924. *Alces americana shirasi* Miller, U.S. Natl. Mus., bull. 128, p. 490.
?1907. *Alces columbae* Lydekker, Field, vol. 9, p. 182 (British Columbia?).
1952. *Alces alces shirasi* Peterson, Roy. Ont. Mus. Zool. and Paleo., Contrib. no. 34, p. 23.

Type specimen. U.S. National Museum, no. 202975.

Type locality. Snake River, Lincoln County, Wyoming.

Geographical distribution. Western Wyoming, eastern and northern Idaho, western Montana, northward into southwestern Alberta and southeastern British Columbia. Occasional occurrence in extreme northeastern Utah has been reported by Durrant (1952).

Characters. A medium-size form with nasal aperture relatively wide. Coloration of the pelage along the back averages paler than other North American forms.

Alces alces andersoni Peterson
Northwestern Moose

1950. *Alces americana andersoni* Peterson, Roy. Ont. Mus. Zool., Occ. Pap. no. 9, p. 1.
P1907. *Alces columbae* Lydekker, Field, vol. 9, p. 18a (British Columbia?).
P1907. *Alces columbae* Lydekker, Zool. Rec., vol. 44, Mamm., p. 69 (Ontario?).
P1915. *Alces alces columbae* Lydekker, Cat. Ungulate Mamm., Brit. Mus. (Nat. Hist.),
     vol. 4, p. 236 (Ontario?).
1952. *Alces alces andersoni* Peterson, Roy. Ont. Mus. Zool. and Paleo., Contrib. no. 34,
     p. 24.

Type specimen. Adult male (skin and complete skeleton) no. 20068, Royal Ontario Museum of Zoology and Palaeontology.

Type locality. Section 27, Township 10, Range 16, Sprucewood forest reserve (15 mi. E. Brandon), Manitoba.

Geographical distribution. Northern Michigan and Minnesota, western Ontario, westward to central British Columbia, north to eastern Yukon Territory and Mackenzie Delta, Northwest Territories.

Characters. A medium-size form differing from other North American forms chiefly in cranial details, especially with respect to the shape of the palate (relatively wider than *americana* and narrower than *shirasi* and *gigas*).

Alces alces americana (Clinton)
Eastern Moose

1822. *Cervus americanus* Clinton, Letters on Nat. Hist. and Int. Resources of New
     York, p. 193.
1835. *Alces americanus* Jardine, Nat. Library, vol. 21 (Mammalia: deer, antelope, camels,
     etc.), p. 125.
1846. *Cervus lobatus* Agassiz, Proc. Boston Soc., vol. 2, p. 188.
1852. *Alces muswa* Richardson, Zool. Herald, Mamm., p. 66.
1873. *Alces lobata* Fitzinger, Sitzber. K. Ak. Wiss. Wien, vol. 68, pt. 1, p. 348.
1884. *Alce americanus* Merriam, Mammals of Adirondacks, p. 138.
1885. *Alces machlis* True, U.S. Natl. Mus., vol. 7, p. 592.
1901. *Alces machlis americanus* Lydekker, Great and Small Game of Europe, etc., p. 46.
1902. *Paralces americanus* Allen, Bull. Am. Mus. Nat. Hist., vol. 16, p. 160.
P1907. *Alces columbae* Lydekker, Zool. Rec., vol. 44, Mamm., p. 69 (Ontario?).
P1915. *Alces alces columbae* Lydekker, Cat. Ungulate Mamm., Brit. Mus. (Nat. Hist.),
     vol. 4, p. 236 (Ontario?).
1915. *Alces alces americanus* Lydekker, *ibid.*, p. 234.
1924. *Alces americana americana* Miller, U.S. Natl. Mus., Bull. 128, p. 490.
1952. *Alces alces americana* Peterson, Roy. Ont. Mus. Zool. and Paleo., Contrib. no. 34,
     p. 28.

Type specimen. Unknown.

Type locality. "Country north of Whitestown" (probably in the western Adirondack region), New York.

Geographical distribution. From Maine and Nova Scotia westward through Quebec to central northern Ontario where it apparently intergrades with *A. a. andersoni*. Introduced into Newfoundland where it is now established.

Characters. A medium-size relatively dark race with a narrow palate relative to length of toothrow.

CHAPTER THREE

PALAEONTOLOGICAL HISTORY

THE ORDER ARTIODACTYLA, to which the moose belongs, has been traced back to the Lower Eocene, although it did not reach its greatest diversity in numbers and importance until the Pleistocene or later. Scott (1937) has pointed out the close relationships of certain Old World and New World members of the family Cervidae in the northern hemisphere, namely wapiti (*Cervus*), moose (*Alces*), and caribou (*Rangifer*). He states (p. 322):

None of these has been found in America in deposits older than the Pleistocene, nor anything that could be ancestral to them; they were all very late immigrants from Asia.
    At least one Pleistocene genus, the Stag-moose (*Cervalces*) was different from any now living. The only known skeleton, now in the Princeton Museum, is in Pleistocene deposits. The skeleton of *Cervalces* is very much like that of the Moose; the bones of the neck, trunk and limbs are almost identical in the two genera, but skull and antlers are very different. The nasal bones are much less shortened than in the Moose, an indication that the proboscis-like muzzle was less inflated. The antlers are unique, though in a general way like those of *Alce*, they are much less palmated and they have, in addition, a great trumpet-like plate of bone on the lower side of each antler; this plate is not known in any other member of the Cervidae. *Cervalces* has not been found in the Old World, yet it must have originated there from the same stock as the Moose and accompanied the latter in its migration to North America.

Thus far *Cervalces* has been taken from Kentucky, New Jersey, Iowa, Nebraska, Ontario, and Alaska (Frick, 1937). Earlier, Hay (1924) reported this genus from Missouri, Oklahoma, Virginia, Illinois, and Pennsylvania. Discussing *Cervalces scotti* from New Jersey, Hay (1923, p. 306) makes the following statement: "It seems certain, therefore, that this stately relative of our existing moose lived after the disappearance of the Wisconsin ice-sheet." Frick (1937) reports that *Cervus, Alces, Cervalces*, and *Rangifer* have been taken from the deeply frozen deposits that overlie the auriferous gravels of the Fairbanks area, Alaska.

    Moose (*Alces*) have also been reported from Quaternary deposits in the eastern, central, and western regions of the United States and Ontario (Frick, 1937). Hay lists fossil records for the following states: Pennsylvania, Illinois, South Carolina (1923); Minnesota, Oklahoma, Iowa (1924); and Ohio and Washington (1927). These records are sufficient to indicate a wide southerly distribution at one time during the Pleistocene. Some of these specimens have been referred to as *A. americana*, while others have been considered as various extinct species.

    The ancestry of *Alces* in the Old World is still uncertain. In recent years various authors have discussed fossil records and applied a confusing array

11

of species to this genus (*Alces* and *Alce*) including *alces, fossilis, gigantea, latifrons, machlis*, and *palmatus*. Of these names, used since 1933, some are obviously synonyms of *Alces alces* and one belongs to another genus entirely. Reynolds (1934) reviews the genus in Great Britain and discusses its occurrence on the European continent as follows (p. 9):

. . . the elk existed on the Continent all through post-glacial times, and [records] show that in prehistoric and late Pleistocene times it ranged all over Northern and Central Europe, extending as far south as Roumania, Northern Italy and the Pyrenees. Its distribution corresponded closely with that of the reindeer. But while, as Boule remarks, the reindeer accompanied the retreating ice, leaving France before the dawn of recent conditions, the elk persisted longer in Central and Western Europe, and its complete disappearance from this region seems more likely to be due to human agency than to climatic change. In the time of Julius Caesar it was abundant in the Black and Hercynian Forests, and was to be found in Bavaria in the Eighth Century and in Flanders in the Tenth. It is still living in East Prussia, and is found in increasing numbers in Finland, Sweden and Norway, and throughout Northern Asia as far as the Pacific.

A study of the available living forms suggests that Asia was probably the centre of dispersal with *pfizenmayeri* approaching the ancestral type. Dispersal westward gave rise to perhaps the smallest existing race (*alces*) which is characterized by a unique development in the species of a much elongated and broadened nasal extension of the premaxilla. A third form may have moved south into Mongolia and Manchuria (*A. a. cameloides*) but detailed knowledge of this supposed race must await further study. Dispersal eastward resulted in more or less gradual and progressive diversions from the ancestral type. In such characters as the relative shape of

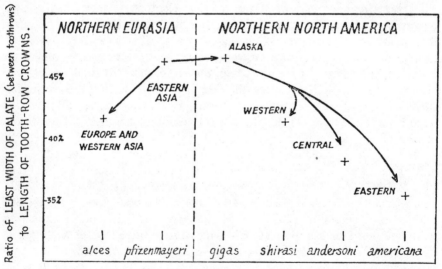

FIGURE 3.   Geographical relationships of the races of *Alces alces* as indicated by the average relative shapes of the palates

the palate, the affinities of *pfizenmayeri* and *gigas* are more similar than any other two geographically adjacent races (Figure 3). The Alaskan moose (*Alces alces gigas*) may have existed in the unglaciated regions of Alaska throughout the latter stages of Pleistocene glaciation. On the other hand, it may be a much later immigrant than the more southern North American races.

CHAPTER FOUR

POST-GLACIAL DISPERSAL IN NORTH AMERICA

THE RECESSION of the great ice sheets following the maximum expansion during the Wisconsin stage of glaciation undoubtedly had a considerable effect in shaping the pattern of redispersal of moose. In an attempt to reconstruct the basic pattern of dispersal that took place, it is most interesting to correlate available fragmentary data on past and present distribution and movements of moose with the disappearance of persistent ice fields.

During the period of the last ice maximum, four distinct *refugia* seem to have been available to moose (Figure 4), which became the centres of origin of the four modern subspecies. The three southern races were separated by the presence of the grassland barriers. The subspecific differentiation of A. a. americana and A. a. andersoni would seem to support the evidence presented by Schmidt (1938) and others for a former eastward extension of a grassland or non-forested belt which would have been an effective ecological barrier to moose. As evidenced by pollen profile studies (Flint, 1948; Sears, 1948; and others) the two eastern areas, indicated as *refugia,* were of the coniferous forest type and thus suitable habitats for moose during that period.

During the intermediate stage of recession when the Laurentide and Cordilleran ice sheets still persisted, the central continental section between was undoubtedly free of ice (Figure 5). This would have allowed early northwestward extension of the range of A. a. andersoni, while at the same time the ranges of A. a. americana, A. a. shirasi, and A. a. gigas would still have been restricted by those persistent ice sheets. Subsequent dispersal seems to have been retarded until a relatively recent date. It seems interesting, if not significant, that the recent extension of ranges (in Ontario, British Columbia, Yukon, and generally northward) was into the areas most recently freed of glacial ice (Figure 6). This would then bring up the point as to whether or not post-glacial dispersal is still going on or has continued up to rather recent times.

Various workers, seeking to understand present distributions of animals and plants in terms of postglacial re-expansions of range, have pointed to changes within historic time as examples of the continuation of this process. There is, naturally, a great deal of this kind of evidence, but owing to the universal disturbance it must be used with extreme circumspection, if at all. (Deevey, 1949, p. 1382)

In Deevey's extensive review of the biogeography of the Pleistocene he repeatedly points out that "it is obviously very dangerous to deal with

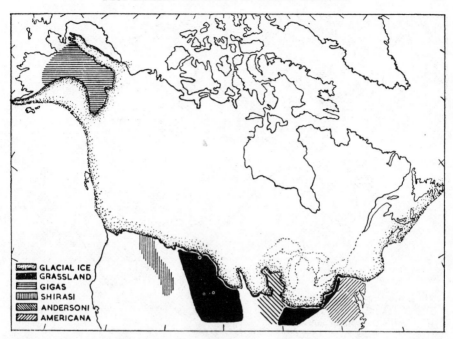

FIGURE 4. The distribution of moose in North America during the greatest extent of Wisconsin glaciation. Limits of glaciation after Flint (1948)

changes in distribution in historic time as continuation of postglacial climatic and biogeographic trends" (p. 1383). He sums up a part of his discussion of this point as follows (p. 1385):

If Antevs (1931) is right in believing that the last ice did not leave the Keewatin and Labrador regions until 7500 to 9000 years ago, and if a relatively long tundra phase preceded the immigration of forests, the age of this immigration falls close to that of the climatic optimum, and there would be no reason to suppose that postglacial re-colonization has ceased.

This whole story, for the documentation of which stratigraphic evidence is sadly missed, reminds one forcibly of the oft-cited fact that many species have extended their ranges up to but not upon the moraines of the last ice sheets. Certain birds appear still to be avoiding the area of the Scandinavian Ice Sheet in Finland (Palmgren, 1938). Surely what they are avoiding is plant communities characteristic of relatively youthful topography and soils, and, when the landscape matures and the appropriate plant communities become established, the birds will follow. In this sense the postglacial extension of range is undoubtedly still going on, but this is not a sense that permits us to operate with observed changes of range within historic time and to draw inferences from them.

Concerning the fact that there have been recent general movements or invasions of moose there can be little doubt. Undoubtedly there was some oscillation in the lines of these dispersal fronts and perhaps even previous waves of invasion, but all available evidence seems to discount any earlier

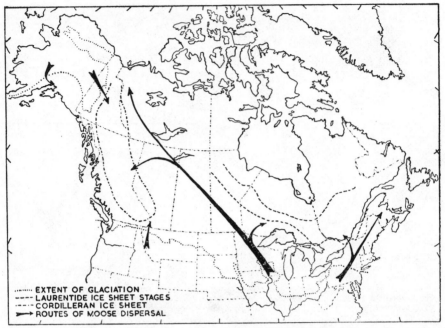

FIGURE 5. The pattern of post-glacial dispersal of North American moose

major immigration into these unoccupied areas, at least within historic time. As to whether or not these recent dispersal movements constitute a continuation of post-glacial re-expansion remains a moot point. If so, it would be of great interest to be able to explain the relatively long lapse in time between the actual disappearance of ice and these major movements of moose which have taken place subsequent to 1875. Perhaps a part of this period of time was required for evolutionary forest succession before a suitable habitat could be developed. Leopold and Darling (1953) have noted the possible effect of a general, slight, Holarctic warming that has been taking place over the last century and point out that certain studies have shown clearly that there has been a progressive widening of the annual rings laid down in the wood of willow in the northern Arctic since 1900. Population pressure especially in the primary direction of redispersal may have influenced the pattern of repopulation. Certainly man's disturbances of the habitat through logging and burning played a major part in the sudden speed of dispersal in some areas.

Unfortunately insufficient data are available to pursue these problems more thoroughly at this time. Nevertheless the fact that these major dispersal fronts involved the coming together of subspecifically distinct populations forces one to conclude that the primary pattern of redispersal was set by

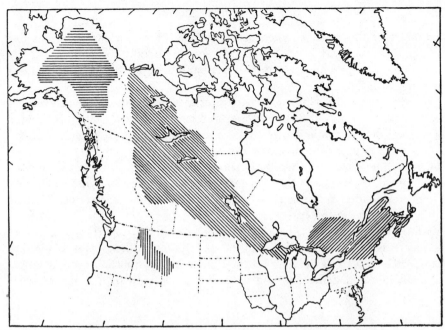

FIGURE 6. Distribution of moose in North America about 1875

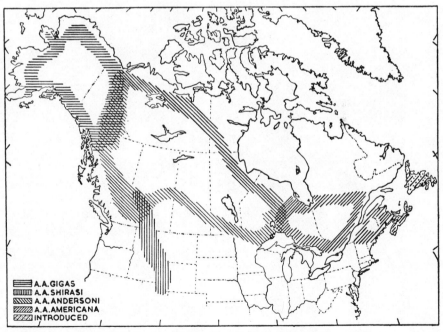

A.A.GIGAS
A.A.SHIRASI
A.A.ANDERSONI
A.A.AMERICANA
INTRODUCED

FIGURE 7. Present distribution of moose in North America

the effect of the disappearance of glacial ice. More recent dispersion has undoubtedly been affected by changes in the habitat brought about by man's influences, which may or may not have diverted the primary pattern of redispersal.

In one sense those parts of the redispersal which were most affected by man's activity (north of Lake Superior and central British Columbia) might be regarded as secondary dispersal fronts inasmuch as they include areas which were more or less by-passed in the primary thrusts of reinvasion. At the same time, however, there has been an extension of range in the general direction of the primary thrust (north to the tree limit) where it seems inconceivable that man's activity could have wrought any serious change in the habitat (Figure 7).

Rand (1948) and others have recently suggested the importance of glaciation as an isolating factor in speciation of birds and other forms. Undoubtedly further research will bear out the fundamental importance of glaciation in taxonomic and general ecological problems of both plants and animals.

CHAPTER FIVE

MOOSE IN THE EARLY HISTORY OF NORTH AMERICA

BY THE TIME of the white man's earliest exploration, moose were apparently already established across the northern regions of the continent. During Jacques Cartier's early exploration of the St. Lawrence River, dating from 1535, he made sketchy records of the indigenous big game but failed to identify several of them by any standards which could be used to establish records of the exact species he encountered (Biggar, 1924). Later authors have considered that one of the species which provided food for Cartier's men, through barter with the Indians, was probably moose (Stephens, 1890; Merrill, 1920), although this is doubted by Seton (1927). Roberval, who visited the St. Lawrence shortly afterward, also fails to identify moose definitely, although his list of animals has been translated to include them (Biggar, 1924).

It was not until 1603 that Champlain began his explorations that produced definite accounts of moose or *orignac*, which he recognized as being quite similar to the European elk (Bourne and Bourne, 1911; Merrill, 1920). Lascarbot (Grant, 1907–14) began his exploration of "New France" a year or two after Champlain, and their early accounts of moose together with those of subsequent explorers and authors have been summarized by Merrill (1920) and Seton (1927). An early account was written by Morton (1632, chap. v) in which he describes the moose in New England.

First, therefore I will speake of the Elke, which the Salvages call a Mose: it is a very large Deare, with a very faire head, and a broade palme, like the palme of a fallow Deares horne, but much bigger, and is 6. footewide between the tipps, which grow curbing downwards: Hee is of the biggnesse of a great horse.

There have bin of them, seene that has bin 18. handfulls highe: he hath a bunch of haire under his jawes: he is not swifte, but stronge and large in body, and longe legged; in somuch that he doth use to kneele, when hee feedeth on grasse.

Hee bringeth forth three faunes, or younge ones, at a time; and being made tame, would be good for draught, and more usefull (by reason of their strength) than the Elke of Raushea. These are found very frequent, in the northern parts of New England, their flesh is very good foode, and much better than our redd Deare of England.

Their hids are by the Salvages converted into very good lether, and dressed as white as milke.

Of this lether, the Salvages make the best shooes, and use to barter away the skinnes to other Salvages, that have none of that kinde of bests in the parts where they live. Very good buffe may be made of the hids, I have seene a hide as large as any horse hide that can be found. There is such abundance of them that the Salvages, at hunting time, have killed of them so many, that they have bestowed six or seaven at a time, upon one English man whome they have borne affection to.

With the beginning of the seventeenth century the increased tempo of exploration and settlement brought about a great exploitation of the moose. More accurate, detailed, and complete accounts were made by the Jesuit missionaries in their *Relations*, in which they referred to moose as *l'élan* or *l'orignal* (Thwaites, 1896–1903, 73 vols.). From these accounts it is quite evident that moose provided one of the more important sources of food and clothing for the Indians and food for the missionaries of the St. Lawrence area, as well as for early travellers and residents across the northern coniferous forest belt (Thwaites, vol. 4, p. 203; vol. 9, p. 25; vol. 36, p. 197). The missionaries frequently refer to hunger and starvation among the Indians and themselves because of failure to obtain moose (Thwaites, vol. 32, p. 41; vol. 39, pp. 113–115; vol. 45, p. 61; vol. 46, p. 227; vol. 55, pp. 151–153). To the Indians, the moose had previously meant food, clothing, and materials for barter with other tribes or for fashioning various implements. The coming of the white man and fire-arms made moose meat and skins important articles of commerce which created an unprecedented exploitation of moose by both Indians and whites (Thwaites, vol. 4, pp. 151–153; vol. 35, p. 33; vol. 45, p. 193).

At Tadousac, a trading post at the mouth of the Saguenay River, there had been 151 skins traded by the Indians in 1646 by the last of May (Thwaites, vol. 28) and more than 500 in 1648 (Thwaites, vol. 32, p. 103).

On Manitoulin Island, in Lake Huron, the Indians were supposed to have killed more than 2,400 moose by use of snares during the winter of 1670–1, according to Nicolas Perrot (Blair, 1911, p. 221); however, the validity of this claim, especially the identification of the animals involved, seems open to doubt. In all probability the Indians killed caribou rather than moose.

In 1672, Denys gave an account of the great killing of moose, relating that, in the territory of the head of the Bay of Fundy and the St. John River, the Sieur d'Aunay in his time (from 1635 to 1650) traded over 3,000 moose skins a year (Ganong, 1908).

The early white travellers also took part in this accelerated destruction of moose. Upham (1905) gives an account of the travels of Groseilliers and Radisson, quoting an instance (p. 505) in which they claim to have killed over 600 moose southwest of Lake Superior in one spring about 1660, with the aid of Indians.

From the Journal of Dollier and Galinée, 1669–70 (Kellogg, 1917, p. 207), the following notation is made: "Meat is so cheap here [near Sault Ste Marie?] that for a pound of glass beads I had four minots of fat entrails of moose, which is the best morsel of the animal. This shows how many these people kill."

This uncontrolled hunting of moose was certain to make drastic reductions in the numbers of moose in the newly settled areas.

By 1721, Charlevoix (Kellogg, 1923, vol. 1, p. 182) remarked on the noticeable decrease in moose in the area of Lake St. Peter: "Let us now return to our hunting; that of the elk would be no less advantageous to us at this day than that of the beaver, had our predecessors in the colony paid due attention to the profits which might have been made by it, and had they not almost entirely destroyed the whole species, at least in such places as are within our reach."

Further south, in Maine (now Norridgewock, Maine) one of the Jesuit writers wrote in 1723 that the Indians had so destroyed the game of their country that for the past ten years they had been unable to secure either moose or deer (Thwaites, 1896–1903, vol. 67, p. 213).

East at Cape Breton, Denys reported in 1672: "This island has also been esteemed for the hunting of moose. They were found formerly in great numbers but at present there are no more. The Indians have destroyed everything, and have abandoned the island, finding there is no longer the wherewithal for living." (Ganong, 1908, p. 187)

This pattern of depletion extended across most of the settled areas with the advance of white populations in eastern Canada and northern United States so that by the beginning of the nineteenth century, the future of moose seemed uncertain in many areas.

CHAPTER SIX

GENERAL POPULATION STATUS

THERE ARE NOT ENOUGH DATA available at present to assess the general status of moose in most of Asia and eastern Europe. In the Scandinavian countries of Sweden and Norway, relatively high moose populations are being maintained in spite of comparatively dense settlement and heavy hunting.

The record is much too vague and incomplete to enable one to define accurately the distribution or status of moose across North America during the early years of invasion by the white man. However, sufficient records are available to give an indication of the distribution about 1875 (Figure 6).

STATUS IN THE UNITED STATES

In general, it appears that the moose was formerly much more abundant in the northern New England and western Great Lakes states than it is now. It is only in these general areas that the moose has disappeared. Apparently the moose was never exceptionally abundant in the western states within historic time; however, it apparently has been showing encouraging increases in recent years.

Since 1937, the United States Fish and Wildlife Service (formerly the Bureau of Biological Survey) has compiled estimates from the various states to give an approximation of the size of existing herds in the United States for each of the following years:

1937–13,346 (U.S., 1939a)   1943–11,803 (U.S., 1946)
1938–16,375 (U.S., 1939b)   1946–16,543 (U.S., 1948)
1939–14,803 (U.S., 1940)   1947–17,900 (U.S., 1949)
1940–11,584 (U.S., 1942)   1948–11,700 (U.S., 1950)
1941–11,840 (Jackson, 1944)

Pennsylvania

"Rhoades omitted moose from his list of Recent Mammals of Pennsylvania, but Dr. Schoepf, the distinguished German traveler, mentioned the black moose as having occurred in Northampton County in 1783; and moose were also reported to him as having been numerous in the Allegheny Mountains between what are now Altoona and Pittsburgh." (Goodwin, 1936, pp. 48–49) "Moose were extirpated from Pennsylvania in 1790 or 1791" (Cahalane, 1942, p. 107). Rhoades (1903) did, however, record fossil remains of moose in the state. Further reference to early records is given by Merrill (1920).

New York

"The moose which once roamed throughout the state has been extinct in New York since the early sixties" (Miller, 1899, p. 302). DeKay (1842) gave the records of distribution in 1841 and thought they were on the increase. The last record Merriam (1884) could find was of an animal killed in 1861. Seton (1927) could locate no evidence that moose ever occurred in the Catskill Mountain region. Grant (1902) discussed the last survivors in New York and urged reintroduction. The legislature of the state appropriated funds to reintroduce moose into the Adirondack region, which was their last stronghold (Hornaday, 1904), but these efforts, according to Merrill (1920) ended in failure.

Connecticut

"There is . . . up to the present time, no proof that moose ever occurred within the state in early days. It is, therefore, of interest to record the discovery of a fragment of moose antlers from an Indian shell heap on Fisher's Island. This indicates a former range farther to the south of its known limits within the historic period and presupposes a former occurrence in Connecticut." (Goodwin, 1935, p. 175) This meagre evidence for occurrence in the state is further supported by Goodwin with a report of a single moose which supposedly crossed over from Massachusetts in the winter of 1933–4.

Massachusetts

Moose were apparently common as far south as this state when it was first settled by the Europeans (Morton, 1632), but have been "practically extinct in Massachusetts since about the beginning of the 19th century but occasional stragglers have been reported in the more mountainous and unsettled regions" (Crane, 1931, p. 272). Several other scattered records have been brought together by Warfel (1937a) and Moore (1944), the latter observing two moose as late as 1942.

Vermont

"In Vermont, Moose were populous in colonial times and furnished an important source of food but, because they were such conspicuous and easy targets, did not long survive" (Cahalane, 1942, p. 107). Warfel (1937b) has summarized the records for the state, where they have been protected by law since 1876. The original population is thought to have become extinct and most of the animals recorded since about 1900 have been strays, immigrants, or releases (Warfel, 1937a, 1937b; Osgood, 1938). No moose were listed for Vermont in the big-game inventories of 1937, 1938, or 1939 (U.S., 1939a, 1939b, 1940); five estimated in 1940 (U.S., 1942); two in 1941

(Jackson, 1944); none in 1943 (U.S., 1946); three animals for both 1946 and 1947 (U.S., 1948, 1949) and 10 in 1948 (U.S., 1950).

New Hampshire

"Moose and possibly caribou continued to exist in northern Vermont and New Hampshire until about 1900, and still on rare occasions they may stray into the upper parts of these states" (Goodwin, 1936, p. 48). Additional records for the state are given by Seton (1927), Jackson (1922), and Cahalane (1942). State-wide estimates have been made as follows (U.S., 1939a, 1939b, 1940, 1942, 1946, 1948, 1949, 1950; Jackson, 1944):

1937—34	1943—43
1938—40	1946—40
1939—56	1947—none listed
1940—52	1948—50
1941—50	

Maine

When Maine was first settled by the white man, moose were apparently common throughout the entire state. Prior to 1904, St. Michael-Podmore (1904, p. 32) states "the State of Maine was 'the sporting paradise' for moose." Hornaday (1904, p. 140) estimated that 3,000 moose were killed by hunters between 1894 and 1902. Aldous and Mendall (1941, p. 5) report that "by 1904 moose were found only in the northern counties. Since then, however, for some unknown reason these animals have appeared more commonly in the southern half of the State. . . . In the extreme northern and western parts of the State, moose are now reported to be rare. . . . At the present time moose are barely holding their own. In a few areas it is quite obvious that they are increasing, but in many others there is a noticeable decrease."

In 1938 Arroll L. Lamson (Walcott, 1939, pp. 268–269) wrote: "There has not been an open season on Moose since 1935 and then it lasted only three days. There are not likely to be any more open seasons in the state of Maine. . . . The number of Moose in Maine today does not exceed twenty-five hundred; there is only a slight increase since they have had complete protection."

Estimates of the numbers of moose in Maine have been compiled by the United States Bureau of Biological Survey (later Fish and Wildlife Service) for the following years (Jackson, 1944; U.S., 1946, 1948, 1949, 1950):

1937—1,839	1943—3,506
1938—1,671	1946—5,000
1939—1,842	1947—6,500
1940—2,103	1948—2,500
1941—2,283	

Michigan

To summarize the history of the moose in Michigan, we may say that early records show they were commonly hunted in the northern part of the state, although possibly they were not so plentiful as in other areas to the east, north and northwest; that the number of moose was very limited in the latter half of the nineteenth century, owing to one or more factors, such as unsuitability of habitat, excessive hunting, and so called phenomenon of 'drift,' or some other unknown influence; and that they are probably as numerous now as they have been at any time during the last sixty years. (Hickie, 1936, p. 632)

The distribution in the state is given by Burt (1946, p. 261): "Formerly over most of the state, but now confined to Isle Royale and a few places in the Upper Peninsula, where the Conservation Department is attempting to reestablish them. . . . It is doubtful if they will ever become an important game animal in the state again."

Between 1934 and 1937 a total of 71 moose were released on the upper peninsula from Isle Royale (Hickie, undated). The fate of this venture remains to be determined.

Murie (1934) received a report that moose had become scarce on Isle Royale in 1880. He states (p. 9): "In former years moose apparently crossed over from the mainland at intervals, but hunting was probably at that time sufficient to prevent the moose from becoming numerous or gaining a foothold." There was no record of moose on the island for several years. Shiras (1935) neither saw nor heard of moose there in 1886. Adams (1909) failed to include them on his list of mammals on Isle Royale; but this omission did not exclude a possibility that there was still a remnant of an original population. In any case, some animals were present on the island a few years later:

According to persons long familiar with Isle Royale, the last influx of moose occurred during the winter of 1912–1913. That winter was so cold that the water between the island and the mainland to the north froze over. The presence of moose on the island the following summer is correlated with conditions of the previous winter, and it is presumed that a few moose crossed over on the ice. (Murie, 1934, p. 10)

Their numbers increased steadily until 1930 when Murie estimated that at least 1,000 animals were present on the island and suggested that perhaps there might be as many as 2,000 or 3,000. He reported the serious food shortage which forecast the dramatic decrease in numbers that followed a few years later. "How many moose were left on the island by 1935 is not known but the number perhaps did not exceed 200. By 1936 the carrying capacity for moose on the island had probably reached its lowest point." (Aldous and Krefting, 1946, p. 296) After about 1937 there was an apparent steady increase in moose again. Aldous and Krefting (1946) estimated 510 moose were present in 1945, and Krefting estimated about 650 in 1947 and felt that the moose were still steadily increasing (personal communication).

Big-game inventories give the following estimates for the entire state of Michigan (U.S., 1939a, 1939b, 1940, 1946, 1948, 1949, 1950; Jackson, 1944):

1937—1,021	1943—265
1938— 221	1946—600
1939— 250	1947—743
1941— 285	1948—775

Wisconsin

Moose were apparently quite abundant in the general area of northern Wisconsin and Minnesota during the early explorations of Groseilliers and Radisson about 1660 (Upham, 1905). Cory (1912) gathered many of the early records for the state and makes the following remark (p. 75): "Moose were abundant in Wisconsin up to the middle of the last century, and more or less common in a few localities at a much later date. It is not unlikely that even at the present time one or two individuals may still be found in the extreme northwestern part of the state." Additional information on occurrence in 1870 is given by Seton (1927). Later records have been collected and summarized by Scott (1939) including reports of a few stragglers as late as 1938. The last reported animal was identified by an ear tag as one of the Isle Royale moose released on the upper peninsula of Michigan. Scott felt that moose might increase in the extreme northwestern part of the state, but at present their status is uncertain.

Minnesota

In the early history of Minnesota, moose were apparently common throughout the northern half of the state as far south as Pine County (Surber, 1932), but their present range has been greatly decreased and now is practically confined to the northernmost tier of counties (Swanson, Surber, and Roberts, 1945). Several records of moose observed or killed between 1897 and 1921 are given by Johnson (1922, 1930). Cahn (1921, p. 121) states concerning moose: "Rapidly nearing extinction in Itasca County, and very seldom seen." Manweiler (1941) discusses the efforts of the Minnesota state government to improve habitat conditions in the region between the Red Lakes and Lake of the Woods, with assistance from the federal government. He felt that "more moose in suitable habitats has resulted" (p. 43).

Surber's concept of the recent status of Minnesota moose was as follows:

At the present time they are increasing in the Red Lake Game Refuge and apparently spreading north and west from that area. That the range of the moose has shifted and continues to shift as years pass by is evidenced by what old settlers relate. We know that they are continually shifting back and forth across the Canadian border, in Minnesota today and Canada tomorrow, and this condition, it is believed, applies to moose living along the entire boundary line from the Pigeon River to Lake of the Woods County. . . .

While the moose has been protected since 1922 it is doubtful if it has increased, taking the state as a whole, to any considerable extent since this law went into effect. (Swanson, Surber, and Roberts, 1945, pp. 22–23)

Estimates for Minnesota are given as follows (Jackson, 1944; U.S., 1946, 1948, 1949, 1950):

1937—4,018	1943—2,672
1938—3,649	1946—4,500
1939—5,193	1947—3,000
1940—2,039	1948—1,100
1941—1,390	

North Dakota

Although no recent records are available for the state, Bailey (1926, pp. 31–32) summarized early records and gives the following information:

From the great forests on the north and east, the moose in the early days entered North Dakota in the Turtle Mountains and along the timbered fringes of the Red River Valley. In 1800, Alexander Henry (1897, pp. 90, 118) stated in his journal that they frequented the mouth of Park River. He also said that the Pembina Hills made a famous country for moose and elk. In 1887, when the writer was at Bottineau, moose were still reported from the Turtle Mountains, and in 1912, records were obtained of some killed there in 1888, 1899 and 1906. . . . It is not improbable that an occasional pair may still stray into these mountains, and if given sufficient protection these moose might stay to restock their old range.

Colorado

The range of moose does not normally extend as far south as Colorado. Occasionally they stray into the state, as evidenced by records given by Seton (1927) and Bailey (1940, 1944). In each case a single moose was observed to be associated with a number of wapiti.

Wyoming

Following early settlement and the decline of moose in the Rocky Mountain states, little was known of the actual status of the remaining animals. It was not until the explorations of George Shiras III from 1908 to 1910 (Shiras, 1912) that a unique and fairly large population of moose was discovered in Yellowstone National Park in Wyoming. In honour of Shiras' discovery and contributions to the knowledge of moose and other wildlife, this mountain race was described as *A. a. shirasi* by Nelson (1914). The number of moose began to increase, especially in Yellowstone National Park after its establishment (Shiras, 1913; Skinner, 1927; Jackson, 1944). Blunt (1950, p. 21) provides information from the annual reports of the State Game Warden:

From the Annual Report of 1908:
"Ten years ago we had but a 'handful' of moose in Wyoming, but today, we have a very respectable number of these animals along the Tetons, on the upper Yellowstone and at the head of the Green River."

From the Annual Report of 1910:

"The open season for moose comes in 1912. But few of our people appreciate the increase of moose during the past ten years. Where a moose was a rare sight, dozens of them are now seen. We cannot boast of large herds; but northwestern Wyoming contains several hundreds. Absolute protection for a number of years accounts for this increase."

Annual Report of 1912:

"The moose that inhabit the mountains of our state are increasing, for I understand these animals are seen quite frequently by hunters, and from all reports I should judge that there are now about 500 head in the state. . . ."

Estimates of moose in Wyoming have been made for the following years (Jackson, 1944; U.S., 1946, 1948, 1949, 1950).

1937—3,360	1943—4,305
1938—3,439	1946—2,500
1939—3,525	1947—2,900
1940—3,500	1948—3,200
1941—3,650	

Wyoming has an open season for moose which has resulted in the legal kill of the following number of moose since 1940 (Wyoming, 1950).

1940— 44	1945—130
1941— 64	1946—206
1942—120	1947—180
1943—190	1948—214
1944—116	1949—377

Cahalane (1948, p. 256) reports that moose are plentiful in Teton National Park although "hunting in the surrounding region during 1945 and 1946 caused a noticeable reduction in the number of park moose."

Montana

In a summary of the early history of big game in Montana, Koch (1941) quotes a record of moose having been killed in 1832 as far out into the plains as the vicinity of Milk and Missouri rivers. No record is available to indicate the relative abundance of moose in the state during early settlement; however, moose apparently decreased markedly until after the establishment of Yellowstone National Park in 1872. The park apparently formed a protected nucleus from which moose have spread northward in Montana. In adjacent areas north of Yellowstone National Park moose increased to such an extent that an open season was declared in 1945 under a limited licence system (Montana, 1942; Cooney, 1946; Couey, 1948). A total of 99 moose were reported killed in 1947 (U.S., 1949) and 55 in 1948 (U.S., 1950).

Bailey (1918) found a few moose in Glacier National Park, although he was told that moose were more numerous than elk in 1895. In 1932 Wright, Dixon, and Thompson (1933) found moose still scarce but apparently increasing in the park. Cahalane (1948) reports that moose are plentiful in both Glacier and Yellowstone national parks. At present moose are widely scattered throughout the mountainous portions of the state (Montana, 1942). Estimates for the total number of moose in Montana have been made as follows (Jackson, 1944; U.S., 1946, 1948, 1949, 1950).

1937–2,187	1943–3,445
1938–2,508	1946–3,900
1939–3,567	1947–3,700
1940–2,800	1948–3,100
1941–3,065	

Idaho

The early status of moose in Idaho, as in many other localities, is obscure. Merriam (1891) reviewed early records and wrote that moose occurred in the Salmon River Mountains in the latter part of the nineteenth century but were nowhere common. Brooks (1906) discussed a restricted population in southeastern Idaho. Davis (1939) has reviewed later records and given the following information (p. 370): "Formerly distributed over much of the mountainous portion of the state; now reduced in numbers and found mostly near Yellowstone National Park and in northern Idaho." Further records for northern Idaho are given by Rust (1946). The following estimates of the number of moose in Idaho seem to indicate definite increases in recent years (Jackson, 1944; U.S., 1946, 1948, 1949, 1950).

1937– 887	1943–1,560
1938– 845	1946–2,200
1939– 785	1947–1,000
1940– 900	1948–1,000
1941–1,109	

Oregon

Although moose do not presently occur in the state, evidence is given by Dice (1919), Seton (1927), and Bailey (1936) which suggests that they occasionally strayed into the Blue Mountains area in former years. Five Alaskan moose were introduced in 1923 but the last survivor was thought to have been killed in 1931 (Bailey, 1936).

Utah

Records of moose occurring within the state have been compiled by Durrant (1952). These records have been confined to the Uinta and Wasatch mountains in the following counties: Cache, Davis, Utah, and Weber. According to Durrant, the occurrences in Utah are "accidental."

Washington

Rare stragglers have been reported in the state by Scheffer (1944). It is suggested that these animals wandered southward from British Columbia (Dalquest, 1948).

STATUS IN ALASKA

Moose occur throughout at least 240,000 of Alaska's 590,000 square miles (Dufresne, 1942). "Although most abundant on Kenai Peninsula . . . and in Rainy Pass, the moose has extended its range well out into the treeless Alaska Peninsula and has also been found within a few miles of the Arctic coast" (Dufresne, 1942). Sufficient records are not available to determine accurately the early status and distribution of moose throughout the vast interior of Alaska, although more recent local references to moose have been made by Osgood and Bishop (1900), Osgood (1904, 1909), Dice (1921), Leopold and Darling (1953), Rausch (1950, 1951), Sheldon (1930), Spencer and Chatelain (1953), Murie (1944), Dixon (1938), Laing and Anderson (1929), Williams, M. Y. (1925), and others.

Toward the end of the nineteenth century, Turner (1886) stated that moose had become plentiful within the previous fifty years and that a single animal killed in the vicinity of Pastolik, near St. Michael, in 1876, was the first instance of an occurrence of the species on the seacoast, north of the Yukon River. A year later, Nelson and True (1887, p. 287) wrote of the moose as follows:

It is unknown near the Arctic coast, but may occur on the Pacific slope of the Alaskan Mountains, in the Cook's Inlet and Copper River district. North of the Alaskan range of mountains, which closely follows the Pacific shore line, the Moose is a well-known animal throughout the interior wherever the spruce and white birch forests occur. They range to the tree limit in latitude 69° and from Bering Sea at the Yukon mouth to the Canadian boundary line. They are more common along the large water-courses, where the heaviest forests are found, than elsewhere, and they are most numerous about the headwaters of the Yukon and Kuskoquim Rivers. . . .

The fur traders and Indians claim that the Moose has been found west of Fort Yukon only within the last twenty-five or thirty years, and that only within the last ten years have they been killed below Anvik and Mission, on the Lower Yukon.

A few years ago a single Moose was shot in the Yukon delta close to the sea, which is the only record I have of its occurrence so far to the west. . . . It is possible that the claims of the natives are true, and that the moose has extended its range to the north-west within the last few decades. . . .

Pike (1896) stated that moose were increasing in numbers from the Yukon boundary along the Yukon River as far west as the junction of the Tanana and up the latter stream to its head.

Porsild (1945) reports that a moose was killed near the Arctic coast of Alaska not far from the Alaska–Yukon boundary in December, 1931. Dufresne (1946) states that the moose of the region north of the Arctic Circle is a smaller animal than the Kenai type (*A. a. gigas*) which suggests the possibility of a westward movement from the Mackenzie Delta region of *A. a. andersoni* or some related form.

According to Stone (1924), no moose had reached the Pacific in south-eastern Alaska, and Seton (1927) and others have not included southeastern

Alaska within the range of the species. However, Dufresne (1942) mapped the distribution of moose indicating that approximately 500 animals were found in that area and later (1946) stated that the moose of the valleys of southeastern Alaska represent an overflow of the British Columbia moose. This seems to suggest another instance of the moose having recently extended its range.

Nelson and True (1887) remarked that it was reported moose had crossed the Alaskan mountains and were found on the Pacific slope about Kenai Peninsula. They felt quite pessimistic about the future of moose as indicated in their statement (p. 288): "The introduction of fire-arms among the natives has rapidly diminished this fine animal, and its extinction in Alaska is but a matter of comparatively few years."

But they not only survived but seem to have expanded westward: "According to reports the moose has but recently appeared in the Cook Inlet region; the older Indians say no moose were there when they were boys; and even within the memory of white men it has moved westward, now being as far out on the Alaska Peninsula as Katmai" (Osgood, 1901, p. 61).

According to Rausch (1951) moose have long been present in the Colville River region since the local natives were told that their fathers and grandfathers had hunted them there.

Brooks (1953) reports the killing of a bull moose on September 20, 1948, at Cape Prince of Wales on Seward Peninsula (lat. 65°36′, long. 168°05′). This apparently constitutes the most westerly record for moose in North America.

Dufresne (1946) states that moose were practically unknown on the Kenai Peninsula prior to the great forest fire of 1883 but that they have since moved into the area and become abundant. He estimates the total population of moose in Alaska at approximately 30,000, although earlier, Palmer (1941) had stated that the Alaska Game Commission estimated a total population of approximately 60,000 animals. Although there is little basis for determining which estimate would be more nearly correct, the trends in recent years would seem to indicate that the number now present would be greater than the lower estimate.

Status in Canada

Although the greatest portion of the moose range in North America is found in Canada, insufficient records have been kept to make a very close estimate of the total number of moose present either now or in the past. Using estimates for the United States and Alaska, Hosley (1949) ventures to guess that Canada's moose population might be in the neighbourhood of 146,000 animals. An attempt at a more accurate estimate would be pure speculation. Nevertheless it seems entirely possible that the estimate should be revised upwards, perhaps even up as high as 300,000. At any rate, it seems conservative to estimate the present population of moose in Canada at something between 200,000 and 300,000. It also seems reasonable to assume that Canada's greatest primitive population probably never exceeded 500,000.

In the following sections, each province is discussed, with the exception of Ontario, which is the subject of a more detailed study in the next chapter.

New Brunswick

Moose were common and were hunted in great numbers during the early explorations of Champlain (Bourne and Bourne, 1911), Lescarbot (Grant, 1907–14), and Denys (Ganong, 1908). For the next period, an excellent review is given by Squires (1946, pp. 36–37):

The first legislature of New Brunswick passed an act for the preservation of the moose in 1786 but the law was permitted to expire in 1792 and the moose continued to be hunted for its hide until it was nearly exterminated. Fisher (1825) wrote "Moose or Elk had been wantonly destroyed for their skins, and in a few years they totally disappeared. A few have lately been seen and a law enacted for their preservation, but can scarcely be reckoned among the present animals of the province." Head (1829) said "The Moose deer . . . is of a race nearly extinct; a few only are killed every year in the spring." Cooney (1832) wrote "now totally extinct in our forest, formerly two hunters could kill 100 a month." Hatheway (1846) stated it a little differently, saying that the moose were almost completely destroyed in the 12 years following 1783, and that those not killed migrated to the Peninsula of Nova Scotia or to the northwest country.

No doubt the great scarcity at this time applied only to the more accessible parts of the Province while the moose remained unmolested in the remote wilderness at the headwaters of the Restigouche and Miramichi. At any rate it is stated that they began to reappear in the New Brunswick forests in 1834–6. They were still hunted for their skins, especially in the spring when there was a crust on the deep snow and every moose in a yard could be killed. The situation became very serious, and in 1877 it was enacted that moose, caribou, and deer should not be hunted from January 1st. to August 1st. This was followed by a closed season from 1888 to 1890. In the latter year hunters were permitted to kill one bull moose, but the closed season on cow moose has continued to the present. A license for non-residents was first introduced in that year. Of course, much illegal hunting continued but many of the persons most responsible for it finally found that there was a great deal more money to be made by guiding and looking after the needs of the non-resident hunters, and they became ardent conservationists. When a license was required for all resident hunters in 1897 and finally to carry a rifle in the woods at any time, it became possible to enforce the game laws much more effectively.

After 1900 moose apparently increased markedly, for by 1920 the number of legally killed animals was 1,596 (New Brunswick, 1921). The annual kill averaged over 1,000 until 1930 (New Brunswick, 1922–31) after which there was a sudden drop to only 447 killed in 1931 and finally to only 205 moose legally killed in the entire province in 1936 (New Brunswick, 1932–7). Squires (1946) and others attributed the great decline in numbers to the effect of winter ticks (*Dermacenter albipictis*). Since 1936 there has not been an open season for moose. However, the game officials have carried out a moose census with the following estimates for the province (New Brunswick, 1938–46):

1937—3,995	1942—10,390
1938—6,065	1943—10,884
1939—8,018	1944—no estimate
1940—8,758	1945— 7,720
1941—8,520	

These estimates are based on the reports of game wardens on their patrols and are, therefore, only approximate, but should give comparative trends.

In the report for 1947 (New Brunswick, 1948, p. 46) the most recent trends are expressed as follows: "Reports received from members of the field staff indicate that the moose situation continues to improve throughout the Province. The increase was particularly evident in the central and northern counties of the Province." Wright (1952) found that there was a high population along a narrow belt in southeastern New Brunswick with the remainder of the province being populated by sparse but slowly increasing herds.

Nova Scotia

Moose were common in the Annapolis Basin, and probably in all the province, at the time of Lescarbot's explorations prior to 1609 (Grant, 1907–14). Denys' 1672 report that the Indians had completely exterminated the moose of Cape Breton Island is followed by a footnote by Ganong (1908, p. 187): "The moose is now abundant on the island, and probably never was really exterminated." Pennant (1784) stated that moose inhabited the Isle of Cape Breton. There seems to be considerable doubt concerning the early status of moose on the island and there has not been an open season there since prior to 1907. In 1928 and 1929 two adults and five calves were placed in Inverness County, Cape Breton, from the mainland (Dale, 1934). In 1947 and 1948 the Dominion government made further introductions of moose from Elk Island National Park, Alberta.

The following summary is given by the report of the Department of Lands and Forests of the province of Nova Scotia for 1933:

Our earliest records indicate that moose were exceptionally plentiful over the entire Province, the Island of Cape Breton included. However, owing to the unrestricted killing carried on at that time which was, in a great many cases, simply for the hide, moose became scarce, markedly so about the year 1825, which condition continued so that in the year 1874 a close season of three years was put into force. This close season, with added prohibition of snaring and hunting with dogs coming into force about 1879, probably saved the moose from extinction at that time.

There does not appear, however, to have been any noticeable increase until about 1907. This is not surprising considering the fact that the benefits of the close season and the forbidden practice . . . [of] snaring and hunting with dogs was offset by the fact that, from 1877 for a period of five years, the season was opened from October 1st to

January 31st, after which time it was further extended by opening it on September 15th. During part of this time each hunter was allowed to kill, regardless of sex, three moose and five Caribou. . . . Some years later this was reduced to two moose and four caribou. . . .

In 1902 the number of moose shot was estimated at 350. In 1907, the first year in which hunters were required to report the kill, the number was 486. This included both sexes. In 1908 the Act was amended, prohibiting the shooting of cow moose and from that period forward there has been a gradual increase in the number of moose, and I think it is generally conceded that moose were the most plentiful about the year 1922. (Nova Scotia, 1934, pp. 45–46)

The report of the Department of Lands and Forests for 1947 (Nova Scotia, 1948) shows that a peak number of moose was killed in 1921 of 1,480; dropping to a low of 890 in 1924; rising to 1,567 in 1931; and dropping again to 809 in 1935. Cameron (1948, p. 94) states that "since that time there has been little if any increase. Woodsmen in the area, however, believe that there has been a slight increase in the past year."

Beginning with 1938, Nova Scotia has had a completely closed season and in 1947 reported that: "All available information obtainable on the problem of the moose population indicates a continued closed season is desireable for the present" (Nova Scotia, 1948, p. 69).

Prince Edward Island

There are no moose on the island now and only vague references are available to indicate that there ever were. Seton (1927) states that moose are known to have been exterminated from Prince Edward Island by man, although as early as 1672 Denys (Ganong, 1908, p. 209) wrote about the island as follows: "As for Moose, there are none of them. There are Caribou, which are another species of Moose." If moose ever occurred on Prince Edward Island, they became extinct there at a very early date, perhaps before settlement by the white man.

Newfoundland

Moose are not indigenous to Newfoundland but have been introduced in recent years. According to reports quoted by Seton (1927) a pair was obtained about 1878 from Nova Scotia and released near Gander Bay. These moose were thought to have died until a bull was killed about 1912 or 1913 which was assumed to have been a descendant of the original pair. About 1904 four or five additional moose were obtained from New Brunswick and released near Grand Lake (Seton, 1927). Seton received reports of general increases and estimated the total population had reached over 2,000 animals. Mr. William E. McCraw of Bishop's Falls, Newfoundland, wrote that moose had "spread fairly well all over the island" (Jan. 26, 1935, Royal Ontario Museum of Zoology, questionnaire files). Mr. R. C. Goodyear of Deer Lake, Newfoundland (Feb. 12, 1934, R.O.M.Z. questionnaire files) gave the following information: "Under Government protection they increased rapidly up until about ten years ago, when poachers began making inroads into the herd. It would appear that there cannot now remain more than about one-third of the number that existed in the year 1924. The herd then increased to several thousand."

Mr. H. W. Walters, Chief Game Warden of Newfoundland, wrote as follows (personal letter, Oct. 14, 1948):

The facts are that Moose were introduced here successfully in 1904 when, according to our records, four Moose were released at Howley. By 1912 Moose were being seen frequently within forty or fifty miles of their release point. By 1930 their range had increased to about one hundred miles from their release point and by 1945 Moose had stretched to other areas of the country, including the Avalon Peninsula. Since 1946 we have had no restrictions on the sale of licences which, in a normal year, now amounts to approximately 5,000. The kill of Moose varies for this number of licences at 1500 to 1600 including the illegal kill. There has been no apparent decrease whatever as the areas showing the greatest kill have consistently maintained their average over the past few years. Any estimation of the numbers now in the country is only guesswork but I would judge that the total stock is not less than 20,000 animals.

Pimlott (1953) has recently reviewed the introduction and spread of moose into Newfoundland. "The history of the population appears to consist of two main periods. The first period of approximately 25 years was one of rapid dispersal and low densities. The second period, which extends to the present time, was one of build-up to high densities." (p. 565) The number of animals known to be killed during open seasons has increased from 747 in 1945 to 3,383 in 1951.

Quebec

Moose were apparently common along both sides of the St. Lawrence River during the explorations of Champlain. In 1663 Boucher (Monti-zambert, 1883) remarked on the numbers of moose at Three Rivers. Apparently the range of moose was being extended northward during that time but little historical data are available since travels and explorations into the northern interior by the Europeans were quite limited. From the Jesuit *Relations* 1660–1, an account is given of the area midway between Tadousac and Hudson Bay along the height of land:

One sees here neither fine forests nor beautiful fields, and the people of these regions know not what it is to cultivate the soil, but live simply as the birds do on what prey they may secure by hunting and fishing. Often in winter, when both fail, they themselves fall a prey to famine—moose and other animals being rare here, because, owing to scanty growth of wood, they find no covert. (Thwaites, 1896–1903, vol. 46, p. 277)

After exploring the Lake Mistassini region between 1892 and 1895, Low (1896, p. 70L) reported as follows: "Caribou and moose, once plentiful in the region, are almost extinct, and can no longer be relied on as a source of food by the Indians. . . ." Grant (1902, p. 229) stated that "there is no record of their ever appearing east of the Saguenay River. . . ." Mr. G. E. LaMotte of Chicoutimi, Quebec (Jan. 17, 1934, R.O.M.Z. questionnaire files), estimated that moose probably entered the Saguenay River area about 1900. In 1895 Dr. R. Bell (Dawson, 1896) explored the Nottaway River (flowing into the south end of James Bay) and reported that moose were confined to the southern portion of that watershed.

Few records have been kept of the status of moose in the province, and of the number killed by hunters. The distribution of moose now apparently extends from between Eastmain and Rupert House on the eastern side of James Bay eastward to Seven Islands, due west of Anticosti Island (personal communications). Bell (1898, p. 376) discussing the migration of moose states that ". . . in the Gaspé peninsula the last interval between its leaving and again returning to the same district was upwards of half a century. . . ." Later, Goodwin (1924) reports moose were common in the same area in 1923. Newsom (1937a) relates that 20 moose were introduced on Anticosti Island between 1895 and 1913 which supposedly increased to 250 animals, although he found only one track during his work there.

The present status of moose in Quebec is uncertain. The Province of Quebec Association for the Protection of Fish and Game, Inc. has followed other conservation-minded groups and individuals in expressing great alarm over the apparent declining number of moose there.

In their annual report (Anon., 1948a) several recommendations for increased protection were given including the following remarks: "This Province probably still has the nearest thing to a 'working supply' of moose in the world. Moose are really rare in Nova Scotia. New Brunswick is so low that moose hunting has been prohibited for several years. Ontario has less than Quebec." (p. 5) "In spite of heavier hunting last year, the legal kill decreased alarmingly. It looks as though we are reaching down near the bottom of the bag, as travellers in the bush report seeing less and less moose." (p. 7)

Manitoba

Between 1694 and 1714 Jérémie (Douglas and Wallace, 1926) reported many moose in the area north of Lake Winnipeg, now called Split Lake and Grass River. Similar reports for the same area are given by Turnor and Hearne for 1774–5 (Tyrrell, 1934) and by Carver (1778). Seton (Thompson, 1886, p. 5) stated that moose in Manitoba were "sparingly distributed wherever the locality is congenial. But it may be described as plentiful in the Duck and Riding Mountains, and in the low country about Lake Manitoba." Still later Preble (1902, p. 43) reports that the moose "occurs in suitable places throughout the region traversed from Lake Winnipeg nearly to Hudson Bay. . . . At Oxford House 60 or 70 miles beyond Robinson Portage, the moose was formerly almost unknown, according to the information received independently from several officers of the Hudson Bay Company, but is extending its range toward Hudson Bay and is now frequently killed near that part." Concerning the region farther south at Island Lake, Anderson (1924a) quotes a letter from Mr. E. T. Blunderl, Island Lake Post, written in 1920, stating that moose were unknown in that area 40 years previously but had gradually appeared in increasing numbers. Tyrrell (1892) and Turner (1906) reported that moose were plentiful throughout most of the forest region of Manitoba. Seton (1927) received a report in 1911 that moose tracks were observed within about twenty-five miles of Churchill (to the south). Seton (1927) estimated that moose occupied about 60,000 of the 70,000 square miles included within the original boundary of Manitoba, at the rate of one moose per square mile. These estimates were based on reports of the great numbers of moose observed and killed in the area north of Winnipeg between 1900 and 1906. At that time there were an estimated 10,000 moose killed annually according to reports quoted by Seton.

In 1914 there were 2,447 moose legally killed and reported in Manitoba; an average of slightly less than 1,500 between 1915 and 1920; 662 in 1921; then dropping steadily to only 257 in 1924 (Jackson, 1926). Criddle (1929) reported moose "tolerably common" about 1928 in the area of Aweme, and a little later Green (1932) reported moose "nowhere plentiful" in Riding Mountain National Park.

Mr. F. M. Mowat visited northern Manitoba in 1947 and 1948 and has provided the following original notes:

Moose appear regularly at the south end of Nueltin Lake and in July 1947 I found fresh droppings at Nileen Rapids at the south end of the Lake. However I am fairly certain that this is the extreme upper limit of their range, and the local population is small. The density of population increases steadily to reach a peak in the country about Fort Hall Lake where the country is very suitable for moose, and an almost complete lack of human predation enables them to hold their own. On the upper Kasmere, and from Fort Hall to the Cochrane River moose droppings were plentiful at every portage. Only four animals were seen, but fresh tracks were found along the shores of all the lakes and lakelets. This area has high repute as moose country in the stories of the Chipeweyan Indians.

Down the Cochrane River to Reindeer Lake and in the entire Reindeer area as far west as Cree Lake, and east to the longitude of Duck Lake, moose are now considered to be very scarce. The entire Indian and native population at Brochet which consists of 350 people hunting over a 29,000 square mile territory, were unable to kill more than 4 moose in the summer and fall of 1948, as far as is known.

To the north east, the northern limit of permanent moose range seems to lie somewhere near Duck Lake where the animals are reputed to be very scarce. At Eganolf Lake a few animals were reported in the fall of 1948.

Soper (1946, p. 151) makes the following statement:

In primitive times the moose was widely distributed in the southern extremity of Manitoba, but it is now confined to the coniferous forest along the Ontario border, and

Spruce Woods Forest Reserve. Only a remnant of the former population remains in the latter area, but it is common to abundant in various parts of the eastern wilderness. This is particularly true of favourable "pockets" east and northeast of Whitemouth Lake and Whiteshell Forest Reserve. In the Early days the species is said to have inhabited Pembina and Tiger Hills and Turtle Mount; in these parts it was perhaps extirpated as long ago as 1890 or 1900, except for rare stragglers from points farther north.

From 1932 to 1941 an average of only 167 moose were legally killed and reported, with a high of 248 in 1932 and a low of 75 in 1936 (Manitoba, 1942). In 1943 and 1944 the reported kill was 170 and 160 animals, after which a closed season for moose was put into effect (Manitoba, 1947). While these figures give no index to the number of moose actually killed nor to the relative state of populations, they do indicate that moose have decreased and have not returned in recent years to anything near their primitive numbers.

Saskatchewan

Preble (1908) compiled the most complete summary of the early exploration of the northern part of the province and made one of the first attempts to outline the northern limits of the distribution of moose in northwestern Canada.

During his explorations he found moose more or less common throughout the central and northwestern portions of the province, but absent from the plains of the north and the northeast corner beyond Reindeer Lake. At that time Preble suggested a northward movement of moose. Tyrrell and Dowling (1896) found moose as far north as Stone River (flowing west into Lake Athabaska) and suggested that this was near their northern limit of range in that section. Buchanan (1920) reported having seen many moose in the vicinity of Churchill River and Reindeer Lake in 1914.

From the annual report of the Department of Natural Resources for 1941 (Saskatchewan, 1942, p. 72) the following excerpts are made: "With the advance of civilization and agriculture, many of our good moose districts have disappeared. . . . Moose are still quite plentiful, and their range is very extensive in that it spreads from the edge of the present populated areas to the extreme northern part of the province. Very few moose are to be found in what was once good moose territory south of the C.N. Railway running to Prince Albert from the Manitoba border." Soper (1946) reports that a few moose still occur on Moose Mountain, which have become an isolated "pocket" south of their present normal range. Between 1913 and 1919 the number of moose legally killed and reported varied from 456 to 1,215 with an all-time high of 1,220 animals reported for 1920 (Saskatchewan, 1914–22). From 1921 to 1928 the average kill reported was about 546 moose annually (Saskatchewan, 1923–30). In 1930 the kill reported increased to 1,163 (Saskatchewan, 1932). Thereafter, the number of moose killed began decreasing almost steadily (Saskatchewan, 1933–46). For the seasons 1944 and 1945 the kill had dropped to 219 and 256 respectively after which the hunting season was closed (Saskatchewan, 1945–7a). In 1947 "the moose population showed some increase during the year particularly in the east central part of the province. . . ." although it was felt that a continued closed season was necessary (Saskatchewan, 1947b).

Alberta

Preble's (1908) review of early explorations and natural history considers the northern portion of Alberta where moose were already widespread in the latter part of the eighteenth century. During 1798–9 David Thompson stayed at Lac la Biche, 105 miles northeast of Edmonton, and reported that in five months the hunters "gave us forty-nine moose all within twenty miles of the (trading) house and a few bull Bisons; whereas on the Stoney region it would be a fortunate trading house that during the winter had the meat of six Moose Deer brought into it, and even that quantity would rarely happen" (Tyrrell, 1916, p. 305).

In 1882 (p. 338) Macoun wrote: "On the Peace River plains and within the Rocky Mountains the Moose is very abundant, and forms the staff of life for the greatest number of inhabitants on that river. . . . At all the Hudson's Bay Company's posts on the Peace river, one or more hunters are constantly employed supplying the residents with meat." From 1907 to 1913 the number of moose reported killed in the organized district increased from 17 to 865 (Alberta, 1908–14). From 1914 to 1924 an average of 1,000 moose were reported killed annually (Alberta, 1915–25). For the next five years the numbers of moose reported killed were not published. By 1931 a total of 2,599 animals were reported legally killed for that year. In the following years moose began to decrease, and certain areas were closed to hunting (Alberta, 1926–35). During the winter months from 1932 to 1935 serious die-offs were reported, many of which were associated with heavy infestations of ticks. For the past few years the over-all status of Alberta's moose population has been uncertain.

In Wood Buffalo Park in northern Alberta, Soper (1942) found moose "more or less commonly distributed" in 1932–4. He estimated that the local Indian population killed approximately 400 to 450 moose each year with little if any appreciable effect on the population. In the parkland belt or "aspen grove section" (Halliday, 1937) lying between the prairies and forested areas, moose were commonly killed by the early settlers (Fowler, 1937); a few were still reported in that area as late as 1925 (Farley, 1925).

A letter from Mr. Tony Lascalles (Banff, Alberta, Jan. 26, 1943; in the Royal Ontario Museum of Zoology files) gives the following information: "Twenty years ago, it is authoritatively said, the sight of a moose in Banff,

Yoho, and Kootenay Parks was quite unusual. Today, moose are extremely abundant, especially in the Bow River valley between Banff and the Continental Divide, and between Lake Louise and the Saskatchewan." The general status of moose in the national parks of southwestern Alberta and adjacent British Columbia has been discussed by Clarke (1940a, 1942) and Cowan (1944, 1946). Banfield (1950, p. 10) makes the following comments on moose in the Waterton Lakes National Park, where he estimates the population at 35 head:

The moose has only recently re-appeared in the Park. Dr. Anderson made no mention of the moose in his report of 1938. That the moose formerly occurred in the area is proven by the large head at the headquarters buildings which was dug out of a swamp in the Stoney Creek area many years ago.

This re-colonization of the Park is in line with a general increase in moose in the area south of the Crow's Nest Pass as reported by E. S. Huestis, Alberta Game Commissioner. E. Beatty, Chief Naturalist of Glacier National Park, reports a recent increase in that Park also.

Moose at present are found throughout most of the province with the exception of the prairie section of the southeast and the settled aspen grove section.

In the annual report of the Department of Lands and Mines for 1943–4 (Alberta, 1945, p. 76) the general status of moose seems to be summarized in the following statement: "Many districts of the Province reported a serious decrease in the Moose population, and many theories have been advanced in an effort to explain this decline. . . ."

British Columbia

Although the earlier status of moose in British Columbia is somewhat obscure, the spread of moose into central British Columbia within comparatively recent years has been fairly well known (Brooks, 1926, 1928; McCabe and McCabe, 1928a, 1928b; Munro, 1947; Hatter, 1947, 1948, 1949; Racey, 1936; Williams, M. Y., 1925). Munro (1947) and Hatter (1948) have traced the spread which began about 1885–95 with dates of entry into various localities. Since this known movement began,

. . . extensive regions have been populated and the invasion has penetrated as far south as the vicinity of Kamloops; as far west as Kitimat, which is on the Granville channel about 40 miles southwest of Terrace and for an undetermined distance north. As with other animal invasions, or successful introductions, moose increased slowly at first, then, in the more favourable localities, with an acceleration that produced over stocking of range and a subsequent decline to a condition approaching a balanced population. (Munro, 1947, p. 151)

Following the rapid increase that took place in several localities, population peaks seem to have been reached between 1926 and 1936 with noticeable declines thereafter (Munro, 1947; Hatter, 1948). In other areas either high populations or general increases seem to continue (Munro, 1947).

Concerning the general movement of moose into central British Columbia, Munro (1947, pp. 151–152) makes the following comments:

So far as I am aware there is no evidence indicating that similar invasions occurred in a remote past. Certainly there were no moose in these regions at the time of the early explorations during the last decade of the eighteenth century, and no records prior to that time are available. No factual explanation has been offered to identify the factors which put into motion, or continued to impel, this movement. The question has often been the subject of debate and various conjectures, such as the reduction of Indian population to the northeast, the decrease of predators in one locality, or the increase of predators in another, and the building of the railway to Prince Rupert, have been offered in explanation of this remarkable invasion.

A second movement of moose was noted by Brooks (1928) which suggests that moose of the Flathead region of the Montana–eastern British Columbia border were moving northward about 1902 and had crossed the Canadian Pacific Railroad by 1907 to meet the central British Columbia invasion later somewhere along the Columbia River.

In northern British Columbia, MacFarlane (1905) reported that between 1865 and 1875 moose were more abundant in the Fort Nelson region than at any time in the following two decades. McConnell (1891) remarked on the great abundance of moose along the Liard River below the mouth of the Dease River in 1887–8 and suggested a recent increase in numbers had taken place in that area. Cowan (1939) reports moose quite abundant in the Peace River district. Swarth (1936) finds moose in "fair abundance" in the region near Atlin. He states (p. 404): "The local belief is that moose have greatly increased in numbers during the past 20 or 30 years." Rand (1944) adds notes on the occurrence and status of moose at specific localities along the Alaska Highway through the northeastern portions of the province. Munro (1949) finds a high winter population in the Vanderhoof region.

Pike (1896) suggested that a third invasion of moose took place beginning about 1870 from northeastern British Columbia along the Liard River into the vicinity of Dease Lake, Telegraph Creek, and as far south as Little Canon on the Stikine River. This movement has apparently been extended to southeastern Alaska in recent years (Dufresne, 1946).

No early estimates of the total moose population of British Columbia have been made, nor has any record been kept of the number of persons hunting moose or of their reported kill. Munro (1947) estimated, on the basis of reports from 511 non-residents and 1,986 licensed trappers in 1942, that the rate of success in hunting was approximately one moose for every 3.4 hunters.

From this figure he calculated that the 6,119 licensed big-game hunters in 1942 would have killed 1,799 moose, and that the total, including those killed by settlers and Indians would have been approximately 3,000. Munro's estimate for 1942 would appear to be conservative for more recent years as evidenced by the fact that in 1946 a total of 1,310 moose export trophy fees were paid compared to 899 in 1945 (British Columbia, 1947, 1948). "Whatever the size of the annual kill may be there is no reason to believe that it has not been within the recuperative capacity of the species to tolerate, for populations generally are being maintained, and some expansion in space is still going on" (Munro, 1947, p. 155).

Hatter (1948) reports that the recent population is not as high as the peak number that was reached ten to fifteen years previously but that in some areas there are too many moose for the existing food supply. "Even under more intensive management it is doubtful if central British Columbia will again realize the high densities that have recently been obtained" (Hatter, 1949, p. 495). Dufresne (1952) ventures to estimate the total population of moose in British Columbia at about 50,000.

Northwest Territories

In a review of the early explorations in the area, Preble (1908) found that moose were commonly encountered by Hearne as early as 1771–2 south of Great Slave Lake. Other early explorers found moose all along the Macken _ie River to its mouth near the tree limit and as far east as Great Bear Lake. Mackenzie (1801) found "plenty of moose" on the northwest side of Great Slave Lake. MacFarlane (1905) remarked that moose were numerous in the "Great Mackenzie Basin" prior to 1861 but were greatly reduced in numbers after about 1866. This reduction was borne out by many witnesses before the committee which inquired into the resources of the "Great Mackenzie Basin" (Canada, 1888). Anderson (1924a) states that moose were reported to be increasing all along the Mackenzie River in 1908 but were thought to be decreasing a few years later. "During 1927–28 and 1930–35 moose were rare in the Mackenzie delta and only a few were killed. . . . According to native informants, moose were formerly more abundant and the present scarcity is attributed to excessive hunting and to the absence of large areas not frequently visited by hunters and dog teams." (Porsild, 1945, pp. 19–20) During MacFarlane's travels he noticed that moose occasionally wandered out on the barren grounds some distance from the limit of trees. Anderson (1924a) reported several additional records of moose wandering out in the barren grounds as far as 30 or 40 miles. Preble (1908) compiled several records during his own explorations and worked out a distributional map for moose which includes the Northwest Territories.

After about 1905 moose apparently began spreading eastward as shown by records compiled by Anderson (1924a). Two moose were reported seen near the mouth of the Rae River, at the west end of Coronation Gulf by 1909 or 1910, where they were apparently quite new and rare to the Copper

Eskimos (Anderson, 1924a). Mr. F. K. Ebner of Yellowknife, Northwest Territories, writes (personal letter, May 3, 1948): "Moose come down to the Arctic coast regularly. The natives killed some there every year I was at Coppermine. The moose evidently come down the Rae or Richardson River. They generally spend the winter about fifteen or twenty miles up the Richardson River, that is to say, that many miles from the settlement Coppermine. One fall six moose out of seven were gotten." Anderson (1924a) gives records of moose having wandered as far east as Chesterfield Inlet by 1923. Although Clarke (1940b) found no definite evidence of moose having occurred in the Thelon Game Sanctuary, he did summarize several reported occurrences in that general area. Manning (1948) found no signs of moose north of Big Sand and Neck lakes, Manitoba, while en route from Reindeer Lake to Baker Lake, Northwest Territories.

Mr. F. M. Mowat spent parts of 1947 and 1948 in south-central Keewatin district and kindly submitted the following notes on moose of that general area:

During late summer and early fall moose are irregularly reported to move out into the barrens as far north on the Kazan River as 61 degrees 30 min. Lat. The Eskimo along the Kazan report that moose are seen nearly every year, but only one or two individuals each year. On Sept. 4, Ohoto, a reliable eskimo of the Kazan band, reported seeing "large moose with very small horns" near the Kazan River at about the latitude already given.

In 1947 Charles Schweder, a trapper at north Nueltin Lake, informed me that he had only once found sign of moose in the barrens. This was in 1946 when he saw fresh tracks in a light snow fall about Oct. 10. The location was about 50 miles south southeast of Kamiluk Lake. In 1947 I found a very old single antler at the north end of Seal Hole Lake which lies just north of Nueltin Lake. From conversations with the Eskimo and with Schweder, it would seem that in the fall single animals wander northward into the barrens, and occasionally get several hundred miles north of heavily timbered country. There is no data on what happened to these animals, but Schweder tells me that once, several years ago, a single moose was seen moving with a small herd of Rangifer arcticus.

Moose occasionally move as far north as Windy River on Nueltin Lake, but the few records from this area are probably for animals that were drifting on into the barrens. During two seasons at Windy River no sign of moose was noted by me.

There is a single record of a moose being killed at the narrows of Nueltin Lake about 1940, but the exact date and data on the person who killed the animal is not available.

During a trip down the Thlewiaza River from Nueltin to the coast, no sign of moose was noted, however the Eskimo along this river report that "a long time ago" moose used to be seen sometimes about Edehon Lake. These Eskimo were quite certain of the identity of the animal, and one man had actually seen a moose at Edehon with his own eyes "many years ago."

The general over-all status of moose throughout the immense area of the Northwest Territories is extremely difficult to evaluate. Additional references to more local areas may be found in Williams (1922, 1933), Fairbairn (1931), Blanchet (1926), Anderson (1937), Hornby (1934), Harper (1932), Clarke (1944), Soper (1942), and works listed in the bibliographies of Preble (1908) and Clarke (1940b).

Yukon Territory

Although moose occur quite commonly throughout the Territory south of its barren lands (Dawson, 1896; Osgood and Bishop, 1900; Osgood, 1909; Camsell, 1906a; Williams, M. Y., 1925; Sheldon, 1911; Merrill, 1920; Clarke, MS; Rand, 1945a, 1945b; and others) their early status and distribution remain shrouded by the lack of definite information on this remote and relatively inaccessible area during the white man's early conquest. The moose of the Yukon are generally conceded to be the Alaskan form (*A. a. gigas*) which now extends throughout the interior area drained by the Yukon River and its tributaries. Pike's (1896) observation on the spread of moose from Upper Liard River into Northwestern British Columbia and the Francis River area, Yukon Territory, suggests the possibility that the central continental form of moose has extended its range into southeastern Yukon Territory to meet the Alaskan form, probably somewhere in the vicinity of the Teslin, Nisutlin, Rose, Ross, and Pelly rivers. This suggestion seems to be substantiated by the following statement by Rand (1945a, p. 49): "Mr. Drury said that old-timers tell of there being no moose in this part of the Yukon, [Canol Road] evidently before 1900. They then appeared and increased, and now they seem to be decreasing."

An evaluation of the present status of moose in the Yukon Territories would be largely conjecture. The number of moose killed by the relatively few inhabitants of the Territory has been amazingly large (Osgood and Bishop, 1900; Osgood, 1909; Merrill, 1920; Clarke, MS, and personal communication; Rand, 1945a, 1945b). The recent practice of legal market-hunting in the Yukon has complicated the evaluation of present moose resources.

CHAPTER SEVEN

DISTRIBUTION AND STATUS OF MOOSE
IN ONTARIO

EARLY HISTORY

PERHAPS THE EARLIEST WHITE MAN definitely to record moose within the boundaries of the area which is now Ontario was Gabriel Sagard, between 1623 and 1624. From his accounts, written in 1632, it appears that moose were quite rare in the Huron country south of Georgian Bay but very common north of there in the early seventeenth century (Wrong and Langton, 1939). There seems too little evidence to indicate that the region south of Georgian Bay to Lake Ontario was ever a part of the normal range of moose within near-recent times.

Moose were apparently fairly common in the western region near Lake of the Woods as early as 1731, at which time the French traders mentioned them in their writings but failed to give any indication of relative abundance or extent of range (Burpee, 1927).

The vast interior of the province remained little known for many years and consequently few early data on the indigenous game animals of the area are available. Philip Turnor travelled from Moose Factory to Lake Superior *via* the Moose and Missinaibi rivers in 1781 but failed to mention moose, although a few other mammals were recorded in his journals (Tyrrell, 1934). That other early explorers of this area did not record moose seems to attest the early absence of the animal from the broad belt extending from the north shore of Lake Superior to James Bay. Shiras (1921, p. 186) stated that there were no moose along the northern shore of Lake Superior at the time of his first visit in 1870. The early use of the names Moose River and Moose Factory would seem to suggest that moose were indigenous somewhere near by, but the names probably came from the Moose Indians who originated in moose country and later migrated to James Bay *via* the Moose River.

DISTRIBUTION AND DISPERSAL

In an attempt to trace the spread of moose in Ontario, some of the earliest available dates of occurrence or absence and estimated entry dates have been plotted (Figure 8). After Figure 8 had been prepared, an early map showing the known distribution of moose about 1888 was discovered in a

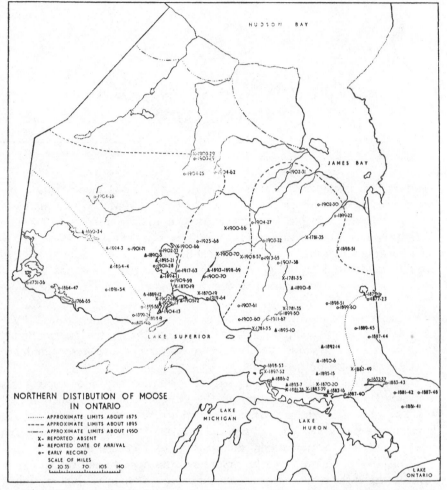

FIGURE 8. The spread of moose into Northern Ontario. Numbers following dates indicate sources listed below. In the list of sources, one asterisk means Royal Ontario Museum of Zoology questionnaires; two asterisks mean special moose questionnaires:

(1) Snyder, 1928, p. 15
(2) Snyder *et al.*, 1942, p. 118
(3) Johnson, J. A.,* 1934
(4) Troke, Ed.,* 1934
(5) McKurdy, Jack (comm. to A. de Vos, 1948)
(6) Bates, M. U.,* 1934
(7) Esket, Harvey A.,* 1934
(8) Pinette, G. J.**
(9) Chief Penassi (comm. to Col. L. A. Deer)
(10) Crichton, V.**
(11) Gresky, Alex**
(12) Edwards, Frank*
(13) Cress, Ed.*
(14) Sawyer, C. E.**
(15) Phillips, Collin**
(16) McIvor, W. J.*
(17) Barr, Peary**
(18) Barr, Peary**
(19) Shiras, 1921, p. 186
(20) Shiras, 1921, p. 186
(21) Beatty *et al.*, 1901
(22) Barlow, 1899, p. 38
(23) Barlow, 1899, p. 38
(24) McInnes, 1899, p. 10
(25) McInnes, 1906c, p. 159A
(26) Camsell, 1906b, p. 152A

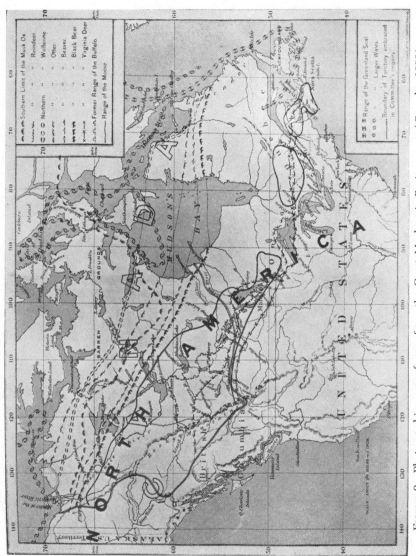

FIGURE 9. Photographic copy of map from the Great Mackenzie Basin report (Canada, 1888)

publication called *The Great Mackenzie Basin: Reports of the Select Committees of the Senate, Sessions 1887 and 1888* which was edited by Chambers (1908). The original report (Canada, 1888) was checked and the original map photographed (Figure 9). No record is available to indicate who was responsible for the preparation of this map. However, Professors John Macoun and Robert Bell were among those who gave evidence at the original sessions and who would have had reliable knowledge of the distribution of moose at that time. Certainly Professor Bell would have known of the presence or absence of moose north of Lake Superior for he had made several geological survey trips in that area prior to 1887.

Shiras has claimed that there were emigrations of moose about 1885 from the east and the west into the area above Lake Superior: "About 1885 a steady movement of the moose westerly from Quebec was observed and a slower easterly migration from northern Minnesota. Eventually these animals commingled and took possession of the entire shore [Lake Superior], later extending into the interior until they reached the waters flowing into Hudson Bay." (Shiras, 1921, p. 186) Writing of the moose of the upper Ottawa River and Lake Kipawa region, Grant (1902, p. 229) provides

(27) Wilson, 1906c, p. 172A
(28) Wilson, 1905, p. 105A
(29) McInnes, 1906b, p. 107A
(30) Wilson, 1906a, p. 240A
(31) Wilson, 1906a, p. 240A
(32) Wilson, 1906b, p. 119A
(33) McInnes, 1906a, p. 213A
(34) McAree, 1901, p. 256
(35) Tyrrell, 1934
(36) Burpee, 1927
(37) Wrong and Langton, 1939
(38) Bowman, C. D. (Ont., 1881, no. 1, p. 35)
(39) Lillie, Henry (Ont., 1883, no. 2, p. 35)
(40) Bolger (Ont., 1887, no. 3, p. 36)
(41) Kickson, J. (Ont., 1881, no. 6, p. 29)
(42) Purvis, F. (Ont., 1881, no. 7, p. 37)
(43) Niven, A. (Ont., 1883, no. 15, p. 43)
(44) Purvis (Ont., 1887, no. 19, p. 49)
(45) Campbell, A. W. (Ont., 1889, no. 27, p. 47)
(46) Bolger, T. O. (Ont., 1885, no. 31, p. 55)
(47) Bolger (Ont., 1886, no. 5, p. 48)
(48) Fitzgerald, J. W. (Ont., 1887, no. 25, p. 42)
(49) Bolger (Ont., 1882, no. 35, no mention)
(50) Niven, A. (Ont., 1899, no. 12, p. 47)
(51) Niven, A. (Ont., 1898, no. 11, p. 51)
(52) Tierman, J. M. (Ont., 1897, no. 8, p. 46)
(53) Tierman (Ont., 1898, no. 10, p. 46)
(54) Niven, A. (Ont., 1891, no. 25, p. 47)
(55) Carver, 1778, p. 114
(56) Stewart, E. (Ont., 1895, no. 65, p. 49)
(57) Speight and van Nostrand (Ont., 1908, p. 102)
(58) Speight and van Nostrand (Ont., 1907, p. 57)
(59) Ont., 1909, p. 16
(60) Speight (Ont., 1903, p. 33)
(61) Niven (Ont., 1907, p. 55)
(62) Prince, L. A. (field notes R.O.M.Z. files)
(63) Phillips and Bonner (Ont., 1917, p. 80)
(64) Crouch (Ont., 1919, pp. 84–86)
(65) Speight and van Nostrand (Ont., 1913, p. 66)
(66) Robinson, 1901
(67) Paulin and Bush (Ont., 1911, p. 95)
(68) Speight and van Nostrand (Ont., 1925, p. 56)
(69) Finlayson (comm. from C. A. Elsey, 1948)
(70) Neelands, 1901
(71) Aldous, F. H. (personal letter)
(72) Anderson, Oscar (personal comm.)

further evidence of the northwestward expansion of their range toward Lake Superior:

Twenty-five years ago they first appeared, coming from the south, probably from the Muskoka Lake country, into which they may have migrated in turn from the Adirondacks. This northern movement has been going on steadily within the personal knowledge of the writer. Ten years ago the moose were practically all south and east of Lake Kippewa, now they are nearly all north of that lake, and extend nearly, if not quite, to the shores of James Bay. How far to the west of that they have spread we do not know, but it is probable that they are reoccupying the range lying between the shores of Lake Superior and James Bay, which was long abandoned.

All available evidence confirms that moose have actually expanded their ranges to meet somewhere north of Lake Superior, but not that moose had previously occurred in that area within recent times. It is not known just when the movements from the east and west met but from examination of Figure 8 it might be estimated that a meeting probably took place about 1900, or shortly thereafter, along a general line projected northward from Lake Superior just west of the Long Lake region.

On special request, Mr. C. A. Elsey, District Biologist for the Ontario Department of Lands and Forests, interviewed several older residents of the Longlac region to determine early records of moose in the area. Mr. Elsey (personal letter, Oct. 13, 1948) writes:

Mr. Finlayson was able to give us first hand evidence since he was with his father when the first moose was killed in the Longlac region. In general Mr. Finlayson's report is as follows: In about 1895 his father and an Indian killed a moose somewhere north of Mobert, Ontario. The next moose signs were seen between McKay Lake and Pagwachuan Lake in 1897 or 1898. He and his father tracked down and killed two moose in the spring of the year in question. At this time the Indians were quite unfamiliar with moose and would not eat the flesh.

The moose population appears to have moved in rather slowly from the east, or south and east. After about ten years (around 1908) the population reached its greatest extent, and since that time has never been as large.

This account is substantiated by reports of the exploration party no. 5 (Neelands, 1901) which explored the region from Jackfish Station on Lake Superior to Long Lake; thence down the Albany River to James Bay. They mention the indigenous big game of the area, stating that caribou are fairly common, and report moose in the Long Lake region only, as follows (p. 157): "Only two or three moose are killed in a year by the Indians who trade at the local post, but they are said to be coming into the district from the east."

Farther west, exploration party no. 6 explored the region from Ombabika Bay at the northeast of Lake Nipigon by Ombabika River and canoe routes to the Albany River, and down the Albany to the mouth of the Kenogami (Robinson, 1901). The report mentions caribou and other wildlife but moose were apparently not encountered.

In the same year party no. 7 explored the region west from Wabinosh Bay on Lake Nipigon up the Wabinosh River and north to the Albany River (Smith, 1901). In a report on the fauna of the area (p. 206) they tell of moose beginning to move in about 1896:

Moose, caribou and black bear are found in this region, but very few are met with. Five caribou, four moose and nine black bears were seen during the summer, which proves to a certain extent that they are not at all plentiful. An Indian who hunts all summer only manages to get a couple of caribou, and then he thinks that he is fortunate.

A few years ago the caribou used to be fairly plentiful, while moose were not to be found at all. About five years ago a couple of moose were killed on Wabinosh Bay. Since that date the moose have been growing more plentiful, while the caribou have been disappearing.

It is possible that there was a minor movement of the western moose from Michigan to Ontario through the Sault Ste Marie region. Snyder et al. (1942, p. 118) give it as the opinion of local residents that it did not take place until about 1889: "According to the recollections of Mr. Frank Shew-felt and Mr. Hugh Erwin, long-time residents of the area, moose did not inhabit the Sault Ste Marie region in 1886. They were both of the opinion that Moose came in from Michigan 'following the White-tailed Deer,' about 1889." Although it seems logical that moose could easily have crossed over in such a manner, it would appear strange that they did not do so before 1886. By that time moose were quite scarce in Michigan (Hickie, 1937; and others) and their absence and subsequent appearance on the Canadian side could be logically correlated with the westward spread of the eastern moose.

FORMER STATUS

Although moose were probably present in fair numbers within the limits of their range at the time of the white man's entry and settlement in Ontario, those areas did not always "abound with moose during the early days." In fact, by 1888 there were probably far fewer moose in Ontario than there are today. Man had so thoroughly exploited this species that it became evident that some protection would have to be afforded to prevent its complete extermination in the province. The seriousness of the situation caused the provincial authorities to close the moose season in the entire province from April 1, 1888, to October 15, 1895, and to appoint a special Fish and Game Commission to investigate the future prospects for the wildlife species of the area. This commission attempted to evaluate the situation of moose and other game by use of questionnaires and by other means. In 1892 the Commission, in its report, foretold the extinction of the species if illegal killing was not stopped (Ontario, 1892, p. 192):

The evidence taken, points to the fact that the protection lately extended to this noble animal has had the effect of materially increasing is numbers, but illegal slaughter continues. . . .

. . . An indiscriminate slaughter of this noble animal has long threatened the total extinction of the race, and it is probable that the time is not far distant when the moose, like the buffalo, will be seen no more in Canada. (Ontario, 1892, p. 318)

There are insufficient records to give an accurate indication of the state of moose populations in the years that followed. Many reports indicate that moose meat was a food for mining and lumbering camps as well as for other residents throughout all seasons for a great many years. The over-all moose population seems to have continued to fluctuate, increasing for a period then decreasing again, in spite of uncontrolled killing and early efforts to conserve them.

Since the early land surveyors frequently commented on the moose situation in their reports, these, together with all other available specific references, were plotted on a map for each year since 1880. Examination of these records did not provide adequate coverage for the entire province, but did give some indication of the situation in the areas covered. That moose were not reported north of Lake Superior prior to 1900 could, of course, be accounted for in part by the scarcity of explorations in that area. But since several early accounts did fail to mention moose there, with no reports to the contrary, it may be assumed that these data are valid supporting evidence for the early absence of moose in that region.

RECENT STATUS

Since 1935, the Royal Ontario Museum of Zoology has sent out annual questionnaires to observers in strategic places throughout the province. Each observer is asked to report on the change in populations by indicating whether the number of moose has increased, decreased, or remained the same during the year in question. On the state of population, the observers are to report whether moose are abundant, scarce, or "as usual," the latter indicating a moderate population. When these opinions are compiled, reduced to percentages, and plotted (Figure 61), the total annual averages indicate that moose were considered to be decreasing from 1935 to 1939, increasing from 1940 to 1943, decreasing from 1944 to 1946, with subsequent indications of an increase following the closed season of 1949. The number of observers reporting moose as abundant dropped from 24 per cent in 1935 to 5 per cent in 1936; increased to 14 per cent in 1937; decreased to 9 per cent in 1939; increased to 14 per cent in 1940; slowly decreased to 3 per cent in 1945; increased to 9 per cent in 1946 and 1947; dropped again to 3 per cent in 1948, but increased to 8 per cent in 1949. The number of observers reporting moose as scarce followed reciprocal trends indicating a general average agreement that, for the province as a whole, moose have remained relatively scarce throughout the entire period (see pp. 209–11) with a general increase following the closed season of 1949.

In 1949 and 1950 a province-wide inventory of moose was undertaken with the Fish and Wildlife Division of the Ontario Department of Lands and Forests. A general approximation of the number of moose present was obtained by individual estimates of the number of animals present in each of the townships or organized trapline areas within the moose range. These estimates were also supplemented by aerial censuses of some sample areas.

In 1949, the total population of moose was estimated at approximately 17,500. In reviewing the limits of the accuracy of this estimate, it was felt that for practicable purposes the total population could be regarded as having fallen between 15,000 and 20,000.

In 1950, the population was estimated at approximately 22,000, or roughly between 20,000 and 25,000. A great part of this difference from the previous year was thought to be a definite increase in the moose population, although the later estimate is regarded as the more accurate of the two. No reliable estimate was obtained from most of the far northern part of the province, known as the Patricia portion of Kenora District; thus the above estimates do not include that area. In 1951 personnel of the Department of Lands and Forests carried out more investigations in a part of the region, as well as in other areas in the province, and estimated that approximately 11,000 animals were present in the western and central portions of the Patricia area, to give a total population of at least 33,000 moose.

By 1952 these investigated areas of Ontario were thought to contain approximately 37,000 moose. In 1953 a still more thorough coverage of the entire province resulted in an estimate of approximately 42,000. It must be remembered, of course, that these are merely estimates based on all the available information that could be brought together concerning an area of approximately 361,000 square miles. While the steady increase in estimated numbers over this period undoubtedly represents, in part, an actual increase in the total population, the fact remains that a significant portion of this increase represents a more accurate knowledge of existing populations.

HUNTING STATISTICS

Ontario has not had such intensive hunting of moose as Nova Scotia, New Brunswick, and Newfoundland. From 1921 to 1937 Nova Scotia issued an average of 9,908 combined moose and deer licences each year which averaged about one hunter for every 2 square miles of the entire province, varying from a low of about one hunter for every 3 square miles in 1924 to a high of one hunter per square mile in 1931. New Brunswick issued an average of 8,023 similar licences each year between 1920 and 1936. This gives an average of about one hunter for every 3.4 square miles, varying from a low of one hunter per 11 square miles in 1936 to a high of one hunter for every 1.7 square miles in 1920. The trend in Newfoundland has been towards increased hunting pressure (Pimlott, 1953). From 1945 to 1951 the average area (square miles) per hunter has been as follows: 14.1, 9.1, 7.0, 5.8, 5.9, 4.8, and 4.0. These licensed hunters were allowed to hunt either moose or caribou. According to the reported kill, caribou constituted from 8.2 to 13.1 per cent of the combined total of moose and caribou taken during this period.

In Ontario, the major portion of the moose range consists of approximately 300,000 square miles, yet an average of only 2,338 moose licences were

TABLE I

MOOSE HUNTING LICENCES ISSUED IN ONTARIO

Year	Resident	Non-resident	Total
1921	1,989	950	2,939
1922	1,584	1,256	2,840
1923	1,098	1,247	2,345
1924	1,385	1,651	3,036
1925	1,291	1,581	2,872
1926	1,359	1,347	2,706
1927	1,379	2,237	3,616
1928	1,371	1,271	2,642
1929	1,356	1,975	3,331
1930	1,548	1,368	2,916
1931	1,446	1,766	3,212
1932	1,135	538	1,673
1933	949	997	1,946
1934*	575	889	1,464
1935	496	680	1,176
1936	542	878	1,420
1937	580	1,043	1,623
1938	471	569	1,040
1939	497	593	1,090
1940	536	755	1,291
1941	611	1,115	1,726
1942	780	795	1,575
1943	854	504	1,358
1944	875	653	1,528
1945	1,282	1,426	2,708
1946	1,694	1,230	2,924
1947	2,270	1,516	3,786
1948	3,000	1,700	4,700
1949	closed	closed	
1950	closed	closed	
1951	1,400	closed	1,400
1952	3,620	closed	3,620
1953†	5,200	600	5,800

*First year non-resident moose licences issued were separate from deer licences.

†Incomplete, estimated.

issued each year between 1921 and 1948 (Table I). This would average about one hunter per 129 square miles, varying from about one hunter per 300 square miles in 1938 to one per 64 square miles in 1948.

During 1948 the Ontario Department of Lands and Forests sent out a special questionnaire to hunters and outfitters which has provided some data on the relative success of hunting (Table II). The number of hunters reported represents slightly more than one-fourth of the total licences issued. From these data it appears that one moose was killed for approximately every 3.5 hunters. In Nova Scotia there was an average of 8.4 licensed hunters for every moose killed from 1921 to 1937, ranging from a low of 5.4 in 1922 to a high of 12.3 in 1937. In New Brunswick similar data (1920–36) show an average of 9.2 hunters per moose killed, varying from

TABLE II

Statistics on Success of Hunting in Ontario for 1948

	Hunters	Man-days hunted	Moose killed	Hunters per moose kill	Man-days hunted per moose kill
Western forest region					
Fort Frances forest district	2	20	1	2.0	20.0
Kenora forest district	132	675	32	4.1	21.0
Sioux Lookout forest district	299	1,761	84	3.6	21.0
Total	433	2,456	117	3.7	21.0
Thunder Bay forest region					
Port Arthur forest district	42	288	12	3.5	24.0
Geraldton forest district	92	324	34	2.7	9.5
Total	134	612	46	2.9	13.3
Central forest region					
Chapleau forest district	239	1,483	51	5.0	29.8
Gogama forest district	32	160	9	3.5	17.7
North Bay forest district	24	135	2	12.0	67.5
Sault Ste Marie forest district	51	323	24	2.1	13.5
Sudbury forest district	39	254	10	3.9	25.4
Total	385	2,355	96	4.0	24.5
Kapuskasing forest region					
Cochrane forest district	42	350	25	1.7	14.0
Kapuskasing forest district	56	386	13	4.3	29.7
Total	98	736	38	2.6	19.4
Northern Ontario	4	12	0		
TOTAL FOR ONTARIO	1,054	6,171	297	3.5	20.8

a low of 5.2 in 1933 to a high of 13.9 in 1931. The fact that Nova Scotia and New Brunswick have issued combined moose and deer licences undoubtedly accounts for the lower rate of success in hunting in these two areas, since many hunters probably did not concentrate on obtaining moose. In Newfoundland, moose hunters enjoyed excellent hunting from 1945 to 1951 where on the average, slightly less than three licences were issued for each moose killed (2.6–3.4 hunters per kill). If based on Pimlott's (1953) adjusted data on the kill, and the caribou hunters were eliminated, the hunters' success would be even higher.

The average number of man-days spent hunting moose in Ontario was approximately 20.8 days in 1948 (Table II).

Since no returns have been required from moose hunters in Ontario it is difficult to determine the number of moose that have been legally killed in Ontario. On the basis of the 1948 questionnaires the kill might be roughly estimated at about 1,100.

Through the excellent efforts of Mr. V. Crichton, Fish and Wildlife Specialist of the Chapleau district, the questionnaires on that district filled out by hunters can be estimated to represent data for about 95 per cent of the hunters of that region. The Chapleau district, outside of the local game preserve, comprises roughly 5,780 square miles. In this area 239 hunters killed 51 moose (5 hunters per moose killed), which represents one hunter for about every 30 square miles and a moose killed in every 113 square miles. Moose hunting conditions in this district appear to have been little above average for areas hunted in Ontario.

Comparative statistics for Nova Scotia, New Brunswick, and Newfoundland are given in Table III.

Following the closed seasons in Ontario during 1949 and 1950, regulations were gradually relaxed to permit increased hunting. The estimated number of licences issued in 1953 (5,800) indicates that the hunting pressure has exceeded the 1948 level to become the highest on record in this province.

TABLE III

COMPARATIVE STATISTICS ON MOOSE KILLED IN NOVA SCOTIA,
NEW BRUNSWICK, AND NEWFOUNDLAND

	Nova Scotia 1921–37	New Brunswick 1920–36	Newfoundland 1945–51
Average annual kill	1,179	899	1,919
Highest annual kill	1,677 (1927)	1,596 (1920)	3,383 (1951)
Lowest annual kill	809 (1935)	205 (1936)	747 (1945)
Av. sq. mi. per moose killed	15	30	18
Greatest av. sq. mi. per moose killed	21 (1935)	136 (1936)	47 (1945)
Least av. sq. mi. per moose killed	10 (1927)	11 (1920)	10 (1951)

CHAPTER EIGHT

RATE OF REPRODUCTION

SINCE THE PRESERVATION of the species is dependent on the interaction of its biotic potential and environmental resistance, the resultant rate of reproduction becomes of vital importance in the general life history and ecology of moose. In this discussion the term fecundity is used to denote the actual rate or number of successful births of offspring compared to the potential rate. The rate of reproduction is here used to include both fecundity and the rate at which young are successfully reared after birth.

FECUNDITY

There is considerable disagreement among various authors concerning the ratio of single and twin calves. Seton (1927) and others have quoted the belief that a cow first produces a single calf and usually twins thereafter. A similar opinion is held for the Old World moose (Lönnberg, 1923). But there seems to be considerable disparity in the ratios found from one locality to another, with little evidence to support the above theory. In Algonquin Provincial Park in 1946 one set of twins and only two single calves were observed during 34 observations of approximately 27 different moose. Two pairs of yearlings were also noted which might be assumed to have been twins. During work in the St. Ignace area in 1947, 243 observations of approximately 100 different moose were made, which included only nine cows with single calves and none with twins. In the same area in 1948, 50 observations of approximately 24 animals included only two cows with single calves and none with twins. Murie (1934) reports that a little less than 5 per cent of 90 cows with calves were accompanied by twins on Isle Royale. Hatter (1948) reports that an average of 12 per cent of the cows with calves in British Columbia were accompanied by twins. In Montana, McDowell and Moy (1942) observed 30 single calves and no twins among 217 moose. Murie (1944) found 9 single calves and 7 sets of twins in the Mount McKinley area of Alaska.

Special record cards were distributed to observers across Ontario in 1947, 1948, and 1949. These cards were designed to facilitate the recording of all observations according to the sex and age of the moose. In 1947, 2,169 observations were recorded: of the animals observed, 214 were cows accompanied by calves less than one year old; 161, or 75 per cent, were single calves; and 53, or 25 per cent, twins. Similar recorded observations showed 61 (85 per cent) single calves and 11 (15 per cent) twins in 1948, and 104 (78 per cent) single calves and 30 (22 per cent) twins in 1949. These data are broken down according to forest regions in Table IV and compared with similar ratios for Newfoundland (Pimlott, 1953) and for Alaska (Spencer and Chatelain, 1953). An examination of these statistics shows considerable variation, both from area to area and from season to season. The combined years 1950–2 show an average of 12.9 per cent twins for Newfoundland and an average of 13.5 for Alaska. A total of records in Ontario indicates that an average of 22.7 per cent twins was observed. These data of course are too meagre and subject to too many influences to warrant critical analysis. Certain factors should be pointed out, however. The data from Alaska are based primarily on aerial counts during winter, while those from Newfoundland are apparently collected between July 1 and November 30. Data from Ontario apply to the entire year, but are heavily weighted toward spring and summer. The data from both Ontario and Newfoundland probably contain an unknown amount of duplication. Winter records are undoubtedly influenced by the early mortality of calves which is possibly significantly higher in the case of twins. It would be most interesting to know to what extent, if any, the rate of twinning is influenced by such factors as the population density of moose and their general nutritional level. Perhaps the low twinning rates observed in Newfoundland, Nova Scotia, St. Ignace Island (Ontario), Isle Royale (Michigan), central British Columbia, and south-central Alaska, can to a large extent be accounted for by the high density of the moose population in those areas. More research along these lines is needed. Unfortunately, the reproductive tracts of females of breeding age have not been sufficiently available to permit of making the basic studies needed. Schierbeck (1929) reports that hunters found only 21 (or 8 per cent) twins in 252 pregnant cows killed during an open season for cows in Nova Scotia. Pimlott (1953) was able to obtain 26 reproductive tracts of mature cows, 23 pregnant, five with twins (approximately 21.7 per cent twins).

On the basis of the limited data available to date, it appears that twinning normally occurs in less than one-third of the successful births with observed rates of between 10 and 25 per cent being common.

Seton (1927) gave no specific records but stated that Indians had reported the rare occurrence of triplets. Mr. Thomas Thorpe, retired District Forester of the Ontario Department of Lands and Forests, reports (personal communication) that on June 5, 1946, accompanied by Mr. S. D. Spence, he observed at close range a cow moose with three calves in Tennyson township in Sudbury forest district. Mr. Thorpe's observations were substantiated with meticulous detail, leaving little reasonable doubt that all three were born to the cow concerned. Mr. D. R. Williams of Sault Ste Marie, Michigan,

TABLE IV
Ratio of Single to Twin Calves

Area	Date	Total cows with calves	% single	% twins
Newfoundland	1950*	77	83.1	16.9
	1951*	146	76.7	23.3
	1951†	9	100.	
	1952*	64	92.2	7.8
	1952†	119	96.6	3.4
Newfoundland average, combined totals	1950–2	435	87.1	12.9
Ontario				
Central Ontario	1947‡	93	72.0	28.0
	1948‡	29	79.3	20.7
	1949‡	76	76.4	23.6
Central Ontario average, combined totals	1947–9	198	74.7	25.3
Northern Ontario	1947‡	26	61.5	38.5
	1948‡	22	95.5	4.5
	1949‡	27	77.7	22.3
Northern Ontario average, combined totals	1947–9	75	77.3	22.7
Midwestern Ontario	1947‡	44	93.2	6.8
	1948‡	4	75.0	25.0
	1949‡	15	86.5	13.5
Midwestern Ontario average, combined totals	1947–9	63	90.5	9.5
Western Ontario	1947‡	50	72.0	28.0
	1948‡	15	80.0	20.0
	1949‡	14	71.4	28.6
Western Ontario average, combined totals	1947–9	79	73.4	26.6
Ontario average, combined totals	1947–9	415	77.3	22.7
Alaska				
Kenai	1951§	158	83.5	16.5
	1952§	130	94.0	6.0
Susitna	1951§	445	86.5	13.5
	1952§	308	90.2	9.8
Copper	1952§	116	82.7	17.3
Alaska Peninsula	1953§	60	66.6	33.3
Alaska average, combined totals	1951–3	1,217	86.5	13.5
Grand average, combined totals	1947–53	2,047	84.6	15.4

Sources: *Pimlott (1953), record cards; †Pimlott (1953), field party; ‡moose record cards; §Spencer and Chatelain (1953).

reports (moose record card) having observed a cow with three calves near Coldwater River, 30 miles northwest of the Montreal River on the shore of Lake Superior, on June 15 and again on June 25, 1947. In all probability the two observations involved the same family. In Sweden, Lönnberg (1923) substantiated the occurrence of triplets by finding three embryos in cows shot by poachers, but comments that such cases are rare.

The reproductive rate of moose is greatly affected by there being a high proportion of so-called barren cows. In Algonquin Provincial Park in 1946, 7 adult cows were observed without calves, and 3 with. In the St. Ignace area in 1947, 14 barren cows (61 per cent) were noted compared to 9 (39 per cent) which were accompanied by calves. In the following year, 1948, only 2 cows were seen with calves and 2 without. Murie (1934) estimated that approximately 50 per cent of the cows on Isle Royale in 1929 and 1930 had no calves. Surber (1932) estimated a barren population of approximately 20 per cent in Minnesota. In a moose census in Nova Scotia, Schierbeck (1929) reports that of 6,175 cows counted, approximately half were without calves. Following this an open season for cows was put into effect for one year in Nova Scotia. A total of 561 cows were killed during a ten-day period in December. Schierbeck obtained reports on the occurrence of pregnant cows and found 273 or 52 per cent were barren. Certain inaccuracies were undoubtedly present in these data but the general trends seem to be quite significant. On the other hand, Pimlott (1935) found 23 pregnant cows out of 26 examined from Newfoundland. On the basis of moose record cards he found that 58 per cent of the 683 cows observed had no calf in attendance while 70 per cent of the 423 cows recorded by his field parties were apparently barren (combined records average 62.5 per cent).

Cowan (1944) found that 66 per cent of 28 cows in Banff National Park and 80 per cent of 22 cows in Jasper National Park had no calves in 1943. In the latter area in 1944, 70 per cent of 40 cows lacked calves, although Cowan (1946) points out certain possible errors in these figures. Later (1950) he summarizes the three years' results of his studies of moose in the national parks of Canada by stating that calves constituted a ratio of 33 per cent of the adult cows in 1943, 25 per cent in 1944, and 22 per cent in 1945. Hatter (1948) reports that in one area in British Columbia the percentage of calves to cows was found to be 28.7.

From Alaska, Spencer and Chatelain (1953) recorded 3,404 female moose of which only 1,157 were accompanied by calves (66 per cent without calves). In this case, however, the yearling females were included with the calfless cows. If the yearling females numbered approximately the same as the observed yearling males (487) the occurrence of calfless cows would be about 60 per cent for south-central Alaska in midwinter.

Data from the moose record cards from Ontario indicate that observers recorded 543 cows in 1947, 61 per cent of which were not accompanied by calves. In 1948, 240 cows were observed, 70 per cent of which were without calves, while in 1949, 403 cows were recorded, 67 per cent of which apparently had no calves. The occurrence of cows without calves is shown by forest regions in Table V.

In appraising this obviously high ratio of apparently barren cows it must be remembered that several uncontrollable factors affect the possible validity of such figures as a representation of actual facts. In the first place, moose frequently leave their calves in hiding or some distance away, especially while feeding. Under such circumstances a casual observer would not be aware of the presence of the calves. On several occasions cow moose were observed feeding on St. Ignace Island with no calf in sight, yet, after careful watching, a calf was noted to appear either during the feeding of the cow or more commonly when she had completed her feeding and was ready to move out of the area. Occasionally residents of Ontario, seeing a cow alone or with only one calf, have concluded that a black bear has killed the cow's only calf, or its twin, whereas the missing calf may only have been hidden by the cow. In general, a cow with calf appears in much

TABLE V

PERCENTAGE OF COWS WITHOUT CALVES OBSERVED IN ONTARIO

Forest region	1947		1948		1949	
	Cows with no calves	%	Cows with no calves	%	Cows with no calves	%
Southern	2	67	6	100	3	60
Central	119	38	90	75	162	68
Northern	46	63	19	46	25	48
Midwestern	103	70	22	78	43	74
Western	60	55	31	67	36	72
Ontario average		61		70		67

poorer physical condition than truly barren cows. Assessment of the general physical condition of a lone cow often enables experienced observers to detect the presence of a hidden calf. When comparing the relative number of calves and yearlings one suspects that in some cases the calf crop must be higher than the above data indicate since in many cases the number of yearlings observed was actually greater than the number of calves. A second important error which is undoubtedly included in the above data is the inclusion of yearling females with adults. It is easy, if unaided by binoculars, to mistake a yearling for an adult, especially if it is alone at a distance.

On the other hand, it seems more than a coincidence that the average rate of calfless cows should be so similar across North America (Newfoundland, 62.5 per cent; Ontario, 64.5 per cent; Alaska, 60 per cent). More detailed studies of reproduction, particularly in the younger age groups, are seriously needed.

Without any valid evidence to the contrary, it must, therefore, be accepted that the rate of reproduction of moose is quite low. All available records indicate that normally less than one-half of the adult cows (two years of age or older) produce calves each year.

FACTORS AFFECTING THE RATE OF REPRODUCTION

It is of fundamental importance to appraise some of the causes of such low productivity in moose. Predation, especially by bears, is frequently considered the primary cause of poor calf crops. Undoubtedly bears do kill a certain number of calves. However, this cannot be considered an important factor here if the data given by Schierbeck (1929) are even approximately correct. If less than one-half the cows were pregnant the answers must be sought elsewhere. No bears are present on Isle Royale, yet Murie (1934) found that half the cows were barren. Pimlott (1953) attempted to assess calf mortality in Newfoundland but found no high losses. Similar studies in Ontario met with the same result. Obviously a part of the answer must involve the success of breeding. In the case of Schierbeck's data the sex ratio was almost three cows for each bull. Such an unbalanced sex ratio is of importance in affecting productivity and will be discussed elsewhere. Nevertheless low calf crops and few twins occur in many areas in Ontario, including St. Ignace Island, where more balanced sex ratios are found. The same is true of Isle Royale. This then suggests that perhaps cows either breed on the average of only every second year or that some reproductive deficiencies must be operating as a limiting factor. The former hardly seems a reasonable explanation since cows are frequently seen accompanied by both a new-born calf and a yearling. It would appear more likely that a high percentage of the young cows fail to produce calves before their third year.

Recent developments in domestic livestock breeding have demonstrated correlations of successful breeding and size of multiple births with nutritional deficiencies and the general physical condition of the animals (Allen, Danforth, and Daisy, 1939; Marshall, 1922; Clark, 1934). Working with white-tailed deer in Pennsylvania, Gerstell (1942) concluded that a decrease in fawn production was correlated with a depletion of food supply. Morton and Cheatum (1946) studied the breeding potential of white-tailed deer in New York and found a great disparity between the northern Adirondack region and southern New York region in the occurrence of barren does and the ratio of single, twin, and triplet embryos. They found that 20.1 per cent of specimens examined from the Adirondack region were barren, whereas only 7.7 per cent were barren from the southern region. The ratio of single, twin, and triplet embryos was 8:2:1 in the Adirondack region and 3:6:1 in the southern region. The authors (p. 246) attribute the difference to the bad effects of poor winter feeding and a deficiency of particular dietary elements in the case of the northern deer:

It is evident that both general malnutrition and a lack of essential specific nutrients may be reflected in lowering rates of reproduction. Study of the ovulation rate of Adirondack deer reveals a significantly lower average than among those from the southern part of New York. The deer from both regions are in their best physical condition during the breeding season.

The lower productivity of Adirondack deer would seem to reflect either or both of the following: (1) persistent effects from the lowered plane of winter nutrition; (2) a prevailing deficiency of one or more dietary elements essential to the highest rate of ovulation and breeding success.

Following continued research along these lines, Cheatum and Severinghaus (1950, p. 188) later reached the conclusion that there was a direct connection between the quality of range and the rate of fertility, and that the latter increased when the number of deer was reduced and the quality of forage improved:

The fertility levels of deer were observed to correspond generally with the quality of their range. Intensive harvests, singly or combined with range improvements, are believed to have resulted in better forage conditions and were followed by increases in fertility.

The data presented indicate that measurements of the fertility of white-tailed deer afford an indicator of trends in population density in relation to range adequacy, although more needs to be known regarding the time lag involved. The measurements of fertility may prove to be a valuable tool to determine where and when more intensive harvests of deer are advisable. It is further suggested that this technique should be investigated for its application to other game or fur-bearer species.

It would seem only logical that moose are affected in a manner similar to deer and that the variation in the essential nutrients available to moose in various localities and habitats may well be affecting the variation in fecundity from region to region. More research is seriously needed along these lines.

CHAPTER NINE

GENERAL LIFE HISTORY

FACTUAL DATA on the general life history of moose are essential to a scientific understanding of the species. Personal field observations and other data obtained during the course of a recent study have been integrated with the findings of previous workers in an attempt to make a summary of our present knowledge of moose.

CALVES

Young moose are usually born during the latter part of May or early June. Kellum (1941) reported the birth of five calves in captivity at Cusino, Michigan, on the following dates: May 12, May 20, May 24, May 25, and June 17. The earliest that Murie (1934) observed a calf on Isle Royale, Michigan, was on May 28. He suggests that most calves are born in June there. In Sweden the European moose is usually born between May 20 and June 15 according to Lönnberg (1923) although he states that records of birth have been made as early as late April in eastern "Prussia."

The earliest a calf moose was observed in the St. Ignace area of Ontario was on May 24, 1948. In 1947 the earliest was on June 16. The cow, also accompanied by a yearling female, had been under observation since May 21 as she and the yearling crossed back and forth from St. Ignace to a small island. She was observed alone on May 29 and was accompanied by the yearling on May 30. Her calf, when observed on June 16, was estimated to be approximately one week to ten days old. On June 5, 1948, a calf was again observed in the same area (Bead Island). The mother was quite small, suggesting that she may have been the same animal that was observed accompanying a cow as a yearling in 1947.

When born, the calves are light reddish brown in colour with a dark dorsal stripe; they have short hair, and lack the spotting found on wapiti and white-tailed deer. The striking features of the calf are the relatively long ears and legs with a short body; a short dark muzzle; and dark areas about the eyes (Figure 11).

The weights of the four normal calves born in captivity at Cusino, Michigan, were 24, 24, 30, and 33 pounds (Kellum, 1941). A fifth calf weighed only 13 pounds at birth but died after only two days.

A cow killed near Pembroke, Ontario, about March 1, 1951, was carrying a foetus weighing nine pounds four ounces (Figure 10). It proved to be a female with the following measurements in millimetres: total length, 554; tail, 18; hind foot, 237; and ear, 83. In this specimen, hair was beginning to show on the lips, on the top of the head, along the back to the rump, and on the lower legs and throat. The "bell" was clearly evident, being one-fourth of an inch long. The teeth had not yet showed signs of eruption.

Soper (1942) examined the foetuses of single calves from two females killed about March 15 and found one measured 12 inches and the other 19 inches. "While perfectly formed in every detail, the uniformly pink skin carried no sign of hair in either instance. According to Indian information, moose give birth to their young in this region [Wood Buffalo Park, Alberta and Northwest Territories] during the latter part of May." (Soper, 1942, p. 142) A foetus taken May 20 on Isle Royale, Michigan, measured 880 millimetres (about 36 inches) and weighed 22 pounds (Murie, 1934). At this stage of development the "tips of the hoofs are soft and white. The incisors have broken through the gums, but the milk premolars have not yet erupted. The foetus is fully haired, and the eyes are open." (Murie, 1934, p. 11)

At birth, moose calves are quite helpless and are usually kept in seclusion for a short period (MacFarlane, 1905; Manweiler, 1941). When found early enough, young moose will frequently approach humans, allow themselves to be handled, and even try to follow them afterward (Merrill, 1920; Couey et al., 1948). According to Couey et al. (p. 309) "the new born moose is nearly mute, only uttering a low-toned grunt when the metal point of the tag pierces an ear." When a few days old, calves have a high-pitched cry which is almost human in quality. This cry was heard on several occasions in the St. Ignace area when young calves were swimming and struggling desperately to keep up with their mothers. "A newly born calf may be caught by handlers for weighing and measuring but after the baby is a few days old it can outrun a man" (Kellum, 1941, p. 5).

RELATIONSHIPS OF MOTHER AND YOUNG

Immediately before the birth of the young, the cow frequently seeks secluded or protected areas such as peninsulas and islands (Seton, 1927; Clarke, 1936; Cowan, 1946). Additional evidence of such habits was found in the St. Ignace area where calves are known to have been born on Bead Island in both 1947 and 1948. The new-born calf may be left in hiding for the first few hours but under such circumstances the cow does not appear to wander far afield. In a personal letter dated May 20, 1953, Mr. George Speidel, Zoo Director of the Washington Park Zoological Garden at Milwaukee Wisconsin, writes concerning a female calf which had been born there: "One thing that was particularly interesting was the fact that the calf nursed the first time while the cow was lying down. . . ." According to

Seton (1927) the calf is able to follow the cow on the second or third day. It is often forced to follow the cow into icy waters at an early age.

About 9:30 P.M., June 5, 1948, a cow with a calf, judged to be less than a week old, was observed on the shore of Bead Island about 100 yards off St. Ignace Island. The cow entered the water and the calf milled about on the shore for two or three minutes, then followed the cow as she started to swim across the channel. The calf was not able to keep up and the cow would turn and swim back toward the calf and turn again to her original course, as if to urge the calf onwards. About midway between the islands the calf began to fall farther and farther behind. However, the cow continued almost to the opposite shore before turning back to meet the calf. The calf could be heard crying in a high-pitched voice, creating considerable anxiety on the part of the observers as to whether or not it would be drowned before it could reach safety. The crossing required between 6 and 7 minutes on the part of the calf. Almost exactly 12 hours later, on the following morning, June 6, the cow and calf were observed to cross the channel back to Bead Island. We hurriedly gave chase in a canoe and were successful in overtaking them and recording the incident with coloured motion pictures. As we approached, the cow stopped near shore to allow the calf to catch up. We noticed that in response to the calf's high-pitched grunts or bleating, the cow answered with several low-pitched grunts. As she reached shore the cow rushed ahead of the calf, leaving it alone on shore momentarily, but soon turned to face us as the calf struggled ashore and into the bush. Mr. Dalton Muir, the photographer, quickly went ashore and attempted to follow them. After going a short distance he suddenly saw the cow coming hastily toward him, but the calf was nowhere in sight. It was not certain that the cow was making a deliberate attack, for when Mr. Muir retreated behind a tree she quickly turned and disappeared into the bush.

On June 18, 1947, a cow with a young calf was observed to swim approximately one-half mile across McEachan Lake on St. Ignace Island. When we approached close to them in a canoe the cow showed considerable irritation by bristling up the hair of her mane, lowering her ears, and giving several nasal snorts. At one point the calf seemed to be resting its nose on the back of the cow as they swam. Cahalane (1939) and others have reported this type of activity as a common occurrence.

All personal observations indicate a strong maternal protective instinct on the part of most cows.

On July 9, 1946, we were patrolling Longbow Lake, Algonquin Provincial Park, Ontario, by canoe, when we discovered a cow feeding a few feet from shore at 9:45 P.M. We were able to manoeuvre our canoe quite close without being detected. The cow continued to feed on the leaves of water shield

(*Brasenia schreberi*) as she moved slowly along. Suddenly she gave two or three low grunts. Much to our surprise she was answered by high-pitched bleats, and a calf immediately came out of the darkness of the bush, entered the water, and swam to the cow. They crossed a small bay, and on reaching the opposite point the calf returned to shore and the cow continued to feed. We manœuvred our canoe into close range and could hear the calf moving around in the bush, occasionally giving a high-pitched bleat. As we moved closer the cow discovered our presence and started ashore, giving two loud grunts. The calf appeared at her side almost instantly. We then moved our canoe directly toward them, approaching within 20 feet, at the same time giving a loud cry to test the cow's reactions. She took a few steps, stopped, gave several low grunts, and whirled as if to turn on us. As she gave another long low grunt the calf immediately started into the bush. The cow hesitated momentarily until the calf had disappeared; then she followed.

While observing a cow moose feeding about 100 feet from shore in the north end of McEachan Lake, St. Ignace Island, Ontario, on July 31, 1947, we found that her calf was playfully romping on the beaches, occasionally dashing into the bush, then running out and splashing into the water. At one point the calf disappeared into the woods and a bull moose, which had been feeding near by, gradually moved between the cow and the calf. As the calf came scampering on to the beach the cow discovered the presence of the bull. She immediately lowered her ears and went charging toward shore. She ran to the calf and nudged it to one side with her nose, and then rushed toward the large bull, who immediately made an expedient retreat.

It is conceded by many that a cow moose will protect her young from natural predators. However, the few opportunities that occur to observe such incidents limit the number of witnessed accounts available in the literature. Murie (1944) reports that a cow which was accompanied by a calf drove off two husky dogs which attacked them in Alaska. On July 6, 1947, we saw a cow and calf standing in shallow water on the east side of McEachan Lake, St. Ignace Island. We noticed that her attention was directed toward something on shore. We then saw a large white timber wolf trot out of the bush to the shore a few feet from the moose. A few seconds later a second typically coloured timber wolf joined its white companion. They made no attempt to attack the moose, nor did they show any interest in them whatever, but instead trotted casually away down the shore. The cow exhibited no visible signs of fear but stood motionless, with bristled mane, watching each movement of the wolves. The calf remained quite close to the cow, which required only six steps to reach shore; there they stood for a few moments before moving slowly into the bush.

Cowan describes the anxiety of a cow disturbed by a bear. "One cow inadvertently disturbed by us when the young was about 4 or 5 hours old forthwith urged it into the lake where it drowned. This was highly abnormal behaviour for a moose confronted by a human disturber and could only be laid to the agitation induced by the presence of the bear." (Cowan, 1946, p. 40)

Several authors have remarked on the protective instinct of cows with calves on the approach of humans (Dixon, 1938; Murie, 1940; Munro, 1947; and others). Working in Montana, Couey et al. (1948, p. 309) came to the following conclusions:

The parental instinct of female moose seems to be stronger than that of a cow elk. Nineteen moose calves were observed on this survey and all but one were at their mother's side or lying near by. It was also learned that a cow moose, when protecting her calf from an invader, will attack a man on foot or on horseback. The cow moose with small calf not old enough to travel, will stand her ground. She will permit approach to within 20 yards of her offspring. Continuation of the approach causes her mane to rise and one ear will drop down on her neck. When the other is dropped, she will charge and strike with both front feet.

Stanwell-Fletcher (1943) reports that Indians in British Columbia believe cow moose will frequently desert their calves completely when unduly alarmed. Little evidence has been found in Ontario to support such a theory. A cow will occasionally desert a calf temporarily when frightened by humans, but no direct evidence has been found of permanent desertion.

Calves generally remain with their mothers throughout the full year. Even during the rutting season the calves continue to remain close by. At that time, according to Murie (1934), the bulls accept the company of the calves along with that of the cow.

There is considerable disagreement as to how long cows continue to suckle their young. MacFarlane (1905, p. 678) says that "suckling is supposed to continue for two or three months." Other authors intimate that calves are not weaned until about the time the next calf is born (Merrill, 1920; Murie, 1934; Stone, 1924; Burt, 1946; Cahalane, 1947). McDowell and Moy (1942) state that weaning takes place in December in Montana. In Sweden, Lönnberg (1923) reports that calves suckle far into the fall of the year. A cow killed on December 6, 1949, after having been injured by a truck near Ear Falls, Kenora District, Ontario, and later received at the Royal Ontario Museum, was still lactating.

Young moose do continue to follow their mothers up to and even beyond the arrival of a new calf the following spring. Most authors agree that pregnant cows attempt to discourage further company of the yearling as the time approaches for the birth of a new calf (Stone, 1924; Murie, 1934; Cahalane, 1939).

The yearlings seem quite reluctant to leave their mothers, causing the cows considerable difficulty in driving them out of the family circle. On June 16, 1947, a cow followed by a yearling was observed swimming across the channel between St. Ignace and Bead islands in Ontario. As they reached the shore of Bead Island the cow turned, lowered her ears, and struck a vicious blow at the yearling with her right front foot, causing the offspring to dodge and fall back into the water. When the cow moved down the shore she was met by a young calf, which had been left in hiding while the cow and yearling were away from the island.

CALF MORTALITY AND SURVIVAL TO YEARLING AGE

In spite of the strong maternal instincts of cow moose, young moose find the first year of their life fraught with danger. While subject to most of the same types of mortality as adults, calves face added perils. Drowning seems to be a fairly common cause of death. Most records indicate some unusual factor in such cases (Murie, 1940; Cowan, 1944) but it seems likely that a high mortality from drowning might go undetected. In recent studies in Ontario no direct evidence was found of unusually high calf mortality. No logical explanation has been found for the occasional appearance of lone calves wandering about on their own (Dymond et al., 1928).

Predation, especially by bears, is commonly thought to be an important factor in the chances of survival of calves. Sarber (1944) prepared a very convincing case from the Kenai Peninsula, Alaska, where he concluded that the extremely low calf crop was attributable for the most part to predation by both black and brown bears. Further studies of the bear-moose relationships were carried out in this general area by Chatelain (1950) who summarizes his findings regarding calf mortality as follows (p. 232):

The percentage of moose calf remains in the scats collected during this study rose steadily from the latter part of May (1.5 per cent) until late July and early August, when it reached its peak (26.3 per cent), and then dropped to nothing in August. Calf hair was found in one dropping in September.

Inasmuch as no attempt was made to secure only very fresh droppings during the first three periods of collection (May and early June, late June, late July and early August) it was believed that the percentages during these periods represented cumulative totals rather than the amount eaten during any particular period. Thus it appeared that bear predation is a gradual procedure, and only by those bears present on the calving areas. Some bears never visit the calving sites.

The bears apparently began eating moose calves shortly after the calving season started. The first calf was noted on May 25, and shortly thereafter the first scat containing calf hair was found. The next period of observation, the latter part of June and the end of the calving season, showed a larger percentage of calf hair (16.2 per cent) in the bear scats, and the end of July showed the largest percentage, as previously mentioned. During August the salmon were spawning and became available as food sources, and in September the berries became ripe.

The decrease of calf hair in August and September scats corresponds with the time that calves become wary and are able to evade predators more easily. This coupled with the fact that no calf carcasses were located or reported that had not been fed upon by bears, indicates that the bears were factors in moose survival, particularly on the calving areas such as Harvey Lake, Russian River, Juneau and Swan Lakes, and Kelley Lake.

Hosley (1949) reviewed other aspects of bear predation on calves, reporting that black bears were considered the most serious predators in Alaska and Montana but that in the latter area their predation was relatively unimportant.

When the question of predation on calves was presented to Ontario observers in a special questionnaire on moose, 74 reported that they had observed definite evidences of bears having killed calf moose, whereas 70 had observed no such evidence. Although bears undoubtedly kill a certain number of calves in Ontario, little direct evidence has been encountered to substantiate the general belief in the seriousness of this predation.

Other predators occasionally take moose calves. Hatter (1945) found that calf moose occurred in 4.6 per cent of the summer scats of coyote or brush wolves in Jasper National Park. He felt that the coyote probably took a part of the calves while they were left in hiding and that carrion was also a possible source of part of the scat material.

In a study of the timber wolves of the Rocky Mountain national parks of Canada, Cowan (1947) compared the statistics from a wolf-infested and a wolf-free area for survival of the young moose to yearling age and concluded that the wolves are not the critical factor influencing the rate of survival. In the wolf-inhabited area yearlings constituted 22 per cent of the adult cows, whereas in the wolf-free areas the ratio was 23 per cent. A more detailed consideration of predation is given in chapter 15.

Some indication of the mortality rate of calves may be obtained by comparing the relative proportion of calves and yearlings. In Jasper National Park, Cowan (1944 and 1946) found that the ratio of calves to adult females was 20 per cent in 1943 and 30 per cent in 1944. The corresponding ratio of yearlings was 16 per cent in both cases. By comparing the number of yearlings with the number of calves a mortality rate of young during the first year might be estimated at approximately 25 per cent in 1943 and 43 per cent in 1944. In Alaska, Spencer and Chatelain (1953) found that the average cow–calf ratio was 100: 31.9 during the summer but was reduced to 100: 23.7 by late winter; indicating a 25 per cent loss by midwinter. A further check on the rate of survival is made by comparing similar statistics from various sources in Table VI. The combined figures recorded in this table indicate an average mortality rate of 29 per cent during the first year.

In analysing the data in Table VI several questions arise. The adequacy and accuracy of these samples is open to question. The variation from year to year and place to place must be considered. However, since the figures represent the largest accumulation of data yet made available, some consideration must be given them. A number of conclusions seem obvious. In the first place, several cases show a greater number of yearlings than calves. Normally there should have been a greater number of calves than reported

TABLE VI
Age Composition of Moose Populations

Area	Date	Adults Total	Adults Cows	Calves Number	Calves % of cows	Calves % of adults	Yearlings Number	Yearlings % of cows	Yearlings % of adults
Banff National Park, Alta.	1943*	67	18	6	33	10	8	29	12
Kootenay National Park, B.C.	1943*	14	7	6	66	43	1	14	7
Jasper National Park, Alta.	1943*	52	22	4	20	8	3	16	6
Jasper National Park, Alta.	1944†	110	48	14	30	13	8	16	7
Montana	1942‡	141	53	30	56	21	23	43	16
Ontario									
Algonquin Park	1946§	21	12	4	33	19	4	33	19
Southern forest region	1947‖	7	3	1	33	14			
	1948‖	9	6				4	67	44
	1949‖	8	5	2	40	25	2	40	25
Central forest region	1947‖	501	212	121	57	24	90	42	18
	1948‖	208	119	35	29	17	33	28	16
	1949‖	456	238	94	40	20	59	25	13
Northern forest region	1947‖	120	71	37	54	30	19	27	16
	1948‖	101	41	24	59	24	25	61	25
	1949‖	125	52	33	62	26	15	29	12
Midwestern forest region	1947¶	367	147	54	37	15	74	50	20
	1948¶	67	28	7	25	11	10	36	16
	1949‖	93	58	17	39	18	4	7	4
Western forest region	1947‖	182	110	65	59	36	22	20	12
	1948‖	97	46	18	39	19	10	22	10
	1949‖	77	50	18	36	23	10	20	13
Ontario average	1947				51	24		33	17
	1948				35	18		34	17
	1949				41	22		22	12
Three-year Ontario average					44	22		32	16
Newfoundland	1950**	226	208	90	43		22		10
	1951**	625	323	189	58		99		16
	1952**	978	575	192	33		216		22
Three-year Newfoundland average					43				19
Grand total and average		4,652	2,452	1,061	43	21	751	32	16

*Cowan (1944).   ‡McDowell and Moy (1942).   ‖Moose record cards.
†Cowan (1946).   §Peterson (1949b).   ¶Peterson (1949b), and moose record cards.
**Pimlott (1953).

in order to produce these number of yearlings. Two main factors seem to affect this ratio between calves and yearlings: (1) During early spring the calves are frequently hidden and later in the season the cows venture forth with young calves more frequently at night. This creates considerable difficulty in observing a true sample. (2) When the yearlings are first driven away from their mothers they have not yet developed a keen fear of humans and consequently wander about and are easy to observe. For example, such a yearling was observed near a salt lick on St. Ignace Island on June 12, 1947, while we were constructing an observation tower. She showed no fear of us whatsoever and returned to the lick at least ten times during the day and did not venture far afield for seven hours in spite of our talking, hammering, sawing, and even shouting at her and approaching quite close to her. On the other hand, it is not always possible to distinguish yearlings accurately, particularly in late winter or if the observer has not been trained.

There is then a possibility that the calf composition may average higher than these figures indicate.

The average figures for the percentage of yearlings in the adult population, ranging between 22 and 34 per hundred adult cows (usually about 32), and between 12 and 22 per hundred adults, seem fairly significant. The average annual increment to the adult population might, therefore, be regarded as rarely exceeding 20 per cent (averaging about 16).

Sex Ratios

The reproductive rate of moose may be affected by the existence of abnormal sex ratios. This is especially true in areas heavily hunted. On St. Ignace Island where moose are protected, the ratio among 50 adults observed was 67 per cent bulls and 33 percent cows in 1947, and of 31 adults 87 per cent were bulls and 13 per cent cows in 1948. The latter was certainly not a true ratio since the observations were restricted to early spring at the time when most cows would have been seeking secluded spots for calving. No logical explanation for such a disparity in survival is readily apparent. Examination of "winter kills" and remains of all carcasses found during the study showed 16 adult bulls and 12 adult cows. These animals had died over a period of several years.

Sex ratio records from Newfoundland, Ontario, and Alaska are given in Table VII.

When considering the broad regions of Ontario and Newfoundland the sex ratios appear near a normal balance of 50:50. Since moose apparently tend toward monogamy (Murie, 1934) and are thinly spread over large areas it seems probable that a reduction in the number of bulls would have a more serious effect on successful breeding than in the case of white-tailed deer. Heavy local depletion of bulls through hunting prior to the comple-

TABLE VII
SEX RATIOS OF MOOSE POPULATIONS

Area	Date	Total	Bulls %	Cows %
Newfoundland	1950*	401	45	55
	1951*	801	53	47
	1952*	1,289	49	51
Newfoundland average	1950–2	2,491	50	50
Ontario				
Southern and central Ontario regions	1947†	508	58	42
	1948†	217	43	57
	1949†	464	48	52
Average	1947–9	1,189	51	49
Northern Ontario region	1947†	120	41	59
	1948†	101	60	40
	1949†	125	58	42
Average	1947–9	346	53	47
Midwestern Ontario region	1947†	367	60	40
	1948†	62	55	45
	1949†	93	38	62
Average	1947–9	522	55	45
Western Ontario region	1947†	182	40	60
	1948†	97	53	47
	1949†	77	35	65
Average	1947–9	356	42	58
Ontario average	1947	1,177	54	46
	1948	477	49	51
	1949	759	47	53
	1947–9	2,413	51	49
Alaska				
Kenai	1951‡	1,329	41	59
	1952‡	998	34	66
Susitna	1951‡	1,362	38	62
	1952‡	1,083	29	71
Copper	1952‡	547	38	62
Alaska average	1951–2	5,319	38	62

*Pimlott (1953).
†Peterson (1949b).
‡Spencer and Chatelain (1953).

tion of a breeding season would undoubtedly result in higher proportions of local unfertilized females. But it is interesting to note that the indicated sex ratio of Ontario moose during the closed hunting season of 1949 (Table VII) shows a continued trend of decrease in the percentage of bulls, a condition which normally might be expected to be reversed by the elimination of the selective drain on the male population. In British Columbia, Hatter (1950) found that, on the basis of data over a three-year period in a heavily hunted area, the bull ratio averaged only 25 per cent. He felt that it had no important influence on the calf crop. The data from Alaska (Table VII) also show a substantially low bull ratio (average 38 per cent).

Pimlott (1953) reports on an unpublished manuscript of Bruce Wright concerning moose in New Brunswick, in which Wright combined data for a three-year period and divided New Brunswick on the basis of browse conditions, to show that on over-browsed areas the bulls were more numerous (53 per cent) while on a normal range the ratio dropped to 44 per cent. More detailed data and studies along these lines seem highly desirable. The high bull ratio observed on St. Ignace Island, Ontario, might lend further circumstantial evidence for such a theory.

GROWTH, WEIGHTS, AND MEASUREMENTS

"There is no other wild animal in America that grows so rapidly as the moose" (Stone, 1924, p. 294). According to Kellum (1941) new-born calves weigh from 25 to 35 pounds and gain from one to two pounds daily for the first month and then increase by from three to five pounds daily during the second month. Skuncke (1949) reports that new-born European moose usually weigh from 22 to 35 pounds, with twins averaging smaller than single calves, sometimes as small as 13.5 pounds. He reports that in Sweden new-born calves have a total length of about 1 metre, and a shoulder height of 700–900 millimetres but that by three weeks a calf will have doubled its weight: 44 to 69 pounds on the average. Data from Sweden indicate an average increase from August to September of about 22 pounds, while gains from September to October average only about 13 or 14 pounds (Gardell, 1947; Skuncke, 1949). Skuncke (1949) reports that in three months a bull calf will have a dressed weight (carcass less viscera) of 99 to 165 pounds and a heifer calf 110 to 176. At about four and one-half months both sexes weigh about the same (averaging 165 to 200 pounds up to 265 pounds dressed weight) but by six months the male usually has grown beyond the female (males averaging 198 to 253 pounds and females 187 to 242). At nine months the dressed weights are usually 264 to 308 pounds for heifers and 242 to 286 for bulls.

A summary of available North American weights and measurements by ages is given in Tables VIII and IX. Because of the great difficulty of getting moose and scales together (Figure 12) relatively few accurate weights are available.

Anthony (1939) states that the Alaskan moose will weigh as much as 1,700 to 1,800 pounds, while other North American moose weigh up to 1,400 pounds. Goodwin (1935) says a large moose killed in Maine weighed

TABLE VIII

WEIGHTS AND MEASUREMENTS OF YOUNG MOOSE
(pounds and inches)

Date	Age (approx.)	Sex	Locality	Source	Subspecies	Weight	Total length	Height shoulder	Hind foot	Tail
May	1 *wk.*		Liard River	Stone (1924)	*A. a. gigas*		37	33		$1\frac{1}{2}$
**	2	F	Wyoming	Denniston (1948)	*A. a. shirasi*		36	32		
**	3	F	Wyoming	Denniston (1948)	*A. a. shirasi*	46	39	33		
**	4	F	Wyoming	Denniston (1948)	*A. a. shirasi*	52	42	34		
June 14	3–4 (?)	M	Isle Royale, Mich.	Murie (1934)	*A. a. andersoni*	67	$44\frac{1}{2}$	$37\frac{3}{5}$	$18\frac{3}{4}$	$1\frac{1}{2}$
June	3–4 (?)	M	Algonquin Park, Ont.	Peterson (1949b)	*A. a. americana*		47		20	
**	5	F	Wyoming	Denniston (1948)	*A. a. shirasi*	57	43	$34\frac{1}{2}$		
**	6	F	Wyoming	Denniston (1948)	*A. a. shirasi*	72	$46\frac{1}{2}$	$34\frac{1}{2}$		
**	7	F	Wyoming	Denniston (1948)	*A. a. shirasi*	84	$46\frac{1}{2}$	37		
*	7			Hornaday (1904)		67	42	37		
**	8	F	Wyoming	Denniston (1948)	*A. a. shirasi*	105	53			
**	9	F	Wyoming	Denniston (1948)	*A. a. shirasi*	110	53	43		
Aug. 10	9–10	M	Isle Royale, Mich.	Murie (1934)	*A. a. andersoni*	153	$56\frac{1}{2}$	$41\frac{3}{4}$	$22\frac{1}{8}$	$1\frac{3}{4}$
Aug. 14	10	F	Isle Royale, Mich.	Murie (1934)	*A. a. andersoni*	183	61	$50\frac{1}{2}$	24	$3\frac{1}{2}$
Sept. 10–18	4 *mo.*(?)	M	Level Mts., B.C.	Allen, J.A. (1902)	*A. a. andersoni*		67	52	$25\frac{1}{2}$	$4\frac{1}{4}$
Sept. 10–18	4 (?)	F	Level Mts., B.C.	Allen, J.A. (1902)	*A. a. andersoni*		$65\frac{1}{4}$	$51\frac{1}{2}$	25	$4\frac{1}{4}$
Oct. 30	5		Kenai Pen., Alaska	Stone (1924)	*A. a. gigas*		88	$67\frac{1}{2}$		4
Dec. 28*	6–7	M	Gogama, Ont.	Peterson (1949b)	*A. a. americana*	283				
Dec. 28*	6–7	F	Gogama, Ont.	Peterson (1949b)	*A. a. americana*	331				
Feb. 23	9	F	Chapleau, Ont.	Peterson (1949b)	*A. a. americana*	375	79		$28\frac{1}{4}$	$4\frac{1}{2}$
June 15	12	F	Isle Royale, Mich.	Murie (1934)	*A. a. andersoni*	280	76	$54\frac{3}{8}$	$26\frac{3}{4}$	$4\frac{3}{8}$
*	12	M	Michigan	Kellum (1941)	*A. a. andersoni*	400–600 av.				
*	12	F	Michigan	Kellum (1941)	*A. a. andersoni*	400 av.				
Aug. 14	15			Hornaday (1904)		330	69	63		
Dec. 28*	18–19	M	Gogama, Ont.	Peterson (1949b)	*A. a. americana*	582				

**Same individual. *Captive animal.

TABLE IX

WEIGHTS AND MEASUREMENTS OF ADULT MOOSE

(pounds and inches)

Date	Sex	Locality	Source and remarks	Weight	Total length	Height shoulder	Hind foot
Alces alces americana							
	M	Maine	Stone (1924)		98	69	
	M	Quebec	Seton (1927)		114	72	31
Nov. 19	F	Algonquin Park, Ont.	Peterson (1949b); animal injured or diseased	442*	95	69	31 3/8
Alces alces andersoni							
Aug. 28	M	Isle Royale, Mich.	Murie (1934) young animal (?)	593*	87 1/4	66 3/4	30
Oct. 18	M	Minnesota	Breckenridge (1946)	1,065	96	71	
June 18	M	Isle Royale, Mich.	Murie (1934)	847*	97 3/4	75	31
Nov. 25	M	Elk Is. Natl. Park, Alta.	Natl. Mus. Can. #10,347	970*	99		
	M	Mackenzie R., N.W.T.	Stone (1924)		99 1/2	66	31 1/2
Sept. 10–18	M	Level Mts., B.C.	Allen, J.A. (1902)		100 1/2	72 1/2	32 1/2
Sept. 10–18	M	Level Mts., B.C.	Allen, J.A. (1902)		100 1/2	71 3/4	32 1/2
June 9	M	Isle Royale, Mich.	Murie (1934)	848*	104	72	31 3/4
Oct. 18	M	Nungesser L., Ont.	R.O.M.Z. #19,912 (stomach contents not included in weight)	1,007*	104 3/4	70 1/2	30
Sept. 17	M	St. Ignace Is., Ont.	Peterson (1949b)	1,177	108	75	32
Dec. 18	M	15 mi. E. Brandon, Man.	Peterson (1950) type specimen	1,060*	108 3/4	75 3/4	32 3/4
Aug. 11	F	Isle Royale, Mich.	A.M.N.H. #93,151		80 1/4		29 1/3
May 20	F	Isle Royale, Mich.	Murie (1934)		81		30
Jan. 20	F	Isle Royale, Mich.	U.M.M.Z. #75,043		83	68 1/2	30 3/4
Nov. 23	F	Harper L., Sask.	Natl. Mus. Can. #8,577		93		30 1/4
Sept. 10–18	F	Level Mts., B.C.	Allen (1902)		93 3/4	71 3/4	31 1/4
Aug. 24	F	Shesley Mt., B.C.	Allen (1902)		100 1/2	70 1/4	30 3/4
July 22	F	Isle Royale, Mich.	Murie (1934)	728*	101 1/2	72	31 1/4
Dec. 6	F	Ear Falls, Ont.	R.O.M.Z. #19,990	800*			31 3/4
Alces alces shirasi							
Sept. 15	M	Yellowstone Nat. Park, Wyo.	A.M.N.H. #98,206		104 1/2		30 3/5
Sept. 21	M	Yellowstone Nat. Park, Wyo.	A.M.N.H. #100,348		109		29 1/2
	F	Yellowstone Nat. Park, Mont.	Montana State Coll.		93		30 1/4
Sept. 27	F	Yellowstone Nat. Park, Wyo.	A.M.N.H. #100,349		100		26 1/2
Alces alces gigas							
	M	Kenai Pen., Alaska	Stone (1924)		103 1/2	76 1/2	33 1/2
	M	Kenai Pen., Alaska	Stone (1924)		106	77 1/2	33 1/2
	M	Kenai Pen., Alaska	Stone (1924)		108	77	33
Sept. 13	M	Funny R., Alaska	A.M.N.H. #125,585		111 1/2	78 1/4	31
Sept. 8	M	Funny R., Alaska	A.M.N.H. #125,587		115	81 3/4	32 3/4

*Weights not including blood or other losses.

over 1,400 pounds. These statements do not seem to be based on recorded weights of definite specimens. Weights for seven adult bulls and two adult cows are given in Table IX.

The most extensive weighing has been carried out in Sweden of what is supposed to be a slightly smaller race of moose than most North American representatives. Most of these weights, however, are listed as either "dressed carcasses," which would be equivalent to "hog-dressed" weights and include the carcass with only the entrails removed; or butchers' weights, in which case the hide, feet, head, and antlers would also be removed. The latter weight would be equivalent to the "dressed weight" of meat. In Table X the minimum, maximum, and average dressed weights for each age up to 14 years are presented for both sexes for two different regions in Sweden. In order to calculate the hog-dressed weight, about 20 to 30 per cent must be added to the dressed weight, or if the total weight (less blood loss) is desired, about 40 to 47 per cent. There seems to be some doubt about whether or not shot-damaged meat is included in the weights from Hällefors, Sweden.

Skuncke (1949) also presents some data on live weights for 342 bulls and 295 cows from the vicinity of Harg, Sweden. He has provided a growth curve (Figure 13) which also shows the relative effects of calves on the weight of the mother.

In certain cases it becomes desirable to be able to compute the total weight of an animal from partial weights. Although inadequate data are available on this point, especially from North America, it is hoped that Table XI will provide some indication of the relationships of dressed weights to total weight. Data on weights of wapiti from Quimby and Johnson (1951) are also included to give some measure of comparison.

When quartered according to the butchers' standard methods, the hindquarters of the moose from St. Ignace Island, Ontario, weighed by the author, were estimated at 303 pounds, or 26 per cent of the total weight, 32.6 per cent of the hog-dressed weight, and 43.5 per cent of the dressed weight. Skuncke states that the hindquarters of the Swedish moose usually weigh 42 to 47 per cent of the dressed weight.

The forequarters of the St. Ignace moose were estimated at 394 pounds; 33.8 per cent of the total weight, 44.5 per cent of the hog-dressed weight, or 56.5 per cent of the dressed weight. In Sweden the forequarters usually weigh 53 or 58 per cent of the dressed weight (Skuncke, 1949).

The hind legs of the St. Ignace Island moose were removed at the hip joints, and together were found to weigh 178 pounds; 15.3 per cent of the total weight, 19.7 per cent of the hog-dressed weight, and 25.6 per cent of the dressed weight.

The forelegs, removed with the shoulder blade attached, together weighed

TABLE X
Dressed Weights of European Moose Killed in Two Areas in Southwestern Berslagen, Sweden*

Age	Hällefors region (July 26–Nov. 6)						Lands of the Uddeholm Company (Sept. 1–Nov. 6)					
	930 bulls			947 cows			177 bulls			129 cows		
	max.	av.	min.	max.	av.	min.	max.	av.	min.	max.	av.	min.
3 *mo.*	128	110	66	158	121	77		165			172	
6	198	154	94	187	143	73		220			216	
9	246	198	156	264	176	143		257			242	
1 *yr.*	334	253	174	359	240	172	462	308	253	361	297	246
2	486	323	209	394	308	231	471	370	306	411	348	224
3	475	370	253	372	319	260	521	409	301	469	365	257
4	530	407	308	455	326	268	495	440	378	400	370	334
5	590	436	277	433	330	222	561	469	332	521	372	279
6	671	458	308	422	332	260	638	493	383	471	374	264
7	649	477	400	378	334	262	594	515	308	407	374	339
8	594	491	297	392	337	279	550	532	451	370	376	363
9	638	502	431	403	339	275	594	550	546	392	378	
10	726	506	317	403	330	308		563	442		378	
11	620	506	348	418	339	249		574	484		374	
12								581			370	341
13								585		385	361	
14		473			319							
18–20							616	561	524			

*Weights from Skuncke (1949) transposed to nearest pounds. These weights do not include viscera, hide, feet, head and antlers, or blood loss, but do apparently include shot-damaged meat.

145 pounds; 12.4 per cent of the total weight, 16.1 per cent of the hog-dressed weight, and 20.8 per cent of the dressed weight.

The remainder of the carcass, including the neck, back, ribs, and pelvis, weighed 374 pounds; 32.0 per cent of the total weight, 41.5 per cent of the hog-dressed weight, and 53.6 per cent of the dressed weight.

Apparently one of the heaviest moose taken in recent years in Ontario was one killed by Mr. Clarence W. McKeen of Kapuskasing, Ontario, in the vicinity of Jumbo Lake, a short distance from the Trans-Canada Highway between Hearst and Longlac, Ontario, in 1948. Mr. McKeen and his companions recognized that the animal was large so they weighed the dressed quarters carefully and submitted statements of all details, officially sworn before a Justice of the Peace (personal communications).

The left side of the animal was dressed according to the butchers' standard method of quartering beef and was well trimmed. The left forequarter weighed 218 pounds and the left hindquarter 167 pounds. Without account-

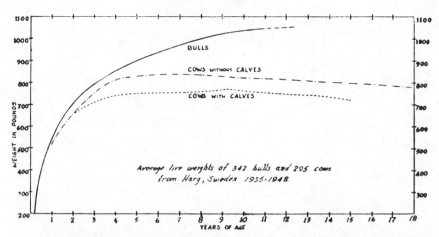

FIGURE 13. Growth curve of European moose, based on 637 moose from the vicinity of Harg, Sweden (from Skuncke, 1949)

ing for the portions trimmed off, which Mr. McKeen estimated to be at least 30 pounds, this animal produced over 770 pounds of dressed meat. On the basis of percentage weights given in Table XI its total weight would be estimated at almost 1,300 pounds. If allowance is made for the weight lost by trimming, it would probably have weighed close to 1,400 pounds.

In Nova Scotia, statistics were taken on the estimated dressed weight of each animal killed during 1935 and 1936. The average given for 1935 was 469 pounds and for 1936, 475 pounds (Nova Scotia, 1936). This would indicate that the moose killed there averaged slightly less than 800 pounds.

PELAGE CHANGE

At birth, young moose of western Ontario appear remarkably light-reddish in colour. Within a few days the coat appears reddish brown, passing later into more brownish tones. The lower abdomen and breast appear greyish. The longer hairs of the upper part of the body develop a greyish base. The juvenile coat is usually lost after two or three months. According to Murie (1934, pp. 11–12) the juvenile coat of the Isle Royale moose is lost by the middle of August except for a few remnants, principally on the face, mane, and legs. "The new coat is dark, grayish brown, with a silvery cast over the shoulders and neck. The face is brown, legs light brown, forelegs darker than hind legs. There is a small, whitish area in the inguinal region."

According to Skuncke (1949) the calf hair is still evident on the under side of the throat in late fall in Sweden and can be identified from its rather thin and soft appearance, lacking, usually, the marked whorls at the base.

By spring, most yearlings observed in the St. Ignace area were markedly

TABLE XI

Weights of Various Portions of Butchered Adult Moose Compared with Wapiti

Area	Sex	Viscera				Skin only				Skin, feet, head, antlers				Total weight (less blood loss)	Hog-dressed carcass (less viscera)		Dressed wt. (less viscera, head, antlers, hide, feet)		
		wt.	% of total wt.	% of hog-dressed wt.	% of dressed wt.	wt.	% of total wt.	% of hog-dressed wt.	% of dressed wt.	wt.	% of total wt.	% of hog-dressed wt.	% of dressed wt.	wt.	wt.	% of total wt.	wt.	% of total wt.	% of hog-dressed wt.
Moose																			
St. Ignace Is., Ont.*	M	250	22.0	27.7	36.0					206	18.0	22.8	29.5	1153	903	78.0	697	60.0	77.2
Minnesota†	M	239	23.0	29.9		80	7.7							1039	800	77.0			
Isle Royale, Mich.‡	M													848			544	64.0	
	M													847			523	61.7	
	F													728			400	55.0	
Sweden (averages)§	M	177+				50–92		9–10	11–15	176		17–31					323–586	55.0	
	F	177–				44–77		10–12	13–16								308–341	53.0	
Wapiti																			
Yellowstone Natl.	M	237	32.0	48.0	61.5	41	5.6	7.1	9.1	108	14.8	21.9	28.0	730	493	68	385	53.0	78.2
Park (averages)‖	F	185	33.0	49.2	59.4	29	5.2	7.7	9.3	66	11.8	17.5	21.2	562	377	67	312	55.0	82.8

SOURCES: *the author; †Breckenridge (1946); ‡Murie (1934); §Skuncke (1949); ‖Quimby and Johnson (1951).

lighter greyish in colour as compared with older adults. The spring coats of both were faded and ragged and much lighter and greyer in colour than at any other time of the year. Shedding was just beginning in early May, with the larger adult bulls being the first to shed. The moult pattern seems to start on the shoulder hump region, proceeding along the sides of the neck and back of the ears and backwards over the body (Figure 14).

Shedding in cows and yearlings follows that of bulls by a few days. In the case of moose of the St. Ignace area the new coat of short hair appears almost black in some older males and deep reddish brown in most other adults. As the hair lengthens, the coat takes on a warmer reddish brown cast toward the fall and early winter. Gradual fading during the winter months, together with continued wearing, completes the transition back to shedding time in early spring.

HAIR STRUCTURE

Studies of the scale pattern of moose hair (Williamson, 1951) have shown that it can be used to distinguish moose from other members of the family *Cervidae*. Compared with that of deer, the species showing the greatest similarity (Figure 15), the scale pattern of moose, along the maximum width of the hair, is more rectangular in shape and more irregularly arranged. It usually has ten or less scales in the maximum width of the hair. The scales lie flatter against the cortex than do those of deer, so that it is more difficult to obtain clear impressions with the method outlined by Williamson. In deer, there are usually more than ten scales in the maximum width of the hair and the scales are more ovoid and slightly raised from the cortex, so that they give a very clear impression in a Gelva medium.

A comparison of the guard hair of moose and deer of comparable size (Figure 16) reveals that the root of the former is usually more cylindrical, ending bluntly on the proximal end rather than being tapered or spear-shaped. The distal end of the guard hair tapers more gradually to the apex, giving a relatively longer attenuated tip in moose. The guard hair of moose appears more glossy than that of deer due to the adhesion or flatness of the scales against the cortex.

In caribou, five or more scales is the maximum width of the hair, and five or less in wapiti, but in each of the latter the shape of the scale patterns along the maximum width of the hair is distinctly different from that of moose (Figure 15).

GENERAL DEVELOPMENT AND ADAPTATION

Tooth Development

The dental formula of adult moose is

$$\text{I}\frac{000}{123} \quad \text{C}\frac{0}{1} \quad \text{P}\frac{0234}{0234} \quad \text{M}\frac{123}{123}.$$

The anterior or first premolar in adults is actually P 2. At birth the in-

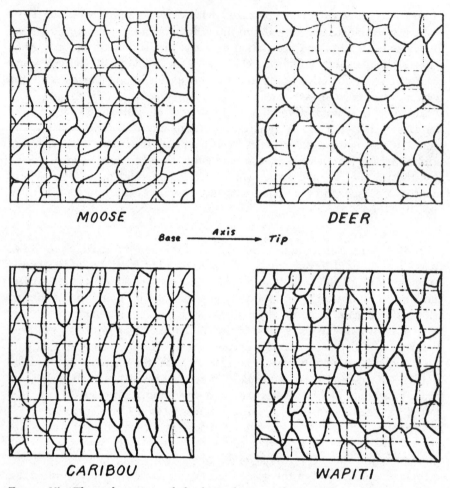

FIGURE 15. The scale pattern of the hair of moose, deer, caribou, and wapiti (after Williamson, 1951)

cisiform teeth are functional and the milk premolars are beginning to erupt (Murie, 1934). Murie found that by June 14 only the first two milk premolars are functional (MP 2 and 3?). The lower jaws of a calf that died in captivity near Sioux Lookout, Ontario, at an estimated age of 3 to 4 weeks show all three milk premolars in place, but MP 2 is barely protruding above the gum line and the two posterior premolars show only slight traces of wear. A male calf, judged to be slightly over one month old, which was found dead in Algonquin Provincial Park on June 27, had three functional premolars. The anterior one is still unworn and free from stain while the last two show definite wear and are heavily stained above the gum (R.O.M.Z. 16681; Figure 17, B).

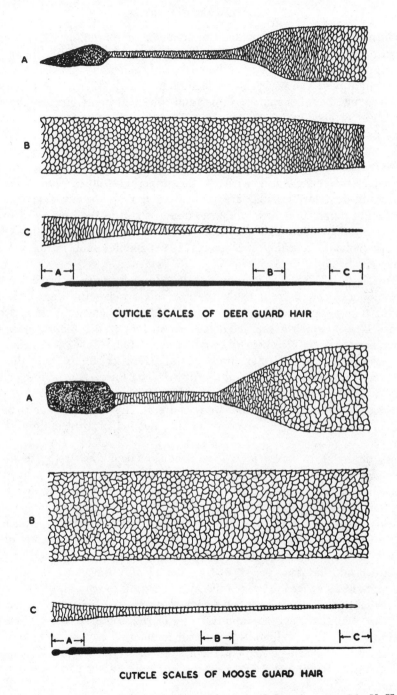

CUTICLE SCALES OF DEER GUARD HAIR

CUTICLE SCALES OF MOOSE GUARD HAIR

FIGURE 16. The structure of the guard hair of moose and deer (courtesy Mr. V. H. H. Williamson)

Murie (1934, p. 11) provides the following information: "A male calf taken on August 10, 1929, has all milk premolars functional, although the last upper milk premolars have been recently emerged and are not quite grown into place. No wear can be seen on any of the teeth. The molars are just forming. The first molars, upper and lower, are emerging through the thin sheet of bone which covers them. The lower first molar seems a little more developed than the upper first molar."

A female specimen from near Red Lake, Kenora District, that died in captivity about August 10–15 shows slight wear on the lower anterior milk premolar and considerable wear on the upper and other premolars. The tips of the first lower molar are protruding though the alveolus and just breaking through the gums, while the upper is still in the process of breaking open the alveolus. The gum still surrounds the posterior portion of the milk premolars. According to Skuncke (1949) the first molar usually erupts about August.

Gardell (1947) reports that by October the calf moose of Sweden have four functional molariform teeth, the first molar being fully erupted. This condition is present in a specimen from St. Ignace Island (R.O.M.Z. 18393; Figure 17, C), which is estimated to be from four to five months old. Two specimens taken on October 10 (one near Red Lake, Kenora District, and the other from Sankey Township, Cochrane District) both show the first molar functional but not yet fully erupted. The lower jaw of a specimen taken near Geraldton, Ontario, on October 19, has four functional molariform teeth that all show marked signs of wear. The second molar is beginning to break through the alveolus but has not yet protruded through the gums.

In a series of 16 lower jaws from Ontario taken during the month of November, all but 3 (the latter taken on November 28 and 29) have the second molar still incased in the gum, although some show evidence of its breaking through the alveolus. The 3 late November specimens show the anterior cusps protruding through the gums. These November specimens have all the milk incisiform teeth still fully functional but the ends of the roots of I_1 are beginning to disintegrate as the permanent tooth pushes forward inside the jaw.

A series of 23 lower jaws taken in Ontario during the month of December are available. In this series 8 specimens show M_2 not yet erupted through the gum, while 15 have the anterior tips of this tooth showing. Fourteen specimens still retain all milk incisiform teeth. In 7 cases both first milk incisors are lost, with permanent teeth showing various signs of eruption, but none fully functional. In 2 cases, the first milk incisor has been recently lost on one side only.

A set of mandibles shipped from Cochrane, Ontario, presumably taken in

January, shows the second molar fully functional with only a slight trace of wear on the anterior cusps. The posterior cusps protrude approximately 17 millimetres above the gum. The right first milk incisor has been lost and the permanent one is just visible beyond the gums. The left side still retains all the milk teeth.

A series of 5 lower jaws taken between January 27 and February 5 in western Ontario (Kenora District) all have the first permanent incisors functional, although they had only recently become fully erupted. In each case there are five functional molariform teeth but M_2 varies in its clearance of the gum from about 5 to 14 millimetres on the posterior cusp. In the least developed ones there is little stain while the most advanced are similar in colour to M_1.

A female calf moose taken on February 23, Township 11B, Chapleau forest district, and a male taken about March 1 in Renfrew County, Ontario, show signs of having recently acquired the first permanent incisors. The milk premolars are moderately to well worn (R.O.M.Z. 19495; Figure 17, D). The upper second molars are protruding only slightly through the gums, although the lower second molars are more advanced. Skuncke (1949) reports that in Swedish moose the second molar usually begins to appear in December and the first milk incisor is usually lost in January or February.

The lower jaws of a male taken on April 20 near Graphic Lake in Kenora District, Ontario, show little change in dentition from the preceding specimens with the exception that the third molar, although not yet broken through the bone covering the alveolus, was obviously about to erupt.

The lower jaws of 3 animals taken during the month of May all show that only the first permanent incisors are present, with the remaining milk incisiform teeth still functional. A female taken in Township 36 near Chapleau, Ontario, on May 11 shows the third lower molars protruding through the alveolus but still not yet broken through the gum. A male from the same locality taken on May 15 and a female taken in Gladstone Township, Algoma District, Ontario, show the anterior cusps of third molars protruding through the gum. In these May specimens the bone surrounding the last milk premolars has broken away, exposing the permanent tooth below. The central roots of milk P_4 have disintegrated and the permanent tooth below is almost in contact with the under surface of the crowns of the upper tooth.

In a yearling female taken June 15, Murie (1934, p. 12) found the following: "The first milk incisor has been shed and replaced by the first permanent incisor. The rest of the milk incisors are still in place. The milk premolars are much worn and being pushed out by the permanent premolars. The first upper molar is fully functional, the second upper molar only partially so. The first and second lower molars are functional. The third molar, upper and lower, has not yet appeared. The third lower molar is slightly more developed than the third upper molar." A series of 4 lower jaws of yearlings taken in June are available from Ontario. Unfortunately, the incisiform teeth are present *in situ* in only 2. Of these, both taken on June 22, one from near Gogama has only the first permanent incisors with the remaining milk incisiform teeth still present, while the other from near Missinaiki has only the second milk incisor on the right side missing and I₂ protruding about one-fourth of an inch beyond the gum. Only the anterior cusps of M_3 are exposed above the gum in each of these June specimens. Further deterioration of the roots of the milk premolars is evident. According to Skuncke (1949) the second incisors are usually replaced in March or April in Sweden, but it is evident that in Ontario, at least, the North American moose does not gain the second incisors until much later.

Of 4 Ontario specimens (lower jaws) taken the first week in July (2 near Elsas, 1 near Fraser River, Cochrane District, and 1 near Ramsay) 2 have only the first permanent incisor with the remaining incisiform teeth still functional. The incisiform teeth of the other two specimens are no longer *in situ*. All the milk premolars are still present but badly worn. In each case the third molar is protruding a short way through the gum (similar to the June specimens discussed above). In the case of Swedish moose, Skuncke (1949) reports that the third incisors are lost during the period from May to July. Of the Ontario specimens examined up to the end of the first week in July, none showed the loss of the third incisor and in only one case was the loss of a second incisor observed (on one side only).

Unfortunately no specimens are presently available that represent the period from the beginning of the second week in July to the end of September (14–16 months). Within this nine-week period a most rapid development takes place. The remaining milk incisors and the milk canine are usually lost and replaced with permanent ones. The milk premolars are lost in most cases and the permanent ones become almost fully functional. The third molar emerges still farther, with the anterior cusp becoming at least partially functional.

By October of the second year most normally developed moose in Sweden have replaced all the milk dentition, although Gardell (1947) reports that occasionally animals from central Sweden do not have a complete permanent dentition at that time. The last tooth to be replaced is apparently the milk canine, which usually is not finished before October of the second year, in Sweden (Lönnberg, 1923).

A series of 12 Ontario specimens taken during the month of October provides some measure of variation for this general region. In two cases the milk dentition has not been completely lost. In one case, that of a male

FIGURE 10. A foetus taken about March 1, 1950, near Pembroke, Ontario

FIGURE 11. A moose calf from near Port Arthur, Ontario, July 31, 1949

FIGURE 12. Weighing a moose killed September 17, 1947, on St. Ignace Island, Ontario

FIGURE 14. A young bull moose showing typical early spring moult pattern, St. Ignace Island, Ontario

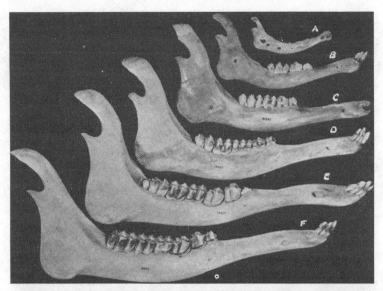

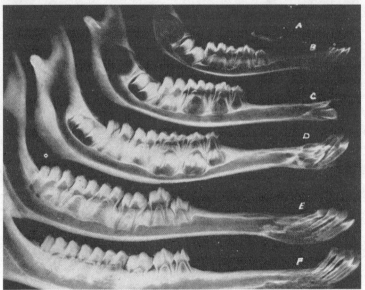

FIGURE 17. Tooth and mandible development in moose

Above: A. Embryo
B. Approximately one month
C. Approximately four or five months
D. Approximately nine months
E. Approximately seventeen months
F. Approximately thirty months

Below: An X-ray photograph of the above specimens
(courtesy of the late Mr. Percy Ghent)

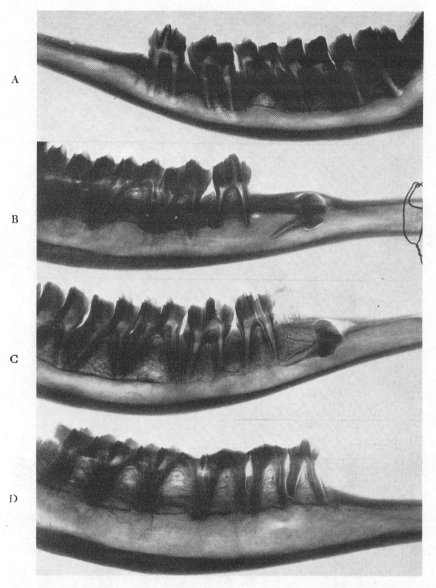

FIGURE 18. Radiographs of moose mandibles

A.   A female 1½ years old showing no sign of either the milk or the permanent P_2

B.   A male 3½ years old showing the permanent P_2 lying horizontal inside the mandible

C.   A male 1½ years old showing the permanent P_2 similar to B above but with the milk P_2 persisting

D.   A normal dentition in an animal judged to be 10–15 years old. Notice the reduction in the size of the pulp cavities, the increase in the space between the roots of the teeth and the ventral surface of the jaw, and also the apparent increase in the thickness of the bone along the ventral surface of the jaw in the older specimens

FIGURE 20. A yearling female at a game lick in early spring, St. Ignace Island. Notice unusual bell. Compare muzzle development with Figure 21

FIGURE 21. An adult bull losing winter coat. Notice bell and muzzle development

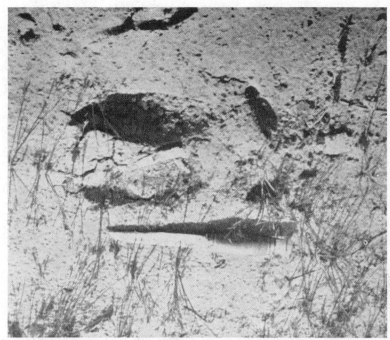

FIGURE 23. Spread toes with "dew claw" tracks, made by a running animal. Notice deer tracks at extreme right centre

FIGURE 22. Normal tracking of moose. The front feet are larger than the rear

FIGURE 24. A yearling bull showing early development of antler which appears as velvet-covered knob

FIGURE 25. A moose showing antler development in early May. Notice bifurcate bell

FIGURE 26. A moose showing antler development in late May

FIGURE 27. Chance association of a cow and bull at a game lick on Simpson Island, Ontario, July 12, 1947

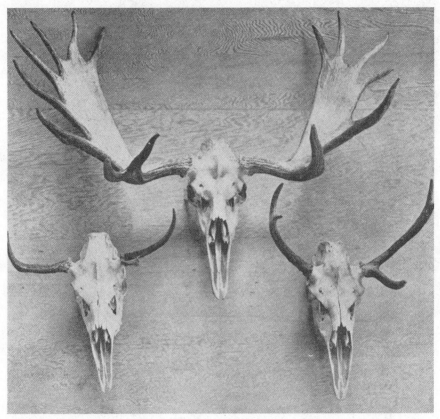

FIGURE 28. Examples of skull and antler development in moose. *Left*: Approximately 18 months. *Centre*: Adult (5 to 6 years). *Right*: Approximately 30 months

from the Cedar Lake area near Sioux Lookout, taken on October 4, the permanent premolars have not yet fully erupted and the milk premolars are still present on the right side. The first two permanent incisors are present but the milk I_3 and canine are still present. In the second case, a male from Marven Township, Cochrane District, only the left milk P_2 remains while none of the permanent premolars are fully erupted; all the milk incisiform teeth have been lost, but the third incisor and the canine are not fully erupted. Of the remaining 10 October specimens the following cases of incomplete eruption are in evidence: P_2, 5; P_3, 3; P_4, 3; I_2, 1; I_3, 4; and C, 8. During this period the canine is still in the process of eruption and revolving into its final position. Inasmuch as the developing incisiform teeth lie with the occlusal surfaces in an approximately vertical plane, these teeth must rotate almost 90 degrees in the process of eruption before reaching the final position. An example of one of the less advanced October specimens (Figure 17, E) was taken on October 9, near Wabaskang Lake, about 30 miles west of Sioux Lookout, Ontario. It had recently acquired permanent upper premolars. The first ones (P^2) are just protruding through the gums and were unworn. The right P_2 has not yet fully erupted and the left protrudes only slightly above the gum line. The second premolar (P_3) protrudes the greatest and P_4 projects slightly above the gum line, indicating a 3–4–2 order of replacement. Skuncke (1949) indicates that this is the normal order of replacement in Swedish moose. In other October specimens from Ontario this order is less pronounced. In all of the October specimens the last cusp of the third lower molar protrudes only slightly above the gum and shows little or no wear.

A yearling male (R.O.M.Z. 19356) taken in November, 35 miles east of Longlac, Ontario, has only two functional upper premolars, the first (P^2) not protruding beyond the alveolus. The former show no signs of wear. The lower premolars are all present but unworn. The third permanent incisors, especially the left, show signs of recent eruption and the canines have not yet fully erupted. The last molars show slight wear on the anterior two cusps only. The first upper (P^2) premolars of a male (R.O.M.Z. 19338) taken on November 12 in Cavendish Township, about 25 miles north of Peterborough, Ontario, are slightly more advanced than the Longlac specimen, protruding only slightly beyond the gum line. Both the third and fourth premolars above and below, as well as the anterior cusps of M 3 are beginning to show wear. The permanent incisiform dentition is complete. In 16 additional lower jaws, taken in Ontario during November, all the permanent teeth are functional except in seven cases in which the canine has not yet reached its final position (in three cases data on the incisiform teeth are not available). Marked wear is in evidence on the crowns of all lower cheek teeth with the exception of the anterior premolar (P_2) and the last cusp of M_3.

In a series of 36 December specimens from Ontario, the full permanent dentition is present with the following exceptions: in two cases (both abnormal) the right milk P_2 is still in place (with the left fully erupted) although in one case the permanent tooth below could not erupt (Figure 18), while in the other the permanent tooth is protruding above the gum and would soon push the deciduous tooth out. In one other instance P_2 is not yet fully erupted. In four cases the canines have not yet rotated to the final position.

Thus by the end of the calendar year, at 18 or 19 months of age, the full permanent dentition is usually in place and is distinguishable from that of older animals chiefly by the relatively unstained premolars and the relatively light wear on the crowns of the cheek teeth. For a further description of the 1½ year-old series, see Appendix A. A specimen approximately 29–30 months of age is shown in Figure 17 for comparison.

Lönnberg (1923), Skuncke (1949), and other Swedish workers have done considerable work on deducing the age of European moose from the amount of tooth wear. The widths of the incisiform teeth have been regarded as suitable criteria in the Old World, but preliminary studies of age determination carried out on Ontario specimens in co-operation with Mr. R. C. Passmore and Mr. A. T. Cringan have shown that the technique does not give a reliable indication of age for moose of this region. The results of these studies may be found in Appendix A.

Abnormal tooth development. In the course of the above-mentioned studies, a check of over 450 adult Ontario specimens (over 16 months of age) shows that the incisiform teeth were available for examination in 320 cases, from which a total of no less than 24 instances of supernumerary incisiform teeth were found (11 cases on the right side, 11 on the left side, and 2 with an extra tooth on both sides). In all but three cases the extra tooth lies in line with the other incisiform teeth. In two instances, the extra tooth is superimposed, lying either above or below the normal row, but in one of these cases the extra tooth is rotated 180 degrees with the occlusal surface facing down instead of up. Among the sub-adults examined, a male calf, taken on January 27 on Big Island, Kenora District, Ontario, has the first permanent incisors in place, while there are still four milk incisiform teeth present on the left side. The first milk incisor had obviously been replaced by the permanent incisor.

In the case of one of the specimens mentioned in the December series (19 months) which retained the right milk P_2, there is no visible evidence that the permanent tooth would have erupted. In four additional cases P_2 is missing with no evidence that either the milk or permanent tooth had ever erupted. An X-ray photograph (Figure 18) of four of these specimens shows that in three cases the permanent P_2 is lying horizontal inside the jaw where it had become incorrectly oriented and had started pushing forward along the inside of the jaw, thus failing to erupt through the bone. In the fourth case there is no sign of either the milk or permanent tooth, both of which apparently failed to develop.

Relatively few cases of serious malocclusions were observed, although considerable variation in the wear-patterns, created by minor malocclusions, was observed. In other cases injury or damage to either the upper or lower series created unbalanced wear on the opposite as well as the adjacent teeth.

Summary of tooth development. Although more data are needed to assess the variation of tooth development in relation to age, the above data are summarized to give tentative criteria for age determination of animals less than 19 or 20 months of age.

Birth. Milk incisors functional. Milk premolars beginning to erupt.

2 weeks. Only two premolars (MP 2 and 3?) functional.

3–4 weeks. All lower premolars in place but MP_2 not fully erupted.

4–6 weeks. Premolars fully functional. MP_2 unworn and only lightly stained.

10–14 weeks. First molars beginning to erupt. Lower ones usually precede the uppers.

4–6 months. First molars fully functional.

6–8 months. Second molars beginning to erupt but may not be visible above gum. No permanent incisiform teeth functional, although milk I_1 may be lost and the permanent one partially erupted.

8–10 months. Second molars nearly to completely functional. First milk incisor lost and replaced by permanent one.

10–13 months. Second molars fully functional. Third molars starting to break through bone and may advance to show anterior cusp projecting throuph gum. Central roots of milk P_4 disintegrated and permanent teeth visible below. Only first permanent incisor functional. Second milk incisor may or may not be lost with permanent tooth coming in.

13–16 months. Third molar partially erupted. All milk premolars are usually lost and permanent ones become at least partially functional. Milk incisors $_2$ and $_3$ and the canine are lost. Permanent I_2 becomes fully functional and I_3 and C may not be fully erupted.

16–19 months. Full permanent dentition usually present but premolars are slightly stained and show obvious signs of recent eruption. Premolars may not be fully erupted in younger specimens. Third incisors and canines may show signs of recent eruptions; the latter may not be fully rotated to final position. P_2 and the rear cusp of M_3 usually show no sign of wear.

Over 19 months. See Appendix A.

Mandible Development

The length of the mandible increases at a rapid rate for the first six months, after which the rate of growth decreases but continues to elongate up to approximately 2½ years (Figure 19). Beyond this age little growth takes place. The anterior portion of the mandible, as indicated by the length of the diastema, elongates rather rapidly up to one year of age, after which a slow but fairly steady rate of increase continues up to about four or five years of age. Most of the elongation of the lower jaw beyond one year of age involves the posterior portion of the jaw (Figure 17). This area must continue to grow in order to provide room for the last two molars. With this growth there is a change in the shape of the ascending ramus. In younger animals the main axis of the ramus is almost vertical. With increase in length of the whole jaw the axis changes as the dorsal portion of the ramus bends backward. On the basis of specimens examined, there seems

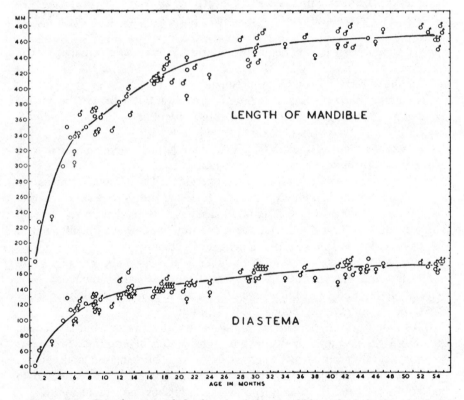

FIGURE 19. Growth curve of the length of the mandible and of the length of the diastema. Length of mandible was measured from the anterior rim of the alveolus to the posterior rim of the ramus (parallel to toothrow crowns). For technique used in determining age of older specimens see Appendix A

to be no significant difference in the rate of growth as between the sexes up to about 4½ years of age.

General Body Development

The "bell" is formed on both sexes, although the greatest development and variation is normally found in bulls (Figure 20, 21, and 25). A female foetus taken about March 1 (Figure 11) possessed a bell, the fleshy portion being one-fourth of an inch in length. Discussing the bell of moose in Sweden, Lönnberg (1923) states that this structure does not usually appear on cows but remarks on its early formation in the unborn young. He gives an example of a female foetus taken in the middle of February, being about 5 months old, with a bell 4 millimetres long and 1½ millimetres thick while the total length of the foetus was about 400 millimetres.

The muzzle of young calves is quite short and "normal" (Figure 10). Denniston (1948) recorded facial length measurements, as well as the others given in Table VIII, of a free-ranging female calf which was fed with a supplementary diet of milk. He found that the facial length was 11 inches during the age of two and three weeks, 12 inches from the fourth to seventh week, and had increased to 14½ inches when measured at the age of eight and nine weeks. By the age of six months the face had elongated considerably but the overhanging muffle does not normally reach full development until after one year of age (compare Figures 20 and 21).

Gardell (1947) discusses the relative proportions of the ear to the length of the head in young moose. He points out that in the fall, in calves of the year, if one ear is pulled down along the nose, the tip of the ear will reach half way down the head, whereas on older animals it reaches only about one-third.

With regard to the general bone development of calves, Skuncke (1949) points out that the elements below the knees are especially porous and are normally dark red inside in contrast to the typically yellow and dense cross-sections of the bones of older animals. He states that it takes at least 12 months before the sutures or symphysis between the three bones of either half of the pelvic girdle are completely fused or "filled in."

In general body proportions, the young moose seems to reach his maximum height early, followed by a gradual extension of body length. The "unusually" long legs serve the moose well in wading in muskeg, water, or snow and in stepping over fallen logs and brush.

The front hoofs are larger than the back ones (Figure 22) and in soft mud, snow, or sand the "dew claws" are frequently brought into play, along with the spreading of the toes, to create an increased surface of footing (Figure 23).

The hoofs of bulls average longer than those of cows and tend to be blunter at the front end. The tracks of cows tend to be sharper at the front end and more nearly circular in outline. Normal variation plus age factors tend to make it difficult to determine sex by tracks alone, however.

Growth and Development

The young male calf may develop small "buttons" during the first year but they rarely protrude beyond the hair line and are lost during his first winter. At about one year of age the yearling male begins the growth of his first set of "spikes." Appearing first as small velvet-covered "knobs" (Figure 24), they gradually lengthen and one or both may fork or merely flatten somewhat on the end. The size and shape of the antlers of yearlings vary considerably. Several authors have erroneously indicated that the yearling moose always develops a simple unbranched "spike" only a few inches in length (Merrill, 1920; Seton, 1927). Spencer and Chatelain (1953) report that of 21 long-yearling class jaws and antlers from Alaska, only two had spike antlers and the remainder had a fork or even a small palm. Lönnberg (1923) found that in moose of Sweden the yearling's antlers were normally a single process but occasionally "strong" individuals had two tines on both antlers, and even three on at least one side were observed.

Field observations in Ontario indicate that most two-year-old bulls exhibit diverse patterns of branching, occasionally with little or no development of the palmate blades (see Appendix B). An example of yearling antlers is compared with those of an animal approximately one year older in Figure 28.

In May the large bulls of the St. Ignace area have advanced antlers measuring nearly a foot in length (see Figures 25, 26). These antlers grow at a remarkable rate, as Manweiler (1941, p. 40) emphasizes:

Maximum body development comes after the sixth year when the antler material formed in the period of a few months is greater than that development in a lifetime by the other even-hoofed mammals [of Minnesota]. Their annual formation is as much a drain on the system of the male as is the production of young to the opposite sex. After the prime of life the antlers become retrogressive and are often characterized by large diameter beam but less total weight and less symmetry.

Lönnberg (1923) and Skuncke (1949) have provided a rather extensive treatment of antler development of moose in Sweden, including tables of measurements and growth, and other records. The antlers of these animals average considerably smaller than those of North American moose and there appears to be a much higher percentage of the "cervina" type of development as opposed to the "palmata" or "shovel" formation found in this country. They point out that the cervina-type antlers lack a more or less complete shovel and the usual very long tines pass out from an almost cylindrical or small flat beam. This type usually bears fewer tines or points than the palmate antler. Apparently moose from Finland also have a high percentage of the cervina-type antlers (Voipio, 1952b).

Lönnberg (1923) points out that the cervina type of antler is probably helped to remain dominant by the fact that animals with longer tines often win in fights with palmate types, when contesting for cows.

In discussing the relative variation in antler size and tine development these authors consider that food supply, lime content of soil, inheritance, and possibly weather all play an important part in determining the size of antlers.

They also devote considerable attention to malformed antlers, pointing out that they are usually caused by injury to the antlers in early stages of development or by abnormalities of the sexual organs through injury, disease, or otherwise.

Freeing of the Velvet

The antlers usually reach full development in August and September at which time the "velvet," or skin, dies and the animal removes it by rubbing the antlers on shrubs and trees. The earliest sign of such activity noted in the St. Ignace area was in the case of a large bull rubbing his antlers against alders on August 19, 1947. At this time only a few patches of velvet had been removed. When the velvet is first shed the antlers appear almost white with the exception of occasional blood stains. By continued rubbing, which marks the onset of the breeding or rutting season, the antlers become stained and appear brown in colour. Complete removal of the velvet usually takes eight or nine days according to Murie (1934).

Lönnberg (1923) reports that in Sweden large bulls are the first to shed their velvet and also the first to drop their antlers.

Shedding of Antlers

Most observers agree that older animals with larger antlers shed them progressively earlier and consequently begin growing new antlers progressively earlier than younger ones. Yearlings and two-year-olds frequently carry their antlers almost to their following birthday. Similar findings are reported from Sweden (Lönnberg, 1923). Hosley (1949, p. 9) states that "the 2-year-old sheds his antlers in April and they are dropped earlier each year following until, in the prime of life, they are lost by late December or early January."

The shedding of antlers in large adults usually starts in December (Merrill, 1920; Kellum, 1941), but at least two instances of shedding prior to the end of November have been reported from British Columbia (British Columbia, 1937).

Newsom (1937b) concluded that moose actually attempt to rid themselves of the antlers by knocking them against trees. He found many shed antlers covered with balsam sap and cites a case where one animal was thought to have returned to a certain tree to knock off the second antler after apparently having dropped the first a few days earlier. Newsom suggests the possibility that this urge to dispose of antlers might be correlated with the passing of an extremely cold period.

Mr. V. Crichton of Chapleau reports (personal communication) having observed one moose for a few days in Abney Township where the animal dropped its 24-point antlers on either January 18 or 19.

On an aerial moose survey of St. Ignace and adjacent islands on February 20, 1948, at least 5 of the 28 animals observed were bulls still carrying antlers. Morse (1946) reports that 2 large bulls were still carrying antlers as late as March 4, in Minnesota.

A total of 100 single shed antlers were found in the St. Ignace Island area in 1947. They were dropped over a period of several years.

Size of Antlers and Age of Moose

No definite criteria have been established for determining the age of moose by antlers; however, measurements of the base near the bur, as described by Cahalane (1932) for deer, should give some indication of age when sufficient specimens of known ages are available (see Appendix B). Lönnberg (1923) points out that the pedicles increase in diameter with the years and become shorter after each shedding.

The Boone and Crockett Club (Ely et al., 1939) compiled a list of moose trophies having the largest spread of antlers. The greatest spread listed was a specimen from Alaska measuring 77⅝ inches across. The largest listed from Canada was 73 inches, a specimen from the Peace River in Alberta. The largest Ontario specimen was taken near Round Lake in the Timagami region in 1910. It was listed as 68⅛ inches but a careful re-examination of this specimen, which is in the Royal Ontario Museum of Zoology, clearly shows a maximum spread of 70⅛ inches. Records show that when first measured as a fresh specimen its spread was 72 inches.

In 1952 the Boone and Crockett Club (Webb et al., 1952) published a new list of record heads based on a different scoring system which attempted to reduce the premium on antler spread and to recognize other features of outstanding antlers such as symmetry, circumference of beam, number of points, and size of the palms. In this new list the record spread remained at 77⅝ inches for an Alaskan moose (*Alces alces gigas*) but this specimen was ranked in sixth position on the new point system of scoring. The highest ranking specimen had a total spread of 75 inches with palms 50 and 46¾ inches long, and 17¾ and 21⅝ inches wide. The smallest circumferences of the beams were 7½ and 8⅛ inches, and 15 points were present on the right side and 18 on the left. A specimen from Yukon Territory taken near Mayo in 1950 ranked in third place with an antler spread of 75½ inches, the largest on record from Canada.

In this later method of scoring, the two races *Alces a. americana* and *A. a. andersoni* were grouped together and the former record spread of 73 inches for the specimen from Peace River, Alberta, was not included since the specimen could no longer be located. It apparently represented the greatest spread ever recorded for the race *andersoni*. The highest ranking specimen under the point system was one from Slave Lake, Alberta, with a spread of 60⅝ inches (ranking first among the combined races). The greatest spread listed for this race was one from Eldersley, Saskatchewan, with a spread of 68½ inches (ranking eleventh among the combined races).

The top ranking eastern moose (*A. a. americana*) was one from Bear Lake, Quebec, with a greatest spread of 65⅝ inches. On the point system employed by the Boone and Crockett Club, this specimen ranked as the fourth from the top of all North American moose (one-eighth of a point below the two Alaskan moose, which were tied for second place). The record for the greatest spread, however, was held by a specimen from Maine (71⅝ inches) followed by the Round Lake, Ontario, specimen (70⅛ inches).

The top ranking Wyoming moose (*A. a. shirasi*) was taken in Fremont County, Wyoming, in 1944 (greatest spread 56⅝ inches), although the largest spread was recorded from Sublette County, Wyoming, (58⅜ inches; ranking in sixth place).

Summary of Antler Development and Phenology

Interesting data on the antler development of a single captive moose given by Kellum (1941, p. 5) are summarized in Table XII.

Male calves may develop buttons the first year. Yearlings may develop simple, sharp, pointed, single spikes, short single spikes with flattened ends, or branched antlers, usually with no more than two points and little or no palm development. Two-year-old bulls may have simple long spikes or branched antlers, frequently with little or no palm development. Older bulls show a great diversity of antler patterns (see Appendix B).

Full development of the antlers is reached in August and September at which time the velvet is freed by rubbing on shrubs and trees. Larger bulls usually free their velvet before younger ones.

Antlers are dropped from November to March, the majority between December and February. Older animals are usually first to lose antlers and progressively younger animals carry antlers successively longer.

BREEDING HABITS

Most authors agree that the rutting or breeding season usually lasts from about September 15 to October 15 (Seton, 1927; and others). Murie (1934)

TABLE XII

Growth and Shedding of Antlers (Records for One Individual)

Age (years)	Velvet shed	Left antler					Right antler				
		Dropped	Points	Weight (lbs-oz)	Length (in.)	Width (in.)	Dropped	Points	Weight (lbs-oz)	Length (in.)	Width (in.)
1-2	Sept. 2	Mar. 7	4	1-2	12.0	10.5	Mar. 4	3	1-2	11.3	9.8
2-3	Sept. 2	Feb. 5	6	2-15	15.3	15.8	Feb. 1	6	2-14	15.3	16.5
3-4	Aug. 30	Feb. 1	8	6-11	22.0	26.3	Feb. 5	7	6-5	22.0	27.0

observed an instance of a bull consorting with a cow on August 23, although he points out that there was some doubt whether this companionship had anything to do with mating, since the sexes were not seen together again until the middle of September (see Figure 27). He was of the opinion that the height of the rut on Isle Royale was toward the end of September, although the rut was still in progress on October 11, a day before his field work was completed.

"On the basis of experimental reindeer studies, Palmer has suggested that a good food supply may advance the onset of the rut and a poor one retard it" (Hosley, 1949, p. 4).

In Sweden, the rut is said to last from the first of September to the first of October (Lönnberg, 1923).

In the course of studies in Ontario, it was not possible to remain in the field during the height of the breeding season; thus personal observations were limited to the beginning of the rut. In Algonquin Provincial Park during 1946, a cow and bull were seen associating on September 18; on September 19 a bull was observed giving low coughing grunts while thrashing his antlers. A second bull was observed acting in a similar manner on September 20, but he was answered by the grunting of a third male. We found that one of the bulls observed on September 20 had pawed out a circular "wallow" or depression. We attempted to move into close range, in the case of the latter three moose, but they apparently had not lost any fear of man for they all departed quickly when we came into the immediate vicinity.

The earliest mating activity observed on St. Ignace Island was on September 16, 1947, beginning at about 7:20 p.m. when a large bull was observed to follow a cow for about one-quarter of a mile. While doing so he gave short low grunts at intervals of a few seconds. Since these two animals were moving in the general direction of a salt lick, we anticipated their destination and moved ahead of them to our observation tower and awaited their arrival. The bull moose arrived on schedule but in the meantime his female companion had disappeared. Since no cows were heard to call or answer calls up to October 3, the impression was gained that the height of the rutting was not reached until after the first of October in the St. Ignace area.

McDowell and Moy (1942) of Montana have made observations on the mating behaviour of North American moose. A part of their account is given here:

On September 27, a large bull and cow were watched for more than three hours. When first observed, they were lying in the high willows of Blacktail Meadow in the Hellroaring drainage. As approached to be photographed, the cow jumped and ran farther into the willows. The bull got up, but didn't immediately follow the cow. The observers were able to approach to within approximately fifty feet of him to take photographs. At this time he began to thrash the brush with his huge antlers and to utter a grunt-like call (oo-oomph, oo-oomph) which was made by opening and closing his muzzle. The cow, hidden in the willows, answered his call with a wail-like call (mew-oo-wa, mew-oo-wa), sounding much like the bawl of a yearling heifer. The bull soon followed the cow. From a bench that ran parallel with the meadow, the observers could look down upon the moose from a distance of about 100 yards, even though the moose were in the high willows.

The bull then approached the cow from the rear and licked her genital organs. He then stretched his neck and opened his mouth as if to bellow, but no sound that could be heard came out. The cow moved off slowly and the bull immediately pursued and tried to mount her. She ran approximately fifty yards and stopped. The bull followed more slowly, but when he caught up with her, he went through the same procedure again without success. This time when she moved, she waded through a narrow lagoon in the willow swamp. The bull followed to a spot across the lagoon from her. At this point, he was again approached to be photographed by one of the observers. He paid little attention, but in the meantime began to dig a wallow. He used his front feet and made rapid progress in the moist soil of the swamp. When he had finished, he urinated in the wallow a number of times, drinking water from the lagoon intermittently. He did not lie down in the wallow, but kept watching the photographer out of the corner of his eye. During the whole procedure the rate of his breathing seemed to increase, a fact that could readily be seen by the movement of his flanks. Next he moved a few yards away and began to thrash the brush with his antlers again. The cow, which by this time had moved approximately 100 feet to one side, wailed, and the bull turned and charged the photographer, his head low and swinging. Fortunately, he stopped at the other side of the lagoon, approximately ten feet away. At this point the observers retired from the field and left the moose to continue their mating in privacy.

Further observations by J. E. Gaab and Robert Neal made on September 25, 1947, in the Absaroka Wilderness area of Montana have been recorded by Thompson (1949, p. 313) as follows:

A mature bull moose was observed pawing in a small area at the base of a rock cliff near the outer margin of a forested area. After a few strokes of pawing, he straddled the depression, bent his body near the ground and urinated into the hole he had pawed out. The bull carried out the alternate operation of pawing and urinating seven times before a female moose appeared from the adjacent timber. As the cow approached, the male moose padded the wallow with a downward motion of his forefeet. He then laid in the wallow and twisted and turned, presumably to cover his body with mud.

When the cow reached the area, she struck the bull with a front foot until he got out of the wallow. The female then laid down and rolled and turned, covering herself with mud. The bull standing by during this procedure, came toward the cow and struck her with a front hoof. When both animals were standing, the bull smelled the female genital region and began rubbing his neck and bell along her back and sides. The cow stood facing away and while the bull continued this action she stamped her rear legs and tossed her head.

When this activity had nearly ceased the cow started to walk away several times, but was stopped each time by a low grunting call from the bull. Finally they walked together into the forested area. Coitus was not executed at this time.

Close examination of the wallow was made after the departure of the moose. A round depression thirty-six inches in diameter and eight inches deep made up the wallow. The soil was damp and had a sparse grass covering. A musky-urine odor prevailed in the area. Two similar wallows were found at distances of thirty and fifty yards from the original wallow.

Other notes on mating behaviour are given by Murie (1934). Much more thorough observations of the rut have been carried out in Sweden (Lönnberg, 1923; Skuncke, 1949).

Formerly thought to be monogamous, the moose is considered by most recent authors to be polygamous to a limited extent, mating normally with one cow for a period, then perhaps with others (Murie, 1934; Burt, 1946; Dufresne, 1946; Cahalane, 1947; Hosley, 1949). Owing to the solitary habits of moose and the distances between animals in many areas, it seems likely that the limited amount of polygamy may well be due to enforced monogamy, rather than to choice.

Hosley (1945, p. 5) quotes the belief that a mature bull can serve up to a dozen cows per season, but the evidence for such a belief is not presented.

Lönnberg (1923) points out that mating happens several times a day and that the bull stays with the cow until her rutting season is over. When the cow shows refusal he seeks another if one may be found in the region. Lönnberg states further that the real rutting time of the cow may last only a few days and if no bull is present or if it has been shot before mating she remains barren. This is pointed out as one of the possible explanations of the relatively large number of barren cows found in Sweden.

The meeting of rival bulls during this period is commonly considered to be the signal for a mighty battle. Many stories of such encounters have been written in sporting magazines and books and Seton (1927) quotes others. No fights were personally observed in Ontario studies. On September 17 a young bull was seen feeding close to a large bull on amiable terms. Murie (1934) had opportunity to observe fighting were it normally common, but saw none. He did observe broken tines and other evidence to indicate that some battling took place. One is led to believe that most such meetings end with a little sparring and much bluffing. Anthony (1939) indicates that active sparring is common in Wyoming. Serious fights undoubtedly do occur, however. Cowan (1946) found cases of mortality due to fighting. Hosley (1949, p. 5) believes such loss to be significant, giving the following example: "In traveling 450 miles in Alaska, Dufresne found the locations where seven pairs of bulls had fought to the death. There were three instances of locked antlers and in the other four cases the skulls were a few feet apart." In some such instances rivals are known to get their antlers so completely locked together that they cannot free themselves and both consequently perish. Shiras (1935) reports having found such a set of locked antlers on St. Ignace Island, and the Royal Ontario Museum has one set taken near Nipigon, Ontario, and another from Shuel Township, Cochrane District, Ontario.

Many writers have remarked about the indifference of a cow when rival suitors are contesting for her companionship.

Palmer reported that the rutting animals are almost invariably in or near clumps of spruce or alder, but rarely out in the more open willow or aspen stands. The cows are said by Seton (1927) to do most of the calling, while the bulls listen and travel. Palmer, however, found both cows and bulls calling. . . .

The call of the moose is seldom heard except during the rut. This call is subdued but clear at distances up to 200 yards. Palmer described the call of the bull as ". . . either a low, moo-like plea broken off short with an upward inflection at the end, or a throaty gulp." He said the call of the cow was ". . . longer and more like that of the domestic cow, but not as loud," and that of the calf ". . . similar to that of the domestic cattle with a moo-like beginning, and ending in a petulant bawl." The call of the cow to her calf was described as a single grunt frequently repeated. (Hosley, 1949, p. 5)

The moose of Sweden are said to call occasionally but are thought to do so less commonly than those of North America (Lönnberg, 1923).

It is only during the rutting season that moose will respond to "birch-bark" calls, rattling of antlers or sticks, and breaking of brush. Much has been written about the art and effectiveness of various means of attracting moose (Merrill, 1920; Stone, 1924; Seton, 1927; and others). Murie (1934) found that moose of Isle Royale commonly responded both to imitated calls of the cow and breaking of branches.

Many observers agree that moose, especially the bulls, travel around more during the breeding season than at any other time of the year. In Algonquin Provincial Park, for instance, moose are said often to venture into areas where they are not seen at any other time of the year. The bulls expend so much energy and feed so little during the rut that they lose up to 150 pounds, according to Kellum (1941). Skuncke (1949) estimates that bulls lose about 6 to 12 per cent of their weight during the rut whereas cows normally increase in weight during this period. He also states that bulls are most active in rut below 10 years of age and cows during the six- to eight-year period.

There has been speculation on the use and significance of the so-called "wallows" or depressions which are found associated with the breeding season (Tanton, 1920; Merrill, 1920; Seton, 1927; Murie, 1934). Such depressions were found on St. Ignace Island even during the summer months. In all probability, two different types of depressions are involved. During the summer it was noticed that moose frequently sought soft, cool, muddy spots in which to lie down. After resting, a fairly deep depression was left. When undisturbed on arising several moose were noted to urinate before moving away. This might account for many depressions that have been reported as not showing signs of having been pawed by moose.

Apparently these depressions are also made by the moose of Sweden, for Lönnberg (1923) states that bulls paw out pits in the ground with their forefeet, where they pass their urine and roll themselves in it. Mating is said to take place near these pits which in Sweden are called *brollgrop*, *brunstgrop* (rut-pit), or in some regions, *trampa*.

"Palmer noted that there were often two holes 6 to 8 feet apart, apparently made by two bulls face to face" (Hosley, 1949, p. 5).

Observations by Mr. J. E. Gaab of the use of "wallows" by moose in Montana are also cited by Hosley.

In the course of freeing the velvet from the antlers, bulls commonly paw up the earth in an apparent state of excitement. The bulls continue to rub their antlers even after the velvet is free. We noticed that when excited by some unrecognized cause moose frequently urinated. It would, therefore, appear that rubbing the antlers, pawing the earth, and urinating in such depressions are sometimes mere nervous reactions or emotional outlets brought on by such excitements as the rut and probably have little other significance with regard to the rut itself, while in other cases they apparently form a normal behaviour pattern during the rut.

The gestation period is generally conceded to be approximately eight months, 240 to 246 days.

Further discussion of the reactions of moose to humans during the rut is given on pages 105–7.

Maturity and Old Age

It is not definitely known when moose reach sexual maturity. Rough indications found in this study seem to substantiate the conclusions reached by several authors that at least a few of the females are successfully bred at the age of 16 months and produce offspring on their second birthday. Lönnberg (1923) reports similar findings from Sweden. The high percentage of barren females would suggest that probably only a small number are mated prior to two years of age. Skuncke (1949) reports that often cows do not become pregnant until they are four years old. On St. Ignace Island an actively grunting adult bull was observed to pass within a few feet of a yearling female on October 1 without any noticeable interest being aroused on the part of either one.

No evidence has been reported of sixteen-month-old bulls successfully mating, although several authors feel that they may be capable of doing so, but are commonly refused the opportunity by larger dominating bulls. The prime of life or maximum development is said to be reached between six and ten years (Lönnberg, 1923; Stone, 1924; Dufresne, 1946). The animals continue to increase in weight and stature beyond full sexual maturity but little is known of the extent of their life span. Stone (1924) postulates that the maximum is near 20 years. Several old skulls were found in the St. Ignace area with teeth so badly worn that it would appear that the animals had reached close to maximum life span.

"Palmer writes of an Alaskan bull that appeared at a camp as a calf and came back each year for 15 years" (Hosley, 1949, p. 9).

Lönnberg (1923) reports on a moose that was tagged as a calf in Sweden and caught again 20 years later. It was still vigorous and had 12 tines on one antler and 11 on the other. Skuncke (1949) reports that a cow in the Stockholm area of Sweden gave birth to healthy calves as late as twenty-one years of age but became so vicious that she had to be killed. He also shows (Figure 13; Table X) that bulls do not reach their maximum weight until they are at least 10 years old, although cows show little increase in weight after four or five years of age.

CHAPTER TEN

GENERAL BEHAVIOUR AND ACTIVITIES

MOOSE SEEM TO BE animals of mixed emotions. Their unpredictable reactions under varying conditions have led to many highly controversial conclusions concerning the relative acuteness of the senses and the normal behaviour patterns. On St. Ignace Island we constructed a makeshift observation tower near a large natural salt lick which afforded excellent opportunity to carry out general behaviour studies.

SENSES

Many uncontrollable factors, such as extremely variable air currents in heavily forested areas, together with the inconsistent behaviour of moose under different circumstances prevent any attempt to evaluate precisely the senses and behaviour patterns. Several generalizations may be made nevertheless. For the most part, our observations seem to substantiate the findings of Murie (1934, p. 15) who concluded that "hearing and smell are highly efficient in moose, and vision somewhat deficient."

Sheldon (1911), Shiras (1912), and others cite examples of moose ignoring obvious stimuli of sight and hearing and reacting to the close approach of humans only when the sense of smell was able to function efficiently. Oberholtzer (1911) concluded that the sound of the human voice was an important stimulus in alerting moose. Murie (1934) also demonstrated the effectiveness of the human voice in creating an immediate reaction. Lamson (1941) concluded that "the powers of hearing of this animal are unequalled." Working with penned animals he found that moose could detect the footsteps of an approaching person 1½ to 3 minutes before the human ear became aware of the first sound. Shiras (1935) performed various experiments which indicate a more highly developed sense of hearing than smell and *vice versa*, under varying circumstances.

In discussing the reactions of moose to stimuli of the senses, Shiras (1912, p. 443) writes as follows: ". . . no antlered animal of the earth is more obtuse and stolid than the moose, and no animal, when finally alarmed, is a greater victim of an increasing and progressive fear than this. At times it seems almost impossible to alarm them, and then when this is accomplished, one wonders whether they ever recover from the shock."

Sheldon (1930, p. 262) states that "after being frightened by scent, moose go much farther without stopping than when frightened by sight."

101

In general the observations carried out in this work indicate that the ears often serve to alert the animal, the eyes to investigate, while the final stimulus, causing immediate reaction, is transmitted by smell. When approaching an animal upwind silently in a canoe we were usually successful in getting within close range. Even when the animal detected our presence, 'rarely did it rush away without stopping and turning to look at us for a second or third time. When travelling noisily upwind through the bush we were occasionally surprised by a moose a few yards ahead watching our every move. Frequently if we stopped and stood silent the moose would continue to watch us, perhaps move a few steps and turn to look again before finally moving away.

We found it exceedingly difficult to move into close range of moose from upwind. Even when animals were observed across a lake as far away as one-half mile, a silent upwind approach usually caused them to become alert or move away before we got within much less than one-quarter of a mile.

When moose were observed as they travelled through the bush, unaware of the presence of humans, they commonly stopped periodically and turned their head and directed their ears in the direction from whence they had come as if they suspected they were being followed.

While observing from our tower at the salt lick we could frequently predict the approach of a second moose by watching the activity of a moose in the lick. It could apparently detect the approach of another animal long before we could see or hear anything unusual.

Apparently the fear of human odour is not as highly developed in yearlings as in adults. On several occasions yearlings would approach quite close to us, even upwind, when we were sitting quiet and unhidden near a trail. After finally becoming frightened and trotting away they frequently returned again in a short time.

One remarkable accomplishment noted in moose was their ability to locate submerged vegetation. Perhaps the sense of touch is involved. On numerous occasions moose were observed to swim out to deep water, then suddenly dive for a few seconds, perhaps become completely submerged, and come up with a mouthful of pond weed (*Potamogeton* sp.). No portion of the plant would be visible from the surface, yet the moose seemed to know where to find it. It is difficult to understand what senses are involved, unless the animal actually touches the plants with its legs.

DISPOSITION, TEMPERAMENT, AND MANNERISMS

The degree of alertness of individuals seems to govern their general behaviour. An alerted or suspicious animal can move through dense bush with an amazing silence. Time after time we found that in spite of careful and constant scanning of the clearing surrounding the salt lick from our vantage point in the tower, we would suddenly discover a moose far out in the clearing without having received any audible warning of its approach. When not alert they could be heard moving through the bush several hundred yards away. When badly frightened there is probably no animal in North America that makes more noise crashing headlong through dense brush.

During the summer months we noticed that when two or more moose came together at the lick they seemed to treat each other with tolerance and indifference and usually entered and departed wholly independent of the other individuals (Figure 29).

Occasionally when two adult bulls met at the lick they would approach each other, put their noses close together, and even "square off" as if to spar, but with a nudge or so each animal would go his own way and appear to ignore further the presence of the other.

Quite frequently two young animals would travel in close association. In most of these cases a yearling would be following a two-year-old. Twins apparently remain together during most of their second year.

On June 12, 1948, five adult bulls and one yearling female were observed in the immediate vicinity of the salt lick at the same time. When the yearling attempted to enter the salt lick she was driven away several times by one or more of the bulls.

Both moose and white-tailed deer were observed drinking side by side from the water of the salt lick. The deer were constantly alert, rushing in and out of the lick area, and constantly watching in all directions as they drank intermittently. This anxiety on the part of the deer did not seem to disturb the moose in the least, for they appeared to ignore the deer completely (Figure 30).

In order to drink from the lick the moose were forced either to spread their front legs in giraffe manner (Figure 31), place one forward and the other backward and bend the knees slightly (Figure 32), or bend both front knees slightly (Figure 33). Several authors have reported that moose commonly kneel down on their front legs to reach low-growing herbs but none was seen to do so during this study.

While photographing moose at night we learned that they are totally indifferent to a spot light. A beam of light could be thrown on them causing their eyes to shine brightly, but they would show no reaction whatsoever and would merely continue normal activity.

When a flash bulb went off at close range each moose almost invariably would make a startled jump, run a few paces, regain its composure, and then return to resume drinking.

The sound of the motion picture camera seemed to cause some anxiety and suspicion on the part of moose, but they soon became accustomed to the new sound. Even the click of a still camera shutter attracted the attention of alerted individuals. Such alerted animals reacted to any sudden noise such as a cry of a bird or splashing of a beaver, whereas when not alerted they paid little attention to such sounds.

During our observations we found that a few individuals would suddenly bolt or leap into a sudden trot only to stop after a few steps and return to normal behaviour without any obvious reason.

The hind foot is commonly used for scratching the head region and bulls were seen using their antlers in all later stages of development for scratching their hind legs.

After consuming great quantities of water from the salt licks most animals urinated frequently. This formed a regular pattern of procedure for undisturbed moose as soon as they left the lick proper. In one case on June 26, 1948, a large bull was timed and found to require 49 seconds to pass his urine.

On two or three occasions frightened moose were noted to stop and urinate on their hind legs by drawing them together. Murie (1934) and others have observed the same behaviour.

We found that when moose became aware of our presence they occasionally started slowly and casually away but after moving a few yards would break into a fast trot.

Moose seem to be much less playful than white-tailed deer. Calves were seen splashing playfully in shallow water but very few adult activities could be definitely classed as playing. Oberholtzer (1911) remarks on the "frolicking" of a few adults.

PROTECTIVE BEHAVIOUR

While working with penned animals in Maine, Lamson (Walcott, 1939) concluded that the keen sense of hearing which allows early detection of possible danger prompts moose to move into a dense cover of trees and stand without motion until the danger is passed. This behaviour pattern seems to be borne out in the present study. On several occasions when frightened at the salt lick moose would run a few yards and stop and stand silent for several minutes before going on or returning to the lick area.

Water is the main refuge of moose when chased by predators. Conclusions reached in this study agree with those of Cowan (1947) that moose regularly make for the nearest water when seeking protection from predators. In this connection it is of interest that the great majority of remains of moose carcasses found in the course of this work were situated in close proximity to water.

FIGURE 29. A bull moose drinking from a game lick while a cow appears alerted by the photographer in a blind, Simpson Island, Ontario

FIGURE 30. Moose and deer use same game lick on amiable terms. Deer normally appear much more nervous and alert than moose

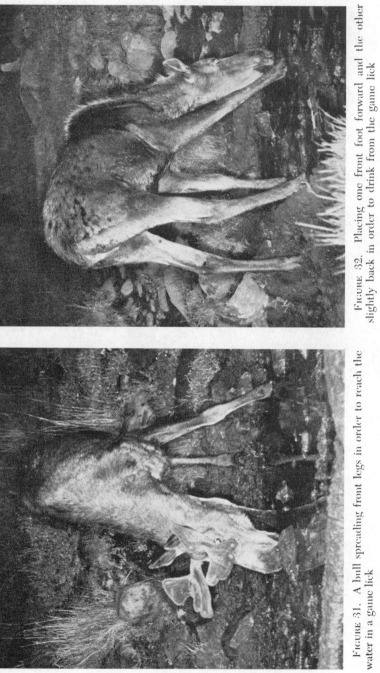

FIGURE 32. Placing one front foot forward and the other slightly back in order to drink from the game lick

FIGURE 31. A bull spreading front legs in order to reach the water in a game lick

FIGURE 33. Bending both front legs slightly in order to reach the ground level

FIGURE 34. Normal swimming attitude

FIGURE 35. Cow and yearling swimming across Moffat Straits, July 12, 1947. Notice that the yearling has more of the back exposed above water

FIGURE 36. Wading ashore with great force

REACTIONS TO HUMANS, AND UNUSUAL BEHAVIOUR

Perhaps the behaviour of moose, as manifested when confronted by human beings, has been the subject of more unnatural history tales than the behaviour of any other mammal in Canada. Every fall one reads of dozens of cases of people being attacked "within an inch of their lives" yet hardly anyone seems to get killed or even hurt. While it is true moose are prone to become reckless and appear belligerent during the rutting season, there are few authoritative records of persons actually being the subject of an unprovoked attack by moose. Many woodsmen have found it expedient to avoid being chased by moose by taking refuge in trees. Unfortunately it is impossible to determine what such moose might have done had the person "being attacked" "stood his ground" or taken other measures to avoid close contact. Hake (1940, p. 33) writes as follows:

. . . I have had numerous moose come toward me under various circumstances but no conclusive proof from which to believe any moose was ever charging me. I have been close to desperately wounded moose and they were lying down in many cases, and I would have thought they were so far gone as to be unable to gain their feet, but I have seen many of them get up with alarming speed and run away from me instead of toward me.

On October 1, 1948, we noticed a rutting bull swimming across the channel from Simpson to St. Ignace Island. I purposely manœuvred to a position on a trail where he would come ashore. When within 30 feet he discovered my presence and immediately showed his indignation by bristling up his mane and lowering his ears. I stood motionless to test his reactions. At first he looked as if he would charge or walk over me but after shaking himself he walked slowly downshore a few feet and bypassed me, soon returning to the trail and resuming his periodic low grunting. I followed close behind (about 75 feet) but the bull seemed indifferent to my presence except for stopping and thrashing his antlers on a small shrub and turning to look at me again before moving slowly on. I followed him until he crossed a long bay and then I gave a loud low grunt. He merely turned to stare at me again for awhile and then resumed his own grunting as he disappeared behind the trees.

At other times of the year the reactions of a moose toward human sights and smells are undoubtedly governed to a large extent by the ainmal's past experience. Instinctive fear of humans appears almost absent in young calves, but becomes quite keen after they become independent adults. Murie (1934, p. 15) concluded that moose become accustomed to human scent and sometimes lose their keen fear of it. "The Isle Royale animals generally turn away when man is scented, but unless the smell is very strong they are not greatly alarmed and often seem unmindful of it. At one salt lick they often wandered all around the blind, hardly noticing my presence, although they undoubtedly had my scent." These conclusions were clearly substantiated during this study. For example, on September 12, 1947, a yearling female was drinking at a salt lick when a large steam tug came through the channel about 200 yards away. Voices from the tug could be heard quite plainly and smoke poured out and spread across the water. The yearling stopped drinking and watched the tug, as if with passing interest, until it was out of sight and then casually resumed her drinking.

Avoiding loud voices and sudden movements and keeping downwind when possible, we found that moose seemed to become accustomed to our constant presence within their habitat. Certainly a few animals became markedly tame and allowed us unusual liberties without showing signs of any keen fear of us.

It has frequently been suggested that the mere presence of humans has been the chief factor in reducing the number of moose in the southern parts of their range. Anderson (1924b) remarks on the ability of large numbers of moose to adapt themselves to settled areas of New Brunswick and parts of Quebec. This adaptability must certainly exist in Sweden and Norway where great numbers of moose are found in these rather densely populated countries. Dr. C. H. D. Clarke also points out (personal communication) the close association of moose and humans in the Banff and Yoho national parks of western Canada. "The moose apparently has few inhibitions regarding the use of settled areas, and wintering populations may build up quite high as noted around Palmer, Wasilla, Kenai and Kasilof [Alaska]" (Spencer and Chatelain, 1953, p. 547). It therefore seems evident that reduction of moose in settled areas results from either the actual killing out of the animals or the unfavourable altering of their habitat, and not so much from the inability of moose to tolerate normal human activities.

In Sweden, Lönnberg (1923) comments on the great difference in the behaviour of moose in different districts especially with regard to the degree of molesting encountered from humans. In agricultural areas he reports that they become "trusting" and will forage very close to people and get inside enclosures, becoming so daring near farms that they can hardly be driven away.

Brown and Simon (1947) found that both calves and adults in Wyoming were belligerent and showed resentment when human would-be benefactors approached too close in midwinter to offer food.

The extremely variable conditions under which moose have been observed have led to many controversial conclusions concerning their reactions toward man. For this reason it is often difficult to distinguish between normal and unusual behaviour. Oberholtzer (1911) remarks on an instance in which he felt a young moose actually sought protection by approaching humans. Cahalane (1945) describes the reactions of a cow to music. A report in *Rod and Gun in Canada* (Anon., 1946, p. 41) tells of a moose that was roped and saddled to be ridden. According to this report, the bull merely folded his legs and lay down and would not arise until unsaddled and left completely alone. Shiras (1935, p. 242) even comments on a semi-tame tobacco-chewing moose that would beg tobacco of anyone that approached. "If this was not forthcoming, he sometimes butted the offender to indicate his displeasure."

SOCIABILITY

The gregarious instinct is less developed in moose than in any other North American hoofed wild mammal. The only well-defined social instincts are exhibited in mother-young relationships and perhaps in yearling relationships with twin brother or sister.

Much has been written concerning the so-called "yarding" instincts in winter, in which social advantages become apparent. As many as 15 or 20 animals have been reported to congregate together in small areas during winter. From reports of authors who have actually investigated winter activities, such large gatherings must not be common, at least in areas where moose are not extremely abundant. Most animals were found to be solitary or in small groups.

In the course of winter aerial census work in Ontario, no more than 4 animals were seen together. The largest assemblage of moose observed during the summer months was 7 animals feeding together in a small bay of McEachan Lake, St. Ignace Island, on July 6, 1947. The second largest number was 6 animals in the vicinity of a salt lick on the same island on June 12, 1947. In both instances each animal seemed to move entirely independent of the others. It seems likely that associations in winter yards may similarly result from some common advantage such as favourable food conditions, and that social instinct plays a minor role in bringing more than family groups together.

SWIMMING AND DIVING

Moose are powerful swimmers. Among North American deer perhaps only the caribou exceed them in speed and endurance. In the St. Ignace area we found we could overtake and keep abreast of moose with two men vigorously paddling a canoe or by use of a boat with an outboard motor. On the other hand, we found we had more difficulty in overtaking woodland caribou, and, in fact, found it impossible to stay abreast of them even with the aid of a boat and outboard motor. When approached, the caribou would put out a burst of speed and turn so sharply that they would pull away from us. Moose were not so prone to attempt to outmanoeuvre us and would persist on their original course unless actually forced to turn by being headed off.

Compared with woodland caribou, adult moose swim lower in the water with the rump usually submerged, although yearlings may have most of the back exposed (Figure 34, 35). When shallow water is reached they are able to wade ashore with incredible power and speed (Figure 36).

Moose have amazing stamina and swim great distances with comparatively little effort. Stone (1924) tells of a moose swimming across Cochamak Bay, Cook Inlet, Alaska, a distance of over 8 miles. Baltzer (1933) reports having seen a bull and cow swim 9 miles across the Bay of Fundy from Cumberland County to Cape Split, with comparative ease. Merrill (1920) quotes reports that moose in Europe frequently swim as far as 12 miles.

Water is definitely one of the preferred elements in the habitat of moose. When feeding on submerged aquatic vegetation they occasionally dive for plants in water over 18 feet deep. They were frequently seen to submerge so completely that not a ripple remained in the water near where they went down. In the majority of cases the rump would float to the top and break water before the animal raised its head. Occasionally animals were seen to make at least a 180-degree turn while completely submerged, and at other times they would seem to roll to one side while attempting to stay under.

The average length of submergence was slightly under 30 seconds. The greatest time actually checked was 50 seconds, although some appeared to remain under slightly longer.

TRAVEL, GAIT, AND SPEED

Moose are able to use their long legs to good advantage in travelling the length and breadth of their habitat. They are able to wade through deep bogs and muskegs where man and many other animals would find travel impossible. When proceeding through such hazardous localities moose seldom become panic-stricken but merely plod steadily along, perhaps resting in brief intervals. When firm footing is reached they may walk casually, break into a sort of stiff-legged trot, or begin a more graceful gait similar to that of a trotter. Unless suddenly frightened they seldom gallop. A cow moose wandered right into our St. Ignace camp on May 29, 1947, and as she approached the cabin, motion pictures were taken of her. As she passed the cabin she suddenly became frightened and galloped over the hill into the bush. Inspection of the individual frames of the movies showed that she truly galloped for a short distance. Certain frames showed all four feet off the ground at once.

Dixon (1938) reports that in Alaska a cow travelling in a normal, undisturbed, slashing trot, crossed one mile in ten mintues. Dr. C. H. D. Clarke (personal communication) states that he checked a moose in Kootenay National Park at 19 m.p.h. for one-half mile in 1943. When Dr. Clarke attempted to speed up, the moose turned off the road. Denniston (1948) and Findley (1951) report that a moose ran 22 m.p.h. in front of a car in Wyoming. Cowan (1947) clocked moose at 27 m.p.h. Cottam and Williams

(1943) report a top speed of 35 m.p.h. for a distance of one-quarter mile.

Moose seldom attempt to jump obstacles. Normally they merely step over or go around. When forced to jump they rear up on their hind feet, place their front feet over the obstacle, and spring or dive over in "standing high jump" fashion. On December 28, 1946, I observed a captive animal of Mr. Joe La Flamme at Gogama, Ontario, jump over a 4½-foot rail fence in such a manner. Lönnberg (1923) states that moose in Sweden can get over obstacles such as fences that are over 6 feet high without great difficulty and even higher in favourable cases.

Thirty inches of uncrusted snow presents little hindrance to active travel by moose, but deep crusted snow is the greatest travel menace they have to face. If moose are forced to move about under such circumstances the sharp ice cuts through the skin of their legs (Wright, Dixon, and Thompson, 1933).

Stanwell-Fletcher (1943, p. 93) reports that in extremely deep snow moose in central British Columbia employed the forelegs as snow-shoes and moved in a kneeling position. "The long forelegs packed the snow before weight was brought to bear, and only the hind legs sank deeply."

The ability to manœuvre a massive set of antlers through a dense forest remains a constant source of amazement. There must be a highly developed sense of depth perception to allow a moose successfully to judge spaces it can clear without striking its antlers against trees. Bulls with large antlers were noted turning their head to one side when passing between trees which were too close together to pass otherwise.

DAILY ACTIVITY

Some moose activity was found at all hours of the day or night; however, the periods of maximum activity centred around nightfall and daybreak. Murie (1934) found a similar pattern of activity on Isle Royale. The least daylight activity was found between 7 A.M. and 4 or 5 P.M. when presumably most animals were lying down chewing their cud. Several animals were disturbed from their resting place during these hours in the course of our work. We noticed that a cow with young left Bead Island late in the afternoon and returned early in the morning almost without exception. This pattern of movement seems to indicate that the animals spent the day on Bead Island and crossed over to St. Ignace Island to feed at night.

Resting places or "beds" were well defined. They were found on many occasions in practically all types of local situations from muddy "pot holes," bogs, swamps, marshes, and hillsides to open grassy swales. In many cases the animals apparently lay down wherever they finished feeding. In others they seemed to return to favourite spots as indicated by small areas containing over a dozen different beds made during successive days.

The routine of daily habits seems to be affected by daily weather as well as by the season. On very windy days moose did not come out to salt licks. Perhaps with the habit of approaching such areas upwind they quickly picked up human scent, but on the other hand we found that even if we did not remain at the blinds on such days there was practically no sign of recent activity when we returned.

A warm still day following a series of cool windy days seemed definitely to increase the activity at the lick during spring and early summer.

We found that there was much more nocturnal than diurnal activity at the salt lick. The majority of daylight visitors were yearlings. Almost without exception each undisturbed moose observed made more than one visit to the salt lick during the night. Some individuals commonly returned two or three times, some as many as seven or eight. Each undisturbed visit averaged between 20 and 30 minutes with some individuals remaining in the vicinity over an hour and a half before leaving. Normally there was an average elapsed time of about one hour between visits.

When the aquatic vegetation became available, there seemed to be a definite decline in activity at the salt lick that we had under more or less constant observation.

Undisturbed periods of aquatic feeding averaged from about 30 minutes to one hour. Certain individuals were observed to return to feed again after an absence of only 10 or 15 minutes.

Aquatic feeding, especially during the day, has led to the erroneous conclusion that insects drive moose into the water for protection.

SEASONAL ACTIVITY

Moose show no well-marked migrations as do wapiti and caribou. The only population shifts which might be distinguished as seasonal movements are found in the mountain regions of the west where there are general altitudinal shifts from winter ranges in the river valleys to poorly defined spring and summer ranges on the higher slopes (McDowell and Moy, 1942; Cowan, 1944; Munro, 1947). Even there, a certain number remain in the lower areas during the spring and summer, especially the cows, calves, and yearlings. Some may even winter near the timberline in areas of alpine fir (*Abies lasiocarpa*) according to Dr. C. H. D. Clarke (personal communication).

The only general seasonal movements observed in Ontario were rather indiscriminate shifts from one local area to another in response to seasonal food supply. In spring there seemed to be temporary concentrations in the vicinity of lakes and streams producing a favourable supply of aquatic vegetation. By the end of August in Algonquin Provincial Park and the Chapleau area we found moose had moved out of local areas where they had been commonly observed earlier in the season. Confirmation of this pattern of movement was given by several local observers.

In the St. Ignace area moose continued to feed on the aquatic vegetation until after the first of October. In the vicinity of several of the larger lakes in west-central St. Ignace Island we found heavy concentrations during the summer months, seeing as many as 25 different individuals in one afternoon, yet signs of winter populations, such as winter droppings, in that vicinity were extremely rare. Inspection of the available winter browse clearly revealed that this area would not support even a moderate winter population. The moose would be forced to move into more favourable localities to spend the winter. It is not known how far moose will move under such circumstances. It has been stated by recent authors that they move only short distances, but this is largely conjecture. In many instances, found during this work, it seemed obvious that at least a few individuals spent all the seasons in one general area.

During fall, winter, and early spring there seems to be general increased activity in the vicinity of "old burned" areas in response to the increased supply of food produced by the young growth.

With the accumulation of deep snow in midwinter, moose are commonly reported to gather in favourable feeding areas and form quite local concentrations which tramp down the snow and form interlaced trails back and forth over a small portion of the forest. This pattern of behaviour is referred to as "yarding." Lonnberg (1923) discusses "yarding," stating that groups of 12 or 15 animals, depending on the population of the region, may come together in *algstard* ("yards") in Sweden. Owing in part to the vague definition of this term, many false impressions have been gained concerning this habit of moose as compared with white-tailed deer. Perhaps a distinction should be made between "voluntary" and "enforced" yarding. The latter is defined here as "one or more animals remaining in a well-defined local area over a period of days because of the great difficulty of movement outside of its boundaries." This seems to be the general but frequently erroneous connotation involved when the term "yarding" is applied. Actually this type of yarding is apparently quite rare over most of the range of moose in North America. Evidently well over 30 inches of normal snow are required to force moose to restrict their movements (Newsom, 1937b; Soper, 1942; and others). In the east a fairly deep heavily crusted snow, which moose break through, would appear to be the chief condition causing enforced yarding.

Voluntary yarding, on the other hand, is a common natural behaviour; one or more animals find themselves in favourable feeding areas and voluntarily remain within either loosely or well-defined limits for at least a few days, presumably in response to advantages. Perhaps this type of activity would not be classified as "true yarding" in the original loose designation of the term as applied to deer. Nevertheless, this behaviour has been so frequently confused with an enforced yarding that some distinction should be made to prevent further confusion, especially with reference to moose.

Undoubtedly it was voluntary yarding that was meant when 97 out of 134 questionnaire correspondents in Ontario reported having seen definite evidence of moose yards. They also reported an average of about three to five moose in each yard.

It seems probable that Soper (1942, p. 142) referred, for the most part, to enforced yarding when making the following statement:

Evidently moose do not yard in this region. I had the advantage of travelling more than 4000 miles in most parts of Wood Buffalo Park during two winters, yet in no single instance did I witness the slightest evidence that moose truly yarded at any period of the winter. Trails were invariably at random through the forest, although, occasionally, in highly favorable localities these were markedly concentrated.

Similar conditions were observed during the aerial moose census work in Ontario, which afforded an excellent opportunity to trace the general movements of moose. There was no marked concentration of moose or of moose tracks which might be construed as representing even voluntary yarding. Morse (1946) reports that several groups of moose were found to remain on the same restricted area for as long as three consecutive days during aerial game census work in Minnesota, although no more than 5 individuals were seen together during the count of 260 moose between March 4 and 13, 1945.

Evidence of only one well-defined concentration that could be clearly classified as a heavily utilized yard was found in the course of this work (see p. 157). In an area of approximately three acres along the northeast shore of McIntosh Lake in Algonquin Provincial Park a total of 391 piles of moose droppings were actually counted on 14,400 square yards of the area. In other words, there was one pile of moose dropping for approximately every 37 square yards, or about 130 per acre.

No accurate check has been made on the average daily number of piles of droppings that are deposited by moose. Mr. Lee S. Crandall of the New York Zoological Society writes (personal communication) that a casual check on a captive moose showed an average of about 4 droppings (24 hours). If this could be considered a tentative index for wild animals, a total of about 32 "moose-days" would have been spent in this restricted locality, roughly equivalent to three acres. Further complicating the appraisal of this yard was the presence of 136 piles of deer droppings. A check of the surrounding vicinity outside the limits of the yard revealed practically no moose droppings. This seemed to indicate that the movements of these animals were closely restricted and that, therefore, this was possibly a case of enforced yarding.

In the Otter Creek valley of St. Ignace Island, Ontario, there were many signs of general heavy winter concentrations of moose, but few indications of more than passing animals during the summer. Since there were no bodies of water near by producing aquatic vegetation it could be assumed that moose were remaining in some more favourable habitat. By the first of October moose and fresh signs of moose activity were again in general evidence all through the valley.

In the final analysis, seasonal movements of moose in the eastern part of its range are restricted to minor local shifts and appear to be correlated with local seasonal food supply.

TERRITORIALITY AND HOME RANGE

The home range concept appears to apply to moose although no conclusive data have been produced to define clearly a "normal" size for such a territory. Seton (1927), Murie (1934), Lamson (Walcott, 1939), Cahalane (1939), Burt (1946), and others have all speculated on the relative size of the home range of moose. Most of the inferences drawn concerning such home ranges are based primarily on the fact that individual animals were repeatedly observed within relatively small localities over a period of a few weeks or during one season. More such evidence could be produced from the present study, yet definite records to substantiate normal individual wanderings are still lacking. The size of home ranges as listed by the above authors probably has little significance since the ecological conditions as well as population pressure appear to govern, to a large degree, the extent of normal movements of moose from one specific area to another. In the areas that provide ample food during all seasons of the year there is little reason to doubt that a moose may remain all its life within a radius of from two to ten miles but such estimates need to be substantiated with more reliable proof before concluding that this is a normal rule.

No definite evidence of a "defended territory" has been found. Perhaps the cow defends her calving territory for a few days, but otherwise the range of individual animals commonly overlaps to a large extent.

CHAPTER ELEVEN

FOOD HABITS

A CONSIDERABLE QUANTITY of available food is required to maintain a healthy moose population. Basing his estimates on feeding experiments with caribou, reindeer, and musk-ox, Palmer (1944) finds that an air dry weight of 35 pounds of food daily is required by adult moose in Alaska (presumably an average for all seasons). Kellum (1941) conducted feeding experiments with captive moose in Michigan and found that when provided with 200 pounds daily they actually consumed 40 to 50 pounds in winter and 50 to 60 pounds in summer. These weights were not dry weights and the greater poundage consumed in summer was thought probably to be the result of a higher water content in the green foods, although it was also considered by Kellum that moose actually eat more during summer while they are putting on considerable weight.

The locations of the principal study areas in Ontario are shown in Figure 37. A more detailed account of the Ontario studies has been given by Peterson (1953).

SEASONAL VARIATION

Considerable seasonal variation is found both in the types of food eaten and in methods of feeding. Winter browsing is restricted to biting off the terminal twigs and branches of both coniferous and deciduous woody plants (Figures 38, 39). Frequently limbs as large as one-half inch in diameter were found to have been bitten off by moose.

The habit of straddling and "riding down" small saplings during winter was found to be quite common in Algonquin Provincial Park, although few such instances of this were noted in the St. Ignace area. Probably this habit is more common in areas of scarce food supply. In Algonquin Park deer compete for many deciduous species, and balsam fir has become greatly reduced through attacks by spruce budworms. Balsam saplings were most commonly found with tops broken off although some deciduous species showed similar injury.

In early spring moose appear to sample the majority of green species as they become available. The habit of chewing the bark from various species seems to reach its climax when the sap is rising, before the trees leaf out.

When trees, shrubs, and various other plants are leafed out, moose commonly grasp the branches a foot or two from the terminal ends and with a

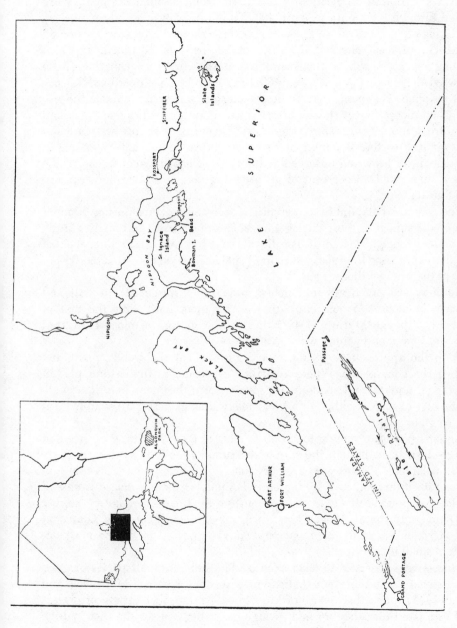

FIGURE 37. Map of the north shore of Lake Superior showing the location of Isle Royale, Michigan, and the St. Ignace Island study area, Ontario. The location of Algonquin Provincial Park is shown in insert, upper left

sideways motion of the head strip the leaves from the branches as they are pulled through the mouth (Figure 40). The utilization of woody plants, by the biting off of terminal twigs, continues throughout the year. In Wyoming, McMillan (1953a) checked the ratio of "nipped" to "stripped" types of feeding on 2,383 willow twigs and found that 52.6 per cent had been browsed during the summer, with 39.9 per cent being nipped and 7.5 per cent stripped. He found that while feeding on willow in summer the undisturbed moose moves slowly, taking a few mouthfuls from one place and some from another with an average rate of movement of three yards every five minutes. In this Wyoming study there was no significant difference in the amount of browsing observed at the edge of a willow copse and in the centre, and about 56 per cent of all browsing was at a level between two and four feet.

The general palatability preferences for woody plants during summer seem to be similar to those during winter. Krefting (1946) has made a study of summer foods of moose on Isle Royale and has found that 19 species of woody plants were browsed and that 12 species formed an estimated 93 per cent of the summer diet.

Conifers are practically untouched from early spring to late fall and apparently moose do not return to feed on them until after the first of October, although Murie (1934) indicates that ground hemlock is utilized in both summer and winter, when available.

With the approach of spring, moose supplement the woody plant diet with herbaceous plants. Where available, especially in the eastern part of the range, aquatic and semi-aquatic plants form the more important bulk of the diet of moose, although a great many upland herbs are sampled but few eaten in quantity.

Aquatic plants are sought long before most of them reach the surface and are used for food through the spring and summer, as long as the plants remain palatable. There was a noticeable decline in aquatic feeding in Algonquin Provincial Park by the end of August, although moose were still feeding on pondweed (*Potamogeton*) in the St. Ignace area after the first of October. In the St. Ignace area, bush honeysuckle (*Diervilla Lonicera*) and large-leaved aster (*Aster macrophyllus*) appeared to be the most important small upland species.

Moose were observed to taste or graze lightly on several species of grass but nowhere was there any indication of serious feeding. McDowell and Moy (1942) found that moose of Montana fed on a great variety of grasses and estimated that they formed as high as 12 per cent of the diet in June (Table XIII). McMillan (1953a) found that only 5.4 per cent of his observations in Wyoming involved feeding on grasses to give a total feeding

FIGURE 39. Typical effect of moose winter browsing on mountain ash. Other species in the background is chiefly mountain maple

FIGURE 38. A balsam fir browsed to a height of about ten feet, Simpson Island, Ontario, 1947

FIGURE 41. A standing quaking aspen that has been "barked" by moose

FIGURE 40. Summer browsed willow. Notice how the leaves are stripped off branches by moose pulling them through their mouth

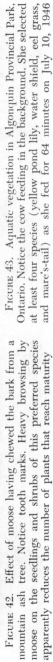

FIGURE 42. Effect of moose having chewed the bark from a mountain ash tree. Notice tooth marks. Heavy browsing by moose on the seedlings and shrubs of this preferred species apparently reduces the number of plants that reach maturity

FIGURE 43. Aquatic vegetation in Algonquin Provincial Park, Ontario. Notice the cow feeding in the background. She selected at least four species (yellow pond lily, water shield, eel grass, and mare's-tail) as she fed for 64 minutes on July 10, 1946

FIGURE 45. *Left*: Balsam poplar, cut and left for moose. *Right*: Effect of a week's browsing. The bark has been removed from the smaller branches

FIGURE 46. Typical winter moose droppings

FIGURE 47. Transition from summer to winter droppings

FIGURE 48. Typical summer moose droppings

TABLE XIII

ESTIMATED AVERAGE PERCENTAGE OF FOODS TAKEN BY
MONTANA MOOSE IN SUMMER AND FALL*

Types of forage	June	July	August	September	October
Shrubs	64	72	81	87	93
Grass-like plants	8	6	5	3	2
Grasses	12	8	4	3	1
Weeds	14	11	6	2	2
Underwater plants	2	3	4	5	2

*McDowell and Moy (1942); Schultz and McDowell (1943).

time of 1.6 per cent. Observations in Ontario would indicate that grasses probably provide less than 1 per cent of the summer food in the east.

More detailed consideration of individual species known to be eaten by moose may be found in chapters 12 and 13.

FEEDING ON BARK

Although the habit of chewing the bark from various trees is carried on from fall to spring, the great majority of instances noted in the St. Ignace area were in late winter or early spring. A few fresh aspen poles were used in construction of an enclosure in September, 1947. On February 22 we found that moose had chewed small portions of bark from two or three of the poles. Kellum (1941) found that captive moose would eat bark from fresh cut trunks all through the winter, although he agreed that it was preferred during spring. Quaking aspen was found to be the species most commonly "barked" on St. Ignace (Figure 41). A great majority of freshly fallen, wind-blown trees showed at least some signs of having been barked by moose. Standing aspens were occasionally barked. Trunks of both quaking aspen and balsam poplar, left near the salt lick in feeding experiments, were almost stripped clean in late May, although quaking aspen was more thoroughly utilized than balsam poplar. The former was rolled over so that it was cleaned of bark on all sides. Kellum (1941) reports that captive moose would kneel down to reach such logs, but we failed to observe this habit at St. Ignace.

Mountain ash was found to be most consistently barked, although mature trees were so scarce that the species does not constitute an important source of this type of food in the St. Ignace area (Figure 42). In Algonquin Provincial Park various species of maples were occasionally barked; however, red maple seemed to be the choice species. A few indications of moose having chewed the bark from balsam fir were noted in both study areas.

Murie (1934) concluded that moose feed on bark by preference during spring, but suggested that winter barking might be an indication of food shortage. These conclusions seem to be borne out by Ontario studies, although it seems doubtful whether the small amount of winter barking observed would necessarily indicate food shortage.

AQUATIC FOOD HABITS

The characteristic habit of feeding on submerged and floating aquatic vegetation has led to a few apparently erroneous conclusions concerning moose. Many have associated the aquatic activity of moose with an attempt to escape pestiferous insects. Others have commonly reported that the chief aquatic food was the roots of water lilies. No evidence was found in Ontario studies to support either theory. In Algonquin Provincial Park many roots were found floating in the vicinity where moose commonly fed, yet none showed signs of having been fed on by moose. This observation is in contrast to the following statement made by Cahn (1937, p. 29): "In a puddle near Camel Lake [Quetico Provincial Park, Ontario] I found the moose pulling up and eating the succulent root system of these plants, and hundreds of huge half-eaten roots were floating on the surface." It appears that moose may, on occasion, consume parts of roots as well as stems and leaves of water lilies. Most of the roots found floating were pulled free of the bottom by moose while feeding on the stems and leaves.

In Algonquin Provincial Park there is such a great variety and abundance of aquatic vegetation that the present moose population has little noticeable effect on the general composition and abundance of the various species (Figure 43). In the St. Ignace area only one aquatic species, pondweed (chiefly *Potamogeton Richardsonii*) provides the great bulk of available food. Other species, which are extremely rare in the area, include the common yellow pond lily (*Nymphaea advena*), eel grass (*Vallisneria spiralis*), and various members of the family Haloragidaceae including *Hippuris vulgaris*. Murie (1934) and Aldous and Krefting (1946) found that the supply of aquatic vegetation was quite low and concluded that the past high populations of moose had been responsible for a great reduction from former years. Unfortunately there is no available record of the former abundance of aquatic species in the St. Ignace area, but it seems likely that it may have been reduced in a manner similar to that on Isle Royale, an explanation which might account for the scarcity of such forms as water lilies.

The relative proportion of aquatic plants in the spring and summer diet of the moose is unknown. McDowell and Moy (1942) have estimated that they provide only 2 to 5 per cent of the diet from June to October in Montana (Table XIII), and McMillan (1953a) estimated that approximately 9.3 per cent of the total feeding time involved aquatic plants.

The summer diet of the moose in eastern North America consists of a much greater percentage of aquatic plants than is indicated for Montana and Wyoming. On several occasions animals were observed to feed on various aquatic plants for over an hour at a time, and in some instances over two hours.

In Algonquin Provincial Park, where a greater variety and abundance of aquatic species are found, we noticed that moose frequently selected a variety of species during one feeding period. There the most important food species included the common yellow pond lily (*Nymphaea advena*), water shield (*Brasenia Schreberi*), sweet-scented water lily (*Castalia odorata*), eel grass (*Vallisneria spiralis*), bur-reed (*Sparganium fluctuans*), and pond-weed (*Potamogeton* spp.).

Horsetail (*Equisetum* spp.) was found in great abundance in Algonquin Provincial Park but was only occasionally browsed by moose. In the Chapleau district of Ontario we found extensive stands of this species that had been closely cropped by moose during July and August, 1946. Wild rice (*Zizania*) was not observed in the Ontario study areas, although it is commonly reported to be fed on by moose when available (Oberholtzer, 1911; and others). Other less important species observed to be utilized in Ontario include the following: *Sagittaria, Eleocharis, Scirpus subterminalis, Carex, Pontederia cordata, Juncus,* and *Nymphaea microphylla*.

The maximum use of common yellow pond lily and eel grass appeared to be reached during June and early July in Algonquin Provincial Park. By the middle of July, water shield was found to be providing the great bulk of aquatic food.

A definite decline in the amount of aquatic feeding, observed in Algonquin Provincial Park during the latter part of August, seemed to be corre-lated with a reduction in palatability. By this time most forms had reached maturity and were becoming tough and soured. In the slow-moving streams and shallow lakes most of the plants had acquired a coating of slime and other debris. Further reduction in the palatability of water lilies was ap-parently caused by the attack of the larva of a chrysomelid beetle (*Donacia*). A similar, but less intensive, infestation was noted in the Chapleau district in August, 1946.

In the shallow waters of Algonquin Provincial Park, moose were not forced to dive to reach ample food. In early spring most animals merely submerged their heads to feed on the young growing plants. By midsummer we noticed that moose rarely reached deeper than about 12 inches, with most animals feeding directly from the surface on floating leaves and stems. In the St. Ignace area moose were observed to feed in water at least 18 feet deep.

The water of Lake Superior is much colder than in the inland lakes and remains clear and free of debris. The earliest aquatic feeding noted on the inland lakes of St. Ignace Island was on June 4. This preceded any observed feeding in the channels of Lake Superior proper by at least one month in 1947. It is not known how long aquatic feeding continued on the inland lakes in the St. Ignace area but moose were still feeding on *Potamogeton* in Lake Superior waters after the first of October.

GAME LICKS

Mineral springs or so-called "salt licks" are utilized by moose wherever they occur. Such areas in the eastern part of their range are usually seeping springs which are normally so thoroughly tramped by constant visits of animals that they appear little more than mud holes with a bit of standing water (see Figures 24, 26, 27, 31, 32, 33).

In New Brunswick a total of 101 samples were taken from 28 licks and analysed by the Physics Department of the University of New Brunswick. A total of 9 elements were detected. A summary of the preliminary study of these samples follows (Wright, 1952):

The spectrographic analysis has given a general picture of the mineral content of the soil and water samples. The soil samples from the different licks do not appear to vary appreciably nor to differ from samples taken in the surrounding area.

The variation in the mineral content of the water samples is much greater, and some additional time might well be spent in further examination of these spectra.

The information that has been recorded to date may be of considerable value for reference purposes in additional investigations connected with this problem. It would not appear on the basis of this analysis to date that the frequent use of game licks by animals can be attributed to their particular mineral content.

In Yellowstone National Park, Wyoming, McMillan (1953a) found that moose were actually eating soil. In one area a "dry lick" was utilized and in another the soil was eaten from a bank of Osidian Creek in a manner which was not due to seepage from a higher level. He was of the opinion that the chlorides and sulphates of sodium and calcium were the minerals sought by moose.

Cowan and Brink (1949) have reviewed the use of licks, especially in the Rocky Mountain national parks of Canada, and made studies to determine the role of the minerals obtained in such licks in the general health of wild animals. After several tests, these authors concluded (p. 387) that:

Our studies have not advanced the general knowledge of the function of natural licks in the physiology of wild ungulates much beyond that already obtained. The results are inconclusive and, taken in conjunction with similar studies of smaller scope made elsewhere in North America, lead to the conclusion (1) that sodium chloride is not necessarily the essential element; (2) that phosphorus is not the essential element in these licks; (3) that trace elements may well be the critical constituents in these natural licks; (4) that to arrive at conclusive results methods such as preference tests will probably be more productive than chemical analysis of the lick soils.

The use of licks by moose appears to reach its greatest intensity in spring. A definite decline in activity was noted at licks in the St. Ignace Island area by late July, although animals continued to visit them until at least October. No sign of activity was noted in one of these well-used licks during a winter visit, although Hosley (1949) reports that Isle Royale moose used similar licks in winter. Cowan and Brink (1949) and other authors concur that little use is made of licks during the winter months. Observations in Ontario substantiate those of other workers that the young of the year seldom if ever use such licks. Well-used licks are apparently less common in eastern North America than in the west, the best known being restricted to the Maritime Provinces and to the islands of Lake Superior and a few scattered localities to the adjacent northwest.

No signs of salt licks could be found in Algonquin Provincial Park and efforts to feed salt by placing out salt blocks brought no response from moose, although they actually approached quite close to several stations. Rock salt was even placed near the natural licks on St. Ignace Island, but moose showed no interest in it and continued to drink from the muddy water. Perhaps the habit of licking commercial salt is acquired over a period of time, for Murie (1934) reports that moose commonly frequent "artificial licks" on Isle Royale. The term "salt lick" seems to be a misnomer. We found no indication of moose licking or eating the soil of such areas in Ontario and the actual salt content seems to vary considerably and frequently appears to be quite low. Murie (1934) had four samples of water and one of mud analysed from licks on Isle Royale. These proved to contain approximate proportions of salt in aqueous extract of from .10 to .25 per cent. The content of these samples was chiefly calcium sulphate and traces of sodium chloride. The mud sample contained much more of the latter than the liquid samples.

Chemical analysis of samples of mud and water from Ontario licks showed such great variation that no more conclusive findings than those outlined by Cowan and Brink could be arrived at (Peterson, 1953).

PALATABILITY PREFERENCE

Several of the less abundant species seem to be preferred, but their low availability prevents them from actually becoming more important items in the diet of moose. The degree of browsing of available foods (Figure 44) gives a partial indication of the palatability preference of moose for various species, but in several instances these expressions of palatability are more or less invalidated. Such species as white birch, mountain ash, and quaking aspen occur in a high percentage of the plots as extremely small seedlings which would be covered by snow during winter, or as mature trees providing no browse within reach of moose. Aspen shrubs and saplings are rare. This

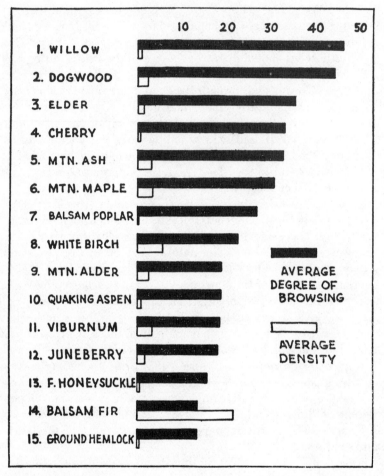

FIGURE 44. Palatability preference for certain moose foods as indicated by the average
degree of browsing found on 1,000 plots in the St. Ignace Island area

scarcity has certainly prevented a true representation of the preference of
moose for quaking aspen.

To obtain further indications of preference, equal-sized branches of
quaking aspen, balsam poplar, white birch, and speckled alder were cut in
the summer of 1947 and left overnight by a well-used salt lick. The next
morning we found that moose had completely stripped the aspen of every
leaf and had chewed off most of the smaller twigs and branches. Balsam
poplar and white birch were browsed only moderately and the speckled
alder was untouched.

In the early spring of 1948 a similar experiment was conducted except that mountain ash was also added to the choice. We were unable to return immediately to check the results, but after an interval of about one week similar results were noted (Figure 45). The mountain ash had been heavily browsed, ranking about second to quaking aspen.

It seems evident that the actual amount of each species of food which moose will consume is correlated and interrelated not only with the palatability and availability of that species, but also with the presence, availability, or absence, in any given area, of all other food plants of various levels of palatability.

STOMACH ANALYSIS

Laboratory examinations of one-quart samples from 24 stomachs of Ontario moose, and one each from Manitoba and Quebec, were made in order to check and verify data on food habits obtained by other methods (Peterson, 1953).

Balsam fir was found in all but three of the stomachs of moose taken from October 19 to May 5, one being from an area in Manitoba where this species does not occur. White cedar occurred in small amounts in four stomachs and as a large portion of one, the latter from a diseased animal. This species occurred in roughly 19 per cent of late fall and winter specimens. Of the total for all months, willow occurred more frequently than any other deciduous species (16 or 66.2 per cent). White birch was found in 11 (42.4 per cent), beaked hazel in 10 (38.6 per cent), quaking aspen in 9 (33.6 per cent), cherry in four cases, dwarf birch and dogwood in two each, and juneberry and maple in only one each.

Hosley (1949) lists the results of examination of one moose stomach from Maine, taken in April, as follows: balsam fir, 45 per cent; birch (sp.?), 45 per cent; maple (sp.?), 1 per cent; northern white cedar, 1 per cent; sheep laurel (*Kalmia angustifolia*), trace; and willow, trace. The average percentage of stomach contents of seven Alaskan moose taken in fall and late winter were as follows (Hosley, 1949): willow, 45; birch, 31; alder, 6; grass and sedge (mainly in one fall stomach), 5; lichens, trace; cranberry, trace; spruce, trace; horsetail, trace; "peavine," trace; mosses and sphagnum, trace.

Spencer and Chatelain (1953) list the following average percentage occurrence of foods from 96 stomachs of moose taken in winter in Alaska: willow, 53; birch, 32; cottonwood, 8; aspen, 4; with seven other species accounting for 3 per cent.

ANALYSIS OF DROPPINGS

From late fall to early spring the droppings of moose are composed of persistent spherical or oblong pellets (Figure 46). Skuncke (1949) points out that the shapes of these pellets are different for the sexes in Sweden, those of the bull being more nearly spherical while those of the cow are more elongate or ovoid. A definite dimorphism has been noted in the droppings of North American moose but apparently the constancy of these sexual differences has not been studied or confirmed here. With the change from winter to summer diet, or *vice versa*, the droppings likewise show a transition (Figure 47), the typical summer droppings becoming amorphous or viscous from the herbaceous diet (Figure 48). Since the needles of the conifer species eaten during winter pass through in an identifiable state, it seemed desirable to obtain still another check on the surprisingly high utilization of balsam.

Careful examination of 1,055 individual pellets showed balsam fir in each (see Peterson, 1953). In Algonquin Provincial Park, where balsam was much less abundant, white cedar and hemlock were eaten in much larger proportions. Hemlock is apparently an important supplement to balsam in the Canadian biotic province. White cedar is sampled freely but is rarely eaten in abundance. Murie (1934) found that moose had eaten the bark from this species during high population levels on Isle Royale. Hosley (1949) points out, from the first two browse analysis surveys on Isle Royale, that the use of white cedar had more than doubled between 1945 and 1948. This was regarded as an indication of heavy over-browsing.

Ground hemlock (*Taxus canadensis*) is apparently too scarce in either locality to constitute an important item in the diet of moose. Murie (1934) reports this species as being a highly palatable moose food during both summer and winter. Murie, as well as Aldous and Krefting (1946), regards it as an important index to general browse conditions. It is still abundant on small islands off Isle Royale and on the Slate Islands in Lake Superior where moose do not occur.

WINTER BROWSE ANALYSIS

Since the food supply during winter is one of the most critical factors in survival, special emphasis has been placed on this phase of study. During 1947 and 1948 a total of 1,000 browse plots, representing approximately 125 miles of browse survey lines, were analysed for the St. Ignace Island area of Ontario. The results of this study have been published in an earlier paper (Peterson, 1953). In order to evaluate certain factors brought out by browse analysis, a comparison of the results on the 1,000 plots with those of similar plots on Isle Royale analysed by Aldous and Krefting (1946) and Krefting (1951) is presented. Although 29 species are listed as available during winter in the St. Ignace area, only 22 were found to have been browsed to any appreciable extent, and 12 species provided 92.3 per cent of all food eaten. On Isle Royale, Aldous and Krefting (1946) found that 34 species were present in 1945 but that only 28 were browsed by moose while the top 12 species provided 92.5 per cent of the foods eaten, although their ratings included some species which do not occur in the St. Ignace area. Krefting (1951) found that the top 12 species provided 91.3 and 96.1 per cent of the diet in 1948 and 1950 with some slight changes in the species involved. When the utilization of the 13 species providing the greatest amounts of food from the St. Ignace area is compared with the Isle Royale results (Figure 49) some interesting conclusions are suggested. One of these is that the availability of a food species is more important in influencing the actual composition of the diet than palatability or individual preference.

In the St. Ignace Island area, balsam fir constituted by far the greatest part of the total winter diet—27 per cent. However, it provided 30.9 per cent of all available food, more than three times the amount provided by any other species. On Isle Royale, balsam fir rated third in the diet of moose in 1945 with 13.6 per cent (about one-half of that for St. Ignace) but provided only 9.8 per cent of the available foods (about one-third of the amount available at St. Ignace). The 1948 browse analysis on Isle Royale indicates that balsam was rated first, constituting 13.5 per cent of the available browse and 21.8 per cent of the total food eaten. In 1950, however, the utilization of balsam dropped remarkably to only 5 per cent of the diet with little indication of reduction in relative availability. Krefting points out that in 1950 balsam fir was evidently affected not only by previous moose browsing but also by severe attacks of the spruce budworm. Some reduction in palatability with a shift of browsing pressure to other species may have influenced this reduced use of balsam fir on Isle Royale. Hosley (1949) reviews the data of Dyer (1948) on 12 "moose yards" in Maine to show balsam constituting 36.7 per cent of the available browse and 54 per cent of the total food eaten. On the basis of 306 plots in southeastern New Brunswick, Wright (1952) found balsam accounting for 50 per cent of the diet.

Quaking aspen was listed as the number one winter food of moose on Isle Royale (16.9 per cent) in 1945, but it provided only 8.7 per cent of the available food. In the 1948 survey it had dropped to fifth place (5.4 per cent of available browse and 9.0 per cent of total food eaten). Hosley (1949) attributes this reduction to the lack of ability of this species to withstand heavy browsing. Krefting (1951) indicates that use of aspen in 1950 moved up to second place (12.8 per cent of diet) but its availability continued to decrease (to 4.7 per cent of available food). Aspen rated only thirteenth in the St. Ignace area since it provided only 1.1 per cent of the available food (see pp. 133, 160, 163).

Most other differences in food ratings between these two areas appear to be expressions of relative availability. The top nine or ten species in the diet in both cases seem to suggest such a correlation.

Assessment of the relative importance of the effect on the available food

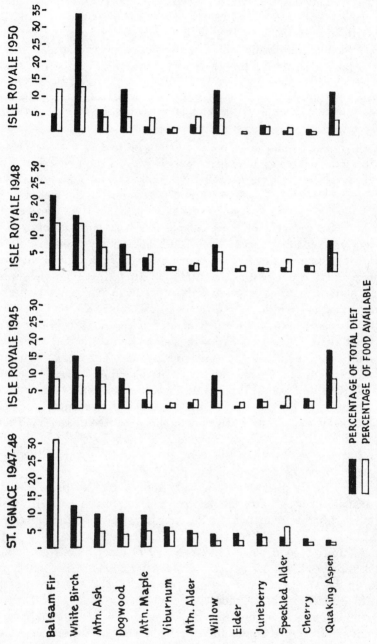

FIGURE 49. The utilization and availability of the principal moose food plants found in the St. Ignace Island area, Ontario, compared with those of Isle Royale, Michigan

supply of the browsing of caribou and deer suggests that the former was insignificant and the latter was of minor over-all importance, although certain species of plants appear to have been significantly affected (Peterson, 1953).

The 12 most important species in the St. Ignace area of Ontario from the standpoint of the percentage of food eaten during winter were found to be ranked in the following order: (1) balsam fir, (2) white birch, (3) mountain ash, (4) red-osier dogwood, (5) mountain maple, (6) high-bush cranberry, (7) mountain alder, (8) willow, (9) red-berried elder (?), (10) juneberry, (11) speckled alder, and (12) cherry.

As indicated by the average degree of browsing, the 12 most highly preferred winter foods were found to be ranked as follows: (1) willow, (2) red-osier dogwood, (3) red-berried elder (?), (4) cherry, (5) mountain ash, (6) mountain maple, (7) balsam poplar, (8) white birch, (9) mountain alder, (10) quaking aspen, (11) high-bush cranberry, and (12) juneberry. Other studies would indicate that quaking aspen usually ranks higher on the preferred list, and that beaked hazelnut and dwarf birch are also included as preferred species when available.

Balsam fir was found to be the most abundant and apparently the most important winter food of moose in Ontario. However, it was practically untouched during the summer months. In the St. Ignace area it occurred on 93 per cent of 1,000 plots and provided 30.9 per cent of the available winter food and 27 per cent of the total winter diet. It was found in varying degree up to 100 per cent in a great majority of the samples of non-summer contents of moose stomachs that were examined, and occurred in 100 per cent of 1,055 pellets from 211 samples of droppings.

DISCUSSION

In a general consideration of the basic importance of food in the ecology of an animal such as the moose, special attention should be devoted to the effects of an inadequate diet on populations of the species. This seems especially important in view of the fact that the effects of malnutrition are frequently obscured by some secondary manifestation.

Assuming that a population of moose is found in an area of inadequate food supply, one might logically contend that the animals would be faced with a choice of either migration or starvation. Little is known of the normal reactions of moose under such circumstances, but it is known that deer will persist in an area when faced with starvation, even though adequate food supplies may be available a relatively short distance away.

The question then rises as to what happens to the population that cannot or does not migrate. If no other factor interferes, death from actual starvation would ultimately result. This manifestation of malnutrition is perhaps the most drastic and most easily recognized. In actual cases, however, the population is usually greatly reduced by other causes such as diseases, parasites, and predators, which frequently combine with malnutrition to lower the number of animals before actual death from starvation is reached. This well-known population phenomenon has been discussed for a great many animals, but one gains the impression that the basic importance of food or lack of food is often not properly appreciated.

Over large areas in Ontario there has existed a low and rather static moose population. Although perhaps not faced with starvation, moose in many areas find a rather marginal food supply, especially in late winter. The failure of moose to show appreciable increases over a period of years in such regions cannot always be logically explained on the basis of constant suppression by such factors as diseases, parasites, or predators, even though no visible signs of starvation may be apparent. If these were limiting factors, one would expect to find a certain amount of marked fluctuation in the population as well as a regular and direct manifestation of one or more of these factors. Furthermore, in adjacent areas where diseases, parasites, and predators should have a similar effect, high populations are often maintained.

The failure of low populations to increase appears to be more directly correlated with a low rate of reproduction. The fact that moose do not increase in some areas while high populations are being maintained in others suggests that the local habitat itself must be influencing this differential rate of reproduction or survival. The most logical correlation within the habitat is with food supply. Perhaps quality, rather than quantity, of available food, is of prime importance in this connection. Morton and Cheatum (1946) have demonstrated a correlation between nutrition and the rate of births in New York deer and have found that in areas of depleted food supply the rate of ovulation is significantly lower than in the more favourable areas. If true for deer, this correlation probably exists for moose as well.

After fertilization the growth and development of the embryo to a healthy birth is dependent on the cow obtaining adequate quantity and quality of nutrition. Even then, food is of basic importance to the cow as well as the calf, for the cow must produce sufficient milk to raise the calf successfully, and at the same time have adequate vitality to protect it from predators.

Although adequate nutritional studies of various moose foods have not yet been carried out, the general food habits of moose indicate that a variety of foods is an essential factor in a balanced diet. A great quantity of poor foods or of only one or two species apparently will not maintain a healthy moose population. While it is well known that the availability of food is a limiting factor affecting the immediate carrying capacity of any given habitat, the role of the habitat (through food supply) in predetermining the potential population level needs further emphasis and investigation.

CHAPTER TWELVE

ANNOTATED LIST OF THE PRINCIPAL MOOSE FOOD PLANTS OF EASTERN NORTH AMERICA

THE FOLLOWING IS A LIST of plants known to have been eaten by moose in the eastern part of their range. Due to the absence of previous ecological studies in much of this area, the primary list has been taken largely from original observations in Ontario and published studies on Isle Royale, Michigan. Other records are added where available. It is no doubt far from being complete, especially with respect to herbaceous species and other plants which may be restricted in distribution beyond the limits of areas which have been more carefully studied to date.

In addition to the above-mentioned sources of information, references have been made to moose foods listed by Pimlott (1953) for Newfoundland, Lamson (Walcott, 1939) and Dyer (Hosley, 1949) for Maine, Cameron (1948, 1949) for Nova Scotia, Wright (1952) for New Brunswick, and Manweiler (1941) for Minnesota.

The list is broken into three broad divisions to allow conventional grouping of the main types of foods. To permit greater uniformity, the botanical nomenclature of the seventh edition of *Gray's New Manual of Botany* by Robinson and Fernald (1908) has been followed in so far as possible.

TREES AND SHRUBS

Taxus canadensis Marsh. Ground hemlock or American yew. Murie (1934) reports this species as being a highly palatable moose food during both summer and winter. It provided 0.7 per cent of the available food and 0.6 per cent of the winter diet in the St. Ignace area of Ontario and was found in 6 per cent of 460 winter dropping pellets in 1947-8, but did not occur in others collected in 1946-7. It is generally heavily browsed but on St. Ignace it is so sparse and most plants so small that little is available by midwinter. It was found in one moose stomach out of 27 examined from Maine (1), Quebec (1), Ontario (24), and Manitoba (1). It was not found in 425 pellets collected in Algonquin Provincial Park, Ontario. This species is considered as an important index to general browse conditions on Newfoundland by Pimlott (1953) and on Isle Royale by Murie (1934) and Aldous and Krefting (1946). The latter found that it provided 5.5 per cent of available food and 4.0 per cent of diet. Hosley (1949) reports that in 1948 it provided 4.2 per cent of the available food and 5.1 per cent of the diet. Reported formerly to have been much more abundant on Isle Royale, it is now much reduced by heavy moose browsing. It is still abundant on small islands off Isle Royale and on the Slate Islands in Lake Superior where moose do not occur.

Pinus Strobus L.   White pine. This species was only occasionally browsed in Algonquin Provincial Park, Ontario. Few mature trees with small traces of browsing were noted in the St. Ignace area. It provided 0.4 per cent of available food and 0.3 per cent of winter diet on Isle Royale in 1945 (Aldous and Krefting, 1946) and 0.6 per cent of available food and 0.5 per cent of diet in 1948 (Hosley, 1949). It occurred as a trace in 2 of 24 moose stomachs from Ontario. No evidence of utilization was noted on Newfoundland by Pimlott (1953), although Wright (1952) lists it as one of the minor foods in New Brunswick.

Pinus Banksiana Lamb.   Jack pine. The jack pine is poor moose food. It was absent in the study area of Algonquin Provincial Park; locally abundant but only occasionally browsed in the Chapleau district of Ontario; and found in less than 0.1 per cent of the plots in the St. Ignace area with no trace of browsing noted. It was reported as unbrowsed on Isle Royale (Murie, 1934; Aldous and Krefting, 1946; Hosley, 1949) but occurred in 3 of 24 moose stomachs from Ontario.

Pinus sylvestris L.   Scotch pine. This is not a normal moose food but it was found in the stomach contents of one animal from Manitoba.

Pinus resinosa Ait.   Red pine. This species is rarely browsed by moose. Traces of browsing were noted only in Algonquin Provincial Park, but it was found in neither stomach contents nor droppings.

Larix laricina (Du Roi) Koch.   Tamarack or larch. No evidence of Browsing was found in regular study plots and only one instance of browse was noted outside of the browse analysis plots on Simpson Island, Ontario. It was reported by Hosley (1949) for Isle Royale and by Pimlott (1953) for Newfoundland as not fed upon.

Picea canadensis (Mill.) BSP.   White spruce. Spruce is normally not a moose food. It is a very common species, providing 6.9 per cent of available winter food in the St. Ignace area and 2.2 per cent on Isle Royale (Aldous and Krefting, 1946), but even traces of browsings were rarely found anywhere. A trace was found in only one moose stomach. None was found in samples of droppings.

Picea mariana (Mill.) BSP.   Black spruce. This species is rarely eaten by moose. It provided 6.6 per cent of available winter food in the St. Ignace area and only 0.8 and 0.6 per cent on Isle Royale winter browse plots. Aldous and Krefting (1946) found that it provided 0.1 per cent of the winter diet and Hosley (1949) indicates it as zero. Only a trace of browsing was found in Ontario. None was found in stomach content samples, but one single occurrence was discovered in the samples of droppings.

Abies balsamea (L.) Mill. Balsam fir. This is apparently the most abundant and most important winter food of moose in the eastern part of its range, but is practically untouched during the summer months. In the St. Ignace area it occurred on 93 per cent of 1,000 plots, providing 30.9 per cent of the available winter food and 27 per cent of the total winter diet. It was found in varying degrees up to 100 per cent in all but three non-summer moose stomachs examined and occurred in 100 per cent of 1,055 pellets of 211 samples of droppings.

On Isle Royale it was considered to provide 8.6 per cent of available food in 1945 (Aldous and Krefting, 1946) and 13.5 in 1948 (Hosley, 1949). Diet percentages were listed for the above at 13.6 and 21.8.

Pimlott (1953) ranked it as one of the top two most important winter foods on Newfoundland. Wright (1953) showed it providing 50 per cent of the diet in southeastern New Brunswick, but ranked it of lesser importance in the remainder of that province. In Maine Dyer (1948) found it providing 36.7 per cent of available food and 54 per cent of winter food eaten in 12 "yards."

Tsuga canadensis (L.) Carr. Hemlock. This species is apparently an important conifer supplement during winter in the eastern portion of the Canadian biotic province. Scattered browsed trees in Algonquin Provincial Park could not always be assigned to moose, although 92 per cent of 85 moose dropping samples of 425 pellets contained hemlock. Over half of these occurrences were in trace proportions indicating that, although it was sampled freely, moose apparently rate it second to balsam fir as a winter conifer food although they seem to prefer it as a staple to white cedar. It was not found in stomach contents examined, most of which were taken beyond the range of this species.

Thuja occidentalis L. White cedar or arbor vitae. Although not a preferred moose food, this species is commonly eaten in winter, usually in small amounts. In the St. Ignace area it provided 3.0 per cent of available winter food and 0.4 per cent of the diet. The corresponding percentages on Isle Royale were 5.8 and 0.7 in 1945 (Aldous and Krefting, 1946) and 4.5 and 1.6 in 1948 (Hosley, 1949). In Algonquin Provincial Park all trees were closely browsed to a height of six feet by deer. Local luxuriant low growth was observed in both the Chapleau and St. Ignace areas of Ontario where deer populations were low. This species was found in 5 of 20 fall and winter stomach samples of moose from Ontario and 1 from Maine. In one case, a diseased animal taken on March 10, 1949, the sample of stomach contents contained a high proportion of this species (64 per cent). It occurred in 94 per cent of the droppings examined from Algonquin Provincial Park, although 69 per cent was trace occurrence and only 5 per cent contained large amounts. In the two lots of dropping samples from the St. Ignace area this species was found in 42 and 29 per cent of the pellets. In these latter cases white cedar did not occur in more than trace or moderate amounts. In general, this species appears to be tasted freely by moose during winter but seldom eaten in great quantity. Murie (1934) found that moose had eaten the bark from this species during high population levels on Isle Royale. Hosley (1949) points out, from the two browse analysis surveys on Isle Royale, that the utilization of white cedar had more than doubled between 1945 and 1948. This was regarded as an indication of heavy over-browsing. Wright (1952) found considerable utilization of this species in New Brunswick.

Juniperus spp. Juniper. Two species are found on both Isle Royale and St. Ignace, the more common *J. communis* (L.) var. *depressa* Pursh., the other *J. horizontalis* Moench. Both are quite sparsely distributed and were not found to be browsed in the St. Ignace area. Aldous and Krefting (1946) also found no browsing on these forms on Isle Royale, although Murie (1934) reports them as "very sparingly browsed."

Salix spp. Willow. This genus is probably one of the most important moose foods in North America. Eaten at all seasons of the year, the winter browse analysis indicated that it formed only 1.4 per cent of the available food but 4.2 per cent of the winter diet in the St. Ignace area, compared to 5.1 per cent available and 9.6 per cent of the diet on Isle Royale in 1945 (Aldous and Krefting, 1946), and 5.1 per cent available and 7.8 per cent of the diet in 1948 (Hosley, 1949). Krefting (1946) estimated that it provided 7.5 per cent of the summer diet of moose on Isle Royale (7.6 per cent of available food). It occurred more frequently than any other deciduous species in moose stomachs examined (66.2 per cent), ranging from a trace to 50 per cent of the contents (Peterson, 1953). It was consistently browsed heavily wherever found. Wright (1952) ranked it in about sixth position in the amount of total food eaten in New Brunswick. It is a widespread genus utilized from Newfoundland to Alaska. In western North America it is apparently much more abundant and thus more important as a moose food there than in the east.

Populus tremuloides Michx. Quaking aspen. This is apparently preferred as food at all seasons by moose. It is frequently "barked" heavily by moose in early spring. Aldous and Krefting (1946) found it to be the number one winter food of moose on Isle Royale in 1945, providing 8.7 per cent of available food and 16.9 per cent of diet. By 1948 these percentages were reduced to 5.4 and 9.0 (Hosley, 1949). In the St. Ignace area it provided only 1.1 per cent of available food and 1.4 per cent of the winter diet (see pp. 160, 163). Krefting (1946) estimated that it provided 9.0 per cent of the summer diet on Isle Royale (8.6 per cent available). It occurred in nine (33.6 per cent) of the moose stomachs examined (Peterson, 1953). In Maine, Dyer found that it provided 2.3 per cent of available food in 12 winter yards and 1.3 per cent of the diet (Hosley, 1949). It was listed as a fairly important food in Newfoundland (Pimlott, 1953) and in New Brunswick (Wright, 1952). It is a widespread species, characteristic of burned areas or successional associations where it is frequently heavily utilized in the form of shrubs and saplings.

Populus grandidentata Michx. Large-toothed aspen. Distinct signs of moose browsing on this species were only light to moderate in Algonquin Provincial Park where it was sparingly distributed. It is of minor importance as moose food.

Populus balsamifera L. Balsam poplar. This is browsed during all seasons, and feeding experiments indicated that it was rated about even with white birch or second to quaking aspen in palatability preference when these three species were offered in equal amounts. It provided only 0.3 per cent of available winter food in the St. Ignace area and 0.7 per cent of winter diet. Corresponding percentages on Isle Royale in winter were 0.6 and 1.0 in 1945, 0.3 and 0.5 in 1948, and in summer (1946), 0.7 and 0.5. No barking of standing or fallen trees was noted, but the bark of limbs and branches that were cut and made available was heavily utilized. It did not occur in samples of stomach contents examined.

Myrica spp. Sweet gale. These forms were rarely browsed in areas studied in Ontario. They are widespread and locally common in shoreline bogs. Pimlott (1953) ranks *Myrica Gale* as a fairly important moose food in Newfoundland.

Corylus rostrata Ait. Beaked hazelnut. Apparently this is a preferred moose food eaten at all seasons and important wherever available in sufficient quantities. It was rare in the St. Ignace area (0.2 per cent available) but consistently browsed (0.7 per cent of diet). It is more common and widespread on the mainland and on Isle Royale, on the latter constituting 4.0 and 4.2 per cent of available winter food and 2.5 and 2.6 per cent of diet in 1945 and 1948. In the summer diet Krefting (1946) found it providing 2.8 per cent of the available food and 2.3 per cent of foods eaten. It occurred in 10 samples of moose stomachs (38.6 per cent of the total examined) in proportions up to 40 per cent of the total contents. Dyer found that in Maine it provided only 0.6 per cent of available food or 0.1 per cent of the diet in 12 winter yards. Wright (1952) ranked it in fifth position for foods eaten in southeastern New Brunswick, but ranked it as of minor importance in the remainder of the province.

Ostrya virginiana (Mill.) K. Koch. Ironwood. Apparently this species is rarely browsed by moose.

Betula lutea Michx. f. Yellow birch. This birch is an occasional food during all seasons where available, but not a preferred species. It is a typical species of climax associations throughout the Canadian biotic province, being abundant in Algonquin Provincial Park where only light moose browsing was noted. It was absent in the St. Ignace area but provided 0.8 and 0.3 per cent of available winter food on Isle Royale (0.6 per cent and 0.2 per cent of diet) in 1945 and 1948 according to Aldous and Krefting (1946) and Hosley (1949). Krefting (1946) estimates that this species constituted 2.7 per cent of the summer diet in the latter area (3.4 per cent available). Pimlott (1953) ranked it as of "lesser importance" as a moose food in Newfoundland, but Wright considered it to be a fairly important food in New Brunswick.

Betula populifolia Marsh. Grey birch. Listed as one of the "chief" foods of moose in Maine by Lamson (Walcott, 1939), this species was also found heavily utilized in parts of New Brunswick (Wright, 1952).

Betula alba L. White birch. Owing to its high availability this form is apparently the most important deciduous species used as food by moose in the eastern part of their range. Widespread and especially abundant in successional stages of forest growth, it provided 8.2 per cent of the available winter food and 12.0 per cent of moose diet in the St. Ignace area of Ontario. Aldous and Krefting (1946) found corresponding percentages to be 9.8 and 14.9 in 1945 and Hosley (1949) reported 13.2 and 15.6 in 1948 on Isle Royale. In his studies of winter yards, Dyer (1948) found it providing 22.5 per cent of the available food but only 5.4 per cent of the diet. Pimlott (1953) regarded it (*B. papyrifera*) as one of the two most important winter foods in Newfoundland. Wright also ranks it in second position in southeastern New Brunswick, where it provided 16.5 per cent of the food eaten. Krefting (1946) estimated it provided 11.8 per cent of the summer diet on Isle Royale (11.3 per cent available). Ranking as a preferred food during all seasons, it was found in 11 (42.4 per cent) of the moose stomachs examined (Peterson, 1953) in addition to one from Maine which contained 45 per cent of this species (Hosley, 1949).

Betula glandulosa Michx. Dwarf birch. This is probably a preferred moose food where available. It was not observed in the study areas of Ontario although it occurred in 2 of the 26 samples of stomach contents examined, in proportions up to 60 per cent of the total contents.

Alnus crispa (Ait.) Pursh. Mountain or green alder. This species is a fairly important food of moose. In the St. Ignace area it provided 3.7 per cent of the available winter food and 4.5 per cent of the diet compared to 2.4 and 2.1 per cent available and 1.7 and 1.7 per cent of the winter diet of Isle Royale moose in 1945 and 1948 (Aldous and Krefting, 1946; Hosley, 1949). In summer it was regarded as providing 1.0 per cent of available food and 0.2 per cent of diet. It was not found in the samples of stomach contents analysed. On Newfoundland it was found to be fairly important moose food (Pimlott, 1953).

Alnus incana (L.) Moench. Swamp or speckled alder. This is apparently an occasional moose food of low quality, that is seldom eaten in great quantity. It was found as a trace in 2 of 26 stomach samples. Widespread and abundant in moist or swampy areas, it provided 5.6 per cent of available winter food (2.7 per cent of diet) in the St. Ignace area, compared to the 3.2 and 3.3 per cent available (0.3 per cent and 0.7 per cent of diet) on Isle Royale in 1945 and 1948 (Aldous and Krefting, 1946; Hosley, 1949). In summer it constituted 1.9 per cent of the diet (1.9 per cent available, Krefting, 1946).

Alnus rugosa (Du Roi) Spreng. Smooth alder. Pimlott (1953) lists this species as one of the minor foods in Newfoundland.

Fagus grandifolia Ehrh. Beech. Apparently this is a relatively poor moose food. Only rare traces of browse were noted in Algonquin Park, Ontario, although Wright (1952) ranked it as the eighth most common food in southeastern New Brunswick.

Quercus spp. Oak. Little is known of the status of oak as a moose food. Murie found that the few red oak (*Q. borealis*) on Isle Royale were heavily browsed, but Aldous and Krefting (1946) did not record this species on their browse plots. It is rather uncommon over most of the range of moose. Heavy browsing was noted on oak in the Sprucewood Forest Reserve of Manitoba in 1949. Wright (1952) lists it as a minor food in New Brunswick.

Physocarpus opulifolius (L.) Maxim. Nine-bark. A rather rare shrub on both Isle Royale and St. Ignace islands, only slight traces of browse being found on the latter.

Pyrus americana (Marsh.) DC. Mountain ash. This is a highly preferred species that formed 4.4 per cent of the available winter food and 9.4 per cent of the winter diet of moose in the St. Ignace area. It was less common in Algonquin Provincial Park. Aldous and Krefting (1946) reported 6.8 per cent available and 12.1 per cent in the winter diet of moose on Isle Royale. Hosley reports similar percentages of 6.6 and 11.6 for the same area three years later, and 4.2 and 5.4 for Maine. Pimlott (1953) ranks *Sorbus* sp. as a fairly important food on Newfoundland and Wright (1952) places it in ninth position in amounts of food eaten in southeastern New Brunswick. Eaten during all seasons, it is consistently barked as a mature tree. Krefting (1946) estimated it provided 11.3 per cent of available summer food on Isle Royale and 11.8 per cent of the diet. It was not found in the samples of stomach contents examined.

Amelanchier spp. Juneberry. Various species are preferred food, which are eaten during all seasons, and which provided 2.6 per cent of the available winter food and 3.1 per cent of the winter diet on St. Ignace, with approximately similar proportions in Algonquin Provincial Park. Aldous and Krefting (1946) found that on Isle Royale they provided 2.2 per cent of the available winter food and 2.9 per cent of the winter diet in 1945, but by 1948 these ratios were reduced to 0.9 and 1.1 according to Hosley (1949). In summer the availability and amount eaten were 2.1 per cent of the total in both cases (Krefting, 1946). *A. bartramiana* was listed as an important winter food in Newfoundland (Pimlott, 1953).

Prunus serotina Ehrh. Black cherry. This species is apparently generally browsed where available, but is not of sufficient abundance to be of much importance.

Prunus virginiana L. Choke cherry. This species is included with the following more common species in the Ontario winter browse analysis.

Prunus pennsylvanica L. f. Fire, red, or pin cherry. This is a preferred food during all seasons, and is generally heavily browsed. It was the most common cherry encountered in the Ontario study areas. Grouped with the above species, cherry formed 0.8 per cent of the available winter food and 1.8 per cent of the winter diet. Aldous and Krefting (1946) list only *Prunus pennsylvanica* from Isle Royale where it provided 2.5 per cent of the available winter food and 2.7 per cent of the winter diet of moose in 1945. By 1948 these percentages were reduced to 1.8 and 1.9 (Hosley, 1949). In Maine it provided 4.5 per cent of the available browse in 12 winter yards and 5.1 per cent of the diet (Dyer, 1948). In Newfoundland and New Brunswick it was regarded as an important winter food (Pimlott, 1953; Wright, 1952). In summer it was regarded as providing 5.7 per cent of the available food and 3.8 per cent of the diet on Isle Royale, Michigan, according to Krefting (1946).

Rhus spp. Sumach. Aldous and Krefting (1946) found *R. glabra* heavily browsed during winter by moose (0.5 per cent available, 1.3 per cent of diet). It was not encountered in Ontario studies, although the above form, as well as *R. typhina*, occurs within the range of moose in this province.

Acer pennsylvanicum L. Striped or moose maple. A preferred moose food, that, although least available, is usually the most consistently browsed of the maples in the eastern section of the Canadian biotic province. In Maine, Dyer (1948) found this species providing 6.0 per cent of the available browse and 4.0 per cent of the total winter diet in 12 winter yards. In New Brunswick it was heavily browsed, ranking in seventh position in total food eaten (Wright, 1952).

Acer spicatum Lam.   Mountain maple. This species apparently ranks below red maple and above sugar maple in palatability preference. Aldous and Krefting (1946) report it as 5.0 per cent of the available winter food and 2.3 per cent of the winter diet on Isle Royale. In a later study, Hosley (1949) reported that these percentages had changed to 4.5 and 3.3. On St. Ignace it provided 4.5 per cent of the available food but formed 9.1 per cent of food browsed. This increase over the amount browsed on Isle Royale suggests some added feeding by deer. However, Dyer's data from Maine indicate that this species ranked second in importance of the moose foods eaten in 12 winter yards (22.2 per cent available and 23.9 per cent eaten; Hosley, 1949). It was classed second to sugar maple as a top producer of summer food (15.4 per cent available and 15.5 per cent of diet) on Isle Royale (Krefting, 1946).

Acer saccharum Marsh.   Sugar maple. This species, which is dominant in the Canadian biotic province, was absent from the St. Ignace area of Ontario, but local stands were present on Isle Royale where it provided 7.0 and 9.9 per cent of the available winter food and 2.7 and 2.8 per cent of the moose diet in 1945 and 1948 respectively. In the Algonquin area of Ontario this species was abundant and consequently showed relatively little effect of winter utilization by moose. It was considered a fairly important food in New Brunswick (Wright, 1952). Krefting (1946) ranked this species as the most palatable species on Isle Royale in summer (9.7 per cent available and 18.4 per cent of the diet).

Acer saccharinum L.   White or silver maple. Wright (1952) found that silver maple was the fourth most common food eaten in southeastern New Brunswick but that it was of minor importance elsewhere in that province.

Acer rubrum L.   Red maple. This is preferred as food by moose during all seasons in Ontario, apparently ranking among the maples second only to striped maple. It was sparse on Isle Royale, where Aldous and Krefting found that it provided 0.1 per cent of the available food and 0.2 per cent of the winter diet in 1945 (0.3 per cent available and 0.4 per cent eaten in 1948; Hosley, 1949). Similar percentages of 0.3 available and 0.2 eaten are shown from Maine. Pimlott (1953) regarded it as one of the lesser important foods in Newfoundland, although Wright (1952) ranked it as the third most important food in New Brunswick.

Tilia americana L.   Basswood. Apparently this species is eaten only occasionally. Only a slight trace of browse was noted in Ontario. It was listed as one of the "principal" winter foods in Minnesota (Manweiler, 1941).

Cornus stolonifera Michx.   Red-osier dogwood. This apparently is a preferred food during all seasons. It was the most common dogwood shrub encountered in Ontario, ranking third as a producer of moose food in the St. Ignace area with 9.4 per cent of the winter diet but only 4.4 per cent available, compared to Isle Royale where it provided 8.3 per cent of the diet in 1945 and 5.6 per cent of the available winter food (Aldous and Krefting, 1946). By 1948 these percentages were reduced to 6.7 and 4.2. It provided 3.9 per cent of the summer food on Isle Royale (4.4 per cent of available food). It occurred in one of the moose stomachs examined from Ontario. In Newfoundland it is of lesser importance as a moose food according to Pimlott (1953).

Cornus spp.   Dogwood. Several species of shrub dogwood including *C. alternifolia* are occasionally browsed. *C. rugosa* was listed as sparse on Isle Royale (0.1 per cent available, 0.2 per cent of the winter diet of moose; Aldous and Krefting, 1946). Krefting (1946) ranked the latter as providing 2.5 per cent of the available food and 1.7 per cent of the diet in summer.

Ledum groenlandicum Oeder.   Labrador tea. This species is rarely eaten by moose. It was found as a trace in one sample of stomach contents from Ontario.

Kalmia spp.   Laurel. This genus is rarely browsed by moose. A trace of browsing was noted in the Algonquin study area. *K. angustifolia* was listed as a trace in one moose stomach from Maine (Hosley, 1949).

Chamaedaphne calyculata (L.) Moench.   Leather leaf. This species is similar in palatability rank to the above. It was found in one sample of stomach contents from Ontario. Apparently it is occasionally more heavily utilized in New Brunswick (Wright, 1952).

Fraxinus americana L.   White ash. This species was quite rare in the Algonquin study area where only slight evidence was found to suggest possible browsing by moose.

Fraxinus pennsylvanica Marsh var. *lanceolata.* (Borkh.) Sarg.   Red or green ash. The status of this form as a moose food is unknown. Aldous and Krefting (1946) found only traces of this species on Isle Royale but saw no evidence of browsing by moose.

Fraxinus nigra Marsh.   Black ash. Aldous and Krefting (1946) found this species poorly distributed and eaten only on rare occasions in winter on

Isle Royale, although Krefting found it providing 2.4 per cent of the summer diet (1.7 per cent available; Hosley, 1949).

Lonicera spp. Fly honeysuckle. This species was usually moderately browsed and sparingly distributed in both the Algonquin Provincial Park and St. Ignace areas of Ontario. In the latter, it provided 0.8 per cent of the available winter food and 0.8 per cent of the winter diet. It was much more abundant on Isle Royale, where according to Aldous and Krefting (1946) it provided 7.8 per cent of the available winter food and 0.2 per cent of the winter food eaten. In the 1948 study these percentages were thought to have changed to 4.5 and 3.1 (Krefting and Lee, 1948). Krefting (1946) indicated that this species constituted 0.5 per cent of the food eaten in summer (1.1 per cent available).

Viburnum alnifolium Marsh. Hobble-bush. This shrub was sparse but widely distributed in Algonquin Provincial Park where a part of the moderate to heavy browsing appeared to be attributable to moose.

Viburnum Opulus L. High-bush cranberry. Fairly common in the St. Ignace area, this species provided 4.4 per cent of the available winter food and 5.2 per cent of the winter diet. On Isle Royale (listed as *V. trilobum*) it provided only 1.4 per cent of the available food in 1945 (1.2 in 1948) and 0.8 per cent of the winter diet (1.2 in 1948). The greater degree of browsing on St. Ignace may be in part attributable to deer. Pimlott (1953) ranked it (*V. trilobum*) among the lesser important foods in Newfoundland. It was not listed among the 19 summer woody plant foods on Isle Royale (Hosley, 1949).

Viburnum cassinoides L. Withe-rod. Cameron (1948) found that moose readily fed on this species in Nova Scotia when available. It was listed as one of the chief foods in Maine by Lamson (Walcott, 1939). Dyer (Hosley, 1949) regarded it as providing 0.3 per cent of available food and 0.2 per cent of diet in 12 Maine winter yards.

Vibernum Lentago L. Sweet viburnum or nanny berry. This species was listed among the chief foods in Maine by Lamson (Walcott, 1939).

Viburnum spp. Viburnum. Various other species were encountered, especially in Algonquin Provincial Park, Ontario, where they could not be properly evaluated as moose foods. Wright (1952) lists this genus among the principal foods in parts of New Brunswick.

Sambucus racemosa L. Red-berried elder. According to Aldous and Krefting (1946) this species provided 1.7 per cent of the available winter food and 0.1 per cent of the winter diet of moose on Isle Royale. In the later study by Krefting and Lee (1948) the availability had increased to

1.6 and the percentage eaten to 0.5. In the St. Ignace area it formed 1.7 per cent of the available winter food, but formed 3.9 per cent of the food actually eaten. This increased degree of browsing on St. Ignace suggests that deer may be in part responsible; however, Cameron (1948) found that a captive moose preferred this species over all others when birch, withe-rod, maple, fire cherry, balsam fir, spruce, and spirea were provided in August. The nature of the pithy limbs and branches makes it difficult to evaluate the degree of winter browsing accurately. Krefting (Hosley, 1949) estimated the summer availability at 3.3 per cent of the total foods but only 1.9 per cent of foods eaten on Isle Royale. Pimlott (1953) ranked it among the lesser important moose foods in Newfoundland.

AQUATIC AND SEMI-AQUATIC PLANTS

Equisetum fluviatile L. (Pipes). Water horsetail. The amount eaten by moose seems to depend on the relative availability of other aquatic species. Available only during spring and summer, it was locally abundant in the Ontario Algonquin Park study area but browsed lightly. It was moderately abundant in the Chapleau area and heavily browsed, but was practically absent from the St. Ignace area. Murie (1934) found it sparse but usually browsed on Isle Royale.

Sparganium fluctuans (Morong) Robinson. Bur-reed. A preferred food species in early June in the streams of the Algonquin study area. Several individual moose were observed to feed on this species for over an hour at a time. It was rarely encountered in the St. Ignace Island area.

Sparganium spp. Bur-reed. Several species were fairly common in the Algonquin area. They were occasionally browsed, principally before the plants had matured. They were not listed for Isle Royale although Lamson (Walcott, 1939) includes this genus among aquatic foods in Maine.

Potamogeton Richardsonii (Benn.) Rydb. Pondweed. This was the most important aquatic species found in the St. Ignace Island area, where it provided the great bulk of aquatic food. Many animals fed for over an hour a day on this species from early June until after the first of October.

Potamogeton spp. Pondweed. Several other species including *P. pusillus* were found, chiefly in Algonquin Provincial Park, where they were locally abundant but aparently browsed lightly. Perhaps the great abundance of other types of aquatic food in that area reduced the amount of feeding on these species. This genus was listed as aquatic food in Maine by Lamson (Walcott, 1939).

Sagittaria spp. Arrow-head. Moose were observed to "sample" these plants on a few occasions in Algonquin Provincial Park. Lamson (Walcott, 1939) lists this genus among Maine moose foods.

Vallisneria spiralis L. Eel grass or wild celery. Apparently this is a preferred species where available. It was encountered as moose food in the streams of Algonquin Provincial Park, Ontario.

Zizania spp. Indian or wild rice. Although not actually observed on the study areas, it is commonly reported to be browsed by moose, especially in the Canadian biotic province of western Ontario (Oberholtzer 1911; and others).

Eleocharis spp. Spike rush. This genus is rarely browsed heavily, although occasionally it is sampled.

Scirpus subterminalis Torr. Water club rush. Occasionally this species was found growing interspersed with other aquatic plants in the Algonquin study area where small amounts were observed to be eaten along with other species. Possibly it is fed on inadvertently.

Carex spp. Sedge. Various sedges, chiefly of this genus, were fairly common in all study areas. No browsing was noted in the Algonquin Provincial Park or the St. Ignace Island areas. They were moderately browsed in the Chapleau area. Murie (1934) reported that moose browsed these plants extensively on Isle Royale during a high moose population period.

Pontederia cordata L. Pickerel-weed. This species was occasionally sampled by moose in Ontario.

Juncus spp. Bog rush. Although sparse and browsed lightly in the Algonquin and St. Ignace study areas, they were in moderate abundance and were moderately browsed in the Chapleau area of Ontario. This genus was sparse and heavily browsed on Isle Royale (Murie, 1934). It was listed by Lamson (Walcott, 1939) as a moose food in Maine.

Nymphaea advena Ait. Common yellow pond lily. A preferred aquatic species during early spring, it is usually fed on extensively when available. Although it is commonly reported that moose feed on the roots of this species, no evidence was found to support these reports. The roots were frequently found pulled free from the bottom of lakes and streams, but in no case had any been fed on by moose. Lamson (Walcott, 1939) reports *N. rubrodisca* among the aquatic foods in Maine.

Nymphaea microphylla Pers. Small yellow pond lily. Browsed lightly to moderately, this water lily is a minor item in aquatic diet in Ontario. It was listed among the chief aquatic foods in Maine (Lamson in Walcott, 1939).

Castalia odorata (Ait.). Woodville and Wood. Sweet-scented water lily. This species is apparently browsed much less extensively than either the common yellow pond lily or the water shield. Only light browsing was noted in areas where it was available. It was sparse but heavily browsed on Isle Royale where other water lilies are also rare (Murie, 1934). It was also listed as important aquatic food in Maine.

Brasenia Schreberi Gmel.   Water shield. This species was the most important aquatic species during late summer in Algonquin Provincial Park, Ontario, where it was locally abundant and extensively fed on.

Cicuta bulbifera L.   Water hemlock. Although the roots of this species are said to be poisonous, Murie (1934) reports that moose on Isle Royale occasionally fed on the leaves.

OTHER PLANTS

Mushrooms.   Murie (1934) reported that moose of Isle Royale were "fond of mushrooms" and found one occurrence in a sample of stomach contents. No evidence of feeding on these plants was noted in Ontario.

Lichens.   Mr. Vince Crichton of Chapleau, Ontario, reported (personal communication) having observed moose feeding on hanging tree species during the winter, and submitted sample specimens. These included two species of *Usnea* (chiefly *U. cavernosa*) and *Alectoria jubata*. (These specimens were kindly identified by Dr. R. F. Cain, Department of Botany, University of Toronto.) The relative importance of lichens as moose food is unknown.

Polypodium sp.   Polypody. This genus was found in one sample of stomach contents from Ontario.

Pteris aquilina L.   Bracken fern. This fern was occasionally browsed in Ontario. Murie (1934) reported it as heavily browsed on Isle Royale.

Asplenium Filix-femina (L.) Bernh. Lady fern. Murie (1934) observed browsing on this species on Isle Royale.

Aspidium spinulosum (O. F. Müller) Sw.   Common shield fern. This species was occasionally browsed in Algonquin Provincial Park, on the St. Ignace Island area, and on Isle Royale.

Osmunda regalis L.   Royal fern. Occasionally browsed.

Osmunda Claytoniana L.   Interrupted fern. Occasionally browsed.

Osmunda cinnamomea L.   Cinnamon fern. Occasionally browsed.

Botrychium virginianum (L.) Sw.   Rattlesnake fern. Occasionally browsed.

Gramineae.   Moose were observed to taste or graze lightly on several species of grass but nowhere was there any indication of serious feeding. McDowell and Moy (1942) found that moose of Montana fed on a great variety of grasses and estimated that they formed as high as 12 per cent of the diet in June. McMillan (1953a) found that in Wyoming grasses were eaten during 5.4 per cent of his summer observations, but that this type of food constituted 1.6 per cent of the total feeding time. Observations in Ontario indicate that grasses probably provide less than 1 per cent of the summer food of moose there.

Arisaema triphyllum (L.) Schott.   Jack-in-the-pulpit. This species was reported as browsed on Isle Royale in summer (Hosley, 1949).

Smilacina trifolia (L.) Desf.   False Solomon's seal. This plant was observed to have been eaten in summer on Isle Royale (Hosley, 1949).

Ranunculus septentrionalis Poir.   Swamp buttercup. According to Murie (1934) this species was occasionally browsed on Isle Royale.

Thalictrum sp.   Purple rue. Murie (1934) reported one observation of feeding on purple rue.

Caltha palustris L.   Marsh marigold. This marigold is commonly eaten according to Murie (1934). A few instances of browsing were noted on St. Ignace Island, Ontario.

Caulophyllum thalictroides (L.) Michx.   Blue cohosh. This plant was listed as a moose food in Maine by Lamson (Walcott, 1939).

Ribes spp.   Currants and gooseberries. In the St. Ignace area, plants of this genus were quite common (23 per cent of all plots) forming 1.9 per cent of the available winter food and 0.4 per cent of the winter diet. On Isle Royale, Aldous and Krefting (1946) found this species formed only 0.2 per cent of the available winter food and a trace of the winter diet.

Potentilla spp.   Cinquefoils or five-fingers. Traces of browsing were observed on this plant in Algonquin Provincial Park. Murie (1934) reported these plants were rare but occasionally browsed on Isle Royale.

Rubus parviflorus Nutt.   Salmon berry. This species was found in local dense stands in the St. Ignace Island area (0.6 per cent of available winter food) where light browsing was noted (0.5 per cent of diet). Aldous and Krefting (1946) did not record winter browsing on this species on Isle Royale but Murie (1934) found maximum utilization in early May before the leaves were fully unfurled. Apparently it is frequently tasted at all other seasons of the year, but is seldom eaten in large quantity.

Rubus spp.   Raspberry. Although not normally regarded as a moose food of any importance, these species appear to be frequently sampled but seldom eaten in quantity. Pimlott (1953) lists *R. idacus* among the minor foods eaten in Newfoundland.

Rosa spp.   Wild rose. Roses apparently provided 0.7 per cent of the winter diet on St. Ignace Island. Murie (1934) found *Rosa acicularis* scarce but heavily browsed on Isle Royale.

Impatiens biflora Walt.   Touch-me-not. Murie (1934) reports that this species was heavily grazed in August after flowering on Isle Royale. A few plants were noted in Algonquin Provincial Park but none had been browsed.

Viola spp.   Violet. Occasionally browsed (Murie, 1934).

Epilobium angustifolium L.   Fireweed. This widespread species, which is common on burned-over areas, was occasionally browsed during summer in all study areas.

Heracleum lanatum Michx.   Cow parsnip. This plant is sparingly eaten (Murie, 1934).

Vaccinium uliginosum. L.   Bog bilberry. One stomach sample from Ontario contained bog bilberry.

Vaccinium spp.   Blueberry. These commonly encountered plants were seldom browsed by moose in Ontario study areas, although they were "browsed in many places" on Isle Royale according to Murie (1934).

Chelone glabra L.   Turtlehead. On one occasion Murie (1934) found this plant eaten.

Dierville Lonicera Mill.   Bush honeysuckle. This plant was one of the important summer food plants of moose in the St. Ignace area, being very common and extensively browsed. It is probably not available during mid-winter. It was found in one stomach sample taken in Ontario on October 19, 1947.

Aster macrophyllus L.   Large-leaved aster. Perhaps this is one of the most commonly available herbaceous plants encountered in Ontario study areas. Considerable heavy browsing was noted in the extensive areas covered by this plant, with moderate browsing noted elsewhere. It was also observed as browsed on Isle Royle, Michigan, and in Maine.

Lactuca canadensis L.   Wild lettuce or horseweed. Hosley (1949) reports this species as being eaten in summer on Isle Royale.

CHAPTER THIRTEEN

FOOD PLANTS OF WESTERN NORTH AMERICA

STUDIES OF THE FOOD HABITS of moose in the western part of their range have not as yet been carried forward to the point where individual species can be treated in detail. The great diversity in the flora from region to region further complicates an attempt to carry out the treatment used for the eastern portion of North America. Lists of foods and their relative palatability have been provided for a few localities which must for the present form the basis of evaluating western food plants.

MONTANA

McDowell and Moy (1942) carried out a study of a summer range of moose in Montana and provided an evaluation of food plants found there. They have defined "proper use factor" as "the average percentage of the available growth of a species which is removed by grazing when the range is properly utilized under the best obtainable management. In browse species having an upright season's growth, height is the base."

The results of these studies were subsequently treated by Schultz and McDowell (1943). Tables XIV and XV give evaluations of the relative abundance and palatability of plants on summer moose range in the Absaroka-Gallatin area of Montana.

Aquatic plants were not fully treated in the above studies; however, water crowfoot (*Batrachium flaccidum*) was considered to be scarce, with a proper use factor of 20, while hornwort (*Ceratophyllum demersum*) and mare's-tail (*Hippuris vulgaris*) were both considered rare, with proper use factors of 5.

An estimated volume in average percentage of the various types of plants utilized by moose in summer is given in Table XIII.

During the fall season buffalo berry (*Shepherdia canadensis*) is reported to be heavily browsed (Hosley, 1949), although Cowan, Hoar, and Hatter (1950) regard this species as unpalatable to moose in British Columbia. Douglas fir (*Pseudotsuga taxifolia*), lodgepole pine (*Pinus contorta*), aspen, and balsam are also considered high in palatability.

WYOMING

On the basis of a three-year study of the summer food habits of moose in the Yellowstone National Park area, McMillan (1953a) found that ap-

145

TABLE XIV

ABUNDANCE AND PALATABILITY OF TREES AND SHRUBS
ON A SUMMER MOOSE RANGE OF MONTANA*

Species	Common name	Abundance†	Proper use‡ factor
Alnus tenuifolia	Alder	M	10
Actaea rubra	Baneberry	S	inc
Amelanchier alnifolia	Service berry	R	inc
Chimaphila umbellata	Pipsissewa	S	inc
Grossularia setosa	Redshoot gooseberry	S	inc
Ledum glandulosum	Labrador tea	S	inc
Lepargyrea (Shepherdia) canadensis	Russet buffalo berry	M	10
Lonicera involucrata	Bearberry honeysuckle	S	15
Menziesia ferruginea	Rusty skunkbrush	R	inc
Prunus melanocarpa	Black choke cherry	S	10
Rhus trilobata	Sumach	S	inc
Ribes lacustre	Prickly currant	S	inc
Ribes petiolare	Western black currant	S	inc
Rosa fendleri	Fendlers rose	S	inc
Rubus parviflorus	White flowering raspberry	M	inc
Salix (1)	Red stem willow	P	15
Salix (2)	Pubescence stem willow	A	65
Salix (3)	Yellowish-green stem willow	A	75
Sambucus melanocarpa	Blackhead elder	S	25
Sorbus scopulina	Green mountain ash	R	inc
Spiraea lucida	Spiraea	P	10
Phyllodoce empetriformis	Mountainheath	R	none
Symphoricarpos orbiculatus	Coral-berry	S	inc
Symphoricarpos racemosus	Snowberry	P	10
Vaccinium membranaceum	Tall huckleberry	S	inc
Vaccinium scoparium	Grouse whortleberry	A	none

*McDowell and Moy (1942); Schultz and McDowell (1943).

†Plants listed from abundant to rare as follows: A, abundant; P, plentiful; M, moderate; S, scarce; R, rare.

‡A percentage of palatability less than 5 per cent is classed as incidental, inc.

proximately 88 per cent of the food consisted of willow browse; 9.3 per cent consisted of aquatic plants, with forbs and sedges accounting for the remainder. He found that of the two species of willow present, feeding on *Salix Geyeriana* was approximately three times more frequent than on S. *Wolfii*. "The fact that S. *Geyeriana* is tall enough in many places to hide the moose while feeding may account for part of the difference in frequency of utilization. S. *Wolfii* is rarely more than three feet tall and can scarcely hide an adult moose even when lying down" (McMillan, 1953a, p. 104).

A summary of the summer foods of the Yellowstone moose is presented in Table XVI.

TABLE XV

ABUNDANCE AND PALATABILITY OF THE MOST IMPORTANT GRASSES AND OTHER
HERBACEOUS PLANTS ON A SUMMER MOOSE RANGE OF MONTANA*

Species	Common name	Abundance	Palatability
Grasses			
Agropyron Smithii	Bluestem	M	10
Agropyron spicatum	Blue wheat grass	R	15
Agrostis alba	Red top	P	10
Agrostis hyemalis	Winter red top	R	inc
Agrostis exarata	Spike red top	M	10
Agrostis idahoensis	Idaho red top	R	inc
Bromus ciliatus	Fringed brome	P	15
Calamagrostis canadensis	Meadow pine grass	M	11
Calamagrostis rubescence	Pine grass	P	11
Catabrosa aquatica	Brook grass	M	15
Danthonia intermedia	Timber oat grass	M	10
Festuca idahoensis	Idaho fescue	M	15
Koeleria cristata	June grass	P	10
Melica bulbosa	Onion grass	S	inc
Oryzopsis hymenoides	Mountain rice	S	11
Phleum alpinum	Alpine timothy	P	15
Poa spp.	Blue grass	S	10
Sporobolus spp.	Drop-seed	S	inc
Rushes and sedges			
Carex atrata	Marsh sedge	P	20
Carex festiva	Ovalhead sedge	M	10
Carex filifolia	Niggerwool	M	inc
Carex alpina	Alpine sedge	M	10
Juncoides parviflorum	Millet wood rush	S	inc
Juncus balticus	Wire rush	S	15
Weeds			
Achillea lanulosa	Western yarrow	M	10
Angelica lyalii	Lyall angelica	S	15
Arnica cordifolia	Heartleaf arnica	A	20
Arnica ventorum	Broadleaf arnica	M	20
Aster townsendi	Townsends aster	M	15
Aster conspicuus	Showy aster	S	15
Balsamorhiza sagitata	Balsam root	M	5
Geranium viscosissmum	Sticky geranium	M	15
Geranium Richardsonii	Cranesbill	S	5
Gaillardia aristata	Gaillardia	S	10
Heracleum lanatum	Cow parsnip	M	10
Hieracium albiflorum	White hawkweed	S	inc
Hydrophyllum capitatum	Ballhead waterleaf	S	25
Lupinus spp.	Lupine	P	10
Lathyrus spp.	Peavine	M	15
Thalictrum fendleri	Fendler meadow rue	M	one instance
Tellima parviflora	Fringecup	M	inc
Helianthus nuttallii	Sunflower	M	15

*McDowell and Moy (1942); Schultz and McDowell (1943).

TABLE XVI

DISTRIBUTION, ABUNDANCE, NUMBER OF OBSERVATIONS, AND PERCENTAGE OF
THE TOTAL OF OBSERVATIONS OF UTILIZATION OF PLANTS EATEN BY MOOSE
IN YELLOWSTONE PARK, WYOMING*

Species	Occurrence	Observations of utilization	Percentage of total observations	Percentage of total feeding time
Shrubs				88.5
Salix Geyeriana	A—W	815	54.5	
S. Wolfii	A—W	300	20.0	
Aquatic plants			17.5	9.3
Heteranthera dubia	P—Sc	78		
Myriophyllum sp.	M—Sc	68		
Potamogeton alpinus	R—TSc	4		
P. pectinatus	M—Sc	52		
Utricularia vulgaris	M—Sc	57		
Chara sp.	R—TSc	2		
Grasses			5.4	1.6
Agrostis hyemalis	S—Sc	6		
Agropyron sp.	S—TSc	18		
Deschampsia caespitosa	R—TSc	3		
Glyceria pauciflora	R—SmC	5		
Bromus ciliatus	S—TSc	3		
Elymus glaucus	S—TSc	3		
Melica bulbosa	R—TSc	3		
Phleum alpinum	M—Sc	4		
Poa sp.	M—Sc	37		
Forbs			0.9	0.5
Fragaria americana	R—TSc	1		
Heracleum lanatum	M—TSc	11		
Potentilla sp.	S—TSc	2		
Miscellaneous			1.6	0.1
Carex sp.	A—W	23		
Equisetum hyemale	R—TSc	1		
Luzula Wahlenbergii	R—SmC	1		

*McMillan (1953a).
SCALE: A—abundant; P—plentiful; M—moderate; S—scarce; R—rare; W—widespread;
Sc—scattered; TSc—thinly scattered; SmC—single small clump.

BRITISH COLUMBIA

Hatter (1948a) lists the following species as the most palatable food
plants in central British Columbia:

Red-osier dogwood, *Cornus stolonifera*
Paper birch, *Betula papyrifera*
Upland willow, *Salix* sp.
Trembling aspen, *Populus tremuloides*
Mountain ash, *Pyrus sitchensis*
Bog birch, *Betula glandulosa*
Saskatoon or juneberry, *Amelanchier florida*
Lowland fir, *Abies grandis*
High-bush cranberry, *Viburnum pauciflorum*
False box, *Pachystima myrsinites*
Maple, *Acer douglasii*
Horsetail, *Equisetum* sp.
Sedge, *Carex* sp.
Yellow pond lily, *Nymphaea polysepala*

In a later study of the nutritional value of moose foods in the same general area Cowan, Hoar, and Hatter (1950, p. 270) conclude as follows:

Nutritive quality and palatability are not necessarily related. Thus *Shepherdia canadensis* and *Picea Engelmanni* are both of good quality, but unpalatable to moose in this area. Further, there is little to choose between the two types of willows analyzed. While one, the upland willow, is a preferred food, the swamp willow is taken in reduced amounts.
Among the palatable species those of highest quality are *Pinus contorta*, *Populus tremuloides*, *Betula papyrifera*, and *Alnus sitchensis*. Those of intermediate quality are *Populus trichocarpa*, *Salix*, *Betula glandulosa*, and *Corylus californica*; while those lowest in nutrients are *Acer glabra*, *Cornus stolonifera*, and *Amelanchier florida*.

The nutrient values other than vitamins, of the 17 species of plants from central British Columbia analysed by these authors, are summarized in Table XVII.

ALASKA

In this region the striking feature of winter foods is the reduction in the number of species available. Willow, two species of birch, and quaking aspen account for well over 90 per cent of the foods eaten. Studies of 1,124 plots following the Aldous system of browse analysis by Spencer and Chatelain (1953) are summarized in Table XVIII. The last six species listed in this table made up only a small fraction of the food available and of the food eaten. Quaking aspen was found to become especially important in areas recently burned over. In one such area they found several hundred moose were subsisting (98 per cent of diet) on this species, which provided 96 per cent of the available food. The average percentage utilization of the current year's growth of aspen on the areas studied was as follows: Kasilof, 1950–50, 1951–46, 1952–39; Kenai, 1950–13, 1951–73 (a small sample), 1952–30; 1947 Burn, 1952–45.

Similar utilization percentages given by Spencer and Chatelain (1953) for Kenai birch are: Kasilof, 1950–55, 1951–53, 1952–66; Kenai, 1950–41, 1951–43, 1952–44; Chickaloon, 1952–22. Willow utilization was as follows:

TABLE XVII

PERCENTAGE COMPOSITION OF MOOSE FOODS FROM CENTRAL BRITISH COLUMBIA*

Common name	Scientific name	No. of samples	Moist-ure	Pro-tein	Ether extract	N-free extract	Min-eral	Crude fibre
Alpine fir	*Abies lasiocarpa*	1	43.43	6.39	12.51	58.41	3.53	19.16
Lodgepole pine	*Pinus contorta*	13	54.30	6.90	8.47	57.23	2.42	24.98
Douglas fir	*Pseudotsuga taxifolia*	13	50.27	6.53	7.83	62.74	3.22	19.91
Spruce	*Picea Engelmanni*	13	47.51	5.40	6.59	60.75	4.01	21.58
Aspen	*Populus tremuloides*	13	46.34	7.10	7.71	52.95	4.16	28.07
Black poplar	*Populus trichocarpa*	7	48.21	6.08	15.26	51.17	3.42	24.07
Mountain maple	*Acer glabra*	1	45.31	5.91	2.42	54.15	4.20	33.32
Swamp willow	*Salix* species†	4	49.77	6.32	5.31	61.92	2.46	23.99
Upland willow	*Salix* species‡	14	46.73	5.91	4.12	55.18	4.35	31.86
Paper birch	*Betula papyrifera*	14	43.75	6.98	8.39	52.01	2.85	29.78
Bog birch	*Betula glandulosa*	6	34.99	6.10	8.23	56.40	2.10	27.17
Red-osier dogwood	*Cornus stolonifera*	13	46.66	4.84	4.89	57.53	4.00	28.75
Service berry	*Amelanchier florida*	13	42.34	5.45	3.17	58.52	4.39	28.52
Hazel	*Corylus californica*	13	45.36	6.58	1.95	59.13	5.77	26.75
Buffalo berry	*Shepherdia canadensis*	1	38.52	14.66	1.98	58.92	3.10	21.34
Beard moss	*Usnea barbata*	1	8.54	2.41	7.31	86.20	1.70	22.38
Alder	*Alnus sitchensis*	6	46.77	9.95	6.57	57.04	2.77	23.68
Aspen (bark)	*Populus tremuloides*			12.66	14.21	43.07	5.81	24.24

*Cowan, Hoar, and Hatter (1950).
†*Salix McCalliana, S. mertillifolia, S. pedicellaris.*
‡*Salix Scouleriana, S. Bebbiana.*

TABLE XVIII

WINTER FOODS OF MOOSE IN ALASKA, 1952*

Species	Kasilof		Kenai		1947 Burn		Chickaloon Bay	
	Avail.	Diet	Avail.	Diet	Avail.	Diet	Avail.	Diet
Willow (*Salix* sp.)	62	66	74	71				
Kenai birch (*Betula kenaica*)	11	15	22	26			86	91
Dwarf birch (*Betula nana*)	13	9						
Aspen (*Populus tremuloides*)	12	10	4	2	96	98		
Alder (*Alnus* sp.)							11	7
Cotton-wood (*Populus tacamahacca*)								
Cotton-wood (*Populus trichocarpa*)								
High-bush cranberry (*Viburnum edule*)								
Red-berried elder (*Sambucus racemosa*)								
Rose (*Rosa* sp.)								
Raspberry (*Rubus strigosus*)								

*Spencer and Chatelain (1953).

Kasilof, 1950–49, 1951–48, 1952–52; Kenai, 1950–41, 1951–43, 1952–44. Studies of the crude protein from samples of willow, birch, and cotton-wood by these authors showed a consistent reduction with increased utilization (willow, no use, 6.13; moderate use, 6.03; heavy use, 5.80; similar percentages for others were, birch, 8.79; 7.94; 7.43; and cotton-wood, 7.28–5.47).

TABLE XIX

RELATIVE PALATABILITY OF SPECIES OF MOOSE FOODS IN ALASKA*

Species	Palatability
Tree birch	100
Ground birch	100
Willows	100
Mountain ash	100
Red currant	100
Black currant	100
Service berry	100
Aspen	75
Cotton-wood	75
Elder	75
High-bush cranberry	75
Alder	50
Carex	50
Fescue	25
Marsh grass	25
Horsetail	25
Rush (*Juncus*)	20
Potamogeton	20
Bur-reed	20
Bunch grass, wheat grass (*Agropyron*), blue grass (*Poa*), and wood rush [(*Luzula*)]	15
Lupine	15
Wild parsnip	15
Raspberry	15
Fireweed	10
Blueberry	10
Pond lily	5
Rye grass	5
Rose	2
Tea (*Ledum*)	2
Twin-flower	2
Cotton sedge	2
Lichens	2
Cranberry	2
Sphagnum	1
Polytrichum	1
Herbaceous dogwood	1
One-flowered pyrola	1

*Hosley (1949).

Willow, by virtue of its abundant availability, stands out as the most important winter food of Alaskan moose.

Hosley (1949) has summarized the work in Alaska of L. J. Palmer, United States Fish and Wildlife Service, and provided a list of relative palatability ratings of moose foods in this region (see Table XIX).

"Other species available but which were refused or were taken only very rarely included devil's club, heather, squawberry (*Menziesia*), spirea, buffalo berry, *Myrica gale,* chaparral, bog rosemary, yarrow, *Cicuta,* monkshood, larkspur, loco, fern, club moss, hawksbeard, crowberry, shrubby cinquefoil, pyrola, fernweed, and marsh marigold" (Hosley, 1949, p. 29).

For further data on foods eaten by Alaskan moose see p. 122.

During late March and early April, moose are said to paw through the snow to feed on lichens, ground birch, willow, and the occasional green shoots of grass clumps, in addition to the usual species browsed above the snow. Apparently grasses play a more important role in the diet of moose in the western part of their range than in the east. Aquatic plants, on the other hand, are apparently taken in lesser amounts.

CHAPTER FOURTEEN

HABITAT STUDIES

As a herbivore, the moose is directly affected by the floral composition of its habitat. Many factors combine to influence the plant life and thereby become important in the ecology of moose. Climate, soils, and time combine to shape the basic factors in the environment. However, several additional factors become interrelated to create considerable variation in local habitats. Chief among these are the various plant associations and their ecological succession, together with the factors which influence them, such as fire, commercial operations of civilization, and the activities of the associated animal communities.

Plant Associations and Ecological Succession

The basis of a favourable habitat for moose is continual forest succession or regeneration. Moose populations apparently reach their maximum in the early stages of succession and decrease as the forest reaches maturity. Many of their important foods are found only in areas where the mature or climax forest has been removed, thus allowing such food species to appear. In dense mature forests, shading by the upper canopy brings about natural pruning of the lower branches and prevents the growth or regeneration of most seedlings and shrubs. Mixed, rather than pure, stands of forest species are usually required for a favourable moose habitat. Although the general environmental conditions found in the St. Ignace area of Ontario are acceptable to moose, there are certain local areas which definitely seem more favourable than others (Figure 50). An excellent example of a good fall and winter area for moose is found in Otter Creek Valley on St. Ignace Island.

Otter Creek Valley, St. Ignace Island, Ontario

This valley comprises roughly two square miles with three small streams traversing parts of it. In addition to evidence of heavy browsing, there are further signs of the attractiveness of this area during the winter months. The number of winter droppings found on the browse analysis plots was 151 per acre compared to 37 per acre for the entire study area including Otter Creek Valley. A total of 47 single shed antlers was found within this two-square mile area compared to 53 for all the rest of the study area. The ratio of freshly dropped antlers to older ones was roughly the same for both

Otter Creek Valley and the total area. On September 16, 1947, no fewer than 40 "beds" where moose had lain down were found during a two-hour hike on the east side of this valley. All of these "beds" appeared to have been made within the previous week. A total of 26 such spots was found on a similar hike through the central and western sections of the valley on September 22.

Parts of Otter Creek Valley had been either logged or burned several years previously. A comparison of the winter browse analysis for Otter Creek Valley with the total for the study area brings out certain features of a favourable winter habitat (Table XX). One of the important factors, suggested by this comparison, is the more nearly equal availability of several preferred food species. In Otter Creek Valley balsam fir does not constitute such a high proportion of the available food and consequently provides a smaller percentage of the diet. This seems further to indicate that the great importance of balsam fir in the diet is more closely related to availability than to palatability.

These data tend to substantiate other general observations which indicate that moose prefer areas producing the greatest variety of available food. Large tracts of land providing only two or three species of food, even in abundant supply, are rarely heavily utilized by moose in Ontario. Smaller "pure stands" are sometimes utilized when other types of food are available near by. Even within local favourable habitats, some of the highest degree of browsing noted was in and around small openings or clearings.

Other characteristics of Otter Creek Valley which reflect favourable conditions for moose are found in a study of the age composition of the principal forest trees (Figure 51). Chief among these are the higher proportions of shrubs and saplings to mature trees.

Age Composition of the Principal Forest Trees of the St. Ignace Area

The forest trees on each plot were classified and recorded by age groups during the winter browse analysis survey. The over-all age composition of the study area is compared with that of Otter Creek Valley in Figure 51. The age pattern for several of the food species preferred by moose in Otter Creek Valley seems to indicate a winter habitat almost ideal for moose.

In considering the general age composition for the islands as a whole, the spruces may be used as indications of the age development of the forests, since they are practically never browsed by moose or deer. Constant heavy browsing by moose has undoubtedly altered the age composition in certain other species.

Over the entire St. Ignace area, seedlings of all species occurred on a higher percentage of the plots than did shrubs. In Otter Creek Valley the reverse was true, with shrubs generally being more abundant than other age classifications, except in the case of spruce and poplar.

TABLE XX

WINTER BROWSE ANALYSIS OF OTTER CREEK VALLEY AND OF AREAS
BURNED IN 1936, COMPARED WITH THE TOTAL ST. IGNACE AREA

Species	OTTER CREEK VALLEY (55 plots)		AREAS BURNED 1936 (55 plots)		TOTAL ST. IGNACE (1,000 plots)	
	eaten %	available %	eaten %	available %	eaten %	available %
Balsam fir	16.4	18.3	1.9	11.0	27.0	30.9
White birch	6.4	4.5	65.6	47.9	12.0	8.2
Mountain ash	4.5	2.7	3.8	1.7	9.4	4.4
Red-osier dogwood	16.7	9.6			9.4	3.3
Mountain maple	25.4	14.1	1.3	.5	9.1	4.5
High-bush cranberry	6.5	6.6	.1	1.0	5.2	4.4
Mountain alder	7.5	10.0	1.0	.7	4.5	3.7
Willow	4.0	2.4	11.9	7.3	4.2	1.4
Red-berried elder	2.5	1.8	4.2	2.4	3.9	1.7
Juneberry	2.7	2.2	.2	.5	3.1	2.6
Speckled alder	.5	7.8	.2	.1	2.7	5.6
Cherry	4.1	2.3	2.9	3.3	1.8	.8
Quaking aspen	.3	.3	6.5	5.3	1.4	1.1
Raspberries	tr*	2.3	.2	4.4	1.2	4.6
Fly honeysuckles	1.2	.9			.8	.8
Balsam poplar	.3	.2			.7	.3
Beaked hazelnut					.7	.2
Roses	.2	2.2	.1	1.1	.7	1.7
Ground hemlock					.6	.7
Salmon berry	.3	.9			.5	.6
White cedar		.1	tr	.1	.4	3.0
Currants and gooseberry	tr	.7	.1	2.9	.4	1.9
White spruce		4.0		7.6	tr	6.9
Black spruce		6.0		1.8	tr	6.6
Nine-bark					tr	tr
Tamarack				.1	tr	tr
Juniper					tr	tr
Jack pine					tr	tr
White pine					tr	tr

*Trace occurrence, less than .1.

There can be little doubt that the age and the species composition, as represented in Otter Creek Valley, is one of the prime factors contributing toward an optimum winter habitat.

Plant Succession in Algonquin Provincial Park

This area is fairly characteristic of the Canadian biotic province in which sugar maple and yellow birch form the climax forest. Moose are largely dependent on the successional stages for a suitable habitat within this

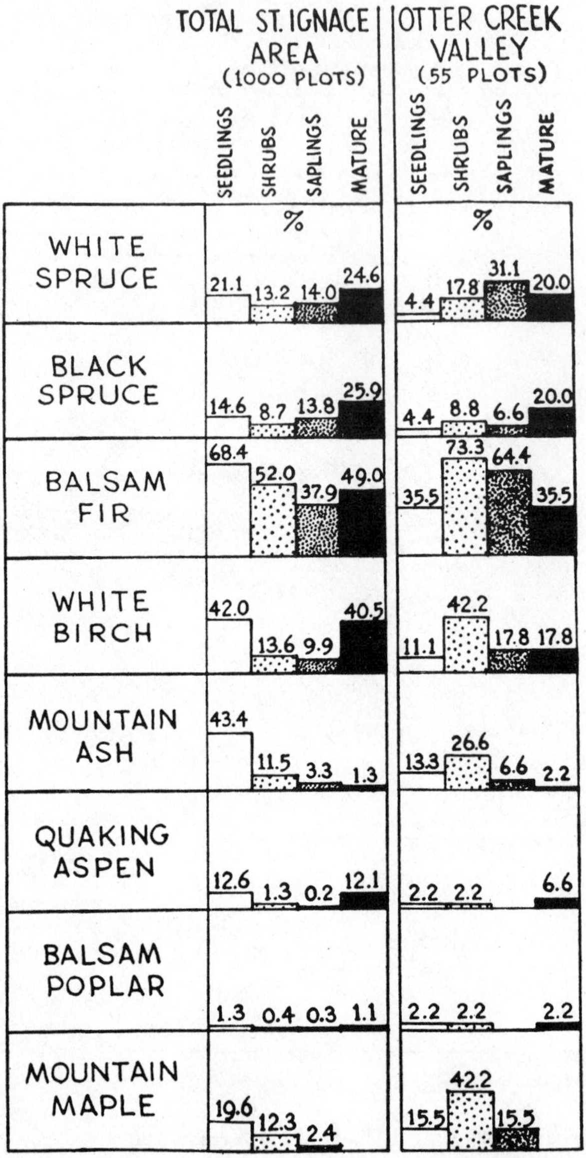

TOTAL ST. IGNACE AREA (1000 PLOTS)

OTTER CREEK VALLEY (55 PLOTS)

SEEDLINGS   SHRUBS   SAPLINGS   MATURE

SEEDLINGS   SHRUBS   SAPLINGS   MATURE

%

%

WHITE SPRUCE
21.1   13.2   14.0   24.6
4.4   17.8   31.1   20.0

BLACK SPRUCE
14.6   8.7   13.8   25.9
4.4   8.8   6.6   20.0

BALSAM FIR
68.4   52.0   37.9   49.0
73.3   64.4   35.5   35.5

WHITE BIRCH
42.0   13.6   9.9   40.5
42.2   11.1   17.8   17.8

MOUNTAIN ASH
43.4   11.5   3.3   1.3
26.6   13.3   6.6   2.2

QUAKING ASPEN
12.6   1.3   0.2   12.1
2.2   2.2   6.6

BALSAM POPLAR
1.3   0.4   0.3   1.1
2.2   2.2   2.2

MOUNTAIN MAPLE
19.6   12.3   2.4
42.2   15.5   15.5

FIGURE 51. The age composition of the principal forest trees in the St. Ignace Island area, based on percentage occurrence of each age classification on the total plots examined

region. Thus shoreline associations and burned areas form important elements in the moose habitat of the Canadian biotic province.

As outlined by Dice (1938, 1943) and others, the chief species that succeed burning are the aspens and white birch. In certain old burned

Figure 50. An example of moose habitat on Simpson Island, Ontario, 1947

FIGURE 52. Balsam fir showing the effect of constant pruning by moose. Pruning has resulted in a temporary increase in actual volume of available browse in this region, although unbrowsed spruce are also increasing

FIGURE 53. Suppression of regeneration of forest species by moose. Small clearings are apparently maintained by heavy browsing

areas a considerable amount of red maple was found associated with these species. Close examination of a small island at the west end of Longbow Lake that had been burned over a year previously revealed that all the chief species of trees had been killed out with the exception of red maple. In a few cases these trees were still alive, while the spruce, white pine, hemlock, balsam, white birch, yellow birch, and sugar maple were all dead. Many of the red maple trees were sprouting from the base of the trunk although the tops were apparently dead. It appears that the resistance of red maple to less intense fires allows this species to maintain itself in certain successional stages of development following fires.

A WINTER "YARD"

A local and well defined winter "yard" in Algonquin Provincial Park afforded an opportunity to check existing conditions in an effort to appraise a few of the factors which attracted or maintained a winter concentration of moose. The area comprised about four or five acres along the northeast shore of McIntosh Lake. About three acres of the area was surveyed and staked into quadrats. The species composition and relative availability of

TABLE XXI

PLANT COMPOSITION OF AN ALGONQUIN PROVINCIAL
PARK WINTER MOOSE "YARD"

(102 plots in a 3-acre area)

Species	Plots present %	Browse available %
White pine	31	1.2
White spruce	8	.7
Black spruce	70	18.7
Hemlock	74	5.7
Balsam fir	100	42.2
White cedar	46	2.8
Beaked hazelnut	17	3.4
White birch	14	1.2
Yellow birch	56	4.8
Speckled alder	8	2.6
Cherry	4	.3
Juneberry	31	1.8
Beech	5	.2
Mountain ash	23	2.5
Striped maple	9	.9
Mountain maple	35	6.5
Sugar maple	15	2.1
Red maple	21	1.1
Hobble-bush	14	1.3

the trees and shrubs in the "yard" based on 102 plots (16½ feet by 16½ feet) are given in Table XXI. A total of 391 piles of moose droppings was counted on 14,400 square yards of the area. In addition, counts of droppings also showed deer, 136; grouse, 16; and rabbit, 1.

The "yard" was situated on the base of a southern slope of a hill forming a long narrow band between a pure climax association of sugar maple and yellow birch on the upper slope and the rocky shoreline of the lake which was fringed by white cedar. The evidences of winter browsing and winter droppings were almost wholly confined to this narrow strip. Their termination at the edge of the hardwood climax was quite striking. The presence of both deer and moose in the area made it impossible to segregate the effect of the browsing of these two mammals. Balsam fir was by far the most abundant and most heavily browsed of all the species present. The habit of riding down or breaking out the tops of shrubs and saplings might give some index to the activity of moose in the area. A total of 164 (24.5 per cent) of the balsam shrubs and saplings had the tops broken out (shrubs 137, or 31 per cent, and saplings 27, or 11.5 per cent) on 0.64 of an acre. In addition, the following shrubs and saplings were found with tops broken by animals: mountain maple, 41; sugar maple, 8; hobble-bush, 3; beech, 2; striped maple, 1; and black spruce, 1.

Since the limits of this area, where there were concentrations of moose in winter, appeared to be closely correlated with the local distribution of balsam fir, there seems little doubt that the heavy utilization of the species corroborates its basic importance in the ecology of moose in the eastern part of their range.

The Effect of Forest Succession upon the Nutritive Values of Moose Food Plants

In central British Columbia, Cowan, Hoar, and Hatter (1950) carried out studies of three stages in forest succession growing under virtually identical conditions of soil and climate, in order to determine the quantity of available palatable browse, the carotene and ascorbic acid content of the available palatable and unpalatable trees and shrubs, and to carry out an analysis of values for moisture, protein, carbohydrate, ether extractives, and total mineral content. Most of their analyses were confined to the winter dormant period. The earliest stage (Area 1) was six years old, the second was an intermediate stage, and the third a mature forest.

In summarizing the results of these studies in British Columbia, the authors concluded (1950, p. 249):

It is determined that the forest changes studied involved a reduction in quantity of palatable browse to about one-third; that there is an increase of carotene values and possibly of total mineral content in the vegetation on more advanced forest areas, but that in ascorbic acid content, ether extractives, total carbohydrates, and proteins, the vegetation upon the younger forest areas is superior to that on the older areas.

It is concluded, therefore, that the declining carrying capacity noted in a forest approaching its climax stage results from decreases in both.the quantity and quality of food produced.

It is further concluded that the most desirable winter range for moose is one upon which there is a variety of palatable species, predominantly in an early stage of growth, but with an intermixture of older forest stands bearing palatable coniferous trees.

The latter conclusion agrees almost identically with that reached by other methods in Ontario studies (Peterson, 1949b).

EFFECTS OF FIRE

Forest fires have undoubtedly been a most important agent affecting forest succession. The wasteful destruction of valuable timber and wildlife and the resultant erosion and flooding are often offset, in part, by the creation of more favourable habitats for moose and other wildlife.

The moose of Isle Royale had so completely depleted their food supply by 1935 that ultimate starvation seemed inevitable. "In 1936 fires burned over approximately one-fourth of the island. These eliminated a large part of the browse supply for 2 or 3 years, but in the long run have been one of the greatest factors in permitting a comeback of the moose. Today the 1936 burned area supplies more browse than the remainder of the island combined." (Aldous and Krefting, 1946, p. 296)

In 1936 a small section was burned on the southwest portions of both St. Ignace and Simpson islands, Ontario. A total of 55 browse plots was analysed in these two areas. The results are summarized in Table XX. White birch is the outstanding species from the standpoint of both the amount available and amount eaten. Next, according to amounts available, were balsam fir, white spruce, willow, quaking aspen, red-berried elder, mountain ash, and cherry. These two small burned areas were providing a significant proportion of the entire islands' available white birch, willow, and quaking aspen.

Moose seem to use these two burned areas for feeding mostly in late fall and early spring. This probably accounts for the low utilization of balsam in these burned areas, since it is eaten only during the winter months. These areas provide little protective cover but they are sufficiently small that moose were able to range out from near-by cover to feed on them.

There are in Ontario some extensive burned areas into which moose rarely venture. Preliminary investigations suggest that large burned-over tracts do not normally become heavily populated by moose until a balanced winter and summer habitat becomes available. Key factors under such circumstances seem to be (1) sufficient variety of foods for all seasons, including (2) aquatic vegetation in summer and (3) balsam fir in winter. Conifers apparently play a much less important role in the winter diet of the moose in the western part of its range.

In Alaska an area of 290,000 acres was burned over near Kenai in 1947. Spencer and Chatelain (1953) carried out studies and state that the original stand, consisting largely of black spruce with scattered aspen trees, furnished an extremely limited range for moose. Following the fire, the aspen, thoroughly interspersed through the original stand, immediately sent up suckers from their roots so that significant aspen browse was produced within two to three years. By 1950 it was estimated that 273 moose were present in the area. Annual increases were as follows: 344 in 1951, 618 in 1952, and 1,111 in 1953. These increases were thought to have resulted from diversions of moose from other wintering areas.

Effects of Lumbering Operations

The over-all effects of various types of lumbering operations cannot be properly evaluated on the basis of past studies and should be the subject of further research. A few generalizations may be discussed, however, in order to present certain aspects of the problem that have been suggested.

The process of forest succession which follows destruction by fire can, to a certain degree, be initiated by certain types of lumbering operations. As suggested by the results of large fires, clean cutting of vast areas appears to reduce maximum utilization by moose for a longer period than other methods of cutting, although this length of time is undoubtedly shorter than that following fire. Selective cutting, on the other hand, frequently fails to reduce the forest canopy sufficiently to allow successional growth. Areas observed in Ontario on which selective cutting had been carried out usually provided little growth of important food plants and in several cases were grown up with dense stands of raspberries.

It seems possible that in the St. Ignace area of Ontario selective cutting of quaking aspen for paper pulp logs may have been one of the factors accounting for the present low supply of the species. However, selective cutting of quaking aspen is probably less important than the browsing of moose and other animals together with the general ecological development of the area.

It seems reasonable to assume that the physical operations of lumbering have little serious detrimental effect on moose unless the animals are shot or wilfully disturbed. In fact, it is frequently reported that moose take advantage of the increased availability of the tops of the freshly cut trees.

In summary, preliminary studies suggest that under most circumstances the clean cutting of smaller spots or strips will normally increase the available food supply and thereby improve the habitat for moose. The effect on moose of various other types of lumbering operations depends on many local conditions and therefore cannot be included in the scope of the present work. Apparently no special study of this subject has been undertaken in North America, although some progress in this direction has been made in Sweden. It seems reasonable to assume that the forestry practices carried on in that country have had a beneficial effect on the habitat of moose. At any rate, moose have increased in number there to such an extent, in spite of high annual kills, that the Government recently established a Royal Commission to inquire into what steps should be taken to prevent and minimize damages to the forests caused by moose (Hamilton, 1947). Certainly the lumbering operations in that country have had little or no detrimental effect on the habitat or numbers of moose.

EFFECTS OF FOREST INSECTS

The habitat of moose is sometimes seriously affected by "outbreak" infestations of forest insects which destroy certain species of food. In areas of heavy outbreak the spruce budworm (*Chloristoneura fumiferana*) has caused remarkably high mortality in balsam fir. The over-all effect of spruce budworm in Ontario has been reviewed in a brief presented before the Ontario Royal Commission on Forestry in 1946 by the members of the Forest Insect Investigation Unit (Canada, 1946).

In many areas spruce budworm has caused over 50 per cent mortality in balsam fir with several instances of 100 per cent. Such drastic reduction in this important winter food undoubtedly has a serious effect on local populations of moose.

As in the case of the destruction of the habitat by fire, there seem to be some compensations in the destruction of balsam fir by spruce budworm. According to Dr. M. L. Prebble, officer in charge of the Forest Insect Laboratory at Sault Ste Marie, Ontario, and others (personal communication) such areas frequently show a rapid regeneration of young balsam fir. In fact, Dr. Prebble has summarized preliminary findings in the following statement (personal letter):

Spruce does not seem to do well when the stand is opened up by budworm killing, despite somewhat heavier killing of balsam fir than spruce. This is an unusual situation which has not always been appreciated by investigators who have sometimes spoken of the spruce budworm as a corrective influence in establishing proper relationship between balsam fir and spruce. Actually, killing of the mature balsam by the spruce budworm seems to have the effect of increasing the balsam content of the succeeding forest.

The speed of balsam regeneration seems to depend on local ecological conditions. Frequently, as pointed out by Dr. Prebble, areas of dead balsam fir will be taken over by a dense growth of raspberries and other quick-growing species which in turn make the establishment and survival of conifer seedlings very difficult. For example, he writes of such an instance as follows: "In one such area that was examined last year [1947] balsam fir seedlings, about seven years old and only about six inches high, were found in fair number under the heavy overgrowth of raspberry, et cetera."

In other areas regeneration is extremely rapid. On this point, Dr. Prebble comments: "At the present time, it appears that much of this advance growth was already established before killing of mature timber and shoots ahead rapidly when the stand is opened by killing."

There can be little doubt that this destruction of balsam fir has limited the winter food supply of moose in Ontario temporarily at least. It seems quite possible that where deer and moose are competing for winter food in the same general area, the reduction of this important moose food creates a change in the habitat which favours deer.

In New Brunswick it is reported that the spruce budworm killed off large stands of balsam between 1915 and 1920 (New Brunswick, 1944). As indicated by the number killed by hunters, the trend in moose and deer populations in that province appears similar to the trend in Nova Scotia where moose generally decreased after 1931 and deer began increasing at a remarkable rate (Nova Scotia, 1948). The relative importance of spruce budworm in the relationship between moose and deer is not known.

In summary, it appears that forest insects, especially the spruce budworm, constitute important factors in the general ecology of moose. The complex role of forest insects in various biotic communities, in terms of their effect on such forms as moose and deer, is as yet poorly understood. Further studies along these lines are needed.

The Effects of Moose on the Habitat

Large herbivores, perhaps as much as any other group, frequently exert a great and noticeable influence on the ecological composition of local habitats or communities. In Sweden the high population of moose or "elk" has caused much damage to forests, especially to reforestation projects (see p. 161). Considerable damage has also been noted in Finland (Kangas, 1949).

Moose in most of North America have never created a similar problem but they apparently have been responsible for definitely altering the forest composition in some areas. The over-all and detailed effects of moose on the general environment cannot be determined in such a short study. A long-time study based on an adequate series of permanently fenced plots should afford data on a great many fundamental factors which directly or indirectly affect both the moose and the habitat. A few of these factors seem apparent on the basis of past studies.

On Isle Royale, Michigan, and perhaps St. Ignace Island, Ontario, moose have apparently been responsible for a great decimation and suppression of ground hemlock. The same applies to the aquatic plants, especially the water lily group. Several species of trees are being browsed to such an extent that normal regeneration is being inhibited or stopped almost completely. This seems especially true in the St. Ignace area of quaking aspen —this species has a very low resistance to browsing, and moose appear to be one of the chief factors responsible for its unusually low occurrence in shrub and sapling stages (Figure 51).

In the case of such species as mountain ash, which rarely attains a very large size it is more difficult to assess the effect of constant pruning by moose. The amount of heavy browsing observed on this species certainly must keep down the number that grow beyond the shrub stage. Aldous (1952) has shown, on the basis of his "clipping" studies, that it does not stand up well to constant browsing.

The species composition of an area is undoubtedly greatly affected by the differing abilities of various species to withstand constant heavy browsing by moose or other mammalian species. Continued close pruning of one species may frequently allow a related, less palatable species to become dominant. This seems particularly true of balsam fir and spruce in certain cases (Figure 52). Constant pruning of the annual growth and even partial destruction of balsam has allowed the unbrowsed spruces to dominate many local areas at a rapid rate.

Recent studies have shown that willow, white birch, beaked hazelnut, pin cherry, and mountain maple are fairly hardy and able to withstand browsing, while quaking aspen, mountain ash, red-osier dogwood, and red-berried elder have a low resistance to browsing (Aldous, 1952; Spencer and Chatelain, 1953; Kangas, 1949).

The preference of moose for semi-open areas or small clearings have frequently been effective in keeping such spaces open by constant browsing (Figure 53). In other areas certain species are so completely destroyed by such heavy use that an entirely new plant association may result.

Such changes may take the form of successional replacement by more hardy or by less palatable forest species. In certain cases moose appear to be a contributing factor in the establishment and maintenance of grassy swales and clearings within a boreal forest community.

Continued over-use results in a lowering of both the quantity and quality of available forage. Studies in Alaska by Spencer and Chatelain (1953) have shown that there is a consistent reduction in the protein content of such species as willow, birch, and cotton-wood with increased utilization by moose. They found that in old willow stands, "utilization will stop when an estimated 50 per cent of the year's growth has been consumed. This appears to be due partly to the growth habit of the bush and partly to the unpalatable nature of the remaining growth. However, younger growths are much more heavily utilized." (p. 545)

Preliminary investigations seem to suggest that in areas where an apparent balance of the moose population with the carrying capacity of the habitat exists, moose tend to help maintain or improve their own habitat conditions. In areas of extremely low populations the habitat usually matures or passes through normal successional stages to become less favourable for moose, while in over-populated areas moose may tend to suppress the regeneration of important moose foods, so that a less favourable forest composition, both in quantity and quality of foods available, may in turn result.

CHAPTER FIFTEEN

RELATIONSHIPS WITH OTHER ANIMALS

WITHIN LOCAL BIOTIC COMMUNITIES, the moose is in constant association with other animals, either directly or indirectly. The following consideration will be restricted largely to a few of the more direct relationships. These fall into two main categories—competitors and predators. In certain cases association with mutual benefit may exist. In others the associations are frequently so indirect or obviously of such minor importance that special attention has not been given them.

An important conflict between moose and other animals is one of competition for food. The most serious competition for food is usually in midwinter, by which time much of the succulent food has either disappeared or been eaten.

The question of predation has been considered, although extensive studies of this subject are much needed. The great diversity of opinions, especially among ecologists and sportsmen, has led to considerable controversy concerning its relative importance. It is not possible to settle this issue on the basis of present knowledge, although some light is shed on the role of predators in reducing the numbers of moose.

WHITE-TAILED DEER

Association, Dispersal, and Relative Abundance

The white-tailed deer of the Great Lakes region has followed a pattern of northward range extension similar to that of the moose (Cross, 1937) and is now commonly associated with the latter throughout much of its range. The greatest concentrations of deer in eastern North America are largely restricted to the Canadian biotic province and the southern fringe of the Hudsonian, although they are sparsely distributed throughout the southern half of the Hudsonian.

Within the Canadian biotic area as defined by Dice (1938, 1943) deer have been increasing at a fairly rapid rate within recent years, while moose have continued at a low level of population or have decreased. As early as 1932 the game authorities of Nova Scotia remarked on the enormous increase of deer and their possible effect on resident moose populations (Nova Scotia, 1932). The number of deer killed in that province has increased from 69 animals in 1918 to 29,280 in 1947 (Nova Scotia, 1948). From 1907 to 1918 the number of moose killed had increased steadily. Subsequently the number fluctuated but showed gradual decreases after 1931. A completely closed season was imposed in 1937 (Figure 54). Since that period the number of white-tailed deer killed increased at a remarkable rate, whereas moose showed some signs of increase but have failed to become numerous enough to warrant an open season (Nova Scotia, 1948).

Similar phenomena were observed in New Brunswick:

In the twenty year period 1890 to 1910 moose and caribou were plentiful in all sections of the province, living in the same kind of habitat and finding sufficient food for their individual requirements. Moose and Caribou do not compete for the same kind of food at any time or season. The deer had made their appearance in the years 1890–91, and were gradually spreading over the central and northern sections, but not yet in very great numbers. At that time they appeared to confine themselves to the big wooded areas rather than to the clearings and settlement areas. The first deer hunting licenses were issued in 1905.

From 1910 to 1930 a remarkable increase was noted in the deer population mostly restricted to the heavy wooded sections. It was during this period that the caribou started to show a gradual decline and eventually they disappeared entirely, the final migration taking place between the years 1920 and 1925, although a few small herds were seen up until 1927–28. The last open season for hunting caribou was in 1918 when less than 500 were shot.

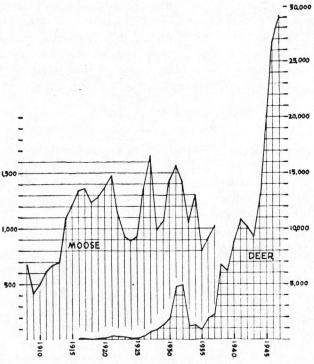

FIGURE 54.   Relative trends in the moose and deer populations (kill figures) of Nova Scotia (data from Nova Scotia, 1948)

It was between the years 1915 and 1920 that the ravages of the spruce bud worm killed off such large stands of fir or balsam, the staple winter food of moose, and forced these game animals to move from the wooded areas in the northern sections of the province to seek their food in the southern counties where the effect of the spruce bud worm was not so severe.

The state of Maine went through the same changes in game population as our province, only at an earlier period in its history, abundance of moose and caribou, introduction and gradual increase of deer in great numbers, followed by falling off in caribou and moose population and final disappearance of each species in the order as named. (New Brunswick, 1944, pp. 40–1)

The moose has not disappeared from Maine and, in fact, has shown recent signs of increase, but the total population remains relatively low in spite of long protection from hunting. The New Brunswick moose populations have shown recent signs of improvement but are still regarded as being too low for an open hunting season (New Brunswick, 1948).

In the Canadian biotic portion of Minnesota, Surber (Swanson, Surber, and Roberts, 1945, p. 23) discusses similar changes in big-game populations as follows:

It is therefore logical to believe the statement often made by old settlers in the region that sixty years ago they [moose] were comparatively scarce in the region eastward of Two Harbors, the common deer at that time being the caribou. As forest fires and lumbering drove out the caribou which were not destroyed by camp hunters, the moose became more common and in turn was replaced over much of its range by the white-tailed deer.

While the moose has been protected since 1922 it is doubtful if it has increased, taking the state as a whole, to any considerable extent since this law went into effect.

In the Algonquin Provincial Park of Ontario deer have become quite numerous while moose have remained relatively scarce in spite of long protection.

At the present time moose are apparently nowhere really abundant within the Canadian biotic portion of Ontario, except possibly in a few local areas east of Lake Superior. In most of the Canadian biotic province deer have recently increased at a rapid rate to create many over-populated deer ranges. An inspection of the map of over-populated or deer-problem areas prepared by Leopold, Sowls, and Spencer (1947) shows that over 95 per cent of these areas east of the Mississippi River are found within this biotic province.

On the St. Ignace group of islands which lie within the Hudsonian biotic province, moose are the dominant species, outnumbering white-tailed deer by approximately eight or ten to one in 1947–8. Both are recent immigrants to these islands, although deer apparently did not appear until about 25 years after moose first arrived.

The relationships between moose and deer are indeed complex and should be the subject of further study, although a few generalizations may be made at this point. During the summer months these two species seem quite compatible from a sociological point of view. They were frequently seen together at salt licks in the St. Ignace area (Figure 30), and they were often seen feeding within a few feet of each other in Algonquin Provincial Park. In the winter "yard" surveyed north of McIntosh Lake in Algonquin Provincial Park droppings of both moose and deer were found, although the two species were probably present in the area at different times. During the aerial survey of the park study area conducted on March 13, 1947, 22 deer were observed compared to 8 moose, although the two species were largely separated into different general areas. No deer were observed in the area where moose were most common. In aerial surveys of St. Ignace Island deer were not observed in local areas frequented by moose. Whether or not these limited observations have any significance is not known.

Competition

The most important ecological relationship between white-tailed deer and moose seems to be one of competition for food. Perhaps in a theoretical "balanced population," these two species could occupy the same general habitat without serious competition. Balsam fir, a winter food of key importance to moose, is generally considered as a starvation diet for white-tailed deer. On the other hand, white cedar rates as an important winter food for deer, while it is only an occasional food of moose, apparently being eaten in great quantity only to avoid starvation.

Of the ten food species listed by Swift (1946, p. 60) as "preferred" by deer only two (mountain ash and red-osier dogwood) are among the ten species providing the greatest amount of moose food in the St. Ignace area, although ground hemlock and red maple, listed among the "preferred" deer foods, are also choice moose foods and become important in the areas where sufficiently available. Hemlock and sumach also provide occasional food for moose as well as "preferred" food for deer.

Among the twenty species listed by Swift (1946) as "second choice" or "good" deer foods of Wisconsin, the following were also found to be among the moderate to choice moose foods: mountain maple, sugar maple, juneberry, cherry, willow, birch, hazelnut, aspen and high-bush cranberry. This list, ranked in Swift's order of deer preference, would be classified differently when considered as moose foods (see pp. 124–8). The remaining half of Swift's list of second-choice deer foods are practically all eaten occasionally by moose where available.

Studies of the fall and winter food habits of deer in northeastern Minnesota by Aldous and Smith (1948) have shown that deer feed on many important species of moose food such as balsam fir, mountain maple, white birch, mountain ash, and beaked hazelnut. They found that in the fall deer fed heavily on willow, quaking aspen, and balsam poplar but that these species were rarely eaten in winter.

In areas where either moose or white-tailed deer become abundant, there is little doubt that direct competition for the available food takes place, especially during the winter months. Given a "balanced ratio between the two" with an equal rate of reproduction, it might be assumed that moose, with the ability to reach higher, could gain the advantage over deer. This rarely seems to be the case within the Canadian biotic area. Rather it appears that the deer, with its higher biotic potential, is able quickly to outnumber the moose. Although unable to reach as high as moose for available foods, deer seem to have gained the upper hand by maintaining such high populations that they have been able to keep regeneration of seedlings and shrubs sufficiently low vitally to affect the food supply of moose. Preliminary studies seem to indicate that as long as white-tailed deer remain the dominant species with such large numbers in Algonquin Provincial Park, moose will not likely become generally abundant, other factors remaining essentially the same. Certainly this seems to have been an important factor in the past, as substantiated by the failure of moose to show any noticeable increase within the Park for a great many years. The failure of moose to regain big-game importance after long protection in Maine and Minnesota seems to reflect similar conditions. It would appear likely that in the once-famous moose-producing provinces of Nova Scotia and New Brunswick, moose will have great difficulty in ever attaining the high populations of former years as long as deer continue to thrive in such abundance. Many other influences make it unwise to attempt further speculation on the relative importance of either direct or indirect competition between deer and moose.

Whether or not the reduction of moose by hunting, diseases, or other factors, has had a significant effect in allowing deer to become dominant is not at present known. In the case of predation it would seem logical to assume that deer, being an easier prey for carnivores, would serve as a "buffer" diverting some predation pressure from moose. In the St. Ignace area several "deer kills" seem to indicate a much higher rate of reduction by wolves than in the case of moose. An examination of 83 wolf scats (79 from the St. Ignace area) showed remains of deer occurring in 45 instances compared to 28 in which remains of moose were found.

Summary

Within most of the Hudsonian biotic province of Ontario, deer have spread out and increased temporarily but apparently have not been able to maintain high populations in competition with moose. Undoubtedly there are several factors in addition to any existing competition that have served to limit deer in that area. In the St. Ignace area the few resident deer certainly find that the heavy moose population has seriously reduced most of the available food with the exception of white cedar. In other localities, especially in those adjacent to the Canadian biotic area, deer have shown several local increases. Possibly the entry of deer into most of the northern parts of the Hudsonian zone has been too recent for serious competition to be in evidence, although this seems doubtful. More data on the present status and possible ultimate future of white-tailed deer in that general region are needed.

In the Canadian biotic province deer have become the dominant big-game species where they have been able to compete successfully with moose for the available food. Direct competition between deer and moose seems to result when either species becomes especially numerous. The deer, with its greater biotic potential, has apparently been particularly adapted for conditions within the Canadian biotic province where it appears to have been an important factor in preventing moose from becoming generally abundant.

Woodland Caribou

As indicated in the discussion of the relationships between deer and moose, caribou were formerly the dominant big-game species throughout the Hudsonian zone of Ontario and the northern sections of the Canadian biotic province. This species is now almost completely absent from the latter area and is much reduced throughout most of the former. According to many older Indian and white residents of the Chapleau area (personal communication from Mr. V. Crichton), caribou were plentiful and moose unknown in that vicinity (apparently including most of the area north of Lake Superior) prior to about 1890.

The present caribou populations of Ontario are low and scattered (de Vos and Peterson, 1951). In the St. Ignace area a few have persisted in spite of invasion by moose and deer and of the development of high populations of the former.

So little is known of the ecology of woodland caribou that it is difficult to evaluate the relationships of the species with moose. In general it appears that direct competition is not a primary factor affecting the decline of caribou. The introduction of moose to Newfoundland has apparently had little detrimental effect on the native caribou herds, according to several reports. The most logical cause for the replacement of caribou by moose and deer seems to be one of change in the habitat. The period of great reduction of caribou and dispersal and increase of moose north of Lake Superior was preceded by the early "opening up" of that area by the building of railroad and subsequent logging and burning. Extensive fires seem to have destroyed the habitat favourable to caribou, and also destroyed the mosses and lichens which are reported to be their important winter foods. Their habitat was in turn replaced by a range ideal for moose.

Dufresne (1946) gives evidence of a similar replacement of caribou by moose in Alaska. He states that after a great fire burned over Kenai Peninsula, Alaska, in 1883, caribou vanished almost completely from the area and moose moved in and increased greatly.

The fact that most of the best-known isolated bands of caribou in Ontario are restricted to the small islands in Lake Superior and Lake Nipigon may well be correlated with the fact that these islands were not burned during big mainland fires. Little is known of the few remaining groups of caribou on the mainland, although recent reports indicate favourable herd conditions in the Red Lake district north of Kenora, Ontario (de Vos, 1948; de Vos and Peterson, 1951).

Perhaps caribou, because of their gregarious habits, require a much larger uninterrupted range than the more solitary moose; thus fire, commercial operations, and other factors have tended to divide and destroy the habitat for caribou while at the same time actually improving the conditions for moose.

WAPITI

Although wapiti have been introduced at several points in eastern North America, they have not increased to a point where they occur in substantial numbers in regions inhabited by moose. In the Rocky Mountains of western North America, wapiti and moose frequently occur together, especially in the national parks of both the United States and Canada. In such areas wapiti have frequently increased to such an extent that direct competition has resulted (Cowan, 1944, 1950). Murie (1951, p. 255) sums up his conception of the competition between these two species as follows: ". . . there is not much direct competition between elk and moose, for, although the moose is a heavy browser and has a somewhat specialized diet, and the elk, too, is a browser and inordinately fond of willows (the mainstay of moose), the moose uses as its winter range certain brushy areas in deep snow that the elk have not yet invaded to any great extent. In the Gros Ventre Basin, however, moose are coming in and are meeting the competition of elk."

Brown and Simon (1947) report that in Wyoming moose and wapiti are not directly competing with one another, although they admit that further increases in populations may create more direct and serious competition. They also report that when the two species occur together under artificial conditions elk are usually sociologically dominant over moose, forcing the latter to give way. Reports of apparently compatible relationships between these two species under natural conditions are common (West, 1941; and others).

McMillan (1938b) observed no antagonism between moose and wapiti and concluded that the only apparent factor which brought them in contact with each other was the presence of food. He sums up an attempt to measure the observed association as follows (p. 165): "The data show that there is an unilateral tendency of association on the feeding grounds. The elk are associated with moose as much as 62 per cent more frequently than could be expected by chance alone, whereas moose are associated with elk as little as 28 per cent as frequently as could be expected by chance. It appears to be evident that elk are using the moose range more heavily, resulting in damage which may seriously affect the Yellowstone moose population."

Timber Wolves

Although timber wolves are probably the most serious natural predators of moose, a thorough appraisal of their over-all effect on normal populations has still to be made. Timber wolves were observed in both major study areas of Ontario (8 in the St. Ignace area and 8 in Algonquin Provincial Park) and their "signs" were quite common. On three occasions during summer field work, wolves were observed in close association with moose without showing any signs of attacking the latter (see also p. 65). On July 12, 1946, a wolf was observed to pass within a few yards of a cow and twin calves feeding in the shallow water of the narrows between Longbow and Rosebary lakes in Algonquin Provincial Park. Each species was aware of the other but neither showed any apparent concern. The wolf was travelling along the shore close to the waterline and appeared to feed on frogs occasionally as it moved along. On July 29, 1946, a timber wolf (possibly the same one observed on July 12) was observed trotting along the north shore of Longbow Lake by my guide and assistant, Mr. Tom McCormick, Jr. As the wolf approached a cow moose feeding on the shoreline, it entered the bush to pass the cow and returned to the shoreline a few yards beyond. From all reports received, it appears that timber wolves may attack moose during the summer months but that such instances are uncommon. In the course of several other observations we found that the howling of wolves even at short distances from moose created no noticeable reaction on the part of the latter. It would appear that normally wolves find sufficient foods available during the summer months to make unnecessary the attacking of such difficult prey as moose.

Two important studies have been made which show some of the relationships between wolves and moose. Murie (1944) has carried out extensive observations on the wolves of the Mount McKinley region of Alaska, and Cowan (1947) has summarized results of research on the timber wolves in the Rocky Mountain national parks of Canada.

Stanwell-Fletcher (1942) reports that in central British Columbia timber wolves were commonly associated with moose in early winter but did not seriously hunt them until the latter part of January when moose found the supply of food running low and were forced to travel in exceptionally deep snow. He reports that several moose had been killed by wolves but also states that in certain cases the wolf had emerged "second best," citing examples of wolves having been injured or killed by moose.

Discussing the relationships between timber wolves and moose, Murie (1944, pp. 186–7) makes the following comments:

It would be highly significant to know the age and condition of the moose killed by the wolves, for possibly they were in a weakened state when killed. In the Mount McKinley National Park the snow depth is usually not great enough to hinder the moose as it does in the part of British Columbia referred to by Stanwell-Fletcher. But even in the latter region, where wolves, which were reported common, were killing the moose, it appeared that moose were not at all scarce.

Wolves perhaps worry many moose which fight them off with such vigor that they are unwilling to expose themselves to the deadly hoofs. However, if any sign of faltering is shown, due to old age, food shortage, or disease, the wolves would no doubt quickly become aware of it, and one would expect them to become more persistent in their attack in hope of wearing down the animal. Moose which are actually known to have been killed by wolves should be closely examined to determine their condition. Unfortunately in many cases the evidence is destroyed.

Granting that adult moose are difficult prey for wolves, one might suspect that young calves would be quite susceptible to wolf attack. However, a cow with a calf is a formidable creature and if molested by wolves would probably put up a vigorous fight to protect her young. I know of one case in which two Huskies, the size of wolves, attacked a cow with a calf. She held her ground beside her newly born calf and drove the dogs away. Nevertheless, we would expect that occasionally a calf would fall prey to wolves.

Although no precise data on survival of calves were obtained, it appeared that many calves were surviving in Mount McKinley National Park. More than half the cows seen, omitting known duplications, were followed by calves. Some interesting observations on calf survival in the ranges of the different wolf families were made.

In an area inhabited by a family of wolves on Savage River a cow and her twin calves were seen on August 14, 1940. She had raised them in an area where wolves traveled daily. During the winter tracks of calves were seen regularly in this general region.

Cowan (1947) presents data on the composition of the moose population in wolf-inhabited and wolf-free areas from which he concludes that wolves are not the critical factor influencing the survival of young moose to yearling age.

According to Murie (1944), Cowan (1947), and others, wolves hunting moose and other big game in winter usually go in "packs" of from 4 to 7 wolves, with a few instances of larger numbers being reported. But during the summer (Cowan, 1947, p. 159): ". . . wolves frequently hunt alone or in smaller groups and a lone wolf is capable of pulling down the largest of the game animals at present occurring in the Rocky Mountains. Several instances of single wolves killing moose and elk were noted."

Judging from several "wapiti kills," Cowan concluded that the usual method of attack was "from the rear and side with the wolf seizing the flank at the point where the leg joins the abdomen. A wound here lets the viscera out, with the opening of large blood vessels and reasonably rapid death" (p. 159). He reports that occasionally attacks were made at the throat or nose of the prey but in no case was there any evidence of hamstringing.

Moose are apparently most vulnerable to attack by wolves in late winter, especially when the snow is deep and sufficiently encrusted to bear the weight of wolves but not moose, or if they are driven onto stretches of ice: "Another hunting technique used in some instances is that of running game out onto the ice of frozen lakes and streams. Under slippery ice conditions ungulates are with difficulty able to run and not infrequently lose their footing and their lives" (Cowan, 1947, p. 161).

On even terms wolves frequently have great difficulty in attacking moose successfully. Cowan found that the top running speed of wolves under optimum conditions was only about 25 miles per hour whereas moose can easily exceed 27 miles per hour. He also reports that in the warmer winter months moose frequently avoid wolves by entering the nearest water where wolves will not follow.

Murie (1944) collected 1,174 wolf scats in the Mount McKinley area and found remains of moose in only 9 of them (.67 per cent of the total number of food items). In Jasper and Banff national parks Cowan (1947) collected 420 scats and found remains of moose in 26 (9 per cent) of the winter scats, and 6 (4 per cent) in the summer scats, giving a total occurrence of 7 per cent in the total annual diet.

From an examination of wolf scats, both summer and winter, Cowan (1947, p. 167) has concluded:

Thus on the basis of the scat analysis as also on the basis of the number of known wolf kills moose constitute the third item in importance in the annual diet, while it is fifth in abundance in the total game population. This is in contrast with conditions reported from the Mount McKinley district of Alaska, where wolves seldom bother moose.

Summer occurrences of moose are all those of moose calf remains. While it is certain that some calves are killed by the wolves, it should be borne in mind that the losses of moose calves to accidents are perhaps higher than similar losses in any other local species of big game. Carrion may well make up a fair part of the calf moose item. More than half of the occurrences of moose in winter scats also consists of calf remains.

In the area discussed by Cowan, several big-game species such as wapiti, deer, bighorn sheep, caribou, and mountain goat were also present, which undoubtedly diverted considerable predator pressure from moose.

An analysis by Mr. V. H. H. Williamson (MSS) of the contents of 30 stomachs of timber wolves taken in Ontario between November and March (Table XXII) shows that moose occurred in roughly 30 per cent of those containing food, compared to an occurrence of 52 per cent for white-tailed deer.

In the St. Ignace Island area of Ontario a total of 76 timber-wolf scats were collected during 1947 and 1948. The identified contents of these by rate are shown in Table XXIII.

The close similarity between the results of the stomach analysis and the scat analysis, regarding the ratio of moose and deer taken, is striking. In the St. Ignace Island area where moose were much more abundant than white-tailed deer, there can be little doubt that the pressure of predation is much greater on the deer than on the moose.

In parts of their range in the east, moose are the primary big-game prey, with only varying numbers of white-tailed deer and occasional caribou to provide alternate big game for the wolves. Consequently it seems logical to assume that a correspondingly higher pressure would be placed on the moose in such areas.

Although the over-all effect of timber wolves cannot be determined at

TABLE XXII

ANALYSIS OF CONTENTS OF 30 STOMACHS OF TIMBER WOLVES
FROM ONTARIO, NOVEMBER TO MARCH*

District	Examined	Empty	Species	Occurrence
Nipissing	10	4	Deer	4
			Varying hare	1
			Porcupine	1
Parry Sound	1		Moose	1
Sudbury	5		Moose	2
			Porcupine	2
			Deer	1
			Red fox	1
			Crayfish	1
Algoma	1		Moose	1
			Varying hare	1
			Porcupine	1
Thunder Bay	4		Moose	3
			Deer	1
Kenora	9	3	Deer	6

*Williamson (MSS).

TABLE XXIII

CONTENTS OF 76 TIMBER-WOLF SCATS, 1947 AND 1948*

Species	Total occurrences	Percentage occurrences
Deer	43	56.6
Moose	27	35.6
Beaver	8	10.5
Varying hare	1	1.3

*Williamson (MSS).

present, it seems significant that the St. Ignace area now supports both a high population of wolves and moose and has apparently done so for some time. Murie (1944) found a similar situation in Mount McKinley National Park in Alaska. Many data are needed on the selective factor of wolf kills. It has been argued that predators normally select the weak and the aged although proof of this logic is usually lacking. A great majority of the skeletal remains of moose found in the St. Ignace area were of old animals with well-worn teeth. The cause of death could not be determined in many cases but in others it was obvious that the animal had died of causes other than predation (Figure 55). If wolves were responsible for the death of many, it would appear that to a certain extent they selected the older weaker animals for prey. Certainly a number of apparently healthy adult animals are taken (Figure 56), but, as pointed out by Murie (1944), "it would be highly significant to know the age and condition of moose killed by wolves." For example, Mr. Joseph Pinette of Kapuskasing, Ontario, found a fresh wolf kill about March 18, 1947, in Seaton Township. He removed one of the lungs, which appeared to be diseased, and forwarded it to the Royal Ontario Museum of Zoology through the district office of the Ontario Department of Lands and Forests. Mr. Pinette remarked that he was of the opinion that the moose was sick, for it did not appear to have "put up much of a fight." He reported that he had examined the carcass for ticks but found none. He also remarked that several of the older moose appeared to suffer from the same lung disorder.

When the lung was examined in the museum laboratory it was found to be so completely filled with hydatid cysts of tapeworms that it seemed incredible that it could have functioned sufficiently to keep the animal alive during normal activity, much less allow it to ward off an attack by timber wolves (see p. 187). Well over 50 per cent of the volume of the lung was occupied by large cysts up to one inch in diameter.

Such examinations of a large series of wolf kills should provide considerable data of value in assessing the true effects of the predation of timber wolves on moose.

BLACK BEAR

The black bear is widely condemned as a killer of moose calves (see pp. 67–8). Such reports are much too persistent to disregard, although concrete evidence of predation is usually lacking. Even reports of bear killing adult moose are not uncommon. Such an account, received by the District Forester's office at Sioux Lookout, Ontario, was reported by letter as follows:

Mr. Peterson, foreman Camp 2, Alexander Clark Company, on the west side of Sturgeon Lake, approximately 40 miles east of Sioux Lookout, reports yearling Moose killed by bear about 100 yards from camp on June 27th, 1947.

FIGURE 55.   Skeletal remains of an adult bull moose that obviously died of natural causes during winter

FIGURE 56. A yearling female killed by wolves during winter

Mr. Peterson reports men heard moose bawling and went to investigate and actually chased bear from moose.

Mr. Vince Crichton, Fish and Wildlife Specialist with the Ontario Department of Lands and Forests, has also submitted information (personal correspondence):

In early June of 1944, train No. 1 was in the siding at Tophet to let train No. 4, east bound to Toronto, by. Tophet is about 20 miles east of Chapleau. While waiting for No. 4 to come, Engineer Hill Gagnon of Chapleau, J. Delaney, trainman of North Bay and Cliff Pearson baggageman of North Bay, these three making up part of the train crew proper, observed a young calf moose come out of the woods near the engine, and following was a bear. The bear caught up with the calf, hit it with it's front paw, and carried the calf off into the woods. The bear did not at any time drag the calf, but carried it.

Although bears do undoubtedly kill a certain number of calves in central Canada, no direct evidence was encountered in our Ontario studies. Most of the fresh summer bear droppings encountered in the field in early spring were examined in gross, but none contained moose material.

Cowan (1946) reports some evidence of predation by bears in the west. In Alaska, however, it is generally felt that the black bear is a serious decimating factor among moose calves, especially on the Kenai Peninsula (Sarber, 1944; Hosley, 1949; Chatelain, 1950).

Insufficient data are at present available to evaluate properly the extent and seriousness of predation on moose by black bear across the continent. Certainly there can be no doubt that bear do occasionally kill moose calves and even adults, but it seems likely that in many cases bear have been accused of killing moose on the evidence of tracks and droppings in the vicinity of moose carcasses, whereas actually they may only have fed on carrion.

Black bear were quite common in both the Algonquin and St. Ignace study areas of Ontario. In the latter, one summer resident reports having trapped over 40 bears with one trap, within a few hundred yards of his fishing camp, in the past 15 years. His report was corroborated to the extent that at least a dozen skulls of these trapped animals were collected in the vicinity of his trap.

It is, however, difficult to conceive that black bear, although numerous, have had any serious effect on the population of moose in the St. Ignace area, for it was rather high in 1947 and 1948. Possibly a small percentage of certain bear populations become "killers" by habit and thus account for a great majority of the known cases of predation on moose. More studies are seriously needed on the relationships between black bear and moose.

COYOTE OR BRUSH WOLF

The brush wolf is found commonly associated with moose in a great part of the latter's range, although it cannot be considered an effective predator of adult moose. Possibly a few calf moose are taken, although no evidence has been found to substantiate this.

Working in the national parks of western Canada, Hatter (1945) found that remains of moose, all assumed to be carrion, were found in both winter and summer coyote scats. He found remains of calf moose, also assumed to be mostly carrion, in 10 out of 218 scats, representing 4.5 per cent of the total scats and 3.7 per cent of 271 items found. Cowan (1944, p. 50) also reports similar results, with moose occurring in 15 per cent of 123 winter coyote scats and in 10 per cent of 49 summer scats.

Five summer scats contained moose remains. Three of these were of calf moose. In one instance the dropping contained calf moose remains associated with the remains of blow flies and their maggots. It seems reasonable to assume that this calf had been dead several days before it was eaten by the coyote. There was nothing to indicate whether the other two calves had or had not been killed by the coyote. Moose frequently hide their young and leave them for more or less extended periods. It would thus be quite possible for coyote to kill calves before the parent could interfere.

OTHER ANIMALS

The moose is commonly associated with a great many forms of animal life within various local communities from one general region to another. Each species has at least some indirect relationships to the moose and its habitat. As it is impractical to discuss even a few of these minor inter-relationships, the following discussion will be limited to those larger forms which appear to have a more direct effect on moose (see also pp. 161–2, 181–92).

In addition to the species listed below several others are found associated with the moose in various parts of its range. The extent of the ecological relationships of moose with the following forms requires additional study: mule deer, Newfoundland caribou, mountain caribou, barren ground caribou, wood bison, domestic livestock, and others.

Beaver

Moose and beaver often appear to be directly associated in a common habitat. In Algonquin Provincial Park, Ontario, where beaver were found in abundance, they appeared to affect moose in more than one way. Beaver dams are responsible for maintaining the water levels in streams and lakes, thus, in turn, allowing aquatic vegetation to be established and maintained as a source of food supply for moose during summer.

Occasionally, flooding of lowlands kills out some moose food plants, but as such, this appears to be of minor importance. On the other hand the maintenance of water levels in swampy areas undoubtedly increases the growth of various plants that moose use for food.

In the St. Ignace area of Ontario, beaver population were comparatively low, and there appeared to be some direct competition for food, especially for quaking aspen. The scarcity of this tree seems to be aggravated by the continued utilization in the past and present by both species. Moose have undoubtedly been responsible, in a large part, for reducing the regeneration of shrubs and saplings, while beaver are systematically removing the mature trees in the vicinity of beaver houses and dams. In more than a few instances we observed that, where beaver had recently cut mature aspen, moose had moved in and competed directly with them by stripping off leaves and chewing the bark from the trunk and the upper branches.

Varying Hare or Snowshoe Rabbit

During the course of studies in Ontario the snowshoe rabbit (*Lepus americanus*) populations were extremely low and thus no opportunity was available to check on possible competition between rabbits and moose. In Alaska, according to Dufresne (1942), the peak populations of snowshoe rabbits often reduce the growth of willow to such an extent that moose face starvation. Similar observations were made earlier by "An Alaskan" (1923). The latter remarked that rabbits were almost bringing famine to moose by feeding so heavily on "willows, birch twigs and leaves, alder bush, aquatic plants etc."

Wolverine

This animal has become so rare in eastern North America that it can no longer be considered a normal associate of moose in this area. Seton (1927) quotes the report of an instance of a wolverine attacking a moose. Cowan (1944) reports an authenticated case of a wolverine killing a bull moose in deep snow in Jasper National Park.

Grizzly and Brown Bear

Various currently recognized forms of either the grizzly or brown bear are found associated with the moose from the Rocky Mountains regions of Wyoming northward to Alaska. Cowan (1944) concluded that in the national parks of western Canada the grizzly bear was more serious than the timber wolf as a summer predator of moose. Brown bear were also considered a serious menace to calves in Alaska (Sarber, 1944; Chatelain, 1950).

Cougar

In the early days prior to settlement, the cougar may perhaps have been a predator of moose in eastern North America. In his account of the natural and civil history of the French Dominions Jefferys (1760, p. 35) makes the following comments:

The elk has other enemies that make as cruel a war on him as the Indians. The most dreadful of these is the Carcajou, or Quincauou, a species of the cat kind, the tail of which is so long as to wrap several times around his body; his hair is of a brownish red. As soon as this hunter comes up with the elk, he leaps upon him, fixes on his neck, round which he twines his long tail, and then cuts his jugular.

The name given the animal by Jefferys implies that the wolverine was the animal in question. However, the description, including that of the tail and colour, leaves little doubt that the cougar was intended.

Within a part of its range in the states and provinces of western North America, the cougar is found in the general vicinity of moose. The extent of its possible predation on the latter has not been thoroughly studied. Young's extensive review of this form (Young and Goldman, 1946) includes only one reference to predation on moose, that of Preble (1908), which was based on reports of Indians in the vicinity of Fort Liard, Northwest Territories. Apparently there is no authentic record of a cougar killing a moose.

CHAPTER SIXTEEN

DISEASES, PARASITES, AND INSECT PESTS

DISEASES

MOOSE ARE SUBJECT to a "moose disease" which seems to be manifested by a large variety of symptoms, including loss of the fear of man, weakened and emaciated condition, aimless wandering or refusal to leave a certain place, partial or complete blindness, travelling in circles, dropping of one ear, holding of the head to one side, partial paralysis of the limbs, and finally inability to rise or stand, followed by death. Thomas and Cahn (1932) described this as a new disease among moose in northwestern Minnesota and the adjacent region of Ontario. They noticed that the outbreak of the disease was coincident with the final metamorphosis of the tick *Dermacentor albipictus* into the adult stage, which occasionally heavily infests moose. They attempted to transmit the disease to guinea pigs and rabbits by using ticks from the dying animals, and found "bodies" in various host cells that they suspected were associated with the disease. They (Wallace, Thomas, and Cahn, 1932) then tentatively placed this "virulent organism" in the *Klebsiella* group but later (Cahn, Wallace, and Thomas, 1932) designated it as a new undescribed organism and gave it the name *Klebsiella paralytica*. This paper was followed by a detailed account of the experimental and cultural work in which they came to the following conclusion: "While we have not proved that *Klebsiella paralytica* is the cause of moose disease, we have presented a series of observations which strongly indicate that it may be the cause. The relationship of moose disease and the disease produced experimentally and discussed in this paper to 'tick paralysis' is suggested." (Wallace, Cahn and Thomas, 1933, p. 29)

Working independently on the disease of moose, Fenstermacher and Jellison (1933) were unable to effect a transmission of the infection in ticks (*Dermacentor albipictus*) to guinea pigs or rabbits and concluded several forces might be co-operating to reduce the vitality of moose for the observed symptoms to be produced. Carrying on further investigations, Fenstermacher (1934a, 1934b) concluded that moose are not affected with a disease of seasonal periodicity since he was able to find dead or sick moose every month of the year except July and August. He further showed that sick or dead moose were not necessarily infested with the tick *Dermacentor albipictus* and concluded that losses among moose were not the result of a single pathogen but rather a combination of factors. His findings were further supported by later studies (Fenstermacher, 1937; Fenstermacher and Olsen, 1942a) with inconclusive evidence that any one major disease caused mortality among moose.

A study of moose diseases in Maine by Lamson (1941) resulted in inconclusive findings similar to those of Fenstermacher and Jellison. He kept several sick moose in captivity and fed them a diet supplemented by foods high in vitamins, with some apparent success. He therefore suggested the possibility of nutritional deficiencies as a cause of moose losses.

Benson (1952) treated a sick moose in Nova Scotia with cobaltus chloride and found that it recovered within one week. He suggests that "moose sickness" may be correlated with cobalt deficiency.

King (1939) studied the brain tissues of diseased moose and found a sub-acute or chronic leuko-encephalitis but concluded there was "no evidence throwing satisfactory light on the etiology of this disease."

Blindness in moose has been reported by Murie (1951), who found "several" blind moose south of Yellowstone National Park in Wyoming.

Bang's disease has been reported in moose of Minnesota (Fenstermacher and Olsen, 1942a, b; 1943). In Montana (Jellison, Fishel, and Cheatum, 1951) further studies of this disease in moose revealed a case from Beaverhead County in which it was suggested that *Brucella abortus* was the probable cause of death. They carried out tests on 44 additional blood samples from moose killed by hunters and found 9 positive cases but the agglutination tests were so low that they were regarded as "of doubtful significance."

Tuberculosis in moose has been reported by Cowan (1951) on the basis of records from animals under semi-wild conditions near Wainright, Alberta.

Hatter (1948a) has reported a disease of the respiratory system of moose in British Columbia.

Cowan (1946) found one case of arthritis in moose in the western parks of Canada. He also suggested that actinomycosis possibly occurs in moose, and later (1951) recorded its occurrence in moose near Banff, Alberta.

Adolph Murie (1934) found cases of necrosis of bony tissue especially of the mandibles and regions adjacent to the upper molars. He reported that the lesions resembled those of necrotic stomatitis, although no causative organism was isolated. O. J. Murie (1951) reports that two moose died in captivity in Wyoming of necrotic stomatitis. He suggests that the infectious agent was *Actinomyces necrophorus* and states (p. 200) that ". . . the only cause to which the disease could be attributed was the oat hay (especially the seeds) fed to them." One instance of tooth decay, with necrosis and swelling of the region of the alveolus in the lower mandible, was found by the author in an adult bull from St. Ignace Island, Ontario. Another similar example from Rolph Township, Renfrew County, Ontario, is shown in Figure 57.

FIGURE 57. Necrosis in the lower jaw of a moose from Rolph Township, Renfrew County, Ontario

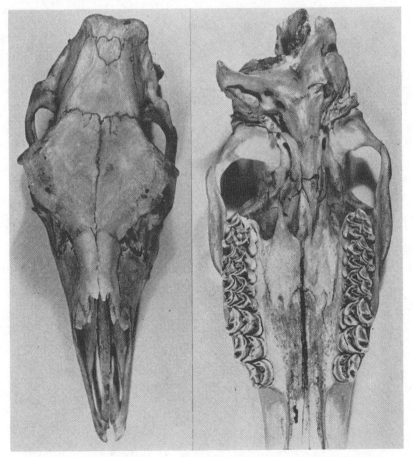

FIGURE 58. Abnormal development of the occipital region of a female moose from Lee Township, Timiskaming District, Ontario. The atlas is completely fused to the occiput

A most unusual abnormality in cranial development was observed in the case of a female 1½ years old taken on November 2, 1952, in Lee Township, Timiskaming District, Ontario (R.O.M.Z. no. 22476; see Figure 58). The atlas was completely fused to the occiput. Apparently the occipital condyles were never functional, as there is no sign of their development. The atlas is fused at an oblique angle in such a fashion as to necessitate the animal's holding its head rather sharply to the left. The entire basal portions of the skull had become asymmetrical. There was no apparent sign of injury and the animal had obviously been able to lead a fairly normal existence for several months. It seems likely that this condition was the result of some pre-natal abnormality.

Contagious warts or tumours affecting the skin only were found in "many cases" of moose from the Chilcotin, Cariboo, and Windermere areas of British Columbia (Cowan, 1951).

Mr. F. J. Johnson, Fish and Wildlife Overseer, of Oba, Ontario, reported (personal communication) that a trapper encountered a diseased cow moose in Wallis Township on March 10, 1949. The animal charged the trapper as he approached but later lay down in the snow. The trapper decided the moose should be killed and reported that it made no attempt to arise before or after it was shot with a .22 calibre rifle. Mr. Johnson later went to the area and secured the lungs, stomach, and head, which were then shipped to the Royal Ontario Museum of Zoology. The animal was heavily infested with ticks. No internal parasites were found in the lungs, but there was evidence that suggested the animal was suffering from pneumonia.

Another interesting case was received from the Geraldton district office of the Ontario Department of Lands and Forests. A sick calf was found lying down in Legault Township. The animal was loaded on a truck and taken to the Pine Ridge base in Geraldton where the animal died after 19 hours. Mr. H. E. Deedo, District Fish and Wildlife Specialist, examined the animal and a part of his report is as follows:

The moose was very heavily infested by ticks. These ticks were all over the animal. Hair could be plucked by the handful from this animal and hair was falling out of the flanks. Upon examination of the roots of the hair there appeared to be something there that looked like dandruff. There was no fight in the moose when captured and the animal was breathing very hard and with difficulty. There was a pocket of green pus more like a thin jelly between the lungs and ribs. Lungs were pinkish with red spots. When hands were placed on the stomach, after the moose died, the fingers easily punctured the stomach casing. When alive there was good movement of the bowels from the moose. The bladder was full and apparently this moose was unable to pass urine as there was no evidence of such while the moose was at the Pine Ridge base. I may add that all the hair on his entire buttock area was rotten. There was a scar on the hump between his shoulders and right on the back bone. The scar was about 4 inches long and there was a scab formed on the wound.

Several observers (personal communications) report that, on the basis of gross examination in the field, the lungs and liver of diseased moose usually show some form of abnormality. Mr. Hugh R. Conn and Mr. J. N. Stevenson, Fur Supervisors of the Indian Affairs Branch of the Dominion Department of Mines and Resources, forwarded reports of several dead moose in the vicinity of Fumerton Lake, 50 miles northwest of Amos, Quebec, during the spring of 1948 (personal communications). Mr. Stevenson was able to obtain one of these carcasses and forward it intact to the Royal Ontario Museum.

Dr. J. F. A. Sprent of the Ontario Research Foundation kindly consented to supervise the autopsy of this specimen. No specific cause of death could be determined, but the results of Dr. Sprent's findings are summarized below:

General appearance. Dismembered carcass. Young female (approximately 20 months old) found dead during March, 1948. Weight approximately 600 pounds.

Carcass. Normal. No external parasites present.

Mucous membrane of head region. Red areas on the nasal mucosa, inner surface of the lips, and outer margins of the gums.

Respiratory system. Trachea and larynx normal, lungs showed red hepatisation and fibrinous pleuritis with adhesions between the costal and diaphragmatic pleural surface.

Circulatory system. The endocardium was a uniform deep red colour. There was no pericarditis.

Alimentary system. The fore stomachs were impacted (weight of entire stomach with contents 117 pounds) but the intestines were normal. Areas of redness were evident on the ruminal mucosa.

Other organs. There was extreme degeneration of the liver and kidneys.

Diagnosis. Acute infectious disease affecting especially the respiratory organs.

Experimental. ½ cc. of the heart blood of the moose was injected intraperitoneally into two guinea pigs; both were dead the next morning. From the heart blood of one of these, bacterial colonies were obtained by culture on blood agar. The colonies were of two types: (1) small round grey colonies; (2) large round yellowish colonies. The former was a large bacterium and probably a contaminant, the latter was a coccobacillus usually associated in pairs. Broth cultures made from these cultures appeared to be harmless when reinoculated into guinea pigs.

Nematodes. Nematodirus sp. *Setaria* sp.

Trematodes. Paramphistomum cervi.

The extent of mortality from disease is not known. The answers to a special questionnaire in Ontario showed that 21 observers had encountered diseased moose during 1946–7, whereas 115 had not. In reply to a question about deaths of moose from past epizootics, 29 observers reported personal knowledge of such occurrences, whereas 90 reported none. When asked if the diseased moose were parasitized by ticks, 37 observers reported ticks on diseased animals and 37 reported no ticks. Observers reporting big dieoffs in the past listed the following years:

1920–0	1924–0	1928–1
1921–1	1925–0	1929–0
1922–1	1926–0	1930–0
1923–2	1927–1	1931–0

1932–0	1938–5	1944–2
1933–4	1939–3	1945–1
1934–2	1940–0	1C46–1
1935–5	1941–3	1947–0
1936–6	1942–2	
1937–5	1943–0	

In spite of considerable research, the specific cause or causes of the diseases of moose have not yet been isolated. It seems probable, as has been suggested, that several factors are involved.

EXTERNAL PARASITES

Dermacentor albipictus. The only external parasite of serious importance that has been reported on moose of North America is this winter or moose tick. As suggested above, the over-all effect of tick parasitism is not yet known. Heavy infestations have been reported from widely scattered areas across Canada in past years. The heaviest infestations were coincident with high populations of moose. Judging from questionnaire reports and other personal communications, general heavy infestations of ticks have not occurred in Ontario in the past ten years, although several reports of heavily infested animals were received during the spring of 1949. Most Ontario observers agree that the heaviest infestations are found in late winter, at which time the host, while bedding down, frequently leaves blood-stained areas in the snow from crushed ticks and tick wounds.

Ticks were observed in the St. Ignace area on June 2, 1947, on a single adult bull which harboured only three visible specimens. In addition one tick was found on May 18 attached to a tuft of moose hair scraped off on the branch of a fallen tree. Two other specimens were collected from the ground in the vicinity of a salt lick on Simpson Island on May 25 and June 1, 1947.

Apparently the heaviest infestations known in Nova Scotia were those reported between 1930 and 1935 (Nova Scotia, 1932, 1936). In Ontario, the last major outbreaks appear to have taken place between 1933 and 1939. Cowan (1944) reported serious tick infestations in moose in the national parks of western Canada in 1943. Hatter (1948a) also reported heavy infestations in British Columbia and concluded that the winter tick "appears to be the most serious parasite of British Columbia moose." According to Cowan (1951, p. 42) "this tick is the most harmful of all moose parasites and probably causes more losses than all other parasites and diseases combined."

In the course of his investigations of wapiti, Murie (1951) found no case in which the effects of ticks could be isolated as the cause of death, although he states (p. 166) ". . . ticks were suspected of being the chief agent in the death of one young moose."

In summary, it seems logical to assume that the most serious effects of tick parasitism are manifested in the reduction of the vitality of moose, making them more vulnerable to other factors, such as diseases, predation, abortion, and malnutrition.

Dermacentor andersoni. The paralysis tick or Rocky Mountain fever tick has been found on moose and other big-game hosts in the drier parts of southern British Columbia and southwestern Alberta (Cowan, 1951).

INTERNAL PARASITES

Sarcocystis sp. A diseased moose killed near Shebandowan, Ontario, on November 12, 1948, exhibited a number of round and oval bodies enclosed in thin capsules in the cardiac muscle of the heart (de Vos and Allin, 1949). Prepared sections of the muscle were submitted for identification to Dr. A. Murray Fallis, Director of the Department of Parasitology of the Ontario Research Foundation. Dr. Fallis concluded that the bodies were a fungus *Sarcocystis.*

A second report of this organism was made by Kelly *et al.* (1950). The host was a captive moose originating in British Columbia. "Autopsy showed marked endocardial hemorrhage with no reason for it. There was no evidence of a struggle, and he was in good condition. There were no ticks on him, nor internally, any hydatid cysts. Heart sections, however, contained small oval patches which have been identified as *Sarcocystis.* Whether this fungus organism, long thought to be a sporozoan, was the cause of death, can only be speculative." (p. 463)

Paramphistomum cervi. Examination of the stomach of an adult bull moose collected on St. Ignace Island, September 17, 1947, revealed a heavy infestation of the rumen fluke. Great numbers were noted to be mixed indiscriminately throughout the food contents and none seemed to be attached to the stomach walls. Similar infestations were found in the stomach contents of an adult bull killed by Mr. L. Hemphill near Elsas, in Gogama forest district, Ontario, October 15, 1947, as well as in a young female found dead near Fumerton Lake (early March, 1948), and a third specimen from near Geraldton, Ontario (late March, 1948). No lesions, which might be attributed to these parasites, were observed in any of these animals. The stomachs of 22 additional animals were examined in connection with studies of food habits, but no rumen flukes were found. In 30 cases examined in Minnesota by Olsen and Fenstermacher (1942) this species occurred in 9 instances. They state that "Seyfarth (1938) reported that calves of *A. alces* infected with large numbers of the rumen fluke, became so emaciated as the results of wide spread destruction of the stratum corneum of the rumen that they had to be killed. No evidence of such lesion was observed in *A. americana*."

Apparently *P. cervi* has no major effect on the adult moose population.

Fascioloides magna. Olsen and Fenstermacher (1942) found this liver fluke in 4 of 33 specimens examined. In one case they attributed the death of the host to this species.

In Ontario studies, this fluke was found in only one instance, although studies by Dr. A. A. Kingscote of the Department of Parasitology, Ontario Veterinary College, have revealed positive tests for *F. magna* from fecal samples of moose collected in the Pipestone Crown Game Preserve (personal communication).

In the one case in which the adult flukes were found in Ontario studies, the host was found dead some 20 miles east of Kenora. Mr. K. Acheson, Regional Forester, provided the following information (personal letter):

This animal had been observed on the ice of Narrow Lake for about a month prior to its death. It would stand almost motionless for long periods. When feeding, it moved only to the edge of the lake to feed on the browse growing on the banks.

Those who first noticed it and reported it to the Department, assumed it had been struck by the train or by a truck. When our officers investigated, they found it apparently capable of providing for itself. When approached, the moose fled into the bush. So we dismissed the matter. Its presence on the lake was reported, however, until its death.

The viscera were kindly forwarded by officials of the Department of Lands and Forests to the Royal Ontario Museum of Zoology. The liver was in turn forwarded to Dr. Fallis at the Ontario Research Foundation who verified the identity of the flukes in question. It seems quite probable that they were a major contributing factor to the death of this animal.

Cowan (1951) records *F. magna* in moose taken near Golden, British Columbia.

Echinococcus granulosus. The hydatid cyst of this tapeworm was the most common parasite found in Ontario studies. Cysts were found in the lungs of a moose killed by Dr. B. J. Woods in Denyes Township, Chapleau forest district, on November 5, 1946. Dr. A. Murray Fallis of the Ontario Research Foundation kindly identified this as well as the following specimens.

A lung of a moose killed by wolves during March, 1947, in Seaton Township, Kapuskasing forest district, and submitted by Mr. Joseph Pinette, was heavily parasitized (see p. 176).

Both the lungs and liver of a moose killed in Kohler Township, Kapuskasing forest district, on October 25, 1947, contained several cysts of this species.

Mr. A. de Vos examined the viscera of a moose shot near Hogarth in Port Arthur forest district on October 17, 1948, and found several cysts.

He also reported (personal letters) two other occurrences of this species, one in the lungs and liver of a diseased moose which he killed near Shebandowan, Port Arthur forest district, on November 12, 1948, and the other in the liver of a moose killed by a hunter near Ear Falls in Sioux Lookout forest district on November 22. These specimens were subsequently submitted to Dr. Fallis for identification.

A sick animal was killed and autopsied near Sudbury for the Department of Lands and Forests on July 12, 1950, by a local veterinarian, who reported the presence of these cysts.

Sweatman (1952) has carried out additional studies in which he found the cysts in 17 cases out of 29 moose examined in Ontario. He also reports on records made on Isle Royale, Michigan, in which 5 out of 8 moose contained *Echinococcus*.

Hadwen (1933), reported this parasite in moose taken at The Pas, Manitoba, in 1929. Law and Kennedy (1933) have reported heavy infestation of hydatid cysts in Ontario moose. Early reports of occurrence in moose from Minnesota were given by Riley (1933, 1939) and Olsen and Fenstermacher (1942) found this species in 12 out of 33 possible cases in that state. Lamson (1941) reported no hydatid cysts in the moose autopsied in Maine, although he stated that a small number of unidentified cestode cysts were observed in the livers of 3 specimens. Hatter (1948a) found *E. granulosus* in moose from British Columbia and concluded it was the only internal parasite that might be seriously affecting the welfare of moose there.

In Alaska, Spencer and Chatelain (1953) found 4 cases out of 11 examined from the Susitna region. Rausch (1952) has expressed a doubt concerning the seriousness of the effects of this parasite on moose in Alaska. He reports it to be common in moose near Palmer, stating that ". . . almost every aged moose is infected and I estimate that the larva may be found in at least 50 per cent of the adult animals" (p. 170)

Rausch (1952) has provided a general review of this parasite in boreal regions. He found no record of its occurrence in moose in the Old World.

Sweatman (1952) has reviewed the distribution and incidence of *Echinococcus granulosus* in man and other animals in North America and has pointed out the close relation between the occurrence of the adult form in wolves (particularly *Canis lupus*) and the larval stage in moose. He found no record of infection in moose in regions where there are no wolves, that is, east of the St. Lawrence River.

Taenia krabbei. Cysticerci were found in the skeletal muscles of a young bull killed April 16, 1947, in Hall Township near Biscotasing in Chapleau forest district. Mr. Donald White, Wildlife Overseer with the Ontario Department of Lands and Forests, reports that when he found the moose, which had been recently killed by a bear, he attempted to dress the animal but found the flesh to be contaminated. Samples of the parasites were kindly examined by Dr. A. Murray Fallis, who tentatively identified them as this species. Since the samples had been previously preserved in formalin no further check or identity could be made by experimental infection.

Cowan (1946) reports this species in caribou from the Rocky Mountain national parks of Canada, but it apparently had not been previously reported in moose.

Taenia ovis. Cowan (1951) groups this species with *T. krabbei* since the cysts are indistinguishable and quotes Hatter (1950) as follows: "35 per cent of the guides hunting in wolf inhabited areas [British Columbia] reported moose with tapeworm cysts in the muscle tissue."

Taenia hydatigena. Olsen and Fenstermacher (1942) report that the cysticercus (*C. tenuicollis*)found in the liver of moose developed into *T. hydatigena* in dogs in 63 days. They found only one case of parasites in skeletal muscles in Minnesota and concluded that they were also *T. hydatigena.* They also reported cysticercus in the mesentery and in the cardiac muscle and found 13 cases of infection in various body localities out of 34 examined. Wardle (1933) also suggests *T. hydatigena* as the form found in the muscles of moose in Alberta. Cowan (1951, p. 50) states that it is ". . . abundant throughout the wolf inhabited areas of Alberta and B.C., scarcer where wolves are absent."

Thysanosoma actinoides. The adult form of this fringed tapeworm was reported by Dikmans (1939) in a moose in Yellowstone National Park. Cowan (1951) found this species in other big game but not in moose in Alberta and British Columbia.

Moniezia benedeni. This species occurred in adult form in the small intestines of 5 of 31 moose examined in northern Minnesota by Olsen and Fenstermacher (1942). Cowan (1951) records it in moose from near Wistaria, British Columbia. Hatter (1948a) reports this genus (presumably this species) in moose in central British Columbia.

Moniezia expansa. Fenstermacher and Olsen (1942a) report this species in one Minnesota moose, but omit it from their list of parasites (Olsen and Fenstermacher, 1942).

Cysticercus sp. Olsen and Fenstermacher (1942) report two occurrences of an additional bladderworm in the liver of Minnesota moose. Wallace (1934) reported a cysticercus resembling *C. cellulosae* in the cardiac muscle of two moose in Minnesota, but these specimens were probably referable to *Taenia krabbei.*

Dr. A. E. Allin found cysts in the sections of cardiac muscle of the moose collected at Shebandowan, Ontario (see p. 186). These sections were submitted to Dr. Fallis, who concluded that they were probably *Taenia* but that further identification was impossible from the material examined.

Trichuris sp. Olsen and Fenstermacher (1942) report the whipworm in one Minnesota moose. Lamson (1941) referred an occurrence of this genus in the moose of Maine to *T. ovis.*

Oesophagostomum venulosum. This nodular worm was reported in the colon of a Minnesota moose in one instance (Olsen and Fenstermacher, 1942).

Haemonchus contortus. Ransom (1911) mentioned the moose as a host of this stomach worm and indicated that he had examined several specimens taken from this host. No further record of this parasite in moose appears to be available.

Nematodirus sp. Nematodes found in the intestines of the specimen from Fumerton Lake, Quebec (see p. 184), and in a calf taken February 23, 1949, from Township 11B in the Chapleau district, were referred to this genus by Dr. Sprent. Cowan (1946, 1951) found this genus (*N. fillicollis*) in the mountain sheep and the mountain goat, but it apparently has not been previously reported in moose.

Nematodirella longispiculata. This intestinal nematode was found in almost half the hosts from Minnesota examined by Olsen and Fenstermacher (1942). Cowan (1946, 1951) reports this species in a single moose examined in the western parks of Canada, and Lamson (1941) also reports it in moose in Maine.

Elaphostrongylus sp. This genus was found in the anterior chamber of the eye of a single moose in Minnesota (Olsen and Fenstermacher, 1942).

Ascaris sp. This genus was reported in one instance in the intestine of a moose from Minesota (Olsen and Fenstermacher, 1942).

Dictyocaulus viviparus. Olsen and Fenstermacher (1942) report this lung-worm in 14 out of 33 moose examined in Minnesota. Lamson (1941) reports *D. hadweni* in moose in Maine, although Olsen and Fenstermacher, as well as others, considered that form to be a synonym of *D. viviparus.*

Wehrdikmansia cervipedis. This legworm has been reported in moose in central British Columbia by Hatter (1948a). According to Cowan (1951) this specimen came from the Ootsa Lake region in 1946.

Setaria labiato-papillosa. Fenstermacher and Olsen (1942a) report this species in the peritoneal fluid of two moose from Minnesota, although Olsen and Fenstermacher (1942) did not include it in their list of parasites for moose.

Setaria sp. An unidentified species apparently of this genus was found in the intestines of the moose from Fumerton Lake, Quebec, autopsied by Dr. Sprent and the writer (see p. 184).

Cephenemyia sp. Olsen and Fenstermacher (1942) found no record of the larval stage of this bot fly in moose in North America. Lamson (1941) reports the occurrence of 11 bots in a moose from Maine taken on May 29, 1937, 1 in the ethnoid cavity, 3 in the posterior nares, and 7 in the pharynx.

A specimen secured in the Sioux Lookout region (11 miles north of McDougall Mills, Ontario) on April 12, 1950, contained a heavy infestation of bots in the throat and posterior nares. Specific identity of these bots has not yet been possible.

Cowan (1951) cites a record from Hatter (1950) of *Cephenemyia jellisoni* from a single moose taken near Quesnel, British Columbia, in 1948.

Warble fly. Apparently the warble fly larva has not been reported in moose in North America. Mr. Harry Mason of Hearst, Ontario, reports (in answer to a special moose questionnaire) that the backs of moose, especially yearlings, are often covered with lumps containing warbles which emerge to develop as adults about May. Other general references by Ontario observers to warble fly larvae in moose suggest that further study of such possible occurrences should be made. Cowan (1946, 1951) reported heavy infestations of *Oedemagena tarandi* in mountain caribou, but did not observe them in moose.

INSECT PESTS

During the warm days of the summer months moose appear to be almost constantly annoyed by various flies and mosquitoes. Although a great majority of the natural history accounts of moose consistently report that moose enter water to seek relief from insect pests, all observations during Ontario studies indicate that they usually enter a body of water either to swim across or to feed on aquatic vegetation. This same conclusion was reached by Murie (1934). Murie cites only one instance in which he felt that a moose actually sought refuge from insect pests by entering water.

Shiras (1935) and Kellum (1941) each report that moose occasionally obtain relief from insect pests by means of a coating of mud which is acquired by lying down in mud holes. Kellum (1941) states captive moose spent hours lying with only a part of their heads above the mud and water of a millpond. Such behaviour was not noted by the author.

Although several species of insects annoy moose, the most serious pest noted in the St. Ignace area of Ontario was the moose fly (*Lyperosiops alcis*). Several specimens of this fly were collected by overtaking swimming moose with the aid of an outboard motorboat and collecting directly from the head region of the moose. Specimens were submitted to Dr. G. E. Shewell of the Division of Entomology, Department of Agriculture, Ottawa who verified their identification. Murie (1934) collected a specimen of this fly from a moose on Isle Royale in 1929 and comments on the fact that since its original description until that time this insect had been regarded as a "lost species." In the original description, Snow (1891, pp. 87–8) made the following comments on the habits of this fly on moose of the cranberry swamps of northern Minnesota:

The flies were noticed first upon skinning the first moose, when a number of them were discovered in the animal's rectum, into which they had crawled for two or three inches in order to deposit their eggs in the excreta. The dejecta upon the ground were also found to contain hundreds of the eggs. Altogether nineteen moose were killed and in almost every case these flies were observed about them, remaining upon their carcasses as long as they lay unskinned, which was often twenty-four to thirty hours. For some time after the death of the animal, the *Haematobiae* could be seen only with difficulty, concealed as they were by the mosquitoes which were incredibly numerous, lingering in clouds upon the dead moose as long as any of its juices could be extracted. The flies seemed to prefer the regions of the head, rump and legs where the hair is shortest.

In the course of our observations we noticed that many of the moose had raw or open spots on their hind legs, especially above the calcaneum. Many of the wounds were from one to two inches in diameter, appearing as pinkish spots except when covered with flies. Later in the fall most moose showed scabs or scars in this same general region from about four to ten inches above the calcaneum. Murie (1934) observed lesions of the same sort on Isle Royale moose, and Shiras (1935) also comments on a similar condition found on moose. Apparently these spots on the hind legs are the result of the persistent feeding of the moose fly (*Lyperosiops alcis*).

Olsen and Fenstermacher (1942) include the black fly (*Simulium venustum*) among the parasites on moose in Minnesota, on the basis of one occurrence on the skin. As they suggest, "the relationship may have been purely coincidental."

CHAPTER SEVENTEEN

ACCIDENTS

WHEN APPRAISING THE OVER-ALL FACTORS contributing to the mortality of moose, it appears that some special attention should be devoted to the deaths resulting from ordinary accidents.

Drowning seems to be an important factor in calf losses, and appears frequently to become significant in adult deaths during early or late winter as a result of falling through thin or bad ice on lakes and streams.

When local observers were asked in a special questionnaire if they had observed cases of moose losing their life by falling through thin or bad ice, 68 reported in the affirmative and 70 in the negative.

Mr. D. Morgan, Fish and Wildlife Overseer at Oba, Ontario, found an adult cow trapped by ice in the Oba River, Irvine Township, during the last week of November, 1947. She had fallen through the ice in the centre of the river and was unable to gain shore because the ice was about three inches thick. Mr. Morgan reports that the animal appeared in excellent physical condition, and he was able to remove the stomach and ship it to the Royal Ontario Museum.

Oberholtzer (1911) remarks on moose falling through thin ice in western Ontario.

Mr. George Phillips, District Forester at Algonquin Provincial Park, related an interesting instance in which he found a cow moose frozen in a lake (personal communication). From the tracks in the snow it was apparent that two moose had started across the lake and had come to the opposite side near the inlet of a creek, where both animals broke through the ice. By sheer strength one animal had broken the ice toward open water and had "ploughed" a trail to the mouth of the creek where it was able to get out. It then, apparently, had circled back on the hard ice of the lake, making several circles of tracks. The second animal, a cow, had almost reached open water but had apparently turned back toward the first moose as if to follow it. As the cow "ploughed" further toward the middle of the lake the ice became thicker. Apparently she finally became exhausted and was completely frozen with only her outstretched head above the ice when found.

A third interesting account which seems worthy of record was received from Mr. Bill McLeod, Deputy Chief Ranger with the Ontario Department of Lands and Forests at Nicholson. He related having observed three or four moose attempt to cross a river on fairly thin ice on an extremely cold morning in early winter. Several attempts were made, but each time the animals would turn back after reaching unsafe ice. One big bull finally ventured as far as midstream, where he broke through. He tried to get back up on the ice, but the water kept splashing and freezing on his antlers. After he had struggled for some time the accumulation of ice on his antlers became so great that he was no longer able to keep his head up, and he finally drowned in the deep water.

Hosley (1949) remarks on the heavy mortality in Alaska from animals venturing out on thin ice on lake outlets, rivers, and creeks. Hatter (1948a) also comments on similar losses in British Columbia.

These observations seem to indicate that such loss of life is not uncommon among moose. Undoubtedly in many cases the animals are able to extricate themselves, but it would seem logical to assume that individuals in poor physical condition would be subject to a higher mortality rate from drowning than those in normal health.

According to Murie (1934), a similar differential mortality applies to moose that become mired in deep marshes and bogs. He found cases of death on Isle Royale which appeared to be the result of animals becoming mired and unable to free themselves. Munro (1947) found similar instances in British Columbia.

The accidental death of bull moose from fighting is another factor difficult to evaluate. In reply to a questionnaire, 56 out of 139 Ontario observers reported having observed instances of moose losing their lives from fighting. No actual cases were observed in our Ontario studies. However, Cowan (1946) concluded that such occurrences must be fairly frequent. During only two seasons of work in the western parks of Canada, he found three instances of males having locked their antlers. Cahalane (1947, p. 45) provides the following account:

When two moose in western Alaska once locked horns, Jack Benson, a game warden, happened to notice them from an airplane. Immediately he ordered the plane to land. The smaller bull was already dead but the other continued to struggle with the carcass to which he was bound. Jack and his assistants lassoed him and after herculean efforts succeeded in sawing off an antler and thus dislodged the dead bull. Free, but annoyed by the loss of his antler and the whole situation, the great moose took after his benefactors. They were able to escape uninjured.

Forest fires cause the death of an unknown number of moose. During the fires in the Chapleau district of Ontario in 1948 a few moose were reported to have been so badly burned that the fire fighters were obliged to kill them.

Collision with trains is a common cause of death. Mr. Vince Crichton, Fish and Wildlife Specialist, has kept a check on the number of moose killed on approximately 127 miles of railroad between Chapleau and White

River, Ontario (personal communications). Seven moose were killed during May and June, 1946, 8 in one week ending July 12, 1947, and 12 in one week ending June 18, 1948. A total of 24 animals were known to have been killed in this area in 1948, and 18 in 1949. He reports that as many as 16 animals were known to have been killed during one spring with a probability that several others had escaped notice. On the railway from Cartier to Chapleau (136 miles) 3 moose were killed in 1948 and 2 in 1949. Mr. A. G. McDonald reports (personal communication) that at least 5 moose were killed by trains on the Canadian Pacific Railway between Amyot and White River, Ontario, during the early part of the summer of 1948. Mr. R. H. Hambly, District Forester from the White River district of Ontario reports (files, Dept. of Lands and Forests) that 16 moose were reported killed in the spring of 1950 between Price and Goudreau on the Algoma Central Railway and between Ryerson and Pic on the Canadian Pacific Railway. He also estimates that about 10 were killed between Bremner and O'Brien near White River. Cowan (1946) estimated that approximately 20 to 30 moose were killed annually by trains in Yoho National Park. Atwood (1952) estimates that up to 200 moose are killed each year by trains in Alaska. Mr. Crichton reports that most moose are killed at night and in the early morning when the animals appear to become confused by the light of the oncoming trains, although a few were known to have been killed during daylight.

Moose are not infrequently involved in collisions with automobiles which add still more to the numbers killed in accidents.

To these more-or-less ordinary accidents there must be added innumerable less common, or unusual, mishaps. It is impossible to determine what the rate of loss from accidents is, but perhaps it should be given approximately the same importance as losses from predation and diseases.

CHAPTER EIGHTEEN

POPULATION STUDIES

ONE OF THE MOST IMPORTANT, yet most difficult, tasks involved in studies of animals under natural conditions is an accurate count or census of populations. The fluctuations in animal populations are often so great from year to year, from season to season, and even from week to week that limited absolute counts become little more than relative indices to changing populations.

Perhaps more important, from the standpoint of field studies, are reliable indices to the normal average and the normal maximum carrying capacities per unit area of various types of habitat. These also fluctuate greatly from one locality to another, but they tend to give a working basis for comparison of population densities or population trends either from area to area or from season to season. "Normal" population density for the purposes of the following discussion is here defined as the average number of animals that voluntarily remain in any given comparatively large unit area during all seasons for a period of years without causing serious damage to the habitat.

POPULATION DENSITY

Moose, being large animals, apparently require a comparatively large minimum area per animal, and the population does not normally increase beyond this density in spite of optimum habitat conditions. Abnormally high moose concentrations usually appear to develop (1) in artificial or natural isolation, for instance on islands, where dispersal is impracticable or impossible (Isle Royale in Lake Superior provides an excellent example); (2) as enforced seasonal concentrations, for instance in restricted winter ranges in the mountain regions; or (3) as temporary responses to particularly favourable habitats.

An examination of examples of these abnormally high population densities should serve to shed some light on more normal population dynamics.

Isolated Populations

On Isle Royale and small adjacent islands, comprising roughly 212 square miles, moose apparently became established as a permanent population rather recently (Murie, 1934). In the absence of either predators or competitors to limit their numbers, they increased steadily but were unable to leave the islands. Murie (1934) estimated that by 1930 the number of moose had increased to at least 1,000, that is, approximately 4.7 moose for every square mile. Murie suggested that this estimate might be low and that the number could conceivably be as high as 3,000 moose, which would represent about 14 moose for every square mile. Since these are mere estimates it is impossible to evaluate accurately the population density that was actually reached, but it seems quite safe to assume that the number did not exceed the maximum estimate and that the normal maximum carrying capacity was exceeded. This over-population so destroyed the habitat that its carrying capacity was seriously reduced for a great many years. Even today the flora shows evidence of this past over-utilization.

It is not known what the population density was at its lowest point following the big die-off. However, Aldous and Krefting (1946) suggest it was probably less than one moose per square mile.

Aldous and Krefting (1946) estimated that moose had increased to 510 by 1945, and that the area had reached the limit of its safe carrying capacity. This estimate represents an average of approximately 2.4 moose per square mile. In 1946 Krefting (personal communication) estimated that their numbers had increased to an average of 2.9 animals per square mile and he felt that continued increases would result in serious over-populations and subsequent destruction of the habitat.

Although the general floral composition of much of Ontario and eastern North America is comparable to that of Isle Royale, such high moose populations have apparently never developed in these regions in the past and there seems little likelihood that such population densities could be developed in the future without a condition of artificial isolation similar to that originally found on Isle Royale.

This consideration of insular populations might be taken as applying also to populations isolated in "pockets," where adverse habitat barriers prevent normal dispersal.

Enforced Seasonal Concentrations

Counts of animals that have been more or less forced to concentrate in restricted areas such as winter ranges in the valleys of the mountain regions cannot be used as a reliable index to the normal carrying capacity of large areas unless the extent of the total annual range of such concentrations of animals can be accurately determined. The total resident population can then be estimated in terms of normal population density. Estimates of the numbers of such temporary concentrations and measurements of the carrying capacities are nevertheless of vital importance. Perhaps the winter concentration of moose reported by Edwards (1952) from British Columbia might serve to illustrate this type of situation. On the basis of 3 consecutive aerial censuses (March 11–13) of a valley of approximately 60 square miles in Wells Gray Provincial Park during which he observed 129, 137, and 111 animals, he estimated the winter population at 2,148, 2,316, and 1,764 animals, or 35.8, 38.8, and 29.4 moose per square mile. He considered an estimate of 2,000 to be conservative.

In eastern North America this type of restricted population density is rarely if ever encountered.

Temporary Concentrations in Favourable Habitats

The most common type of high concentration encountered, especially in the east, appears to be the result of response to particularly favourable conditions in the local habitat. Temporary high population densities are commonly found in such areas as salt licks, favourable aquatic feeding localities, old burned-over or cut-over areas, and restricted "pockets" of other favourable habitats.

On St. Ignace Island, Ontario, it was calculated that at least 10 different moose visited one salt lick during the summer of 1947, with as many as 6 being present at the same time. As many as 23 moose were observed in a single afternoon on a trip from Duncan Cove to the north end of McKeachan Lake and return. The evidence of winter concentrations in Otter Creek Valley is still another example of local temporary concentrations in response to a favourable habitat, evidence which cannot be used alone as a basis for estimating the total population density of St. Ignace Island.

Cowan (1944, p. 18) gives the following information on summer population density in Banff National Park:

On June 8 a strip count of moose along 110 miles of the Banff Jasper Highway was taken and a figure of 4.5 moose per square mile arrived at. From comparison of this with other ecologically equivalent areas the above density was judged to be fairly characteristic. The heaviest concentration encountered was at the head of Siffleur River. Here on July 15 it was estimated to be 11 per square mile. However, the presence of a well used muck lick in the vicinity may have induced an artificial concentration.

From Jasper National Park, Cowan (1944, p. 31) reports as follows:

Moose were found in all parts of the park visited but with two exceptions they were uncommon. At the junction of the Rocky and Medicine-tent rivers there was evidence of a heavy population although but few were seen. However, the heaviest concentration encountered anywhere, during the summer, was that of Mowitch Creek near Little Heaven Summit. Here on August 16 the moose population was found to be close to 8 per square mile.

On the basis of aerial and other counts, Spencer and Chatelain (1953) have provided examples of observed winter densities of moose in south-central Alaska (see Table XXIV).

In all probability these observed densities are a direct reflection of the suitability of the winter habitat, with the higher densites beng restricted to relatively small and particularly favourable areas.

TABLE XXIV

WINTER DENSITIES OF MOOSE IN SOUTH-CENTRAL ALASKA*

Moose per sq. mile	Size of area	Locality
0.14	223 sq. mi.	?
0.8	150	Kenai Peninsula (1947 Burn)
4.3	127	Kenai Peninsula (1947 Burn)
5.1	331	Susitna Valley
7.4	90	Kenai and Kasilof
11.4	?	Matanuska Valley
57.5	9	?

*Spencer and Chatelain (1953).

Estimation of Average Population Densities

Frequently it is highly desirable to have some sort of an estimate of a moose population present in a large area. Perhaps of greatest importance in this regard is an estimation of wintering populations. Before general comparisons of estimates from different regions can be considered, some basic differences encountered between populations found in the mountain regions of western North America and those further east should be recognized. In the west, the winter ranges may be completely distinct from the areas normally occupied during other months, whereas in the east there may be little or no seasonal separation into well-defined regions. In addition, the wintering ranges of moose in the western areas often contain rather extensive stands of highly palatable winter moose foods (particularly willow) while the winter foods of moose in the east are more or less randomly dispersed over wide areas.

In other words, observed winter densities per unit area in the east probably represent something approaching the average annual population density, whereas moose in the west are perhaps occupying less than half the normal annual range. In any attempts to take a census of winter populations, a much higher percentage of the total population can be located, or observed, in the west than in the east. This may be resulting in a tendency for estimates by western observers to be relatively high and by eastern observers, relatively low.

Population Densities in Eastern North America

Seton (1927) estimated the original moose ranges for all North America at 3½ million square miles and a primitive population of 1 million animals, or 1 moose for every 3.5 square miles.

An error in Seton's estimates that has often been cited should be corrected at this point. Citing the data of Shiras (1923), Seton refers to an estimate of 300 moose for St. Ignace Island, Ontario, which he indicates as being about 30 square miles in size, to give an estimated 10 moose per square mile. Actually the island comprises some 110 square miles which would give a rate nearer 2.7 moose per square mile.

Seton also estimated that there were about 60 thousand moose present within a part of the original boundaries of Manitoba, at the rate of 1 moose per square mile. These estimates were little more than guesses.

Manweiler (1941) estimated that there was 1 moose per 3 square miles in the best moose range of Minnesota. By use of an aerial census method Morse (1946) estimated that a total of 260 moose were present on 494 square miles of the Red Lake Game Preserve district of Minnesota (1 moose per 1.5 square miles). He reports that the highest concentration found was 1.8 moose per square mile on a 52 square-mile area. On March 14, 1946, a census was taken by Morse of the entire northwest angle, comprising 133 square miles, in which the population was estimated at 42 (1 moose per 3.1 square miles).

During the period from 1929 to 1934, the province of Nova Scotia would have had to have almost 1 moose for each square mile to support a 10 per cent kill. The highest kill recorded from that province was 259 in Annapolis County (1,285 square miles) in 1926 (Table XXV). This represented a moose killed for every 5 square miles of the county. Assuming a 10 per cent kill, the population density would have been roughly 2 moose per square mile. Since this high rate of kill was not maintained, it appears that it probably exceeded an assumed 10 per cent. The highest average rate maintained from 1908 to 1937 was in Halifax County, Nova Scotia (2,063 square miles) where an average of 222 moose were killed each year at the average rate of 1 moose for each 9.3 square miles. At this rate one might assume that about 1 moose per square mile was an average normal maximum density for habitat conditions found in Nova Scotia. Temporary average densities of 2 or more moose per square mile apparently could not be maintained in large areas over a period of years in that province. Presumably those data would apply equally well to maximum densities for moose in most other areas in eastern North America.

At present, the highest known densities of moose in eastern North America are to be found in Newfoundland. A fairly accurate record of the number of animals killed between 1945 and 1951 has been kept and is provided by Pimlott (1953; see Table XXVI). On an area approximately 35,000 square miles the number of moose killed annually has risen almost constantly from 747 in 1945 to 3,383 in 1951. The average area per moose killed for the entire area has decreased from 47 square miles in 1945 to 10 in 1951. During this period one region of 5,800 square miles shows an average of 1 moose

TABLE XXV

STATISTICS ON MOOSE KILLED IN NOVA SCOTIA FROM 1908 TO 1937*

County	Sq. mi.	1908–17		1918–27		1928–37			1908–37	
		Av. kill	Sq. mi. per kill	Av. kill	Sq. mi. per kill	Av. kill	Sq. mi. per kill	Minimum sq. mi. per kill	Av. kill	Sq. mi. per kill
Halifax	2,063	210	9.8	258	8.0	196	10.5	6.2	222	9.3
Annapolis	1,285	104	12.3	162	7.9	119	10.8	5.0	129	10.0
Shelburne	979	78	12.6	115	8.5	81	12.1	5.5	92	10.7
Queens	983	84	11.7	108	9.1	71	13.8	7.1	87	11.2
Yarmouth	838	50	16.7	77	10.9	60	13.9	7.1	62	13.5
Guysborough	1,611	63	25.6	103	15.6	146	11.0	7.9	104	15.5
Hants	1,229	56	21.9	84	14.7	74	16.6	8.7	71	17.1
Digby	970	53	18.3	68	14.2	48	20.2	9.5	56	17.2
Lunenburg	1,169	49	23.9	62	18.9	54	21.6	12.3	55	21.2
Colchester	1,451	37	39.2	59	24.6	97	15.0	11.2	65	22.5
Pictou	1,124	12	93.7	44	25.5	88	12.7	7.4	48	23.4
Antigonish	541	2†	271.0	10	54.1	31	17.4	12.6	19	28.0
Kings	842	23	36.6	37	22.8	30	28.1	13.4	30	28.1
Cumberland	1,683	40	42.1	41	41.0	68	24.7	17.0	49	34.0

*Data computed from Nova Scotia (1948).

†Two animals reported killed in one year.

killed per 11 square miles, while three others with a combined area of 14,700 square miles averaged 1 moose killed for every 13 square miles. In 1951 a total of 1,068 moose was killed in the Exploits region (7,300 square miles). A break-down of this area (see Table XXVI) shows the highest kill of 1 moose for every 2.4 of 710 square miles.

While it is impossible to gain a reliable estimate of the actual density of moose from these figures, one might speculate, with some justification, on the minimum density that would be required to produce the above-mentioned kills.

Since the total trends have shown a consistent increase for the period discussed, one might assume that not more than 10 per cent of the population has been harvested (assuming a maximum annual increment of 20 per cent, one-half bulls). On this basis, for the whole range in Newfoundland, the population would have to average 1 moose per square mile in order to sustain the harvest as indicated for 1951. On the other hand, most of the kills (3,026) were made on only about 60 per cent of the total area. This would then require a density of about 3 moose for every 2 square miles. Even higher densities would be required to sustain the 1951 rate of kill as indicated in some of the sub-divisions of the Exploits region; however, calculations on these smaller units are quite likely to be misleading.

TABLE XXVI

AREA PER MOOSE KILLED IN NEWFOUNDLAND*
(square miles)

Region	Size of area	1945	1946	1947	1948	1949	1950	1951	Av.
Northern	5,900	1,475	281	84	56	46	40	109	79
Western	5,800	21	14	11	10	12	9.3	6.5	11
Exploits	7,300	28	18	20	12	12	9.5	6.8	13
Gander	3,100	50	32	25	12	12	9.6	6.4	13
Eastern	4,300	49	27	17	13	11	7.9	7.4	13
Fortune Bay	4,400	138	52	31	25	27	20	21	30
Burgeo	4,200	525	263	221	233	150	84	78	150
Annual kill	35,000	747	1,213	1,476	2,081	1,937	2,686	3,383	1,919
Av. area per kill		47	29	24	17	18	13	10	18

Subdivisions of Exploits region	Size of area	1951
Annieopsquotch	1,850	92
Noel Paul	600	3.0
Sandy	630	4.2
Rattling Brook	710	2.4
Badger–Millertown	1,120	5.7
Notre Dame	780	7.6
Hall's Bay	960	9.0
Baie Verte	650	325

*Data from Pimlott (1953).

In other words, Newfoundland apparently has at present an over-all average moose density of at least 1 per square mile with the probability that it averages 2 or more per square mile on a greater percentage of its moose range.

In the province-wide moose inventory taken in Ontario in 1950, the average density was estimated for each of the forest districts in the major portion of the moose range lying north of the French River and the north shore of Georgian Bay; in a total of some 175,000 square miles, the density varied from a high of 1 moose per 4.8 square miles in one district to a low of 1 per 26 in another. In the best moose range, a block of six adjacent forest districts representing approximately 50,000 square miles, independent estimates from each of the forest districts were compiled and expressed in terms of square miles per moose with the following results: 4.8, 5, 5, 5, 5.5, and 5.6.

In summary, it appears that in eastern North America an average density of 1 moose per 5 square miles might be regarded as a "normal" average density for a great portion of the range. One moose per square mile is probably a relatively high density under most conditions, while 2 or more moose per square mile represent an approach to maximum carrying capacity for most large regions. While much higher densities undoubtedly occur in restricted areas, at least temporarily, they have not been observed on large areas (1,000 square miles or more) in eastern North America on a sustained basis.

Population Densities in Western North America

McDowell and Moy (1942) estimated there was less than 1 moose per square mile on the area studied in Montana.

In British Columbia, according to Hatter (1952, p. 58), "Aerial counts along an 85-mile strip this March made by Mr. P. W. Martin revealed a moose density between Bridge Lake and Deadmans Creek of 6.5 animals per square mile. The lowest count of several flights made in the forested plateaus area of the interior revealed 1.5 moose per square mile." In an area of about 2,350 square miles in central British Columbia, Hatter estimated that approximately 7,000 moose were present at an average rate of about 3 moose per square mile.

Cowan (1946, p. 30) reports an estimated moose density in Jasper National Park as follows:

At Willow Creek the presence of 30 horses on the range presented the opportunity of an experimental census of moose population. On May 25 and 26 an extensive survey of the winter range there yielded 9 moose and 18 horses. On this basis 15 moose were estimated to be present on the 18 to 20 square miles. Counts of fecal deposits of the two species yield the figure of 21 moose as the winter population on the same area. Warden Burstrom assures me that the latter figure is far below actual conditions at the time of greatest concentration. He places the population on this area during the later winter as approximately 40 moose or roughly 2 per square mile. It is quite probable that the fecal pellet does not serve as an accurate basis of comparison and consequently does not give satisfactory results.

Estimates of the numbers of moose in Alaska by the Alaska Game Commission (Palmer, 1941) were 60,000, although Dufresne (1946) estimated only 30,000. Palmer (1944) estimated the average population density of specific areas in Alaska as 1 to 1.5 animals per square mile. More recent studies by Spencer and Chatelain (1953) have provided some specific examples of population densities in south-central Alaska (see Table XXIV). In one area of 25 square miles they found that 440 moose had eaten approximately 50 per cent of the year's increment of food in one and one-half months. They estimated that in order to utilize this area properly for five winter months, 132 animals would be the desirable maximum, or that 5 to 6 moose per square mile is the maximum carrying capacity of a good range properly used.

These estimates are roughly 50 per cent higher than those made in studies in Ontario. Remembering, however, that in the east the winter ranges are largely the same as the summer, these estimates might be considered fairly comparable for average moose habitats.

Population Densities in Europe

For the past few years Sweden has apparently maintained one of the highest moose populations of any comparably sized area in the world. Lubeck (1947) reports on the kill for 1945 and 1946 and corrects the area in each district to include only the area suitable for moose. His data for 1946 have been transposed from Swedish to standard square miles in Table XXVII which gives a break-down of the average square miles per moose killed for the various districts of Sweden. In the best moose-producing area, 785 moose were killed in 1,639 square miles, or 1 moose for every 2.1 square miles. The population density for this area might be roughly estimated by assuming that the kill was between 10 and 20 per cent of the total adult population. Since this area has supported a similar kill for

TABLE XXVII

STATISTICS ON MOOSE KILLED IN SWEDEN DURING 1946*

Province	Square miles	Number moose killed	Sq. mi. per moose killed
Uppsala	1,639	785	2.1
Västmanland	2,162	817	2.6
Södermanland	2,019	723	2.8
Örebro	2,885	875	3.3
Stockholm	2,467	717	3.4
Östergötland	3,244	819	4.0
Kalmar	3,464	586	5.9
Skaraborg	2,473	394	6.2
Kronoberg	3,108	450	6.9
Kopparberg	9,598	1,346	7.1
Halland	1,368	153	8.9
Alvsborg	3,997	431	9.3
Värmland	6,379	663	9.3
Gävleborg	6,421	605	10.6
Göteborg och Bohus	1,419	129	11.0
Jönköping	3,746	302	12.4
Blekinge	1,007	74	13.8
Jämtland	12,124	785	15.5
Kristianstad	1,799	114	15.8
Malmöhus	619	29	21.4
Västernorrland	8,813	290	30.4
Västerbotten	15,300	197	77.7
Norrbotten	20,272	50	405.4
TOTAL	116,323	11,334	Av. 10.3

*Data computed from Lubeck (1947).

several years and a larger kill since 1946, this figure cannot logically exceed 20 per cent, which would indicate a density of at least 2.4 moose per square mile. Assuming a 10 per cent kill, the average density for all moose-producing areas of Sweden in 1946 would be roughly 1 moose per square mile. During the high kill of 1941 and 1948 Sweden must have had several areas producing over 5 moose per square mile.

In Norway an average of about 1,024 moose was killed each year from 1889 to 1930 (Olstad, 1934). When a part of Olstad's data is examined (Table XXVIII) it becomes apparent that for that entire period the best

TABLE XXVIII

STATISTICS ON MOOSE KILLED IN NORWAY, 1889–1930*

County	Sq. mi.	1889–1902		1903–1916		1917–1930			1889–1930	
		Av. kill	Sq. mi. per kill	Av. kill	Sq. mi. per kill	Av. kill	Sq. mi. per kill	Minimum sq. mi. per kill	Av. kill	Sq. mi. per kill
Vestfold	592	25	23.3	47	12.5	45	13.0	8.5	39	15.2
Nord Trondelag	4,738	324	14.6	325	14.6	185	25.6	10.9	278	17.0
Akershus	1,406	82	17.2	70	20.2	34	41.2	10.1	63	22.3
Buskerud	2,520	106	23.8	109	23.2	100	25.2	12.5	105	23.9
Sör Trondelag	2,562	91	28.1	136	18.8	92	27.9	14.5	106	24.1
Opland	3,322	109	30.5	105	31.7	124	26.8	14.9	113	29.5
Telemark	2,627	62	42.3	105	24.9	79	33.3	16.3	82	32.0
Östfold	963	35	27.7	36	26.9	15	65.9	18.2	28	34.4
Hedmark	6,670	140	47.6	250	26.6	167	39.3	21.8	186	35.9
Nordland	2,083	11	196.5	25	82.0	3	801.1	54.8	13	161.4
Vest Agder	534			2	222.5	4	121.4	12.7	2	222.5
Aust Agder	2,637	3	753.3	13	198.2	2	1,318.5	94.1	6	425.3

*Data computed from Olstad (1934).

moose-producing area is Vestfold County with a forested area of about 592 square miles, which has maintained a rate of 1 moose killed for every 15.2 square miles. The same county produced Norway's highest rate of kill for any one year (1930) of 1 moose killed for every 8.5 square miles. In other words, Norway maintained an average annual kill of about 1,000 moose on 30,652 square miles. On the basis of an assumed 10 per cent kill, Norway must have had an average of at least 1 moose for every 3 square miles. Possibly this average rate might compare favourably with that of many regions of eastern Canada.

CENSUS METHODS

Due to the solitary habits of moose and to the nature of their habitat, population numbers are extremely difficult to obtain by ordinary field work. In the course of Ontario studies, two main approaches to this problem were taken. All moose observations during field work were recorded on base maps and, wherever possible, careful notes were taken on the diagnostic features of the appearance of each animal in order to distinguish individuals and avoid duplication in tallying the actual counts.

The second method consisted of taking aerial censuses by flight strips during winter.

Algonquin Provincial Park Study Area

In the course of field investigations, 34 moose observations were made which were estimated to represent at least 26 different individuals. Nine other moose were reliably reported by local observers. Most field work was done in the township of Bishop, Devine, and the eastern half of Butt, and a total of 25 moose were recorded during the summer of 1946. Since much of the area could not be visited, it was impossible to estimate the average population density for these townships on the basis of summer field investigations.

On March 13, 1947, an aerial census was made of this area, comprising about 185 square miles. Flight strips at 1.25 mile intervals were made in a Department of Lands and Forests aircraft. A total of 8 moose and 22 deer was observed. An estimated 20 to 25 per cent coverage was obtained. The presence of many moose tracks in areas where we saw no moose plus the fact that the aircraft was a bit too fast for accurate census work indicate that the estimated coverage might be approximately correct. The highest concentration observed was 5 moose in Devine Township, an area of about 75 square miles. If the coverage estimate is reasonable, a total of 20 to 25 moose would give a population of 1 moose per 3 to 3.8 square miles. This seems to compare favourably with a total of 15 moose recorded in this township during the summer of 1946. The average for the total census area of Bishop, Devine, and Butt townships was estimated to be between 32 and 50 moose, or roughly 1 moose per 5 or 6 square miles. In the parts of this area visited during the summer of 1946, we recorded 25 moose.

This same general area was covered by a second aerial census on February 3, 1949. A total of 6 moose was counted, compared to 8 seen during the 1947 census.

From general flights over the park during winter it became readily apparent that the census area was about the best moose-producing region in Algonquin Provincial Park.

St. Ignace Island Study Area

On April 3, 1947, a systematic aerial coverage of St. Ignace and Simpson islands in a three-seater Piper Cruiser aircraft was completed in about three hours. Flight lines were flown at one-mile intervals. No moose were actually observed, although tracks were abundant in many areas on both islands. Several factors seem to have contributed to the unsatisfactory results of this survey (see pp. 208–9). The chief factor was undoubtedly the late date of survey: by the first of April the snow had melted from many patches of ground, and concentrations of animals in such areas would be extremely difficult to see from the air.

During summer field work in 1947 a total of 243 moose observations were made, which represented an estimated 100 individual animals.

On February 18, 1948, an aerial census of Simpson Island was carried out in a Norseman aircraft owned by the Department of Lands and Forests. With an estimated 20 per cent coverage, 6 moose were observed, which would give a total of 30 moose, or 1 moose per square mile. During the summer of 1947 a total of 30 individuals were recorded on Simpson Island.

Bad weather and heavy snow prevented an aerial survey of St. Ignace Island on that date, but provided excellent opportunity to test the accuracy of the aerial survey census method. A fresh heavy snowfall continued during the afternoon of February 18 and all day on February 19. On February 20, a bright clear day made it possible to locate all fresh tracks whether the animals could be located or not. Flight lines at about half-mile intervals were flown north and south across St. Ignace Island.

Saugstad (1942) reports on experimental big-game aerial census work in North Dakota in which it was estimated that a strip of about one-eighth of a mile could be effectively covered by an observer on each side of the plane at an altitude of about 375 feet. At this rate two observers should effectively cover a strip one-fourth of a mile in width. Flight strips at half-mile intervals should, therefore, give a 50 per cent coverage. In Ontario the nature of the forest cover, especially in areas with a high percentage of mature conifers, prevents the observer from locating all moose within such strips. To check on the accuracy of this method, all sets of fresh tracks were recorded in instances where animals were not actually observed during the flight over St. Ignace Island on February 20. A total of 28 moose and 55 additional sets of fresh tracks were recorded. This would indicate that there must have been at least 83 moose on areas covered by the census, or a total of 166 animals on St. Ignace Island. At this rate the population density would be estimated at the rate of 1.6 moose per square mile. During the summer of 1947 an estimated total of 70 animals was observed on the portions of the island that were covered during field work.

From study of the data on winter browse analysis it seems apparent that the population density was near the normal maximum carrying capacity, at the estimated rate of 1 moose per square mile on Simpson Island and 1.6 moose per square mile on St. Ignace Island. The accuracy of these estimates should be checked by further research with aerial survey methods.

Black Bay Peninsula Survey

The southern portion of this peninsula lies immediately west of St. Ignace Island in Lake Superior, Ontario, where it forms about 195 square miles of a Crown game preserve. During January and February, 1950, officers of the Department of Lands and Forests, Port Arthur forest district, carried out three aerial surveys of this area to check on the moose population. The results of these aerial surveys, compiled by Mr. G. C. Armstrong, District Biologist (typewritten reports, Fish and Wildlife Service, Dept. of Lands and Forests, Toronto, Ontario) show totals of 15, 14, and 18 moose observed when flying at two-mile intervals on January 18, February 19, and February 22. If the effective coverage per flight line is estimated at one-fourth of a mile, the area sampled might be considered at between 10 and 15 per cent. At this rate the estimated population on the basis of these surveys would be between 100 and 150, 90 and 140, or 120 and 180, and the population density might be estimated roughly between 1 moose per square mile and 1 per 2 square miles.

Armstrong's final estimate of approximately 135 moose for this area seems as reasonably accurate as can be arrived at with present methods.

Aerial Census Techniques

This type of census appears to be the most reliable and practical method of estimating moose populations yet devised, although additional studies are needed in order to standardize techniques and thereby obtain reliable and comparable results. Personnel of the Ontario Department of Lands and Forests have conducted experiments in taking aerial censuses by means of a helicopter which show even greater promise of satisfactory results. In fairly open or hardwood forests absolute counts are possible, but in dense conifer areas moose are often difficult to see unless they are moving about. It was estimated that on St. Ignace Island, where conifers are dominant, only about one-third of the animals could be located on regular flight strips.

On February 5, 1947, a reconnaissance flight was made over an area of about 2½ townships north of Wanapitei Lake in the Sudbury District, in which 27 moose were counted in less than one hour of flying time (Figure 59). The area was principally a second-growth aspen and white birch association with scattered conifers. No systematic coverage was made, but the animals were quickly located by following tracks in the fresh snow that had fallen the night before. An accurate census can undoubtedly be carried out under such circumstances.

The following are important considerations in the technique of taking an aerial census of moose with conventional types of aircraft.

1. The aircraft should accommodate a pilot and two observers and have safe flying speeds below 100 miles per hour.

FIGURE 59. Two moose in mixed hardwood and conifer forest as they appear from an aircraft. North of Wanapitei Lake, Sudbury District, February 5, 1947

2. Flights should be made within one day following a snowfall sufficiently heavy to obliterate old tracks. This is especially important in areas of dense conifers.

3. The best conditions for observation can apparently be obtained on bright days or in the hours around noon.

4. Careful flight plans should precede the census, and include the preparation of flight lines on a detailed large-scale map, using the best possible landmarks and runs of less than 10 miles in length where possible.

5. The distance between flight lines should be governed by the percentage of coverage desired. (One-mile intervals give approximately 25 per cent coverage with two observers.) Greater than 25 per cent coverage seems necessary to obtain reliable indications of abundance in areas of dense mature conifers.

6. Altitudes between 300 and 700 feet seem to be the optimum for observing moose.

7. Animals, and sets of fresh tracks where no animals are observed, should be counted during each flight run. These counts should not be tallied or plotted on a base map during the flight run, but during the turn at the end of each run in order to prevent the observer from being forced to lose sight of the census strip long enough to overlook the presence of animals or tracks.

8. Most observers must have considerable experience in flight observation before they become skilled enough to produce reliable results.

FLUCTUATIONS IN POPULATIONS

Since the rate of reproduction in moose is rather slow, one would not expect to find violent fluctuations. The only data available that can be used to show possible population trends are figures on the number killed by hunters, kept by only a few provincial governments (Figure 60), and data compiled by observers across Ontario in answer to questionnaires on general opinions of annual population trends (Figure 61). Since so many variable factors may be influencing these data they must be considered as only rough indications of trends.

One of the most interesting features of the figures on the number killed (Figure 60) is the apparent general agreement of trends among the four Canadian provinces. Perhaps most significant is the general drop in numbers killed in all four provinces about 1922–4.

The last peak population reached in both Nova Scotia and New Brunswick in 1930–1 seems to have coincided with a peak population reached on Isle Royale. The subsequent low populations reached between 1935 and 1937 also seem to agree with trends in the population on Isle Royale. If the opinions of Ontario observers, given in answer to questionnaires, can be

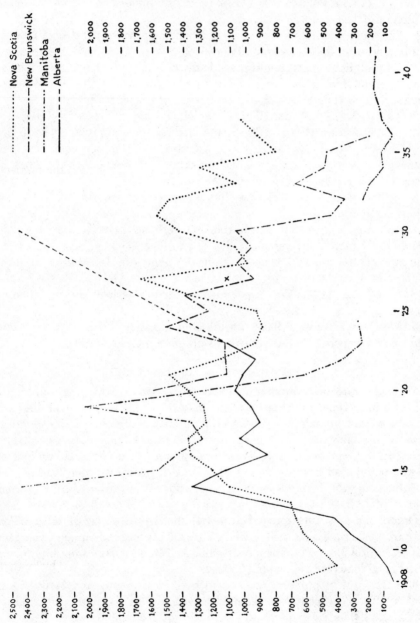

FIGURE 60. Trends in number of moose killed by hunters in four Canadian provinces

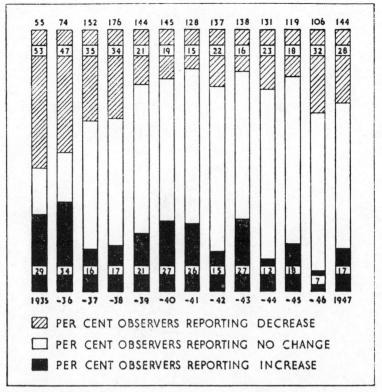

FIGURE 61. Trends in population changes of moose in Ontario, based on answers to
annual questionnaires of the Royal Ontario Museum of Zoology

used as an index, this general low in moose numbers was also experienced
in this province (Figure 61).

When the opinions on population trends of these observers are plotted,
there is a suggestion of a peak increase in 1941 followed by a general
decrease to 1946 or 1947.

A further check on trends in the fluctuations of moose populations can
be made by examining statistics on the number of moose killed in Sweden
(Lubeck, 1947; Hamilton, 1947; Sweden, 1947, 1949) and Norway (Salvesen,
1929; Olstad, 1934). Data from these sources have been plotted in Figure 62
for comparison with the North American data summarized in Figure 60.
Perhaps the most significant point in this comparison is the fairly close
agreement between the data for both continents on the fairly well-defined
decline in the numbers of moose following 1920. In various parts of Norway,
completely and partially closed hunting seasons were enforced during this
period. In Sweden a completely closed season was enforced from 1920 to

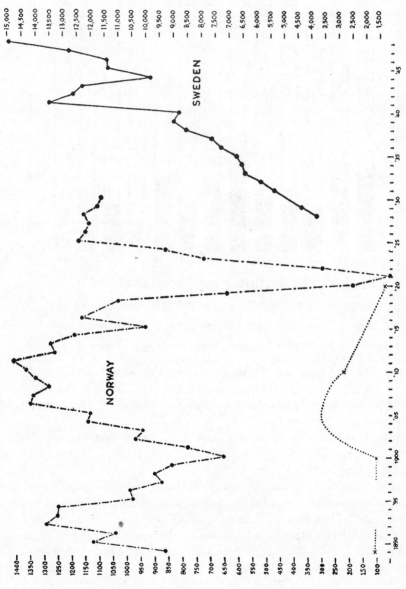

FIGURE 62. Trends in number of moose killed in Norway and Sweden. Scale on left for Norway and on right for Sweden

1928. Since that time the kill in Sweden has continued to increase almost steadily with the exception of a brief decline following an unusual high in 1941. A preliminary tabulation of the figures for 1948 indicates a total of 14,912 animals killed (Sweden, 1949). On the basis of data compiled by Lubeck (1947) this rate indicates that on the average 1 moose was killed for 7.77 square miles of forested area in all Sweden. The 1941 peak in that country corresponds roughly with a high in Ontario, as indicated by the opinions of observers given in answer to questionnaires (Figure 61). Otherwise the trends in fluctuations in Sweden, as indicated by statistics on the numbers killed, show little indication of short-term cyclic periodicity. Unfortunately recent data on the numbers of moose killed in Norway are not available at present. For the early part of the period covered, there seems to be general agreement in population trends in Norway and Sweden.

In summary, it appears that on the basis of the available data from both Europe and North America, moose tend to show fairly well-marked fluctuations. The available data, especially those from North America, are influenced by so many variable factors that they cannot be considered reliable indices to actual populations. These data are, therefore, not suitable for critical analysis. Cyclic periodicity cannot be demonstrated from them, although it appears possible that long-term fluctuations may be being influenced by shorter periodic cycles.

CHAPTER NINETEEN

MANAGEMENT

THE MOOSE, like many other forms of wildlife, is a natural resource, of economic and aesthetic importance to man. Like other living resources, it is renewable. If such renewable resources are to be conserved, the harvest must be managed with a view to obtaining a sustained annual yield. Management of moose may be regarded as a specialized form of animal husbandry, in so far as the maintenance of breeding stock and the harvest of the annual surplus is concerned. As in the case of other forms of animal husbandry, the first essentials are a reasonably accurate knowledge of the size and age composition of existing herds, the rate of annual production, and the carrying capacity of the available range. These primary essentials should be carefully determined by the most modern, practicable, and scientifically sound methods. These requirements continue to present a challenge to workers in wildlife research and management.

Once the status of the populations and the carrying capacity of the ranges are determined, two major approaches form the basis for practical management policies: (1) control of human decimating factors (harvest, etc.); and (2) control (maintenance or improvement) of the habitat. Past management policies in North America have been largely restricted to the first approach.

Few practicable management programmes, other than these two, have been demonstrated. Attempts at controlling natural decimating factors such as predators, diseases, and parasites have been instituted in various regions, but their practicability has not been clearly established in terms of sustained increases in moose production. Attempts have been made at stocking or restocking areas where there are no moose or where the animals are scarce or impoverished, but most of them have yet to be proved completely successful ventures. Newfoundland, however, apparently provides an exception. In instances of over-population, resulting in serious harm to the local habitat, it seems logical that a reduction in numbers would be desirable. In areas normally opened and accessible to hunting this usually poses no serious problem, but public sentiment, politics, existing regulations and policies or interpretations of the same tend to prevent or hinder practices that are biologically sound. It is also difficult to reduce populations or manipulate sex ratios by harvesting females because of similar resistance from uninformed or sceptical public sentiment.

It becomes increasingly obvious that as yet we know relatively little about the management of such wild species as moose, and we have a long way to go before it can be said that moose populations are being managed on a scientifically sound basis.

INVENTORY OF EXISTING POPULATIONS

No completely satisfactory census method has yet been devised. Aerial census during midwinter seems to be the most efficient method available (see pp. 208–9) but this still leaves much to be desired. More research on standardization of this method is needed.

Ground counts often provide useful indications of populations but can hardly be used as a practicable method of ascertaining total populations over large areas.

On the basis of our as yet meagre knowledge of population dynamics, it appears that about one or two moose per square mile in comparatively large areas (possibly over 1,000 square miles) constitute what normally might be considered a relatively high population of moose in eastern North America. Apparently five or more moose per square mile have rarely if ever been maintained over a period of years in North America under normal conditions. Population densities reached on restricted winter ranges in western North America and on Isle Royale, Michigan, might be considered exceptions. In the latter, however, the population level was abnormally increased through enforced isolation and lack of natural decimating factors.

"Actually in the field of management we are more concerned with some reliable index rather than an actual count of populations. Something is needed which can be used to follow the relative changes that take place from year to year." (Peterson, 1949a, p. 73) As yet such a system has not been satisfactorily devised. Several approaches may be made to such a problem.

The use of annual questionnaire returns by regular qualified observers stationed across the range of moose gives one tool which indicates broad trends in population changes. Unfortunately, however, it has not yet been possible to test critically the degree of accuracy or reliability of such a method.

Returns filled out by hunters provide another approach to analysing population trends but here again an entirely satisfactory system has not yet been devised. Voluntary returns have, for the most part, proved unsuccessful, while compulsory returns are often equally unsatisfactory largely owing to the inherent difficulty of enforcing such regulations. It seems evident, nevertheless, that some form of compulsory return is particularly desirable in the case of moose. Such returns are needed not only to secure data on trends in population changes but also to give some measure of the annual kill and thereby provide some basis for regulation of the harvest.

An annual or other regular appraisal of the habitat by the browse analysis method gives some indication of trends in the abundance of moose. Such a system is best applicable to local areas, especially where population densities are reaching the maximum safe carrying capacity. Wider application to larger areas has not yet been attempted but such experiments seem desirable.

In the case of white-tailed deer, studies in various types of habitat of the productivity of females during the period from fertilization to the birth of offspring have opened up relatively new approaches in appraising the relative abundance of populations in terms of the carrying capacities of ranges (see pp. 60–1). Fundamentally similar approaches might be applied to moose, but would undoubtedly prove less practicable than in the case of deer because the numbers of moose are comparatively low, so that it is difficult to secure adequate samples of female reproductive tracts from areas to be studied.

Many other approaches to methods of determining relative abundance have been attempted in wildlife studies which might well be applicable to moose. Counts of droppings, tracks, and other signs of animal activity provide useful tools, but as in the case of many other systems, sufficient research has not been carried forward to a point where a statistically sound sampling method can be adopted and applied on a practicable basis.

ESTIMATION OF ANNUAL INCREMENT AND SIZE OF HARVEST

A measure of the average rate of reproduction is highly desirable from the standpoint of management. Harvests should be set in such a manner that the annual number of animals taken by the hunter does not exceed the number that reach shootable age. From a study of available data on the sex and age composition of moose populations (see pp. 67–70), it appears that the average annual increment, as measured by the ratios of yearlings to adult populations, usually falls between 12 and 25 (averaging about 15, 16, or 17 per cent). If only bulls are to be taken by the hunter, the normal safe kill must remain roughly between 6 and 12 per cent of the total adult population in order to maintain adequate breeding stock. If both sexes could be killed perhaps these figures could be doubled and a normal breeding population still maintained.

CONTROL OF HUMAN DECIMATING FACTORS

Man's interest and activity have created the need for management of wild species. Basically, however, most management centres around control by regulation of man's activities rather than direct control of the species in question.

Regulation of Hunting Seasons

This form of management has long been used as a basic control of the harvest of wild species. As hunting pressure has increased, the tendency has been toward greater restriction on the length of open seasons. A decrease in the numbers of moose has forced a closure of all moose hunting in many areas. Hunting during late winter, when moose were at a disadvantage owing to crusted snow, and hunting during the height of the rutting season were particularly devastating practices that seriously reduced the numbers of moose. Recent seasons have been restricted to the fall when supposedly the rut was over. In some areas, however, late September finds the rut still in progress and the bulls recklessly bold and easy targets for hunters.

Regulation of the Kill

Hunting seasons may be regulated in various ways in the interest of moose conservation and management. In some areas the general population level may be such that cropping a restricted number of animals would be beneficial and wise. The most efficient approach to such a situation would suggest a limitation of the kill by limiting the number of hunters. The difficulties thus involved have led to an alternate system of manipulation of seasons by closing certain areas, zoning, alternating open and closed seasons, shortening the seasons, and enforcing other local regulations. While these practices, which are designed to control or limit the number of animals killed, are undoubtedly simple to administer, they are grossly inefficient in regulating the harvest in such a way that maximum safe utilization can be maintained annually.

Protection of the Females

A basic problem in wildlife management has arisen through over-protection of the females. In areas where moose populations are exceeding the normal carrying capacity of the habitat, the harvesting of males only has proved ineffective in reducing herds to a safe level. Experience in Europe has shown that high populations of moose can be safely maintained by harvesting both sexes. This also provides a more efficient utilization of the available surpluses which may otherwise be wasted or even prove detrimental to the species. Legislation is seriously needed which will allow game administrators and managers to utilize regulations for the harvesting of cows by hunters when and where needed. For a more detailed discussion the reader is referred to such works as Schierbeck (1929), Skuncke (1949), Clarke (1952), Voipio (1952a), and others.

Restriction of Hunters

It appears almost inevitable that the days of unlimited hunting for moose must soon pass from most of North America. By its very nature the moose is a solitary animal requiring considerable space in which to survive. If the maximum production of moose is to be obtained, hunting must be closely regulated: not necessarily by reducing the number of moose killed but rather by distributing hunting pressure more evenly.

Protective Regulations

It has been necessary to introduce many additional regulations to prevent unsportsmanlike destruction of moose. Such practices as "poaching," "jack-lighting," shooting from aircraft, shooting swimming animals, meat-hunting for camp kitchens, and many others have been a serious threat to the future of moose. Game preserves, parks, and other sanctuaries have been established for the protection of such species as moose with the idea of providing increased production to replenish surrounding areas. While such areas do provide protected nuclei of populations, their value in restocking adjacent areas has not been sufficiently studied to demonstrate their effectiveness in this matter. Certainly mere protection does not in itself ensure increased numbers of animals.

In some cases such regulated areas produce an over-population which presents an equally, if not a more, serious problem from the management standpoint. Over-populations for even a short period may damage the habitat to such an extent that it cannot recover for several years.

Protective regulations should include some measure of protection for the habitat as well as for the animals in question. Certainly there should be some semblance of balance between the number of animals present and the carrying capacity of the habitat. More attention must be given to the potential productivity of the habitat in appraising the need for protective regulations.

CONTROL OF HABITAT

Manipulation of habitats to produce greater percentages of near-optimum conditions for wildlife offers perhaps the greatest opportunity for increasing the annual production of certain desired species. In the case of moose, several stages of forest successions must be maintained in order to produce a favourable habitat. Areas of second growth produce the greatest quantity of food.

Fire has been the chief factor initiating forest succession. Although usually extremely wasteful of forest resources, it continues to be one of the best producers of habitats suitable for moose. In some cases, however, its benefits are nullified when repeated fires practically destroy the entire supply of humus in the soil. Over most of the range of moose in North America, controlled burning as a management practice would be extremely difficult to carry out. In only a relatively small percentage of the area would the benefits derived offset the damages involved to the extent that burning could be recommended as a regular procedure.

About the only other practicable measure available for the manipulation of moose habitats is the use of certain types of commercial logging operations so as to be of value to moose and other wildlife. Preliminary studies indicate that clean cutting of small strips or spots (of possibly one square mile or less) alternately through the forests provides the maximum benefits to moose. Selective cutting usually fails to reduce the forest cover sufficiently to initiate a complete cycle of the desired stages in forest succession. Clean cutting of vast areas greatly increases the length of time required for such areas to reach a stage where maximum use can be made of them.

Other measures for improving the habitat, such as providing for the aquatic requirements of moose by using dams or other means of maintaining water levels or water supply, offer some promise in limited areas. For the most part such improvements can only be gained as a by-product of some other programme for conserving or using water, rather than as a practical venture in moose management.

In certain areas habitat improvement might be integrated with reforestation projects, although this approach has been largely unexplored as far as moose are concerned in North America. In Sweden, however, it appears that moose have benefited by that country's reforestation as well as forest management programmes.

CONTROL OF NATURAL DECIMATING FACTORS
Predators

Apparently an increase in the numbers of moose resulting directly from control of predators such as wolves or bears has not yet been demonstrated. While local control is undoubtedly desirable in certain instances, state or province-wide bounty systems probably have little if any beneficial effect on moose populations. At any rate it seems almost certain that any benefit that might occur would not justify, or compensate for, the expense involved in bounty payments. The over-all effects of predators on moose need much more study before the situation can be properly evaluated and appreciated.

Control of predators should be regarded as a less desirable management measure than control of the habitat or of decimation by man, if for no other reason than the fact that present-day control measures cannot be effectively carried out on a practicable basis across the range of moose.

Competitors

Some measure of control over competitors may frequently be desirable. In the northeastern part of the continent, the white-tailed deer has replaced the moose as the dominant big-game animal. In some areas control of predators might well have the effect of furthering the encroachment of deer into areas which have been predominantly moose ranges. If it proves desirable to maintain moose populations in certain regions, a heavy harvest of deer in such areas would probably prove beneficial to moose.

Under rigid protection in such areas as national parks in the west, the wapiti or American elk has increased to a point where serious competition with the moose may be taking place. In such cases a reduction or control of the numbers of elk seems highly desirable not only from the standpoint of moose but of other species of wildlife as well.

Diseases, Parasites, and Accidents

Controls of other natural decimating factors are difficult to effect. Moose normally harbour a number of internal parasites. Practicable control measures must, of necessity, be largely restricted to preventing the introduction of new parasites. An example which might be cited is the liver fluke (*Fascioloides magna*) which was thought to have been brought into Ontario with wapiti introduced from outside the province. Once such parasites become firmly established in large populations it becomes extremely difficult to carry out an effective programme of control.

It is equally difficult to establish control over diseases and accidents.

STOCKING AND RESTOCKING

Trapping big solitary animals like moose usually becomes a difficult and expensive enterprise. Relatively few attempts have been made. Stocking was successfully carried out on Newfoundland. Restocking in New York proved a failure and perhaps similar efforts in northern Michigan will ultimately be regarded as failures too. More recent attempts at restocking on Cape Breton Island and in certain areas in Wyoming cannot as yet be evaluated.

MOOSE IN CAPTIVITY

When taken as young calves moose are quite tractable. As they reach maturity they usually become difficult to handle, especially the bulls during the rutting season. There are many accounts in the literature about training moose to harness to pull sleighs, particularly in Sweden, beginning with the reign of Charles IX (shortly after 1600). Some of these accounts assert that moose were capable of travelling over 200 miles in one day. But attempts to domesticate the moose have all failed.

In North America a few attempts to train moose to harness have met with varying degrees of success. Accounts of such attempts, as well as of other early efforts to raise moose in captivity may be found in the writings of Powell (1855), Thompson (1886), Merrill (1920), and Seton (1927).

Attempts to rear moose in zoological gardens have met with only limited success. In most cases the captive animals tend to develop gastric disorders because of the difficulty of providing foods equivalent to those they feed on in the wild. Stott (1948) found that captive moose showed a strong preference for such exotic foods as Australian blackwood acacia trees, oranges, and bananas.

Moose have been successfully trapped in the wild in efforts to stock or restock various areas as well as to provide specimens for zoological gardens. For accounts of the methods that have been employed in trapping, the reader is referred to papers by Hickie (undated) and Grasse (1950). Studies of captive animals are also provided by Kellum (1941). But to confine the monarch of the northern woods is to rob him of his kingdom. A captive shackled in a small enclosure cannot portray the majestic splendour of a full-grown bull, carrying his antlers proudly as he roams through the lakes, streams, and forests of his native haunts.

A STUDY OF MANDIBULAR TOOTH-WEAR AS AN INDEX TO AGE OF MOOSE

R. C. Passmore,[*] R. L. Peterson, and A. T. Cringan[†]

The recent intensification of scientific interest in moose, brought on primarily by a real need for a sounder approach to management, has served to focus attention on several serious gaps in our knowledge of this species. Among the most urgent requirements in this regard is a method of determining the age of individual animals, in order to permit assessment of such important and interrelated factors as population structure, reproductive rates, and survival rates. Any comprehensive estimate of harvestable surplus should be based on a knowledge of these attributes of the population that are related to its age composition.

Characteristics of the teeth of the lower jaw have been used to determine age in some cervine species. Severinghaus (1949) has described criteria for determining the age of white-tailed deer, based on the development and wear of the teeth of the lower jaw. Murie (1951) has similarly found that characteristics of the lower jaws of wapiti are, within limits, diagnostic of age. In addition, Skuncke (1949) has indicated that certain features of the lower jaw of the Swedish moose (*Alces alces alces*) can be used to determine age. The possibility that the lower jaws of the two subspecies of moose (*A. a. andersoni* and *A. a. americana*) found in Ontario might be used in age-determination prompted the present study.

When the season for moose was reopened in Ontario in the fall of 1951, after two years of closure, opportunity arose for examining many specimens in the flesh and for obtaining moderate numbers of lower jaws. During September, 1953, all specimens gathered to date, including those in the collections of the Royal Ontario Museum of Zoology and Palaeontology, were examined from the standpoint of patterns of wear displayed by the cheek teeth of the lower jaw. Although the sample was small, numbering only 108 specimens with adult dentition, some preliminary grouping of similarly worn material was achieved and estimates of age were assigned to these groups. The results of this examination were sufficiently rewarding that the authors felt justified in making a province-wide appeal for addi-

[*]Division of Research, Department of Lands and Forests, Maple, Ontario.
[†]Division of Fish and Wildlife, Department of Lands and Forests, Sioux Lookout, Ontario.

tional material during the 1953 open season for moose. The response to this appeal was particularly gratifying.

The authors wish to make grateful acknowledgment of the assistance given by many persons in collecting and preparing the material discussed in this paper. We particularly wish to express our gratitude to the field staff of the Division of Fish and Wildlife, Ontario Department of Lands and Forests, through whom most of the collections were made, to the hunters who kindly donated the lower jaws of their moose, and to the many persons on the staff of the Royal Ontario Museum of Zoology and Palae-ontology and of the Southern Research Station, Ontario Department of Lands and Forests, who assisted with the tasks of cleaning, cataloguing, and tabulating associated with this study.

METHODS

From the beginning it was realized that to undertake a study of the relationship between age and tooth-wear would involve working from un-knowns towards assumptions which could not be verified without a large series of specimens of known age. However, it was reasoned that specimens of known age would be of value only if rate of wear were shown to be reasonably uniform with age in wild, unmarked individuals. In view of the fact that there seems little possibility that an adequate number of specimens of known age will become available in the near future, we have felt justified in attempting to classify our material by arranging it on the basis of in-creasing degree of wear. By restricting the sample to individuals taken at only one season of the year one might reasonably expect that the dentitions of animals of similar age would be sufficiently similar to form discernible groups.

Since the early development of the dentition is described fully in chapter 9 of this book, only the adult dentition of the lower jaw is dealt with in this study.

Four hundred and twenty lower jaws were carefully arranged in series in order of increasing average degree of wear, and the resultant groups of similarly worn specimens were termed "wear-classes." These were numbered I to IX.

Four hundred and one of the jaws in the series were from animals col-lected during the autumn or early winter. Jaws of nineteen animals taken at other times of the year were used in that portion of the series in which wear-classes were considered to include more than one age-class.

In the description of wear-patterns of the group defined in this study, the nomenclature of the teeth follows the basic dental formula of mammals as used elsewhere in this publication, and as described for white-tailed deer by Riney (1951).

Reference will be made frequently to "dark" and "light" dentine. If an unworn cheek-tooth from a young moose is sectioned through a dorso-ventral plane, it will be found to consist of a thin outer layer of enamel over a layer of white dentine varying in thickness from less than one millimetre in the peaks of lingual crests to more than 2.5 millimetres in the wall of the body of the tooth. This initial or primary dentine takes on very little stain after it is exposed by wear. By contrast, the substance which is apparently laid down within the tooth as wear progresses (see Figure 18) stains a brown or dark-brown colour when exposed. The result is that a well-worn occlusal surface appears to have around it a whitish rim, com-posed of enamel and primary or "light" dentine, and an inner core of dark material which is referred to here as "dark" dentine. On the lingual crests of the molars, where elongated areas of dark and light material are exposed during the early stages of wear, widths of "dark lines" and "light lines" will be compared. The two faces of these crests which slope down toward each other and toward the centre of the tooth will be referred to as the "opposing" faces.

From the pattern of wear which develops on occlusal surfaces, it is apparent that the enamel is much harder than the dentine, and that light dentine is slightly harder than dark dentine. The result is that broad wear-ing surfaces develop a decided concavity which is referred to here as "scooping" or, in the case of long narrow crests, as "troughing."

Measurements recorded for each jaw included:

Length of lower jaw. Measured from the anterior-most point of the jaw (excluding teeth) to the posterior rim of the angle, on one side only.

Length of diastema. The distance between the alveoli of the canine and the first premolar (P_2) measured on one side only.

Length of toothrow. Greatest length of toothrow crowns of the lower cheek-teeth, measured on one side only.

Width of posterior buccal crest of the second molar. Greatest width measured across the occlusal surface of the crest, and recorded as the average of the measurements from the left and right sides of the jaw.

Height of posterior buccal crest of second molar. The height from the base of the crown, which is well defined by a line of constriction at the point of union with the roots, to the occlusal surface; recorded as an average height for the left and right teeth.

Width of first incisor. Greatest width across the tooth measured on one tooth only.

General Variation

Although the main purpose of this paper is to draw attention to certain similarities which exist within groups of our material, some consideration of the types of variation encountered is warranted.

It was anticipated that subspecific differences in rates of development and/or wear might influence the results of this work but no such differences could be detected on the cheek-teeth. Some individuals of the eastern sub-species (*A. a. americana*) did exhibit more rapid wear on the incisiform teeth.

The types of variation evident in the pattern of wear on the cheek-teeth appeared to be individual in nature and usually involved excessive wear on one portion of the toothrow while the remainder received relatively little wear. Excessive wear of this type was found on many specimens in each of several categories, including excessive wear on the anterior, the middle, or the posterior portions of the toothrow and on the lingual or buccal sides. Lighty worn specimens commonly displayed great variation in the degree of wear evident on P_2, while older, heavily worn specimens commonly showed variability in the degree of wear on M_1. In a few cases there was a marked difference between the amount of wear on the left and right sides of the same jaw. In certain instances in which unbalanced wear was obviously caused by abnormalities or necrosis in one side of the jaw, the specimens were set aside as unsuitable for inclusion in this study.

A great many of these variations in distribution of wear were probably caused by variations in width of palate or conformation of the upper tooth-row. Unfortunately, we had access to the skulls of only a small percentage of our specimens. The cause of extremely light wear on P_4 of the left mandible of specimen 19293 was traced to an abnormal lateral displacement of P^4 in the upper toothrow of the same side. No doubt some other cases of abnormal wear might have had similar explanations had all the corresponding skulls been available for examination.

Skuncke (1949, p. 130) has indicated that the hardness and weight of the bone of the lower jaw may be used as an index to the probable rate of wear of the teeth, suggesting that the rate is slower in jaws of denser harder material. The extent of variation in hardness of the mandibles was not examined in our material and therefore remains as a potential cause of unexplained variation in degree of wear.

Other types of variation observed in the over-all conditions of the mandible were associated with increasing age. Examination of Table XXIX will reveal that means of measurements of the total length of the mandible continued to increase throughout the first five wear-classes. Although a great deal of this elongation took place in the anterior portion of the jaw (the increase in means of lengths of diastema from Class I to Class V equalled 30.9 millimetres, while the same figure for total length of mandible was 46.5 millimetres) there was apparently also some increase in the length of the jaw posterior to the third molar. In addition, there was a tendency for the obtuse angle between the mandible and the ascending ramus of the mandible to become greater, during the period under dis-cussion (see Figure 17).

TABLE XXIX

Measurements of the Lower Jaws of Moose by Wear-Classes

		I	II	III	IV	V	VI	VII	VIII	IX
Width of post. buccal crest of M₂, mm.	Mean	4.2±.053	6.1±.049	7.0±.048	7.9±.049	8.6±.050	9.1±.071	9.5±.067	(10.6)±.239	10.0-····
	Range	2.8-5.1	5.4-7.2	6.1-7.8	7.3-8.6	7.8-9.4	8.5-9.9	8.7-10.4	9.4-13.3	
	Stan. dev.	.476	.378	.361	.348	.368	.409	.395	.929	
	Number	80	60	58	50	55	33	35	15	20
Height of post. buccal crest of M₂, mm.	Mean	21.7±.108	19.0±.105	17.6±.126	16.0±.102	14.1±.093	12.7±.100	11.3±.152	8.4±.432	6.6±.293
	Range	19.6-23.8	17.2-21.1	16.1-19.8	14.5-17.7	12.3-15.6	11.5-13.7	9.2-12.9	3.5-11.8	3.9-9.3
	Stan. dev.	.968	.810	.960	.721	.688	.574	.925	1.93	1.28
	Number	80	60	59	50	55	33	37	20	19
Ratio of the width to height of post. buccal crest of M₂ (%)	Mean	19.2±.304	32.1±.310	40.0±.418	49.5±.500	60.1±.533	71.5±.806	85.3±1.48	(121.0)±7.22	123.0-···
	Range	12.8-25.0	27.6-38.7	34.3-47.0	42.9-57.8	53.5-71.5	63.9-83.1	70.6-106.2	94.3-197.0	
	Stan. dev.	2.73	2.40	3.16	3.54	3.95	4.61	8.72	27.0	
	Number	80	60	57	50	55	33	35	14	20
Width of first incisor, mm.	Mean	12.4	12.3	12.3	12.1	12.1	12.0	11.8	11.6	11.5
	Range	11.5-14.0	11.2-13.0	11.3-13.5	10.3-13.1	11.0-13.5	11.5-12.6	11.1-12.9	11.0-12.5	9.3-12.6
	Number	59	37	41	36	35	19	31	18	14
Length of lower jaw, mm.	Mean	421.0	451.0	462.0	464.0	467.5	467.6	464.1	466.1	470.0
	Range	389-450	435-470	444-478	446-486	444-489	443-488	437-482	451-483	455-481
	Number	51	31	30	28	27	17	22	8	9
Length of diastema, mm.	Mean	141.3	160.5	166.0	169.5	172.2	173.7	173.1	176.4	177.5
	Range	120-160	148-181	154-188	148-185	157-190	159-189	150-189	163-196	166-192
	Number	75	56	53	46	52	31	37	20	17
Length of toothrow, mm.	Mean	170.0	166.0	168.0	167.8	167.1	165.8	162.3	163.8	161.4
	Range	165-175	158-175	157-181	160-175	159-177	158-172	158-170	158-173	154-171
	Number	9	32	38	35	38	21	21	10	12

There was evidence (Table XXIX) that, at about the time the lower jaw had completed its elongation, reduction in the length of the toothrow began. Wear on the occlusal surfaces of the teeth of the lower jaw gradually reduced their heights below the point of maximum length (along the axis of the toothrow) of the tooth. The fact that the teeth did ordinarily continue to keep close contact with one another indicated that some slight and gradual shifts in their location along the mandible must have taken place. Resultant shortening of the toothrow of older animals was clearly evident in our material.

Our observations indicated that wear on the incisiform teeth of moose in Ontario was ordinarily much less rapid than that of moose in Sweden (Skuncke, 1949) and that it was not sufficiently uniform to be of direct value in assessing age. The means of measurements of width of the first incisor, recorded for each class in Table XXIX, showed a reduction of only 0.9 millimetres from Class I to Class IX. This was in contrast with Skuncke's (1949, p. 123) Figure 104 which indicates reductions in width of the first incisor approximating 4–5 millimetres during the life of the Swedish moose. Skuncke's reference to incisiform teeth worn so that they resemble tusks which no longer touch each other after about the sixteenth year (1949, p. 129 and Figure 102) describes a condition of wear advanced well beyond that of our most-worn specimens. Figure 63 illustrates normal degrees of wear encountered in young (Class II) and old (Class IX) moose in Ontario, and in one eastern specimen of intermediate age (Class V) which was considered to show abnormally rapid wear.

It is reasonable to suppose that when both upper and lower cheek-teeth have become reduced in height, through progressive wear, the maxillae and mandibles must be brought into closer approximation to enable mastication to take place. Since, as already indicated, the incisiform teeth did not commonly become greatly modified by wear, some change in their position was necessary in order to allow the molariform teeth to occlude. Whereas in young animals the incisiform teeth protruded upward from the line of the mandible at a moderate angle, in older animals this angle was reduced so that the axis of the incisiform teeth, particularly that of the canines, formed a very small angle with the axis of the mandible.

WEAR-CLASSES

The wear-classes as first designated did not include all the jaws in the series. Except for the clear division between classes I and II, there were some specimens that displayed wear which was intermediate in degree between consecutive classes. Each intermediate specimen was later re-examined and assigned to whichever adjacent wear-class it most resembled. The following descriptions and illustrations (Figure 64) of each class refer

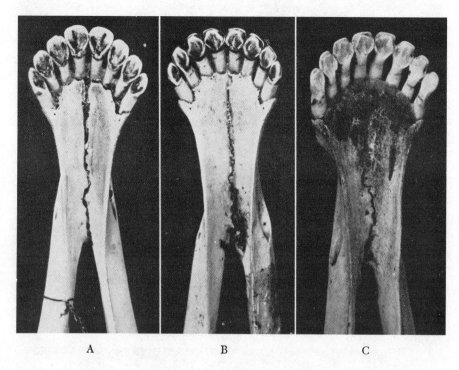

A   B   C

FIGURE 63. Wear on incisiform teeth: A. Light wear, young (Class II); B. Abnormal wear, moderate age (Class V); C. Moderate wear, old (Class IX)

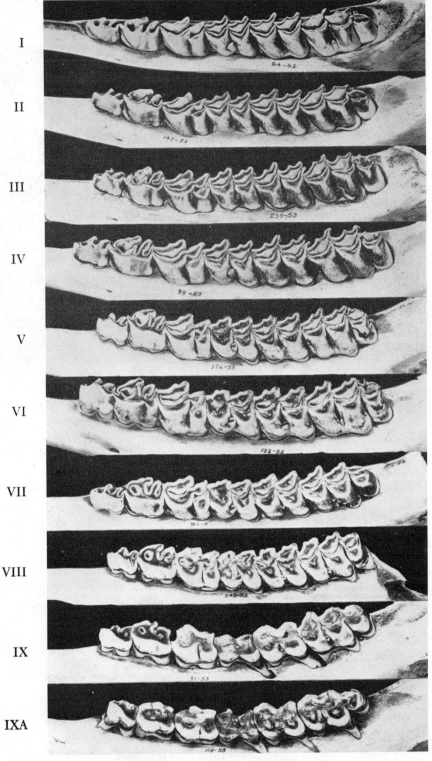

I

II

III

IV

V

VI

VII

VIII

IX

IXA

FIGURE 64. Series of jaws displaying wear typical of wear-classes I to IX, and (at bottom) the most heavily worn jaw in the series. All specimens are *A. a. andersoni*

to the average degree of wear displayed by the original members of the classes. Specimens subsequently assigned to these wear-classes are included in the measurements given in Table XXIX.

The reader is reminded that the primary criterion used in assigning jaws to a specific wear-class was *total amount of wear* on the cheek-teeth. Thus, although the specimens shown in Figure 64 were chosen as representing the average degree of normally distributed wear for each class, individual patterns of wear within classes showed some variation with regard to detailed location of the wear.

Wear-Class I: 82 Specimens

The newly erupted premolars were lightly stained in all cases and showed very little wear. The third molar, though frequently heavily strained, was also very lightly worn. The gum line was still high around the posterior cusp of M_3, and in some cases partially covered the occlusal surface of that cusp. Eruption of M_3 was far from complete, with the result that the alveolus was still open around the base of the tooth. The relative position of M_3 gave it the appearance of being cradled in the angle formed by the mandible and the ascending ramus of the mandible.

The width of the dark lines of the lingual crests of M_1 did not exceed the width of the light lines. Only very fine lines of dark dentine were exposed on the occlusal surfaces of the buccal crests of M_1 and M_2, and these were respectively chevron-like and crescentic in shape.

The Class I specimen shown in Figure 64 was typical of well developed and moderately worn members of this class.

Wear-Class II: 58 Specimens

Although all specimens in this class displayed some degree of cradling of the posterior portion of the third molar, the dentition of this class was otherwise fully adult and fully stained.

Wear on the premolars was still light. The enamel of the lingual crest of P_3 was commonly worn through only on the highest point of the crest. In 31 cases, dentine had been exposed on this crest along a length exceeding five millimetres. The dentine line on the lingual crest of P_4 extended along the whole length of the crest in 31 specimens.

The lines of dark dentine exposed on the lingual crests of the molars were not greater than the widths of the light lines, except in the case of the opposing faces of the lingual crests of M_1. At least one of these faces displayed a dark line whose width exceeded that of the adjacent light lines. In a few cases the enamel had not been worn through along the whole length of the lingual crests of M_3.

The areas of dark dentine exposed on the occlusal surfaces of the buccal crests of the molars were broadly chevron-shaped in M_1, with that of the posterior crest approaching a deltoid shape, chevron-shaped in M_2, and narrowly crescentic in the buccal crests of the anterior and middle cusps of M_3.

Wear-Class III: 48 Specimens

Elongation of the posterior portion of the mandible had progressed sufficiently that M_3 was no longer markedly cradled, and in about half the specimens of this class no cradling was discernible.

Exposure of dentine along the lingual crests was complete on P_4 but incomplete on P_3. The occlusal surface of the anterior buccal crest of P_4 was worn so that some concavity was observed, but in no case did the greatest width of the trough so formed exceed 4 millimetres. The occlusal surface of the posterior buccal crest of P_4 was worn much broader than in Class II, and was concave.

Wear on the lingual crests of the molars had increased beyond the Class II level so that the dark lines exposed on both the opposing faces of these crests of M_1 were conspicuously broader than the light lines. The same faces of the lingual crests of M_2 were similar to those described for M_1 in Class II. The enamel of the lingual crests of the anterior and middle cusps of M_3 had been worn through along their whole length.

The occlusal surfaces of the buccal crests of the molars had worn broader so that the area of dark dentine exposed was broadly chevron-shaped on M_2 and chevron-shaped on M_3.

The posterior cusp of M_3 had received very slight wear.

Wear-Class IV: 35 Specimens

Elongation of the mandible had progressed sufficiently that there was no longer any suggestion of cradling and the gum line had settled well down around the base of the posterior cusp of M_3.

The lingual dentine line of P_3 was usually complete and joined anteriorly with that of the buccal side. Slight troughing, such as would permit sliding a pencil point along its length, was apparent on the buccal side of P_3. The lingual crest of P_4 was worn noticeably broader and lower than in the previous class, and a moderate trough, approximately 4 millimetres in greatest width, was formed in the occlusal surface of the anterior buccal crest of that tooth.

The dark lines of the opposing faces of the lingual crests of M_1 were now about twice as wide as the light ones, and those of the other two faces were broader, often conspicuously so, than the light lines. The heights of these crests had usually been reduced by wear to within 3 millimetres of the buccal crests. The dark lines on the opposing faces of the lingual crests of M_2 were broader than the light lines and one of them, usually the anterior, was conspicuously broad. Other dark lines of the lingual crests of M_2 and M_3 were approximately the same width as the light lines.

The shape of the dark dentine exposed on the buccal crests was broadly chevron-like in M_3, very broadly chevron-like to deltoid in the anterior crest of M_2, and squatly deltoid in the posterior buccal crest of M_2. The posterior cusp of M_3 was moderately worn.

Wear-Class V: 50 Specimens

Although the range of variation in total amount of wear was broader in this class than in those preceding it, several characteristics were common to all specimens. Primarily, the class was characterized by broad, deep scooping on the buccal sides of P_3, P_4, M_1, and M_2. The buccal crests of M_3, though frequently displaying a considerable degree of concavity, were still more chevron-like than deltoid in shape and hence did not have great breadth.

Secondarily, the lingual crests of the premolars and molars were worn broader and lower. In 24 specimens, the anterior infundibulum of P_3 was isolated by a continuous line of dentine. All four faces of the lingual crests of M_1 were conspicuously broad. The dark lines of the lingual crests of M_2 were all broader than the light lines except in the case of the posterior face of the posterior cusp, so that those crests now resembled those of M_1 in Class III. The dark lines of the opposing faces of the lingual crests of M_3 were commonly slightly wider than the light lines.

The lingual crests of M_1 were worn down almost to the level of the buccal crests. The anterior infundibulum was still intact in 41 specimens but was partially worn away on at least one side of the other 9 jaws. The anterior cusp of M_1 appeared to be the portion of the toothrow most likely to receive disproportionately heavy wear and therefore its condition was often not a reliable indication of the total amount of wear on the toothrow.

Wear-Class VI: 24 Specimens

The deep, broad concavity of the buccal sides of the occlusal surfaces was more pronounced in this group than in Class V, particularly since this condition was now present on M_3.

The buccal crests of M_3 were worn so that the deltoid shape of the dark dentine and their great width made them resemble those of M_2.

The anterior infundibulum of M_1 was intact on 2 specimens, partially or completely worn out on at least one side of 17 jaws, and completely worn out of both sides of 5 jaws. The posterior infundibulum, though shallow and very narrow, was intact in all specimens.

The anterior infundibulum of P_3 was isolated by a complete line of dentine in all specimens except one, which was worn abnormally lightly on the lingual sides of the premolars.

The lingual crests of M_2 resembled those of M_1 in Class IV. The Class VI specimen shown in Figure 64 was abnormal in this respect—apparently a portion of the posterior lingual crest of M_2 had been chipped off. The lingual crests of M_3 were variable in this class, but commonly displayed dark lines which were conspicuously broad on the opposing faces.

Wear-Class VII: 33 Specimens

This was the first class to show heavy wear along the whole occlusal surface of the toothrow. No high sharp crest remained. The height of the buccal crests of M_1 above the gum line was less than their width. On M_2 the height commonly exceeded the width by only 1 to 2 millimetres.

The lingual crest of P_4 was worn low but the anterior infundibulum was not isolated by dentine in any specimen. The anterior infundibulum was worn out of M_1 in all cases, while the posterior infundibulum of that tooth remained intact on 13 specimens, was partly worn away in 18, and completely gone in 2 cases. The infundibula of M_2 were commonly intact but shallow.

The lingual crests of M_3 were similar to or slightly more worn than those of M_1 in Class IV. The posterior cusp of M_3 was worn so that considerable dark dentine was exposed, particularly on the buccal side.

Wear-Class VIII: 16 Specimens

The proportion of dentine to enamel visible on the occlusal surface of the toothrow had increased appreciably over that of Class VII. The anterior infundibulum of P_4 was isolated by dentine or worn away completely. Both infundibula of M_1 had been worn away in all cases, and the anterior infundibulum of M_2 was commonly partially worn away.

With the exception of the posterior cusp of M_3, the widths of buccal crests of all molars exceeded the heights of the same crests above the gum line.

Wear-Class IX: 19 Specimens

All specimens in the modal group of this class displayed extremely heavy wear. The anterior cusp of M_1 was worn almost to the gum line on the buccal side. The anterior infundibulum of P_4 was commonly worn completely away, as was the anterior infundibulum of M_2. The posterior infundibulum of M_2 was no longer intact and, as in the case of the Class IX specimen shown in Figure 64, was sometimes worn completely away. The lingual crests of M_3 had been worn down to the level of the buccal crests and, in some cases, the enamel edges of the infundibula separating them were no longer intact.

Any tendency toward abnormal distribution of wear had usually become pronounced by the time wear had progressed to the level of this class.

Necrotic lesions appeared to have developed very readily when excessive wear had reduced the height of any tooth below that of the normal gum line.

Ages of Wear-Classes

Although, as already stated, our material contained no specimens from animals whose date of birth was known, the process of development of adult dentition is sufficiently well documented that one can be certain that animals taken in the autumn and displaying the final stages of development of adult dentition are, for all practical purposes, 1½ years of age. Our material contained 82 such specimens whose characteristics have been described under Class I. These provided a known starting-point from which to work upward through consecutive classes in an attempt to assign ages to each.

Examination of Table XXIX will show that the standard errors of the means of widths and heights of M_2 and of their ratio were somewhat larger for Class I than might have been expected on the basis of corresponding standard errors of the next few classes. One might expect that a class which is known to be homogeneous for age would display great uniformity in these measurements. However, one must consider the fact that at this early age the crests of M_2 were still high and relatively narrow. It can therefore be assumed that relatively small amounts of wear, such as might take place during periods as short as one or two months, would be capable of producing considerable change in the measured dimensions of the tooth. From the discussion of developmental changes, in chapter 9 of this publication, it will be seen that variations of one to two months in the dates at which wear on M_2 commences may be expected to occur quite commonly. Although the very rapid wear of this period probably accounts for the large variation in this class, some variation is to be expected, in any case, because of differences in the original size of the tooth. Our investigations indicated that individuals which had a relatively long toothrow were also likely to have teeth that were large in all respects.

In Table XXIX it will be observed that the means of both width and height of the posterior buccal crests of M_2 indicate that wear had advanced rapidly during the year-long interval between Class I and Class II. There was, moreover, a complete separation between the ranges of classes I and II in the measured width of the posterior buccal crest of M_2. It will also be noted that Class II was more uniform with regard to the two measurements taken on that crest. Such a condition might have been anticipated in view of the fact that moderate differences in dates of eruption would now account for only a small proportion of the total time that the tooth had been subject to wear.

Of the 60 specimens in Class II, 58 showed striking uniformity in degree of wear. In view of the magnitude of the discernible differences in the degree of wear on these specimens and that of the modal group of Class III, it seems highly probable that all of the 58 original specimens were 2½ years of age. The 2 specimens moved into this class from the cline between Class II and Class III were of more doubtful age, but the probability that they were actually 2½ years old seems strong. Data for this class have been plotted above the value of 2½ years on the ordinates of Figures 65 and 66.

The modal group of Class III contained 48 specimens which showed considerable uniformity in total amount of wear on the mandibular cheekteeth. It seems probable that all of these specimens were the same age, 3½ years. Of the 10 specimens which lay between the original Class II and III, 8 resembled the characteristics of Class III more than those of Class II. We doubt, however, whether this provided sufficient evidence to warrant the assumption that each was in fact 3½ years old. Some of these specimens might more properly have been included in Class II. Three specimens which were more heavily worn than those contained in the original Class III were placed in this class on the basis of greater similarity to Class III than to Class IV. The appropriate data for Class III have been plotted on Figures 65 and 66 above the points on the ordinates representing 3½ years.

Of the 50 specimens in Class IV, 35 fell within a modal group which had a range of variation in total wear somewhat greater than that of Class III. It is assumed that the probability that all these animals were actually 4½ years old is moderately strong. Of the 13 specimens which fell between the original Classes III and IV, 10 showed greater similarity to Class IV conditions of wear. The possibility that at least a few of these animals were actually only 3½ years of age is too strong to be overlooked. Five specimens which were more heavily worn than the specimens within the original Class IV appeared to fit this class better than the next. We were aided in the task of setting upper limits on the latitude of Class IV by having, in addition to the specimens in the series, those from two moose which had been taken during the spring period. The fact that the amount of wear displayed by these specimens was intermediate between that of the last few specimens in Class IV and the first few of Class V gave some assurance of the correctness of our choice. The appropriate mean values calculated from the measurements of the Class IV specimens have been plotted above the 4½ year points on the ordinates of Figures 65 and 66.

If we can assume that there is justification for the ages assigned to Classes I to IV, the means of the measurements plotted in Figure 65 become of interest. It will be noted that the rates of change of both height and width measurements have decreased progressively with age. This, no doubt, is a reflection of the greater occlusal area of the toothrow in the older animals.

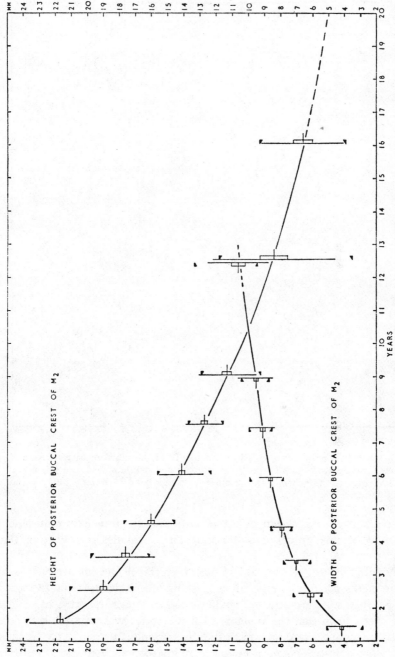

FIGURE 65. Changes in the width and height of the posterior buccal crests of M_2 with increased age. Two standard errors and one standard deviation are shown on either side of the means with the observed range lying between the black triangles

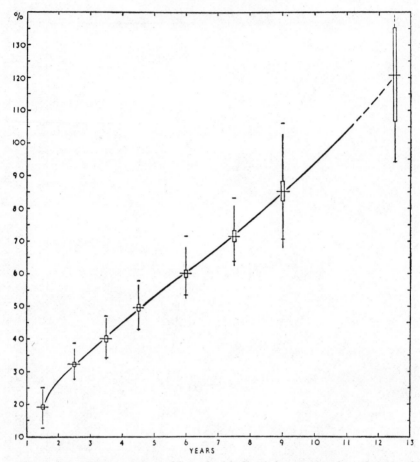

Figure 66. Relation of the width to the height of the posterior buccal crests of M_2 with increased age. Two standard errors and one standard deviation are shown on either side of the means with the observed range lying between the upper and lower horizontal bars

Similar amounts of abrasion might be expected to cause less reduction in the height of the crowns and hence result in smaller increases in their width.

Although the ranges and the standard errors of the means of the M_2 measurements and their ratio failed to show any real loss of uniformity in Class IV, it was apparent from detailed examination of the occlusal surfaces of the cheek-teeth that the remainder of the series was beginning to form a continuous cline, as compared to the discontinuous tendency of the lower end of the series. Such circumstances might come about as a result of individual differences in rates of wear which could permit some individuals of an age-class beyond 4½ years to overtake, from the standpoint of total wear, lightly worn individuals of the next higher age-class.

Beyond Class IV no large groups of specimens in the series showed sufficient uniformity of wear to justify assigning a single age-class to a group. Although classes V to IX were all assumed to cover multiple, overlapping age-classes and there were no longer obvious discontinuities in the series which suggested the ages which should have been assigned, the authors felt that there was reasonable justification for attempting to place tentative age-limits on the remainder of the classes. The early classes in the series provided a basis, from the standpoint of both the visual estimation of wear and the changes in measurements attributable to wear, for estimation of ages in the remainder of the wear-classes. The relatively smooth shape of the curves of Figures 65 and 66 lends support to these estimates.

The original Class V contained 50 specimens which displayed a range of variation considerably greater than that found in any of the previous classes. There was some temptation to subdivide this group on some arbitrary basis such as the remaining width of the anterior infundibulum of M_1, but close appraisal of the total amount of wear on specimens making up the group showed that no subdivision was warranted. Since all the 5 specimens which were more lightly worn than the specimens of the original class did show greater wear than the 2 spring specimens already mentioned, there is some probability that the youngest specimens included in this class were 5½ years of age. Three specimens that were worn more heavily than the specimens in the modal group were included in this class. We estimate that a high proportion of the material contained in this class was from animals which were 5½ or 6½ years of age and have therefore used the six-year line (suggesting that the class is divided more or less equally between these age-classes), in plotting the appropriate data in Figures 65 and 66.

Although we feel that the assignment of ages to classes I through IV has been accomplished accurately without material of known age, the limits of age assigned to classes V to IX must not be construed as anything more than tentative estimates until specimens of known age have been fitted into the series.

The 24 original specimens of Class VI displayed a range of variation only slightly larger than that of the modal group of Class V. Four specimens which were less heavily worn than those within the original class and 5 specimens which were more heavily worn were included in the final class. We estimate that the ages of individuals in Class VI varied from 6½ to 8½ years with a possibility that most of the specimens were actually 7½ years old. The means of measurements for this group have been plotted in Figures 65 and 66 on the line representing average age as 7½ years.

Of the 38 specimens in Class VII, 33 were essentially uniform in degree of wear, while 1 was less heavily worn and 4 exceeded the modal degree of wear but did not approach that of the next higher class. We estimate that this class included mainly animals $8\frac{1}{2}$ and $9\frac{1}{2}$ years old but that some specimens of $10\frac{1}{2}$ years may also have been included. The means of measurements for the class have been plotted in Figures 65 and 66 on a line which would indicate their average age as 9 years.

Class VIII originally contained 16 specimens to which 2 lightly worn and 2 heavily worn specimens were added. As might have been expected, the range of variation in this group was large. Tentative estimates of limits of age included the age-classes from $10\frac{1}{2}$ to $15\frac{1}{2}$ years. Data for Class VIII have been plotted in Figures 65 and 66 on a line representing an average age of $12\frac{1}{2}$ years. The means for width of the posterior buccal crest of M_2 and for ratio of width to height on the same crest began to lose significance in this group due to the fact that on 4 of the 20 animals no measurement of width could be made.

Due to the inward curvature of the lower extremities of the sides of the infundibulum, the width of the buccal crest increased rapidly, as suggested in Figures 65 and 66, prior to the disappearance of the infundibulum.

The 20 specimens (including one intermediate) which were more heavily worn than those of Class VIII were assigned to Class IX and tentative estimates of the age-classes represented included those from $14\frac{1}{2}$ upwards. Nineteen of the specimens in this class had a measurable height of buccal crest of M_2 remaining, and the mean for this measurement is plotted in Figure 65 on a line indicating an average age of 16 years.

Lacking more positive information it is perhaps presumptuous, but none the less interesting, to speculate on the upper limit of age of the specimens contained in this series. Our most-worn specimen, 115–53, has been compared to a photograph (Skuncke, 1949, Plate 56) of the lower jaw of a female Swedish moose known to have been 20 years old. Wear-patterns were similar, though the total amount of wear was somewhat greater on the Ontario specimen. The heights of crowns appeared to be similar but the infundibula of P_4 and M_3, which remained intact in the Swedish specimen, had been worn completely away in the specimen from Ontario. Provided that grossly similar rates of wear may be assumed, this comparison would indicate that our most-worn specimen had reached an age of at least 20 years. Since this specimen showed much more wear than most of the Class IX material it was probably three or four years older than most of the remainder of the class. Assignment of a tentative average age for Class IX of 16 years is supported by both the fit of the curve through means of heights in Figure 65 and by the estimated age of 20 years for the above-mentioned specimen.

APPENDIX B

STUDIES OF MOOSE ANTLER DEVELOPMENT
IN RELATION TO AGE

A. T. Cringan[*]

GREAT NEW AREAS of biological investigation have been opened up due to the development of precise techniques for determining age. One such field in the case of cervids is the study of antler development in relation to age. Good information on this phase of the biology of white-tailed deer, wapiti, and European moose has become available during the past few years. A technique evolved for determining the age of Ontario moose (*Alces alces andersoni* and *A. a. americana*) has enabled the collection of the material which forms the basis of this paper.

White-Tailed Deer

The mean antler beam diameter of New York deer by age-classes increases quite rapidly until deer are 3½ years old, and more slowly up to the age of 7½ (Severinghaus *et al.*, 1950). There is considerable overlapping of the beam diameter measurements of individual antlers between age-classes, so that these measurements cannot be used as a reliable index to age. New York deer have also been examined for distribution of antler points in relation to age, and much variation has been found (Anonymous, 1948c). Bucks 1½ years old had from 2 to 10 points, 2½ years old from 2 to 11 or more, and 3½ years old from 4 to 11 or more. Mean point counts showed a definite increase each year up to 3½ years, but overlapping between age-classes renders the point count, by itself, unsuitable for age-determination purposes.

Wapiti

Antlers of wapiti belonging to one age-class are probably more similar as to conformation than those of white-tailed deer. This is probably due to the greater constancy of the antlers of typical adult wapiti. Antlers of most wapiti 1½ years old are simple spikes, but some are slightly forked at the tips (Murie, 1951). Each antler of 2½- and 3½-year-old wapiti usually bears 4 or 5 points, yet there may be fewer than 4 or as many as 6. Shape

[*]Fish and Wildlife Division, Department of Lands and Forests, Sioux Lookout, Ontario.

of the pedicle and size of the antler are the main distinctions between the antlers of wapiti of these two ages. Succeeding antlers are usually of the typical 6-point form. There is some evidence that a wapiti's antlers may regress after it has reached its prime. One captive wapiti grew its best antlers when about 12 years old, and became senile three years later.

EUROPEAN MOOSE

The typical antlers of a Swedish yearling (1½ years old) are a pair of spikes (Skuncke, 1949). Antlers bearing 2, even 3 points and slight palms, may occur, but 85 out of 96 yearlings in one sample had simple paired spikes. Moose 2½ years old usually bear 2 points on each antler, but frequently 3 or 1. The antlers of Swedish moose in all older age-classes exhibit extreme variation in the number of their points owing to the existence of moose having a "cervina," or "pole-horn" type of antlers, some of which produce paired spikes throughout their lives; and of moose bearing a "palmata," or "shovel-horn" type of antlers, which tend to carry more points. Still, mean point counts seem to show marked increases up to the age of 6 to 8 years.

Weight and beam circumference are other antler qualities of Swedish moose which have been shown to be related to age. Skuncke believes that the maximum antler is grown around the moose's sixth to eighth year, after which the weight decreases, and with it, but more slowly, the beam diameter.

Skuncke stresses the fact that there is much variation in antler development, both between individuals of the same age, and in the regularity in increase of one bull's antlers from year to year. Among the causes contributing to such variation are factors inherent in the individual bull, and temporary injuries.

Interesting data on the successive antlers of two captive moose are presented. One moose grew a heavier antler, with the same, or greater, number of points, and equal, or greater, beam circumference, each year until he was 9½ years old, when he died. The other produced his greatest number of points when he was 7½ years old, his heaviest antler at 8½, and his thickest beam at 10½. This moose died at the age of 13, after showing a fairly regular decline in point count and rather irregular declines in beam circumference and weight, the latter to a level about equal to the weight of his antlers at 3½ years.

ONTARIO MOOSE

Collection of Data

Measurements of the antlers of 62 bull moose from Ontario have been collected. Age-determinations were performed by the technique described in Appendix A. The mandibles of 19 of them are in the collections of the Royal Ontario Museum of Zoology and Palaeontology and of the Department of Lands and Forests, and the age of the other 43 was determined by the author in the field, during the 1953 open seasons. Antler measurements, including greatest spread, normal point count, greatest palm width and length, and minimum beam circumference, were made in accordance with instructions for the Boone and Crockett Club's North American Big Game Competition (Webb *et al.*, 1952). All the antlers were measured by the author, except one pair, the largest in the series, which was measured by Mr. G. Whitefield.

The sample is inadequate for any definitive work. The number of specimens for certain age-classes and groups is much too small to indicate the normal range of individual variation. Also, the sample is heavily weighted by 1953 specimens, and since variations due to the effect of weather on nutrition could reasonably be expected from year to year, a better temporal sample is desirable.

Characteristics in Relation to Age

Each of the five antler qualities selected for measurement should demonstrate some relation to age, on the basis of Skuncke's findings. This expectation has been generally fulfilled in every case.

The greatest antler spread, shown in Table XXX, increases from a

TABLE XXX
DISTRIBUTION OF GREATEST ANTLER SPREAD:
MEASUREMENTS BY AGE-CLASSES
(Basis: 62 Ontario specimens)

Antler spread (inches)	$1\frac{1}{2}$	$2\frac{1}{2}$	$3\frac{1}{2}$	$4\frac{1}{2}$	$5\frac{1}{2}$–$6\frac{1}{2}$	$6\frac{1}{2}$–$8\frac{1}{2}$	$8\frac{1}{2}$–$10\frac{1}{2}$	$10\frac{1}{2}$–$15\frac{1}{2}$	Total
$14\frac{1}{8}$–21	2								2
$21\frac{1}{8}$–28	13	2							15
$28\frac{1}{8}$–35		5	6			1			12
$35\frac{1}{8}$–42			2	3	2	3			10
$42\frac{1}{8}$–49		1			4	3	2	2	12
$49\frac{1}{8}$–56				1	2		3	1	7
$56\frac{1}{8}$–63						1	2		3
$63\frac{1}{8}$–70							1		1
TOTAL	15	8	8	4	8	8	8	3	62
Minimum	$14\frac{1}{4}$	$22\frac{3}{8}$	29	$35\frac{1}{4}$	$36\frac{5}{8}$	$31\frac{7}{8}$	$44\frac{5}{8}$	$47\frac{3}{8}$	$14\frac{1}{4}$
Mean	$23\frac{3}{8}$	$31\frac{7}{8}$	34	$42\frac{1}{4}$	$45\frac{5}{8}$	$43\frac{5}{8}$	$53\frac{3}{4}$	$49\frac{3}{8}$	
Maximum	$27\frac{3}{4}$	$44\frac{3}{8}$	$39\frac{7}{8}$	$51\frac{1}{8}$	$55\frac{7}{8}$	$58\frac{5}{8}$	70	$51\frac{7}{8}$	70

mean of 23⅜ inches in the 1½-year age-class to 45¾ inches in the 5½–6½-year age-group, then fluctuates between 43 inches and 54 inches. The greatest mean spread and the four greatest individual spreads occur in the 8½–10½-year age-group. Antler spreads of all 39 moose which were 3½ years old or older were greater than the largest spread among the yearlings.

The mean count of normal points of age-classes and groups, Table XXXI, increases from 4.0 in the yearling class to a maximum of 21.1 in the

TABLE XXXI

DISTRIBUTION OF ANTLER POINTS BY AGE-CLASSES

(Basis: 62 Ontario specimens)

Antler points (both antlers)	Age-class (years)								Total
	1½	2½	3½	4½	5½–6½	6½–8½	8½–10½	10½–15½	
1—1	2								2
2—1	5								5
2—2	4								4
3—2	3	1							4
4—3	1	2	1						4
4—4	1	2	1						4
5—4		2	1	1					4
5—5				1					1
7—3						1			1
6—5					1				1
6—6						1			1
7—6			1	1					2
8—6					2				2
8—7		1	2	1	1	3	1		9
9—7						1			1
9—8					1		2	1	4
9—9					1		1		2
10—9					2				2
11—8								1	1
11—10						1			1
12—9						1			1
12—11						1			1
12—12							1	1	2
13—12							1		1
14—11							1		1
16—12							1		1
TOTAL	16	8	6	4	8	9	8	3	62
Minimum	1—1	3—2	4—3	5—4	6—5	7—3	8—7	9—8	1—1
Mean (combined)	4.0	8.5	11.1	11.3	15.9	16.5	21.1	20.0	
Maximum	4—4	8—7	8—7	8—7	10—9	12—11	16—12	12—12	16—12

8½–10½-year group, and declines slightly in the next higher age-group. The three greatest individual point counts also occur in the 8½–10½-year age-group. The point counts of all moose 4½ years old or older that were examined exceeded the greatest point count of any yearling included in this sample. Furthermore, 10 out of 11 moose in the 8½–15½-year age-groups had point counts which exceeded the greatest point count of any moose 4½ years old or less.

There is much variation in the antler palms of moose of the same age-class, owing to the existence of "palmata" and "cervina" types of antlers, and so the measurements of palms seem to show greater overlapping than those of the other antler qualities. Only 8 out of 30 of the yearling antlers examined were palmed, and only 3 of 15 yearlings in the sample bore paired palmed antlers. Both antlers of all the older moose examined were at least slightly palmed.

Mean palm width, Table XXXII, and length, Table XXXIII, both increase

TABLE XXXII

DISTRIBUTION OF GREATEST ANTLER PALM WIDTH: MEASUREMENTS BY AGE-CLASSES

(Basis: 121 antlers from 61 Ontario specimens)

Palm width (inches)	Age-class (years)								
	1½	2½	3½	4½	5½–6½	6½–8½	8½–10½	10½–15½	Total
0–4	29	4	3	1					37
4⅛–8	1	10	7	3	3	7			31
8⅛–12			4	4	12	7	9	3	39
12⅛–16					1	4	6	3	14
TOTAL	30	14	14	8	16	18	15	6	121
Minimum		2¾	3¼	3⅛	5	5¾	8⅝	8⅞	
Mean		4⅝	6¼	7⅛	9⅜	9¾	11⅝	11⅜	
Maximum	5⅛	7⅛	10⅛	9¼	13⅛	15⅜	14¾	14½	15⅜

with age, from 4⅝ inches by 13⅛ inches in the 2½-year age-class, up to 11⅝ inches by 31¼ inches in the 8½–10½-year age-group, then decline very slightly in the 10½–15½-year age-group. The widest individual palm was on one antler of a moose belonging to the 6½–8½-year age-group, and the two longest palms were from one moose in the 8½–10½-year age-group. Moose of the 8½–15½-year groups seem to have distinctly wider antler palms than those of the 1½–2½-year classes, and longer palms than most moose in the 1½–4½-year classes.

TABLE XXXIII

DISTRIBUTION OF GREATEST ANTLER PALM LENGTH
MEASUREMENTS BY AGE-CLASSES
(Basis: 121 antlers from 61 Ontario specimens)

Palm length (inches)	Age-class (years)								
	1½	2½	3½	4½	5½–6½	6½–8½	8½–10½	10½–15½	Total
0–6	26								26
6⅛–12	4	7	2						13
12⅛–18		5	7	1	1	1			15
18⅛–24		2	5	6	5	8			26
24⅛–30				1	10	5	7	2	25
30⅛–36						4	6	4	14
36⅛–42							1		1
42⅛–48							1		1
TOTAL	30	14	14	8	16	18	15	6	121
Minimum		7¼	9⅝	17	16⅛	16¾	25¾	25⅜	
Mean		13⅛	16½	21	24¼	25¼	31¼	31	
Maximum	7½	22	22	25⅝	29¼	33⅛	45¾	34⅜	45¾

TABLE XXXIV

DISTRIBUTION OF MINIMUM ANTLER BEAM CIRCUMFERENCE:
MEASUREMENTS BY AGE-CLASSES
(Basis: 123 antlers from 62 Ontario specimens)

Antler beam circumference (inches)	Age-class (years)								
	1½	2½	3½	4½	5½–6½	6½–8½	8½–10½	10½–15½	Total
2⅝–3½	6								6
3⅝–4½	14	1							15
4⅝–5½	8	10	12	1					31
5⅝–6½		5	4	5	6	10		1	31
6⅝–7½				2	10	4	13	3	32
7⅝–8½						4	2	2	8
TOTAL	28	16	16	8	16	18	15	6	123
Minimum	3⅛	4¼	4¾	5½	5⅝	5⅞	6⅞	6½	3⅛
Mean	4⅛	5¼	5⅜	6	6⅝	6¾	7¼	7⅛	
Maximum	5⅜	6⅛	6⅛	6¾	7½	8	8½	8⅛	8½

Mean antler beam circumference, Table XXXIV, increases most rapidly between the first and second years, from 4⅛ inches to 5¼ inches, then more slowly to a maximum of around 7¼ inches during the eighth to tenth years, and appears to decrease slightly thereafter. The greatest beam cir-

cumference measured was that of one antler of a specimen classified as
8½–10½ years old. All the antlers of yearling moose that were measured
had smaller diameters than the smallest antler of any moose 4½ years old or
older that was checked, and the largest antler beams of moose 2½ and 3½
years old were smaller than the smallest antler beam of any moose 8½–15½
years old that was measured.

Characteristics Indicative of Age

As already noted, there are breaking points in each of the series of five
antler qualities measured, which seem to separate two groups of old and
young moose, leaving an intermediate overlapping group. These breaking
points have been used, key-fashion, to reassess the age of the 62 specimens
examined, on the basis of their antler characteristics. The results of this
procedure are given in Table XXXV.

By using this procedure, it was possible to determine the age of 14 out
of 16 yearlings. The antler characteristics of yearlings—the small spread,

TABLE XXXV

MOOSE AGES DETERMINED FROM ANTLER CHARACTERISTICS
COMPARED TO THOSE DETERMINED BY TOOTH-WEAR

(Basis: 62 Ontario specimens)

Age-class antler basis	Age-class (years): tooth-wear method								
	1½	2½	3½	4½	5½–6½	6½–8½	8½–10½	10½–15½	Total
1½	14								14
1½–2½	2								2
2½		2							2
2½–3½		4	3						7
2½–6½		1	1	1	1				4
2½–8½		1		1		2			4
3½			2						2
3½–8½			2			1			3
4½–8½				1	1	1			3
4½–10½				1	1	1	1		4
4½–15½						1			1
5½–8½					1				1
5½–15½					2	3	7	3	15
TOTAL	16	8	8	4	6	9	8	3	62
Range of antler-based age determinations	1½–2½	2½–8½	2½–8½	2½–10½	2½–15½	2½–15½	4½–15½	5½–15½	

low point count, and usual lack of palmation—are a fairly sound indication of their age.

The method of determining the age of older moose on the basis of antler characteristics yields results that are much less precise. The age of 11 out of 16 moose, judged on the basis of tooth-wear to have been $2\frac{1}{2}$ and $3\frac{1}{2}$ years old, was assessed to within one year by their antler characteristics. Using this method, it was not possible to judge the age of any older moose in this sample within less than two years of its age-class or group. Sixteen out of 26 moose judged to be $5\frac{1}{2}$ years old or older by their tooth wear, were also classified as at least $5\frac{1}{2}$ years old by their antler characteristics.

Contrast between Swedish and Ontario Moose

The results of Skuncke's and the author's approaches to the problem of antler development in relation to age are not directly comparable, except possibly in the case of point counts. Swedish and Ontario moose exhibit striking differences in point counts. The incidence of yearlings with paired spikes is 85 out of 96 in Sweden, and only 2 out of 16 in the Ontario sample. Paired spikes occur fairly often in Swedish moose up to the age of $5\frac{1}{2}$ years, and occasionally beyond, but no Ontario moose in this sample, except yearlings, bore a single spike. There is also probably a difference in the total number of points commonly attained by Swedish and Ontario moose. Only 1 out of 378 moose from Hällefors tabulated by Skuncke bore more than 18 points, while 11 of 62 in the author's sample carried more than 18 points. (These differences may be partly accounted for by differences in point classification. I do not know what system Skuncke used.)

Skuncke speculates that the best moose antler in Sweden is produced during the sixth to eighth years of the animal's life. Each of the criteria used in this study of Ontario moose suggests that the best antlers are to be found on moose from $8\frac{1}{2}$–$10\frac{1}{2}$ years old. The rate of retrogression in antlers of older moose in Ontario requires much further study.

LITERATURE CITED

ADAMS, CHARLES C.
1909. Ecological survey of Isle Royale, Lake Superior. Rept. Board Geol. Sur. for 1908. Hallenbeck Crawford Co., Lansing, Mich., pp. 1–468.

AGASSIZ, LOUIS, and J. ELLIOT CABOT
1850. Lake Superior, its physical character, vegetation, and animals, compared with those of other and similar regions. Gould, Kendall and Lincoln, Boston, Mass., pp. 1–428.

ALBERTA
1908–35. Dept. Agr. Ann. Repts.
1941–5. Dept. Lands and Mines Ann. Repts.

ALDOUS, C. M., and H. L. MENDALL
1941. The status of big game and fur animals in Maine. Maine Coop. Wildlife Res. Unit, Univ. Maine, Orono, Me., pp. 1–24.

ALDOUS, SHALER E.
1944. A deer browse survey method. Journ. Mamm., vol. 25, no. 2, pp. 130–136.
1952. Deer browse clipping study in the Lake States region. Journ. Wildlife Mgt., vol. 16, no. 4, pp. 401–409.

ALDOUS, SHALER E., and LAURITS W. KREFTING
1946. The present status of moose on Isle Royale. Trans. 11th N. Am. Wildlife Conf., pp. 296–308.

ALDOUS, SHALER E., and C. F. SMITH
1948. Fall and winter food habits of deer in northeastern Minnesota. Wildlife Leaflet 310, U.S. Dept. Int., pp. 1–10.

ALLEN, EDGAR, CHAS. H. DANFORTH, and EDWARD A. DAISY
1939. Sex and internal secretions. 2nd ed. Williams and Wilkins, Baltimore, Md., pp. 1149–1196.

ALLEN, J. A.
1902. Mammals collected in Alaska and northern British Columbia by the Andrew J. Stone Expedition of 1902. Bull. Am. Mus. Nat. Hist., vol. 19, art. 21, pp. 521–567.

"AN ALASKAN"
1923. The moose butchers of Kenai. Am. Forests, vol. 29, no. 360, pp. 719–20, 750.

ANDERSON, R. M.
1924a. Range of moose extending northward. Can. Field-Nat., vol. 38, no. 2, pp. 27–29.
1924b. The present status and future prospects of larger mammals of Canada. Scottish Geogr. Mag., vol. 40, pp. 321–331.
1937. Mammals and birds of the western Arctic district, Northwest Territories, Canada. Canada's Western Northland. Can., Dept. Mines and Resources, pp. 97–122.
1946. Catalogue of Canadian Recent mammals. Natl. Mus. Can., Bull. no. 102, Biol. ser. no. 31, pp. 1–238.

ANONYMOUS
1946. Riding by cowboy. Rod and Gun in Canada, vol. 48, no. 6, p. 41.
1948a. Report of the Big Game Committee. Prov. Quebec Assoc. for the Protection of Fish and Game Inc., Ann. Rept., pp. 5–8.
1948b. Questions you hunters ask! New York State Cons. Dept., Pittman-Robertson Res. Proj., 28-R, leaflet, pp. 1–4 (mimeo.).

ANTEVS, ERNEST
1931. Late-glacial correlations and ice recession in Manitoba. Geol. Sur. Can. Memo 168, pp. 1–76.

247

ANTHONY, H. E.
1939. The moose: description and distribution, and hunting the Wyoming moose. North American Big Game. Charles Scribner's Sons, New York, pp. 263–265, 278–284.

ATWOOD, B. H.
1952. Moose vs. the "iron horse." Outdoor American, vol. 17, no. 2, pp. 10–11.

AUDUBON, JOHN J., and JOHN BACHMAN
1851. The viviparous quadrupeds of North America. V. G. Audubon, New York, vol. 2, pp. 1–334.

BAILEY, ALFRED M.
1940. The moose in Colorado. Journ. Mamm., vol. 21, no. 1, p. 96.
1944. Records of moose in Colorado. Journ. Mamm., vol. 25, no. 2, pp. 192–193.

BAILEY, VERNON
1918. Wild animals of Glacier National Park. Mammals. U.S. Dept. Int., Natl. Parks Serv., Govt. Printing Office, Wash., D.C., pp. 1–102.
1926. A biological survey of North Dakota. N. Am. Fauna, no. 49, pp. 1–226.
1930. Animal life of Yellowstone National Park. Chas. C. Thomas, Springfield, Ill., and Baltimore, Md., pp. 1–241.
1936. The mammals and life zones of Oregon. N. Am. Fauna, no. 55, pp. 1–416.

BALTZER, BEN. E.
1933. Swimming power of moose. Rod and Gun in Canada, vol. 35, no. 6, p. 22.

BANFIELD, A. W. F.
1950. The mammals of Waterton Lakes National Park. Wildlife Mgt. Bull., Dept. Resources and Development, Can. Wildlife Serv., ser. 1, no. 1, pp. 1–43.

BARLOW, A. E.
1899. Report on the geology and natural resources of the area included by the Nipissing and Temiscaming map-sheets. Geol. Sur. Can., Ann. Rept., 1897, vol. 10, pp. 1I–302I.

BEATTY, DAVID, et al.
1901. Exploration survey party No. 8 report. Report of the Survey and Exploration of Northern Ontario, 1900. Toronto, pp. 189–207.

BELL, ROBERT
1898. On the occurrence of mammoth and mastodon remains around Hudson Bay. Bull. Geol. Soc. Am., vol. 9, pp. 369–390.

BENSLEY, B. A.
1913. A Cervalces antler from the Toronto interglacial. Univ. Toronto Studies, Geol. ser. no. 8, pp. 1–3.

BENSON, D. A.
1952. Treatment of a sick moose with cobaltous chloride. Journ. Wildlife Mgt., vol. 16, no. 1, pp. 110–111.

BIGGAR, H. P.
1924. The voyages of Jacques Cartier. Roberval's voyage. Pub. Publ. Arch. Can., no. 11, pp. 1–330.

BLAIR, EMMA HELEN (tr. and ed.)
1911. The Indian tribes of the upper Mississippi Valley and region of the Great Lakes: as described by Nicolas Perrot, etc. The Arthur H. Clark Co., Cleveland, Ohio, vol. 1, pp. 1–372.

BLANCHET, G. H.
1926. Great Slave Lake area: Northwest Territories topographical survey. Can., Dept. Int., pp. 1–58.

BLUNT, FLOYD M.
1950. "Untitled notes on moose in Wyoming." Wyo. Wild Life, Wyo. Game and Fish Comm., vol. 14, no. 1, p. 21.

BOSTOCK, JOHN, and H. T. RILEY (trs.)
1855. The natural history of Pliny. Translated with notes and illustrations. Henry G. Bohn, London, vol. 2, book 8, chap. 16, pp. 263–264.

BOURNE, A. N. and E. G. BOURNE (trs. and eds.)
1911. The voyages and explorations of Samuel de Champlain (1604–1616) together with the voyage of 1603. Courier Press, Toronto, vol. 2, pp. 1–229.
BRECKENRIDGE, W. J.
1946. Weights of a Minnesota moose. Journ. Mamm., vol. 27, no. 1, pp. 90–91.
BRITISH COLUMBIA
1937. Report of Provincial Game Commission for the year ended December 31st, 1936. Prov. B.C., Dept. Attorney-General, Victoria, B.C., pp. 21–58.
1947. Report of Provincial Game Commission for the year ended December 31st, 1946. Prov. B.C., Dept. Attorney-General, Victoria, B.C.
1948. Report of Provincial Game Commission for the year ended December 31st, 1947. Prov. B.C., Dept. Attorney-General, Victoria, B.C.
BROOKS, ALLAN
1926. Past and present big-game conditions in British Columbia and the predatory mammal question. Journ. Mamm., vol. 7, no. 1, pp. 37–40.
1928. The invasion of moose in British Columbia. Murrelet, vol. 9, no. 2, pp. 43–44.
BROOKS, HARLOW
1906. The Idaho moose. N.Y. Zool. Soc. 10th Ann. Rept., pp. 201–216.
BROOKS, JAMES W.
1953. A record of North America's most westerly moose. Journ. Mamm., vol. 34, no. 3, pp. 396–397.
BROWN, ROBERT C., and JAMES R. SIMON
1947. Notes on wintering moose. Wyo. Wild Life, Wyo. Game and Fish Comm., vol. 11, no. 6, pp. 4–8, 38.
BUCHANAN, ANGUS
1920. Wildlife in Canada. McClelland, Goodchild and Stewart, Ltd., Toronto, pp. 1–264.
BURPEE, LAWRENCE J. (ed.)
1927. Journals and letters of Pierre Gaultier de Varennes de la Vérendrye and his sons. Champlain Soc., Toronto, pp. 1–548.
BURT, W. H.
1946. The mammals of Michigan. Univ. Mich. Press, Ann Arbor, pp. 1–288.
CAHALANE, VICTOR H.
1932. Age variation in the teeth and skull of the white-tail deer. Cranbrook Inst. Sci., Sci. Pub. no. 2, pp. 1–14.
1939. Deer of the world. Natl. Geogr. Mag., vol. 76, pp. 463–510.
1942. Wildlife vistas of the eastern highlands. Audubon Mag., vol. 44, no. 2, pp. 101–111.
1945. The moose. Cranbrook Inst. Sci. News Letter, vol. 14, no. 7, pp. 70–74.
1947. Mammals of North America. The Macmillan Co., New York, pp. 1–682.
1948. The status of mammals in the United States national park system, 1947. Journ. Mamm., vol. 29, no. 3, pp. 247–259.
CAHN, ALVIN R.
1921. Mammals of Itaska County, Minnesota. Journ. Mamm., vol. 2, no. 2, pp. 68–74.
1937. The mammals of the Quetico Provincial Park of Ontario. Journ. Mamm., vol. 18, no. 1, pp. 19–29.
CAHN, ALVIN R., G. I. WALLACE, and L. J. THOMAS
1932. A new disease of moose. III. Science, vol. 76, no. 1974, p. 385.
CAMERON, AUSTIN W.
1948. Report of ecological studies conducted in the Liscomb Game Sanctuary. Rept. Dept. Lands and Forests, 1947, Nova Scotia, pp. 93–117.
1949. Report on biological investigations of game and fur-bearing animals in Nova Scotia, 1948. Rept. Dept. of Lands and Forests, 1948, Nova Scotia, pp. 5–28.
CAMSELL, CHARLES
1906a. Report on the Peel River and tributaries Yukon and Mackenzie. Geol. Sur. Can., Ann. Rept., 1904, vol. 16, pp. 1CC–49CC.

1906b. County around the headwaters of the Severn River. Geol. Sur. Dept., Summ. Rept., 1904, Ottawa, vol. 16, pp. 143A–152A.

CANADA
1888. Report of the select committee of the Senate appointed to inquire into the resources of the great Mackenzie Basin. Session 1888. Ottawa, pp. 1–310, plus maps.
1939. Native trees of Canada. Rev. ed. Dept. Mines and Resources, Bull. 61, Ottawa, pp. 1-210.
1946. Forest entomology in the province of Ontario. A brief presented before the Ontario Royal Commission on Forestry. Forest Insect Investigations Unit, Div. Ent., Sci. Serv., Dept. Agr., Ottawa, pp. 1–134.

CARVER, JONATHAN
1778. Travels through the interior parts of North America in the years 1766, 1767 and 1768. J. Walter, London, pp. 1–543.

CHAMBERS, ERNEST J. (ed.)
1908. The Great Mackenzie Basin. Reports of select committees of the Senate. Sessions 1887 and 1888. Ottawa, pp. 1–80, plus map.

CHATELAIN, EDWARD F.
1950. Bear-moose relationships on the Kenai Peninsula. Trans. 15th N. Am. Wildlife Conf., pp. 224–233.

CHEATUM, E. L., and C. W. SEVERINGHAUS
1950. Variations in fertility of white-tailed deer related to range conditions. Trans. 15th N. Am. Wildlife Conf., pp. 170–189.

CLARK, R. T.
1934. Studies on the physiology of reproduction in the sheep. I. Ovulation rate of the ewe as affected by the plane of nutrition. II. The cleavage stages of the ovum. Anat. Rec., vol. 60, pp. 125–159.

CLARKE, C. H. D.
MS Biological reconnaissance of the Alaska military highway with particular reference to the Yukon Territory and the proposed national park therein. 1944, pp. 1–43.
1936. Moose seeks shelter for young. Can. Field-Nat., vol. 50, no. 4, pp. 67–68.
1940a. Wildlife investigation in Banff National Park, 1939. Ottawa, pp. 1–26 (mimeo.).
1940b. A biological investigation of the Thelon Game Sanctuary. Natl. Mus. Can., Bull. no. 96, Biol. ser. no. 25, pp. 1–133.
1942. Wildlife investigations in Banff and Jasper National parks in 1941. Natl. Parks Bur., Ottawa, pp. 1–21 (mimeo.).
1944. Notes on the status and distribution of certain mammals and birds in the Mackenzie River and Western Arctic area in 1942–43. Can. Field-Nat., vol. 58, no. 3, pp. 97–103.
1952. The sacred cow. Northern Sportsman, vol. 7, no. 6, pp. 10–12.

COONEY, ROBERT
1832. A compendious history of the northern part of the Province of New Brunswick, and the District of Gaspe in Lower Canada. Halifax, N.S. (Original not seen.)

COONEY, ROBERT F.
1946. Montana. Pittman-Robertson Quarterly, U.S. Dept. Int., Fish and Wildlife Serv., vol. 6, no. 1, pp. 11–12.

CORY, CHARLES B.
1912. The mammals of Illinois and Wisconsin. Field Mus. Nat. Hist., Zool. ser., vol. 11, no. 153, pp. 1–502.

COTTAM, C., and C. S. WILLIAMS
1943. Speed of some wild mammals. Journ. Mamm., vol. 24, no. 2, pp. 262–263.

COUEY, FAYE M., et al.
1948. Montana. Wildlife survey and management. Pittman-Robertson Quarterly, U.S. Dept. Int., Fish and Wildlife Serv., vol. 8, no. 3, pp. 306–311.

COWAN, IAN MCTAGGART
1939. The vertebrate fauna of the Peace River district of British Columbia. Occ. Papers B.C. Prov. Mus. no. 1, Victoria, B.C., pp. 1–101.
1944. Report on game conditions in Banff, Jasper and Kootenay national parks. Ottawa, pp. 1–72 (mimeo.).
1946. Report of wildlife studies in Jasper, Banff and Yoho national Parks, 1944, and parasites, diseases and injuries of game animals in the Rocky Mountain national parks, 1942–1944. Ottawa, pp. 1–84 (mimeo.).
1947. The timber wolf in the Rocky Mountain national parks of Canada. Can. Journ. Res., sec. D, vol. 25, no. 5, pp. 139–174.
1950. Some vital statistics of big game on overstocked mountain range. Trans. 15th N. Am. Wildlife Conf., pp. 581–588.
1951. The diseases and parasites of big game mammals of western Canada. Rept. Proc. 5th Ann. Game Conv., Vancouver, B.C. Game Dept., pp. 37–64.
COWAN, I. McT., and V. C. BRINK
1949. Natural game licks in the Rocky Mountain national parks of Canada. Journ. Mamm., vol. 30, no. 4, pp. 379–387.
COWAN, I. McT., W. S. HOAR, and JAMES HATTER
1950. The effect of forest succession upon the quantity and upon the nutritive values of woody plants used as food by moose. Can. Journ. Res., sec. D, vol. 28, pp. 249–271.
CRANE, JOSSELYN
1931. Mammals of Hampshire County, Massachusetts. Journ. Mamm., vol. 12, no. 3, pp. 267–273.
CRIDDLE, S.
1929. An annotated list of the mammals of Aweme, Manitoba. Can. Field-Nat., vol. 43, no. 7, pp. 155–159.
CROSS, EWART C.
1937. The white-tailed deer of Ontario. Rod and Gun in Can., vol. 38, no. 9, pp. 14–15, 32.
DALE, BONNYCASTLE
1934. Midnight moose calling. Rod and Gun in Can., vol. 36, no. 5, pp. 14–15, 27, 31.
DALQUEST, WALTER W.
1948. Mammals of Washington, Univ. Kan., Pub. Mus. Nat. Hist., vol. 2, pp. 1–444.
DAVIS, WILLIAM B.
1939. The recent mammals of Idaho. The Caxton Printers, Ltd., Caldwell, Idaho, pp. 1–400.
DAWSON, G. M.
1896. Summary report on operations of the geological survey for the year 1895. Geol. Sur. Dept., Ottawa, vol. 8, pp. 1A–154A.
DEEVEY, EDWARD S., Jr.
1949. Biogeography of the Pleistocene. Bull. Geol. Soc. Am., vol. 60, pp. 1315–1416.
DEKAY, J. E.
1842. Natural history of New York. Zoology, pt. 1, Mammalia. D. Appleton and Co. and Wiley and Putnam, New York, pp. 1–146.
DENNISTON, R. H., II
1948. Notes on the behaviour of the Wyoming moose, *Alces americana shirasi*, in the Jackson Hole area, 1947–1948. Prog. Rep., Univ. Wyo., Laramie, Wyo., pp. 1–15 (mimeo.).
DE VOS, A.
1948. Status of the woodland caribou in Ontario. Sylva, Ont. Dept. Lands and Forests, vol. 4, no. 1, pp. 17–23.
DE VOS, A., and A. E. ALLIN
1949. Some notes on moose parasites. Journ. Mamm., vol. 30, no. 4, pp. 430–431.

DE Vos, A., and RANDOLPH L. PETERSON
1951. A review of the status of woodland caribou (*Rangifer caribou*) in Ontario. Journ. Mamm., vol. 32, no. 3, pp. 329–337.

DICE, LEE R.
1919. The mammals of southeastern Washington. Journ. Mamm., vol. 1, no. 1, pp. 10–22.
1921. Notes on the mammals of interior Alaska. Journ. Mamm., vol. 2, no. 1, pp. 20–28.
1938. The Canadian biotic province with special reference to mammals. Ecology, vol. 19, no. 4, pp. 503–514.
1943. The biotic provinces of North America. Univ. Mich. Press, Ann Arbor, pp. 1–78.

DIKMANS, G.
1939. Helminth parasites of North American semi-domesticated and wild ruminants. Proc. Helminthological Soc. Wash., vol. 6, pp. 97–101.

DIXON, JOSEPH S.
1938. Birds and mammals of Mount McKinley National Park. Fauna of the Natl. Parks of the U.S., U.S. Dept. Int., Natl. Park Serv., Fauna ser. no. 3, pp. 1–236.

DOUGLAS, R., and J. N. WALLACE (trs.)
1926. Twenty years of York Factory, 1694–1714: Jérémie's account of Hudson Strait and Bay. Transl. from French edition of 1720. Thorburn and Abbott, Ottawa, pp. 1–42.

DUFRESNE, FRANK
1942. Mammals and birds of Alaska. Circ. no. 3, U.S. Dept. Int., Fish and Wildlife Serv., pp. 1–37.
1946. Alaska's animals and fishes. A. S. Barnes and Co., New York, pp. 1–297.
1952. Too many moose. Field and Stream, vol. 57, no. 5, pp. 54–57, 115–116.

DURRANT, STEPHEN D.
1952. Mammals of Utah. Univ. Kans. Pub., Mus. Nat. Hist., vol. 6, pp. 1–549.

DYER, HAROLD JACOBSEN
1948. Preliminary plan for wildlife management on Baxter State Park. Master's thesis, Univ. Maine, pp. 1–79 (vide Hosley, 1949).

DYMOND, J. R., L. L. SNYDER, and E. B. S. LOGIER
1928. A faunal survey of the Lake Nipigon region, Ontario. (Contrib. Roy. Ont. Mus. Zool., no. 1), Trans. Roy. Can. Inst., vol. 16, pt. 2, pp. 232–291.

EDWARDS, R. Y.
1952. An aerial moose census. B.C. Forest Service (Victoria) Res. Notes no. 23, pp. 1–9.

ELY, ALFRED, et al.
1939. North American big game. Boone and Crockett Club. Charles Scribner's Sons, New York, pp. 1–533.

FAIRBAIRN, H. W.
1931. Notes on mammals and birds from Great Slave Lake. Can. Field-Nat., vol. 45, pp. 158–162.

FARLEY, F. L.
1925. Changes in the status of certain animals and birds during the past 50 years in central Alberta. Can. Field-Nat., vol. 39, no. 9, pp. 200–202.

FENSTERMACHER, R.
1934a. Further studies of diseases affecting moose. Univ. Minn. Agr. Exp. Sta., Bull. 308, pp. 1–26.
1934b. Diseases affecting moose. Alumni Quarterly, vol. 22, no. 3, pp. 81–94.
1937. Further studies of diseases affecting moose. II. Cornell Vet., vol. 27, no. 1, pp. 25–37.

FENSTERMACHER, R., and W. L. JELLISON
1933. Diseases affecting moose. Univ. Minn. Agr. Exp. Sta., Bull. 294, pp. 1–20.

FENSTERMACHER, R., and O. W. OLSEN
1942a. Further studies of diseases affecting moose. III. Cornell Vet., vol. 32, no. 3, pp. 241–254.

1942b. Diseases affecting moose. Cons. Volunteer, Minn. Dept. Cons., vol. 5, no. 27, pp. 46–48.

FINDLEY, JAMES S.
1951. A record of moose speed. Journ. Mamm., vol. 32, no. 1, p. 116.

FISHER, PETER
1825. Sketches of New Brunswick,—by an Inhabitant. Saint John, N.B. Reprint. First History of New Brunswick by Peter Fisher, Saint John, 1921. (Original not seen.)

FLEROV, C.
1931. A review of the elks or moose (*Alces* Gray) of the Old World. Comptes Rendus de l'Académie des Sciences de l'URSS, pp. 71–74.

FLINT, RICHARD FOSTER
1948. Glacial geology and the Pleistocene epoch. John Wiley and Sons, New York, pp. 1–589.

FOWLER, R. L.
1937. Changes in the natural history of the High River district, Alberta. Can. Field-Nat., vol. 51, no. 2, pp. 15–16.

FRICK, CHILDS
1937. Horned ruminants of North America. Bull. Am. Mus. Nat. Hist., vol. 69, pp. 1–669.

GANONG, WILLIAM F. (tr. and ed.)
1908. The description and natural history of the coasts of North America (Acadia) by Nicolas Denys. 1672. Champlain Soc., Toronto, pp. 1–625.

GARDELL, TORSTEN
1947. Arskalv eller äldre älg? Svensk Jakt, Svenska Jägareförbundets Tidskrift, Stockholm, Arg. 85, N:R 9, pp. 293–296.

GERSTELL, RICHARD
1942. The place of winter feeding in practical wildlife management. Pa. Game Comm., Res. Bull. no. 3. (Original not seen.)

GOODWIN, GEORGE G.
1924. Mammals of the Gaspé Peninsula, Quebec. Journ. Mamm., vol. 5, no. 4, pp. 246–257.
1935. Mammals of Connecticut. State Geol. and Nat. Hist. Sur., Bull. 53, pp. 1–221.
1936. Big game animals in the northeastern United States. Journ. Mamm., vol. 17, no. 1, pp. 48–50.

GRANT, MADISON
1902. Moose. Seventh rept. N.Y. Forest, Fish and Game Comm., 1901, pp. 225–238.

GRANT, W. L. (tr.)
1907–14. The history of New France, by Marc Lescarbot. 3 vols. Champlain Soc., Toronto.

GRASSE, JAMES E.
1950. Trapping the moose. Wyo. Wild Life, Wyo. Game and Fish Comm., vol. 14, no. 5, pp. 12–18, 36, 38.

GREEN, H. U.
1932. Mammals of the Riding Mountain National Park, Manitoba. Can. Field-Nat., vol. 46, no. 7, pp. 149–152.

HADWEN, S.
1933. [untitled note] Proc. Helminthological Soc. Wash. *in* Journ. Parasit., vol. 19, p. 83.

HAKE, GEORGE ALEXANDER
1940. Man versus moose. Privately published, Devlin, Ont., pp. 1–46.

HALL, E. RAYMOND
1934. Mammals collected by T. T. and E. B. McCabe in the Bowron Lake region of British Columbia. Univ. Cal. Pub. Zool., vol. 40, no. 9, pp. 363–386.
1936. Identity of the Bowron Lake moose of British Columbia. Murrelet, vol. 17, p. 71.

1946. Zoological subspecies of man at the peace table. Journ. Mamm., vol. 27, no. 4, pp. 358–364.

HALLIDAY, W. E. D.
1937. A forest classification for Canada. Forest Serv. Bull. 89, Can., Dept. Mines and Resources, pp. 1–50.

HAMILTON, HARRY
1947. Balansen Mellan Skogsvård Och Algvård. Svensk Jakt, Svenska Jägareförbundets Tidskrift, Stockholm, Arg. 85, N:R 5, pp. 164–170.

HARPER, FRANCIS
1932. Mammals of the Athabaska and Great Slave Lakes region. Journ. Mamm., vol. 13, no. 1, pp. 19–36.

HATHEWAY, C. L.
1846. The history of New Brunswick. Fredericton, N.B., pp. 1–81.

HATTER, JAMES
1945. A preliminary predator-prey study with respect to the coyote (*Canis latrans*) in Jasper National Park. Ottawa, pp. 1–41 (mimeo.).
1947. Preliminary report on moose investigation in British Columbia. Proc. Game Conv., B.C. Game Dept., pp. 20–28.
1948a. Summarized interim report on a study of the moose of central British Columbia, 1946. B.C. Game Comm. Rep., 1946, pp. DD44–DD52.
1948b. A progress report on moose investigations in central British Columbia. Proc. 2nd Ann. Game Conv., B.C. Game Dept., pp. 23–31.
1949. The status of moose in North America. Trans. 14th N. Am. Wildlife Conf., pp. 492–501.
1950. The moose of central British Columbia. Wash. State College, unpub. thesis, pp. 1–356. (*vide* Cowan, 1951; Pimlott, 1953.)
1952. Some trends in the hunting and harvest of moose and mule deer in British Columbia. Rept. Proc. 6th Ann. Game Conv., Vernon, B.C., B.C. Game Dept., pp. 57–61.

HAY, OLIVER P.
1923. The Pleistocene of North America and its vertebrated animals from the states east of the Mississippi River and from the Canadian provinces east of longitude 95°. Carnegie Inst. Wash., pp. 1–499.
1924. The Pleistocene of the middle region of North America and its vertebrated animals. Carnegie Inst. Wash., pp. 1–385.
1927. The Pleistocene of the western region of North America and its vertebrated animals. Carnegie Inst. Wash., pp. 1–346.

HEAD, SIR GEORGE
1829. Forest scenes and incidents in the wilds of North America. London. (Original not seen.)

HENRY, A., and D. THOMPSON
1897. New light on the early history of the great Northwest. The manuscript journals of Alexander Henry and of David Thompson 1799–1814. Ed. by E. Coues. New York, vol. 1.

HICKIE, PAUL F.
Undated. Michigan moose. Mich. Dept Cons., Game Div., pp. 1–57.
1936. Isle Royale moose studies. Wildlife Restoration and Conservation. Proc. N. Am. Wildlife Conf., pp. 396–399.
1937. A preliminary report on the past and present status of the moose *Alces americana* (Clinton), in Michigan. Papers Mich. Acad. Sci., Arts and Letters, vol. 22, pp. 627–639.

HOLLINGSWORTH, S.
1787. The present state of Nova Scotia with a brief account of Canada and the British Islands on the coast of North America. Creech, Edinburgh, 2nd ed., pp. 1–221.

HORNADAY, W. T.
1904. The American natural history. Charles Scribner's Sons, New York, pp. 1–449.
HORNBY, JOHN
1934. Wildlife in the Thelon River area, N.W. Territories, Canada. Can. Field-Nat., vol. 48, no. 7, pp. 105–111.
HOSLEY, N. W.
1949. The moose and its ecology. Wildlife Leaflet 312, U.S. Dept. Int., Fish and Wildlife Serv., pp. 1–51.
JACKSON, C. F.
1922. Notes on New Hampshire mammals. Journ. Mamm., vol. 3, no. 1, p. 14.
JACKSON, HARTLEY H. T.
1944. Big-game resources of the United States, 1937–1942. Res. Rept. no. 8, U.S. Dept. Int., Fish and Wildlife Serv., pp. 1–56.
JACKSON, V. W.
1926. Fur and game resources of Manitoba. Industrial Development Board of Manitoba, Winnipeg, pp. 1–55.
JEFFERYS, THOMAS
1760. The natural and civil history of the French Dominions in North and South America. Part I—Containing a description of Canada and Louisiana. Printed for Thomas Jeffreys at Charing-Cross, London, pp. 1–246.
JELLISON, WILLIAM L., CHARLES W. FISHEL, and E. L. CHEATUM
1953. Brucellosis in a moose, Alces americanus. Journ. Wildlife Mgt., vol. 17, no. 2, pp. 217–218.
JOHNSON, CHARLES E.
1922. Notes on the mammals of Northern Lake County, Minnesota. Journ. Mamm., vol. 3, no. 1, pp. 33–39.
1930. Recollections of the mammals of northwestern Minnesota. Journ. Mamm., vol. 11, no. 4, pp. 435–452.
JOSSELYN, JOHN
1674. New England's prospect, an account of two voyages to New England. London, pp. 1–279.
KANGAS, E.
1949. On the damage to the forests caused by the moose, and its significance in the economy of the forest. Eripainos: Suomen Riista, vol. 4, pp. 62–90. (English summary pp. 88–90.)
KELLOGG, LOUISE PHELPS (ed.)
1917. The journey of Dollier and Galinée 1669–1670; by René de Bréhaut de Galinée. Reprint of English version. In Early narratives of the Northwest, 1634–1699. Scribner's, New York, pp. 167–209.
1923. Journal of a voyage to North America, translated from the French of Pierre François Xavier de Charlevoix. R. R. Donnelley and Sons, Chicago (for the Caxton Club), 2 vols., pp. 1–362; 1–379.
KELLUM, FORD
1941. Cusino's captive moose. Mich. Cons., Mich. Dept. Cons., vol. 10, no. 7, pp. 4–5.
KELLY, ARTHUR L., LAWRENCE R. PENNER, and RAWSON J. PICKARD
1950. Sarcocystis in the moose. Journ. Mamm., vol. 31, no. 4, pp. 462–463.
KING, LESTER S.
1939. Moose encephalitis. Am. Journ. Pathology, vol. 15, no. 4, pp. 445–454.
KING, MAJOR W. ROSS
1866. The sportsman and naturalist in Canada. Hurst and Blackett, London, pp. 1–334.
KOCH, ELERS
1941. Big game in Montana from early historical records. Journ. Wildlife Mgt., vol. 5, no. 4, pp. 357–370.
KREFTING, LAURITS W.
1946. Isle Royale summer moose browse survey, 1946. Prog. Rept., Fish and Wildlife Serv., pp. 1–12 (vide Hosley, 1949).

1951. What is the future of the Isle Royale moose herd? Trans. 16th N. Am. Wildlife Conf., pp. 461–470.

KREFTING, LAURITS W., and FORREST B. LEE
1948. Progress report, moose browse investigations on Isle Royale National Park, May. Fish and Wildlife Serv., pp. 1–34 (*vide* Hosley, 1949).

LAING, H. M., and R. M. ANDERSON
1929. Notes on mammals of upper Chitina River region, Alaska. Natl. Mus. Can., Bull. 56, Ann. Rept. for 1927. *In* Birds and mammals of the Mount Logan Expedition, 1925, pp. 96–107.

LAMSON, ARROLL L.
1941. Maine moose disease studies. Master's thesis, Univ. Maine, Orono, 1941, pp. 1–61 (typewritten).

LAW, R. G., and A. H. KENNEDY
1933. *Echinococcus granulosus* in moose. N.Y. Vet., vol. 14, pp. 33–34.

LEOPOLD, A. STARKER, and F. FRASER DARLING
1953. Effects of land use on moose and caribou in Alaska. Trans. 18th N. Am. Wildlife Conf., pp. 553–560.

LEOPOLD, ALDO, LYLE K. SOWLS, and DAVID L. SPENCER
1947. A survey of over-populated deer ranges in the United States. Journ. Wildlife Mgt., vol. 11, no. 2, pp. 162–177.

LOCKHART, J. G.
1890. Notes on the habits of the moose in the far north of British America in 1865. Proc. U.S. Natl. Mus. vol. 13, no. 827, pp. 305–308.

LÖNNBERG, EINAR
1923. Sveriges jaktbara djur. Svenska Jordbrakets bok, Albert Bonnier, Stockholm, Häft. 1, pp. 1–65.

LOW, A. P.
1896. Report on explorations in the Labrador Peninsula along the East Main, Koksoak, Hamilton, Manicuaga and portions of other rivers in 1892–93–94–95. Geol. Sur. Can., vol. 8, pp. 1L–387L.

LUBECK, R.
1947. Algstatistiken. En liten korrigering. Svensk Jakt, Svenska Jägareförbundets Tidskrift, Stockholm, Arg. 85, N:R 2, pp. 72–73.

LYDEKKER, R.
1907. The British Columbian moose. The Field, London, vol. 109, p. 182.
1915. Catalogue of the ungulate mammals in the British Museum (Natural History), Artiodactyla. Brit. Mus. (Nat. Hist.), vol. 4, pp. 1–432.

McAREE, JOHN, et al.
1901. Exploration survey party No. 10 report. Report of the Survey and Exploration of Northern Ontario, 1900. Toronto, pp. 250–285.

McCABE, T. T., and E. B. McCABE
1928a. The Bowron Lake moose, their history and status. Murrelet, vol. 9, no. 1, pp. 1–9.
1928b. The British Columbia moose again. Murrelet, vol. 9, no. 3, pp. 60–63.

McCONNELL, R. G.
1891. Report on an exploration in the Yukon and Mackenzie basins, N.W.T. Geol. and Nat. Hist. Sur. Can., Ann. Rept., 1888–1889, vol. 4, pp. 1D–163D.

McDOWELL, LLOYD, and MARSHALL MOY
1942. Montana moose survey, Hellroaring–Buffalo–Slough Creek unit (1942), pp. 1–72 (typewritten).

MACFARLANE, R.
1905. Notes on mammals collected and observed in the northern Mackenzie River district, Northwest Territories of Canada, with remarks on explorers and explorations of the far north. Proc. U.S. Natl. Mus., vol. 28, no. 1405, pp. 673–764.

McINNES, WILLIAM
1899. Report on the geology of the area covered by the Seine River and Lake Sheban-dowan map sheets comprising portions of Rainy River and Thunder Bay districts, Ontario. Geol. Sur. Can., Ann. Rept. (new ser.), 1897, vol. 10, pp. 1H–65H.
1906a. Region on the north-west side of Lake Nipigon. Geol. Sur. Dept., Ottawa, Summ. Rept., 1902–4, vol. 15, pp. 208A–213A.
1906b. The Winisk River, Keewatin District. Geol. Sur. Dept., Ottawa, Summ. Rept., 1903, vol. 15, pp. 100A–108A.
1906c. The upper parts of the Winisk and Attawapiskat rivers. Geol. Sur. Dept., Ottawa, Summ. Rept., 1904, vol. 16, pp. 153A–160A.
MACKENZIE, ALEXANDER
1801. Voyages from Montreal, on the River St. Lawrence through the continent of North America, to the Frozen and Pacific oceans in the years 1789 and 1793. London, pp. 1–412.
McMILLAN, JOHN F.
1953a. Some feeding habits of moose in Yellowstone Park. Ecology, vol. 34, no. 1, pp. 102–110.
1953b. Measures of association between moose and elk on feeding grounds. Journ. Wildlife Mgt., vol. 17, no. 2, pp. 162–166.
MACOUN, JOHN
1882. Manitoba and the great north-west. World Publishing Co., Guelph, Ont., pp. 1–687.
MANITOBA
1942. Ann. Rept. Game and Fisheries Br. for the fiscal year ending April 30th, 1942. Dept. Mines and Nat. Resources, pp. 1–66 (mimeo.).
1947. Ann. Rept. Game and Fisheries Br. for the fiscal year ending April 30th, 1947. Dept. Mines and Nat. Resources.
MANNING, T. H.
1948. Notes on the country, birds and mammals west of Hudson Bay between Rein-deer and Baker lakes. Can. Field-Nat., vol. 62, no. 1, pp. 1–28.
MANWEILER, J.
1941. The future of Minnesota moose. Cons. Volunteer, Minn. Dept. Cons., vol. 3, no. 15, pp. 38–45.
MARSHALL, F. H. A.
1922. The physiology of reproduction. London, Longmans, Green and Co., pp. 1–770.
MERRIAM, C. HART
1884. Vertebrates of the Adirondack region, northern New York. Trans. Linnaean Soc., vol. 2, pp. 9–214.
1891. Results of a biological reconnaissance of south-central Idaho. N. Am. Fauna, no. 5, pp. 1–113.
MERRILL, SAMUEL
1920. The moose book. 2nd ed., E. P. Dutton and Co., New York, pp. 1–366.
MILLER, GERRIT S., Jr.
1899. A new moose from Alaska. Proc. Biol. Soc. Wash., vol. 13, pp. 57–59.
1912. Catalogue of the mammals of Western Europe (Europe exclusive of Russia). Brit. Mus. (Nat. Hist.), pp. 1–1019.
1924. List of North American Recent mammals, 1923. Bull. 128, U.S. Natl. Mus., pp. 1–673.
MONTANA
1942. Hellroaring-Slough Creek moose investigations. Bien. Rept., Mont. Fish and Game Comm., pp. 44–45, 93.
MONTIZAMBERT, EDWARD L. (tr.)
1883. Canada in the seventeenth century. From the French of Pierre Boucher 1664. Desbarats, Montreal, pp. 1–84.

MOORE, CLIFFORD B.
   1944. Moose in western Massachusetts. Journ. Mamm., vol. 25, no. 3, p. 310.
MORSE, MARIUS A.
   1946. Censusing big game from the air. Cons. Volunteer, Minn. Dept. Cons., vol. 9, no. 52, pp. 29–33.
MORTON, GLENN H., and E. L. CHEATUM
   1946. Regional differences in breeding potential of white-tailed deer in New York. Journ. Wildlife Mgt., vol. 10, no. 3, pp. 242–248.
MORTON, THOMAS
   1632. New English Canaan or New Canaan, containing an abstract of New England. 3 books, 2nd book, Charles Green, Amsterdam.
MUNRO, J. A.
   1947. Observations of birds and mammals in Central British Columbia. Occ. Papers B.C. Prov. Mus. no. 6, pp. 1–165.
   1949. The birds and mammals of the Vanderhoof region, British Columbia. Am. Midl. Nat., vol. 41, no. 1, pp. 1–138.
MURIE, ADOLPH
   1934. The moose of Isle Royale. Misc. Pub., Mus. Zool., Univ. Mich., no. 25, pp. 1–44.
   1940. Ecology of the coyote in the Yellowstone. Fauna of the Natl. Parks of the U.S., U.S. Dept. Int., Natl. Parks Serv., Cons. Bull. no. 4, pp. 1–206.
   1944. The wolves of Mount McKinley. Fauna of the Natl. Parks of the U.S., U.S. Dept. Int., Natl. Parks Serv., Fauna ser. no. 5, pp. 1–238.
MURIE, OLAUS J.
   1951. The elk of North America. Stackpole, Harrisburg, Pa.; Wildlife Mgt. Inst., Washington, D.C., pp. 1–376.
NEELANDS, E. V.
   1901. Geologist's report of exploration survey party No. 5. Report of the Survey and Exploration of Northern Ontario, 1900. Toronto, pp. 147–157.
NELSON, E. W.
   1914. Description of a new subspecies of moose from Wyoming. Proc. Biol. Soc. Wash., vol. 27, pp. 71–74.
NELSON, E. W., and F. W. TRUE
   1887. Mammals of northern Alaska. Pt. 2 in Rept. upon natural history collections made in Alaska 1877–1881. Arctic ser. no. 3, U.S. Govt. Printing Office, Washington, pp. 227–293.
NEW BRUNSWICK
   1921–5. Ann. rept. of the Crown Land Dept. for the years ending Oct. 31, 1920–4. Fredericton, N.B.
   1926–48. Ann. rept. of the Dept. of Lands and Mines for the years ending October 31st, 1925–47.
NEWSOM, E. M.
   1937a. Mammals on Anticosti Island. Journ. Mamm., vol. 18, no. 4, pp. 435–442.
   1937b. Winter notes on the moose. Journ. Mamm., vol. 18, no. 3, pp. 347–349.
NOVA SCOTIA
   1932–48. Rept. of the Dept. of Lands and Forests for years 1931–47.
OBERHOLTZER, ERNEST C.
   1911. On the habits of moose. Proc. Zool. Soc. London, pp. 348–364.
OLDMIXON, JOHN
   1741. The British Empire in America, containing the history of the discovery, settlement, progress and state of the British Colonies on the continent and islands of America. 2nd ed., London, vol. 1, pp. 1–567. (1st ed., 1708.)
OLSEN, O. W., and R. FENSTERMACHER
   1942. Parasites of moose in northern Minnesota. Am. Journ. Vet. Res., vol. 3, no. 9, pp. 403–408.
OLSTAD, O.
   1934. Elgin I Norge, en statistisk undersolkelse skrifter utgitt av Det Norske Videnskaps. Akademi I, Oslo 1. Mat.-Nat. Klasse 1934, no. 4, pp. 1–123.

ONTARIO
   1881–1903. Crown Land Ann. Repts.
   1892. Ont. Game and Fish Comm. Warwick and Sons, Toronto, pp. 1–483.
   1907–8. Ont. Dept. Lands, Forests and Mines Repts.
   1909. Ont. Game and Fisheries Ann. Rept.
   1911–48. Ont. Dept. Lands and Forests Ann. Repts.
   Undated. "Ontario Forest Atlas." Dept. Lands and Forests, 17 maps.
OSGOOD, FREDERICK L., JR.
   1938. The mammals of Vermont. Journ. Mamm., vol. 19, no. 4, pp. 435–441.
OSGOOD, W. H.
   1901. Natural history of the Queen Charlotte Islands, British Columbia; Natural
      history of the Cook Inlet region, Alaska. N. Am. Fauna, no. 21, pp. 1–87.
   1904. A biological reconnaissance of the base of the Alaska Peninsula. N. Am. Fauna,
      no. 24, pp. 1–86.
   1909. A biological investigation in Alaska and Yukon Territory. N. Am. Fauna, no. 30,
      pp. 1–96.
OSGOOD, W. H., and LOUIS B. BISHOP
   1900. Results of a biological reconnaissance of the Yukon River region. N. Am. Fauna,
      no. 19, pp. 1–100.
PALMER, L. J.
   1941. Animal and plant resources of Alaska. Wildlife Leaflet 176, U.S. Dept. Int.,
      Fish and Wildlife Serv., pp. 1–12.
   1944. Food requirements of some Alaska game mammals. Journ. Mamm., vol. 25,
      no. 1, pp. 49–54.
PALMGREN, P.
   1938. Zur Kazalanalyse der ökologischen und geographischen Verbreitung der Vögel
      Nordeuropas. Arch. Naturgesch., N.F., vol. 7, pp. 235–269 (vide Deevey, 1949).
PENNANT, THOMAS
   1784. Arctic zoology. London, vol. 1, pp. 1–200.
PETERSON, RANDOLPH L.
   1949a. Management of moose. Proc. 39th Conv. Internat. Assoc. Game, Fish and
      Cons. Commissioners, Winnipeg, Man., pp. 71–75.
   1949b. A study of North American moose with special reference to Ontario. Ph.D.
      thesis, Univ. Toronto (471 pp. typewritten).
   1950. A new subspecies of moose from North America. Occ. Papers Roy. Ont. Mus.
      Zool., no. 9, pp. 1–7.
   1952. A review of the living representatives of the genus Alces. Contrib. Roy. Ont.
      Mus. Zool. and Paleo., no. 34, pp. 1–30.
   1953. Studies of the food habits and the habitat of moose in Ontario. Contrib. Roy.
      Ont. Mus. Zool. and Paleo., no. 36, pp. 1–40.
PIKE, WARBURTON
   1896. Through the subarctic forest. Edward Arnold, publisher to the India Office,
      New York, pp. 1–295.
PIMLOTT, DOUGLAS H.
   1953. Newfoundland moose. Trans. 18th N. Am. Wildlife Conf., pp. 563–579.
PITTMAN-ROBERTSON QUARTERLY
   1946. U.S. Dept. Int., Fish and Wildlife Serv., Wash., D.C., vol. 6, no. 2, pp. 1–89.
PORSILD, A. E.
   1945. Mammals of the Mackenzie Delta. Can. Field-Nat., vol. 59, no. 1, pp. 4–22.
POWELL, JAMES E.
   1855. "Untitled letter regarding moose in Maine." Proc. Acad. Nat. Sci. Philadelphia,
      vol. 7, pp. 343–344.
PREBLE, E .A.
   1902. A biological investigation of the Hudson Bay region. N. Am. Fauna, no. 22,
      pp. 1–140.
   1908. A biological investigation of the Athabaska Mackenzie region. N. Am. Fauna,
      no. 27, pp. 1–574.

QUIMBY, DON C., and DONALD E. JOHNSON
1951. Weights and measurements of Rocky Mountain elk. Journ. Wildlife Mgt., vol. 15, no. 1, pp. 57–62.

RACEY, K.
1936. Notes on some mammals of the Chilcotin, British Columbia. Can. Field-Nat., vol. 50, no. 2, pp. 15–21.

RAND, A. L.
1944. The southern half of the Alaska Highway and its mammals. Natl. Mus. Can., Bull. no. 98. Biol. ser. no. 27, pp. 1–50.
1945a. Mammal investigations on the Canol Road, Yukon and Northwest Territories, 1944. Natl. Mus. Can., Bull. no. 99, Biol. ser. no. 28, pp. 1–52.
1945b. Mammals of Yukon, Canada. Natl. Mus. Can., Bull. no. 100, Biol. ser. no. 29, pp. 1–93.
1948. Glaciation, an isolating factor in speciation. Evolution, Internat. Journ. of Organic Evolution, vol. 2, no. 4, pp. 314–321.

RANSOM, B. H.
1911. The nematodes parasitic in the alimentary tract of cattle, sheep, and other ruminants. Bull. 127, U.S. Dept. Agr., Bur. Animal Industry, pp. 1–132.

RAUSCH, ROBERT
1950. Notes on the distribution of some Arctic mammals. Journ. Mamm., vol. 31, no. 4, pp. 464–466.
1951. Notes on the Nunamiut Eskimo and mammals of the Anaktuvuk Pass region, Brooks Range, Alaska. Arctic, vol. 4, no. 3, pp. 147–195.
1952. Hydatid disease in boreal regions. Arctic, vol. 5, no. 3, pp. 157–174.

REYNOLDS, S. H.
1934. A monograph on the British Pleistocene Mammalia. *Alces*. Paleo. Soc. Monogr., London, vol. 87 (suppl. pp. 1–16).

RHOADES, S. N.
1903. The mammals of Pennsylvania and New Jersey. Privately published, Philadelphia, pp. 1–266.

RILEY, WILLIAM A.
1933. Reservoirs of *Echinococcus* in Minnesota. Minn. Med., vol. 16, pp. 744–745.
1939. The need for data relative to the occurrence of hydatids and of *Echinococcus granulosus* in wildlife. Journ. Wildlife Mgt., vol. 3, no. 3, pp. 255–257.

RINEY, THANE
1951. Standard terminology for deer teeth. Journ. Wildlife Mgt., vol. 15, no. 1, pp. 99–101.

ROBINSON, A. H. A.
1901. Geologist's report of exploration survey party No. 6. Report of the Survey and Exploration of Northern Ontario, 1900. Toronto, pp. 162–172.

ROBINSON, B. L., and M. L. FERNALD
1908. Gray's new manual of botany. A handbook of the flowering plants and ferns of the central and northeastern United States and adjacent Canada. 7th ed., American Book Company, New York, pp. 1–926.

RUST, HENRY JUDSON
1946. Mammals of northern Idaho. Journ. Mamm., vol. 27, no. 4, pp. 308–327.

ST. MICHAEL-PODMORE, P.
1904. A sporting paradise, with stories of adventure in America and the backwoods of Muskoka. Hutchinson, London, pp. 1–273.

SALVESEN, SIGVALD
1929. The moose and red deer in Norway. Journ. Mamm., vol. 10, no. 1, pp. 59–62.

SARBER, HOSEA R.
1944. Report of the moose studies, National Moose Range, Kenai Peninsula, Alaska, 1944. U.S. Dept. Int., Fish and Wildlife Serv., pp. 1–10. (mimeo.).

SASKATCHEWAN
1914–23. Report of the Chief Game Guardian on matters relating to game protection,

the administration of the Game Act, and the development of the Provincial Museum during 1913–23.

1925–30. Report of the Game Commissioner on matters relating to game protection, the administration of the Game Act, and the development of the Provincial Museum during the years ending April 30, 1925–9.

1931–47a and b. Ann. Rept. Dept. Nat. Resources.

SAUGSTAD, STANLEY
1942. Aerial census of big game in North Dakota. Trans. 7th N. Am. Wildlife Conf., pp. 343–345.

SCHEFFER, VICTOR B., and W. W. DALQUEST
1944. Records of mountain goat and moose from Washington State. Journ. Mamm., vol. 25, no. 4, pp. 412–413.

SCHIERBECK, OTTO
1929. Is it right to protect the female of the species at the cost of the male? Can. Field-Nat., vol. 43, no. 1, pp. 6–9.

SCHMIDT, K. P.
1938. Herpetological evidence for the postglacial eastward extension of the steppe in North America. Ecology, vol. 19, no. 3, pp. 396–407.

SCHULTZ, W., and L. McDOWELL
1943. Absaroka-Gallatin moose study. Pittman-Robertson Quarterly, vol. 3, no. 2, pp. 71–77.

SCOTT, W. E.
1939. Rare and extinct mammals of Wisconsin. Wis. Cons. Bull., Madison, vol. 4, no. 10, pp. 21–28.

SCOTT, WILLIAM B.
1937. A history of land mammals in the western hemisphere. Macmillan Co., New York, pp. 1–786.

SEARS, PAUL B.
1948. Forest sequence and climatic change in northeastern North America since early Wisconsin time. Ecology, vol. 29, no. 3, pp. 326–333.

SETON, ERNEST THOMPSON
1927. Lives of game animals. 4 vols. Doubleday Doran, New York, vol. 3, pp. 1–780.

SEVERINGHAUS, C. W.
1949. Tooth development and wear as criteria of age in white-tailed deer. Journ. Wildlife Mgt., vol. 13, no. 2, pp. 195–216.

SEVERINGHAUS, C. W., H. F. MAGUIRE, R. A. COOKINGHAM, and J. E. TANCK
1950. Variations by age class in the antler beam diameters of white-tailed deer related to range conditions. Trans. 15th N. Am. Wildlife Conf., pp. 551–570.

SEYFARTH, M.
1938. Pathogene Wirkung und innerer Bau von Paramphistomum cervi, Deutsche tier. Wehnschr. XLVI, pp. 515–518.

SHELDON, CHARLES
1911. The wilderness of the upper Yukon. A hunter's explorations for wild sheep in sub-arctic mountains. The Copp Clark Co., Ltd., Toronto, pp. 1–354.

1930. The wilderness of Denali: explorations of a hunter-naturalist in northern Alaska. Charles Scribner's Sons, New York, pp. 1–412.

SHIRAS, GEORGE, III
1912. The white sheep, giant moose and smaller game of the Kenai Peninsula, Alaska. Natl. Geogr. Mag., vol. 23, no. 5, pp. 423–493.

1913. Wild animals that took their own picture. Natl. Geogr. Mag., vol. 24, no. 7, pp. 763–834.

1921. The wild life of Lake Superior, past and present. Natl. Geogr. Mag., vol. 40, no. 2, pp. 113–204.

1923. The increase of game on limited refuges. Am. Forests, vol. 29, no. 359, pp. 670–671.

1935. Hunting wild life with camera and flashlight. 2 vols. Natl. Geogr. Soc., Wash., D.C., vol. 1, pp. 1–450.

SIMPSON, GEORGE GAYLORD
1945. The principles of classification and a classification of mammals. Bull. Am. Mus. Nat. Hist., vol. 85, pp. 1–350.

SKINNER, M. P.
1927. Moose becoming a common sight in Yellowstone National Park. Journ. Mamm., vol. 8, no. 2, p. 163.

SKUNCKE, FOLKE
1949. Algen, studier, jakt och vård. P. A. Norstedt and Söners, Förlag, Stockholm, pp. 1–400.

SMITH, ALEXANDER H.
1901. Geologist's report of exploration survey party No. 8. Report of the Survey and Exploration of Northern Ontario, 1900, pp. 198–207.

SNOW, W. A.
1891. The moose fly—a new Haematobia. Can. Ent., vol. 23, no. 4, pp. 87–89.

SNYDER, L. L.
1928. The mammals of the Lake Abitibi region. A faunal investigation of the Lake Abitibi region, Ontario. Univ. Toronto Studies, Biol. ser. no. 32, pp. 7–15.

SNYDER, L. L., E. B. S. LOGIER, and T. B. KURATA
1942. Faunal investigation of the Sault Ste. Marie region. (Contrib. Roy. Ont. Mus. Zool. no. 21), Trans. Roy. Can. Inst., vol. 24, pt. 1, pp. 97–165.

SOPER, J. DEWEY
1942. Mammals of Wood Buffalo Park, northern Alberta and District of Mackenzie. Journ. Mamm., vol. 23, no. 2, pp. 119–145.
1946. Mammals of the northern great plains along the international boundary in Canada. Journ. Mamm., vol. 27, no. 2, pp. 120–153.

SPENCER, DAVID L., and EDWARD F. CHATELAIN
1953. Progress in the management of the moose of south central Alaska. Trans. 18th N. Am. Wildlife Conf., pp. 539–552.

SQUIRES, W. AUSTIN
1946. Changes in mammal population in New Brunswick. Acadian Naturalist, Bull. Nat. Hist. Soc., N.B., vol. 2, no. 7, pp. 26–44.

STANWELL-FLETCHER, JOHN F. and THEODORA C.
1942. Three years in the wolves' wilderness. Nat. Hist., vol. 49, no. 3, pp. 136–147.
1943. Some accounts of the flora and fauna of the Driftwood Valley region of north central British Columbia. Occ. Papers B.C. Prov. Mus. no. 4, pp. 1–97.

STEPHENS, HIRAM B.
1890. Jacques Cartier and his four voyages to Canada. Drysdale, Montreal, pp. 1–163.

STONE, ANDREW J.
1924. The moose: where it lives and how it lives. In The deer book, by Theodore Roosevelt and others. Macmillan Co., New York, pp. 291–325.

STOTT, KEN, Jr.
1948. Moose notes. Zoonooz, Zool. Soc. San Diego, vol. 21, no. 7, pp. 3–4.

SURBER, THADDEUS
1932. The mammals of Minnesota. Minn. Dept. Cons., pp. 1–84.

SWANSON, GUSTAV, THADDEUS SURBER, and THOMAS S. ROBERTS
1945. The mammals of Minnesota. Minn. Dept. Cons. Tech. Bull., no. 2, pp. 1–108.

SWARTH, HARRY S.
1936. Mammals of the Atlin region, northwestern British Columbia. Journ. Mamm., vol. 17, no. 4, pp. 398–405.

SWEATMAN, GORDON K.
1952. Distribution and incidence of Echinococcus grandulosus in man and other animals with special reference to Canada. Can. Journ. Publ. Health, vol. 43, pp. 480–486.

SWEDEN
1947. Algar fällda 1947 (och 1946). Svensk Jakt, Svenska Jägareförbundets Tidskrift, Stockholm, Arg. 85, N:R 12, p. 423.
1949. Preliminär uppgift över antalet under tillåten jakttid fällda älgar år 1948, länsvis. Svensk Jakt, Svenska Jägareförbundets Tidskrift, Stockholm, Arg. 87, N:R 1, p. 26.

SWIFT, ERNEST
1946. A history of Wisconsin deer. Wis. Cons. Dept. Pub. no. 323, pp. 1–96.

TANTON, T. L.
1920. Depressions found on moose trails and their significance. Journ. Mamm., vol. 1, no. 3, pp. 142–143.

THOMAS, L. J., and A. R. CAHN
1932. A new disease of moose. 1. Preliminary report. Journ. Parasit., vol. 18, pp. 219–231.

THOMPSON, ERNEST E.
1886. A list of the mammals of Manitoba. Trans. Man. Hist. and Sci. Soc., no. 23, pp. 1–26.

THOMPSON, W. K.
1949. Observations of moose courting behavior. Journ. Wildlife Mgt., vol. 13, p. 313.

THWAITES, RUBEN G.
1896–1903. Jesuit relations and allied documents, 1610-1791. 73 vols. Burrow Brothers, Cleveland.

TURNER, J. P.
1906. The moose and wapiti of Manitoba. Trans. Man. Hist. and Sci. Soc., no. 66, pp. 1–8.

TURNER, L. M.
1886. Contributions to the natural history of Alaska. Arctic ser., U.S. Govt. Printing Office, no. 2, pp. 1–226.

TYRRELL, J. B.
1892. Report on north-western Manitoba with portions of the adjacent districts of Assiniboia and Saskatchewan. Geol. Sur. Can., Ann. Rept., 1890–1, vol. 5, pt. 1, pp. 1E–235E.

TYRRELL, J. B. (ed.)
1916. David Thompson's narrative of his explorations in western America 1784–1812. Champlain Soc., Toronto, pp. 1–580.
1934. Journals of Samuel Hearne and Philip Turnor. Champlain Soc., Toronto, pp. 1–611.

TYRRELL, J. B., and D. B. DOWLING
1896. Report on the country between Athabasca Lake and Churchill River. Geol. Sur. Can., vol. 8, pp. 1D–120D.

UNITED STATES
1939a. Big-game inventory of the United States, 1937. Wildlife Leaflet BS–122, U.S. Dept. Agr., Bur. Biol. Sur., Wash., D.C., pp. 1–13 (mimeo.).
1939b. Big-game inventory of the United States, 1938. Wildlife Leaflet BS–142, U.S. Dept. Agr., Bur. Biol. Sur., Wash., D.C., pp. 1–11 (mimeo.).
1940. Big-game inventory of the United States, 1939. Wildlife Leaflet BS–175, U.S. Dept. Int., Fish and Wildlife Serv., Wash., D.C., pp. 1–11 (mimeo.).
1942. Big-game inventory of the United States, 1940. Wildlife Leaflet 207, U.S. Dept. Int., Fish and Wildlife Serv., Wash., D.C., pp. 1–10 (mimeo.).
1946. Big-game inventory of the United States, 1943. Wildlife Leaflet 283, U.S. Dept. Int., Fish and Wildlife Serv., Wash., D.C., pp. 1–11 (mimeo.).
1948. Big-game inventory of the United States, 1946. Wildlife Leaflet 303, U.S. Dept. Int., Fish and Wildlife Serv., Wash., D.C., pp. 1–13 (mimeo.).
1949. Big-game inventory of the United States, 1947. Wildlife Leaflet 321, U.S. Dept. Int., Fish and Wildlife Serv., Wash., D.C., 3 pp. (mimeo.).

1950. Big-game inventory of the United States, 1948. Wildlife Leaflet 321 [?], U.S. Dept. Int., Fish and Wildlife Serv., Wash., D.C., 3 pp. (mimeo.).

UPHAM, WARREN

1905. Groseilliers and Radisson, the first white men in Minnesota, 1655–56, and 1659–60, and their discovery of the upper Missippi River. Coll. Minn. Hist. Soc., St. Paul, vol. 10, pt. 2, pp. 449–594.

VOIPIO, PAAVO

1952a. How shall we get our moose population palmated in type? Suomen Riista, vol. 7, pp. 52–59.

1952b. One-sided levying of males, a disastrous procedure for the development of game stocks. Suomen Riista, vol. 6, pp. 66–82, 188–189 (1951).

WALCOTT, F. C.

1939. The moose: hunting the Canada moose. North American Big Game. Charles Scribner's Sons, New York, pp. 266–272.

WALLACE, F. G.

1934. Parasites collected from the moose, *Alces americanus*, in Northern Minnesota. Journ. Am. Vet. Med. Assoc., vol. 94, pp. 770–775.

WALLACE, G. I., ALVIN R. CAHN, and L. J. THOMAS

1933. *Klebsiella paralytica*, a new pathogenic bacterium from "moose disease." Journ. Infectious Diseases, Am. Med. Assoc. Press, 535 North Dearborn St., Chicago, pp. 386–414.

WALLACE, G. I., L. J. THOMAS, and ALVIN R. CAHN

1932. A new disease of moose. II. Proc. Soc. Exp. Biol. and Med., vol. 29, pp. 1098–1100.

WARDLE, R. A.

1933. Cestodaria and Cestoda in Canadian animals. Can. Journ. Res., vol. 8, p. 325.

WARFEL, H. E.

1937a. Notes on some mammals of western Massachusetts. Journ. Mamm., vol. 18, no. 1, pp. 82–85.

1937b. Moose records for Vermont. Journ. Mamm., vol. 18, no. 4, p. 519.

WEBB, S. B., M. BAKER, F. K. BARBOUR, D. ELY, and A. C. GILBERT

1952. Records of North American big game. Boone and Crockett Club. Charles Scribner's Sons, New York, pp. 1–178.

WEST, RAYMOND M.

1941. Elk of the northern Rocky Mountain region. Field Notes on Wildlife. U.S. Forest Serv., vol. 2, no. 9, pp. 1–32 (mimeo.)

WHITE, J. H., and R. C. HOSIE

1946. The forest trees of Ontario and the more commonly planted foreign trees. 2nd ed., Ont. Dept. Lands and Forests, pp. 1–81.

WILLIAMS, ARTHUR BRYAN

1925. Game trails in British Columbia: big game and other sport in the wilds of British Columbia. Charles Scribner's Sons, New York, pp. 1–360.

WILLIAMS, M. Y.

1922. Biological notes along fourteen hundred miles of the Mackenzie River system. Can. Field-Nat., vol. 36, no. 4, pp. 16–66.

1925. Notes on life along the Alaska-Yukon boundary. Can. Field-Nat., vol. 39, no. 4, pp. 69–90.

1933. Biological notes, covering parts of the Peace, Liard, Mackenzie and Great Bear river basins. Can. Field-Nat., vol. 47, no. 2, pp. 23–31.

WILLIAMSON, V. H. H.

1951. Determination of hairs by impressions. Journ. Mamm., vol. 32, no. 1, pp. 80–84.

MSS Monthly progress reports. Div. Res., Ont. Dept. Lands and Forests, Maple, Ont., 1950–1 (typewritten).

WILSON, ALBRED W. G.

1905. The country west of Nipigon Lake and River. Geol. Surv. Dept., Ottawa, Summ. Rept., 1901, vol. 14, pp. 96A–105A.

WILSON, W. J.

1906a. Reconnaissance surveys of four rivers southwest of James Bay. Geol. Surv. Dept., Ottawa, Summ. Rept., 1902, vol. 15, pp. 222A–241A.

1906b. The Nagagami River and other branches of the Kenogami. Geol. Surv. Dept., Ottawa, Summ. Rept., 1903, vol. 15, pp. 109A–120A.

1906c. The Little Current and Drowning rivers, branches of the Albany, east of Lake Nipigon. Geol. Surv. Dept., Ottawa, Summ. Rept., 1904, vol. 16, pp. 164A–173A.

WRIGHT, BRUCE S.

1952. A report to the Minister of Lands and Mines on the moose of New Brunswick. Northeastern Wildlife Sta., Fredericton, N.B., 43 pp. (typewritten).

WRIGHT, GEORGE M., J. S. DIXON, and B. H. THOMPSON

1933. A preliminary survey of faunal relations in national parks. Fauna of the Natl. Parks of the U.S., U.S. Dept. Int., Natl. Parks Serv., Fauna ser. no. 1, pp. 1–157.

WRONG, GEORGE M., and H. H. LANGTON (ed. and tr.)

1939. The long journey to the country of the Hurons by Father Gabriel Sagard [1632]. Champlain Soc., Toronto, pp. 1–411.

WYOMING

1948. Game harvest continues rise. Wyo. Wild Life, Wyo. Game and Fish Comm., vol. 12, no. 3, pp. 4–11, 34–39.

1950. The 1949 big game harvest. Wyo. Wild Life, Wyo. Game and Fish Comm., vol. 14, no. 8, pp. 5–11, 32–33.

YOUNG, STANLEY P., and EDWARD A. GOLDMAN

1946. The puma, mysterious American cat. Am. Wildlife Inst., Washington, pp. 1–358.

INDEX

Abies
 balsamea, 131
 grandis, 149
 lasiocarpa, 110, 150
Abnormality: of behaviour, 66; cranial,
 183; of tooth development, 86f., 226
abortus. See Brucella
Accidents, 193–195, 220
Acer
 douglasii, 149
 glabra, 149f.
 pennsylvanicum, 136
 rubrum, 137
 saccharinum, 137
 saccharum, 137
 spicatum, 137
Achillea lanulosa, 147
Achlis, 3
acicularis. See Rosa
Actaea rubra, 146
actinoides. See Thysanosoma
Actinomyces necrophorus, 182
Actinomycosis, 182
Activity: daily, 109f.; diurnal, 110; general,
 101–113; nocturnal, 110; seasonal,
 110–113
Adaptation, general, 79–90
advena. See Nymphaea
Aerial moose census, 107, 112; techniques,
 208–209
Age
 antler development in relation to, 92,
 289–246
 composition: of forest trees, Ontario,
 154, 156; of moose populations, 69
 determination, 86; by number of antler
 points, 242; by tooth wear, 223–238
Agropyron, 148, 151
 Smithii, 147
 spicatum, 147
Agrostis
 alba, 147
 exarata, 147
 hyemalis, 147f.
 idahoensis, 147
Alaska, 9, 11, 13, 29ff., 41, 55ff., 60, 65,
 67f., 71ff., 92, 97, 99, 106, 108, 149f.,

152, 160, 163, 170, 172, 174, 176f.,
 179, 188, 195, 198f., 203
alba. See Agrostis; Betula
Alberta, 9, 33, 39f., 63, 68f., 74, 92f., 186,
 189, 203
albiflorum. See Hieracium
albipictus. See Dermacentor
Alce, 5, 12
 americanus, 10
Alcelaphus, 5
Alces, 5, 12
 alces, 8, 12, 186
 alces alces, 6ff., 12, 223
 alces americana, 6, 8, 10, 12, 14, 73f.,
 93, 223, 226, 239
 alces americanus, 10
 alces andersoni, 6, 8, 10, 12, 14, 30, 73f.,
 93, 223, 239
 alces bedfordiae, 7
 alces cameloides, 6f., 12
 alces columbae, 10
 alces gigas, 6, 9, 12ff., 30, 44, 73f., 92
 alces pfizenmayeri, 6f., 12f.
 alces shirasi, 6, 9, 12, 14, 27, 73f., 93
 americana, 11, 187
 americana americana, 10
 americana andersoni, 10
 americana gigas, 9
 americana shirasi, 9
 americanus, 10
 americanus gigas, 9
 americanus shirasi, 9
 bedfordiae, 7
 columbae, 9f.
 fossilis, 12
 gigantea, 12
 gigas, 9
 latifrons, 12
 lobata, 10
 machlis, 10, 12
 machlis americanus, 10
 machlis angusticephalus, 7
 machlis bedfordiae, 7
 machlis gigas, 9
 machlis jakutskensis, 7
 machlis meridionalis, 6
 machlis tymensis, 7

267

272

INDEX

122ff., 131, 155ff., 161ff., 167f.;
Douglas, 145, 150; lowland, 149
Fire, 159–160, 167, 170
Fireweed, 144, 151
Five-fingers, 143
flaccidum. See *Batrachium*
florida. See *Amelanchier*
fluctuans. See *Sparganium*
Fluke: liver, 187; rumen, 186
fluviatile. See *Equisetum*
Fly: black, 192; bot, 191; moose, 191f.;
warble, 191
Foetus, 62, 63, 89
Food
aquatic, 118–120
habits, 114–128, 158
plants: of Alaska, 149–152; aquatic,
semi-aquatic, and other, 140–144; of
British Columbia, 148–150; of eastern
North America, 129–144; of Montana,
145–147; of western North America,
145–152; of Wyoming, 145–148
shortage, 118
supply, 128
weight of, consumed daily, 114
See also Feeding; Forest; Plants; Trees
Forbs, 148
Forest: climax, 155; fires, 159–160, 167,
170; insects, 161f.; succession, 160,
and effect on nutritive value of food,
158f.; trees, age composition of, 154
fossilis. See *Alces*
Fox, red, 175
Fragaria americana, 148
France, 12
Fraxinus
americana, 138
nigra, 138
pennsylvanica lanceolata, 138
Fringecup, 147
fumiferana. See *Chloristoneura*

Gaillardia, 147
aristata, 147
Gait, 108f.
Gale. See *Myrica*
Galloping, 108
Game licks. *See* Licks
Gastric disorders, 221
Gelva, 79
Geographical relationships, 12
Geranium
Richardsonii, 147
viscosissmum (sticky), 147
Gestation period, 99
Geyeriana. See *Salix*
gigantea. See *Alces*

gigas. See *Alces; Paralces*
glabra. See *Acer; Chelone; Rhus*
Glaciation, 14–18
Gland, metatarsal, 6
glandulosa. See *Betula*
glandulosum. See *Ledum*
glaucus. See *Elymus*
Glyceria pauciflora, 148
Gooseberry, 143, 155; redshoot, 146
Gramineae, 142
grandidentata. See *Populus*
grandifolia. See *Fagus*
grandis. See *Abies*
granulosus. See *Echinococcus*
Grass, 116f., 123, 142, 148, 152; blue, 147,
151; blue wheat, 147; brook, 147;
bunch, 151; June, 147; marsh, 151;
meadow pine, 147; onion, 147; pine,
147; rye, 151; timber oat, 147; wheat,
151
Grassland barriers, 14
Grass-like plants, 117
Great Britain, 12
Gregariousness, 107
groenlandicum. See *Ledum*
Grossularia setosa, 146
Growth, 72–77
Growth curve: European moose, 77; length
of mandible and diastema, 88
Grunting, 105

Habitat, 164; appraisal of, 216; control of,
218–219; effects of moose on, 162;
studies, 153–164
hadweni. See *Dictyocaulus*
Haematobiae, 192
Haemonchus contortus, 190
Hair: scale pattern of, 79ff.; structure of, 79
Haloragidaceae, 118
Hare, varying, 175, 179
Harvest, size of, 216
Hawksbeard, 152
Hawkweed, white, 147
Hazelnut, 150, 168; beaked, 123, 133, 155,
157, 163
Hearing, sense of, 101
Heather, 152
Helianthus nuttallii, 147
Hemlock, 124, 131, 157, 168; ground, 122,
124, 129, 155, 162, 168; water, 142
Heracleum lanatum, 144, 147f.
Heteranthera dubia, 148
Hides: 32f.; for clothing, 20; for leather, 19
Hieracium albiflorum, 147
Hippuris vulgaris, 118, 145
History, early, of moose in North America,
19–21